The Distinctive Surnames of North Staffordshire

II

Occupations, Trades, Position and Rank

Edgar Tooth

ACKNOWLEDGMENTS

I would like to thank the following for their invaluable assistance in the compilation of this book: The staff at the William Salt Library, Stafford, Stafford Record Office, Hanley Reference Library (Arts and Archives), Newcastle under Lyme Public Library, Meir Public Library, the Family History Societies at Audley and Betley, and the Keele History Department.
The distribution maps for Bott, Earp, Lightfoot and Plant have been reproduced by courtesy of David Hey of Sheffield University. David Horovitz, as usual, has been a mine of information on numerous obscure placenames.
My special thanks go to Mrs Florence Daniels for transferring the original typescript to computer.

Carding p. 280

NOTE:
THE MAPS AT THE BEGINNING OF EACH CHAPTER SHOW THE DISTRIBUTION
OF SURNAMES AT THE TIME OF THE 1666 HEARTH TAX RETURNS

CHURNET VALLEY BOOKS
6 Stanley Street, Leek, Staffordshire ST13 5AG 01538 399033
www.thebookshopleek.co.uk

© Edgar Tooth and Churnet Valley Books 2002
ISBN 1 897949 80 4

INTRODUCTION

Theer's mony folk as ses theer's nowt
But pots and pits in Staffordshire
Wi' smould'ring bonks and cracking chunks
An' grime an' grit in Staffordshire.
Such folk are foos an' wunner know
The rain comes dine in Staffordshire
To wesh away the dusty clay
An' mak all clane in Staffordshire.

So runs the opening verse of an anonymous dialect poem about the county of Staffordshire with obvious allusions to the two main industries which have dominated the area since the advent of the Industrial Revolution in the eighteenth century, namely, pottery and mining. Yet to these must be added a third - ironworking, as hinted at by Arnold Bennett in a short story from *The Grim Smile of the Five Towns*, entitled 'Beginning the New Year': *"We are a stolid and a taciturn race, we of the Five Towns. It may be because we are geographically so self-contained; or it may be because we work in clay and iron"*.

This is the situation in a nutshell. In geological terms, of course, our county had been prepared for the development of these three industries thousands of years ago, for waiting to be exploited beneath the beautiful Staffordshire landscape lay bountiful supplies of clay, coal and ironstone. Some of the earliest evidence for the presence of these industries in our region comes from excavations undertaken at the Roman site of Holditch near Chesterton, where more than 30cwt of pottery have been discovered dating back to the first century AD, and where coal and ironstone were being worked during the 2nd century AD. At another Roman site at Trent Vale, occupied by the Romans during the 1st century, excavations have brought to light an up-draught kiln and a substantial assortment of artefacts including flagons, cinerary urns, platters, storage pots, bowls and lampholders.

During the Middle Ages, when our surnames were in the process of becoming hereditary, the manufacture of pottery was not restricted to any one region of the country, since pots were made wherever clay was available. Moreover, the local potters simply extracted their own clay out of the ground, as and when it was required for use. For instance, at a session of the Tunstall manor court in 1369, Robert le Potter of Burslem *"came into court and gave the lord twelve pence to have licence to get earth for making pots until the feast of Michaelmas following"*.

Yet at this particular juncture in the proceedings, the occupational term "potter" did not necessarily refer to a craftsman who made pots from clay, because it has to be borne in mind, that the commoner table utensils during the Middle Ages were often made of wood or metal. In fact, a bell-maker was often dubbed "bell-founder", "girdler" or "potter". Locally, the medieval potter was sometimes equated with the "thrower", that is, an artisan who worked or shaped the clay on a potter's wheel, as demonstrated by William le Potter, charged 6 pence for a licence to make earthen pots at Tunstall in 1348, who is almost certainly identical with William le Thrower, present at the manor court in 1363. By extension, the "thrower" was occasionally lumped together with the "turner" in the sense of someone who fashioned wooden objects such as bowls and dishes on a lathe. Here the relevant examples are from the Inquests on the Audley estates, where William le Throwere of Betley (1298), is alternatively styled William le Torner in 1307. These instances pre-date by three centuries such occurrences as 1644, John Browne, dishthrower of Norton-in-the-Moors, and 1659, William Bankes, dish turner of Haughton near Stafford.

Both Thrower and Turner have other scenarios. Thrower could apply to an employee in the clothing trade, who worked with filaments of silk, converting them into silk thread, whilst many north Staffordshire families called Turner can trace their ancestry back to some medieval turnspit in a scullery, a jouster in a tourney or even a nickname for a hunter who could run down and "turn" the hare he was pursuing. Robert Turnehare, assessed at Hilderstone in the 1327 lay subsidy rolls, obviously practised this little trick to perfection, relying no doubt on his speed off the mark.

With regard to the situation in coal-mining, the medieval "collier" was a charcoal burner, not a miner, and this is the meaning inherent in the surname Collier. It was the "collier" who supplied the necessary charcoal to fire the furnaces and forges, operated by the local "smiths", hence the expertise and knowledge in this complicated woodland craft of Richard le Colier, resident in the village of Alton in the Churnet Valley in 1332, would have been invaluable to his local community. Furthermore, charcoal was the only fuel used for iron-working until Dud Dudley discovered a method of using pit coal about 1620, a date which is considered to mark the end of the medieval period in iron mining. Collier in its modern sense of "coal-miner" was not in common usage until the 1500s. The usual medieval term for a coal-miner was the Old French word "mineur", but this is very rare for north Staffordshire: 1424, John Mynour of Haywood near Eccleshall. Despite all this, it may turn out that the more apposite names for a coal-miner or pit worker in our region may well be Delf and Delves, as outlined in Volume 1.

By the 14th century ironstone was being mined at Talke, Chesterton, Tunstall, Knutton and Longton. However, during this period the centre for marketing the local ores and iron was Newcastle-under-Lyme, as indicated by the town's Ironmarket. Elyas le Ironmongere of Newcastle (1294), was clearly a merchant or dealer involved in this trade, and his name lives on as Iremonger; 1583, Letice Iremonger of Standon.

These surnames, connected with pottery, coal and ironstone mining, are just a foretaste of the ancient crafts and trades, which have become enshrined in our local nomenclature. There are scores more besides, and all, in their own inimitable way, capture the essence of an era when society was built upon the basis of land ownership - the Age of Feudalism. This was the political system, perfected by the Normans on their Continental estates in Normandy, and which they transplanted wholesale across the English Channel in the decades following their resounding victory at Hastings in 1066. The Normans remained masters of our country for a sufficiently long time to leave a deep impression, not only on the political, legal and social structure, but also on our language and process of name-giving. The Celts, Romans, Angles, Saxons, Jutes and Vikings had all left their own mark earlier, but the Norman legacy was far more pervasive, affecting all strata of society from the very highest overlords down to the most humble peasant.

Our north Staffordshire forebears, conversing in their traditional Anglo-Saxon dialect, tinged with Old Norse, were suddenly bombarded on all sides by a strange new nasalized speech. With the gradual but inevitable assimilation of the Normans into our medieval society, our language was slowly but surely transformed and enriched by an immense corpus of French words encompassing the entire sphere of human activity. Miraculously, at the very pinnacle of the feudal hierarchy, the old Saxon words "king, earl, lord and lady" remained intact, but the overwhelming majority of terms relating to government and to the highest administration are of French origin. These high-ranking officials included "chancellor, treasurer, chamberlain, marshal, castellan, mayor, spencer, constable, steward" with the various steps in the scale of rank represented by "prince, peer, duke, marquis, baron, viscount". French was for so long part and parcel of the language of the law court, that it is hardly surprising, that the major portion of the legal vocabulary comes from the language of the conquerors. Hence the prevalence of "judge" or "proctor" - "attorney and provoker of suits in an ecclesiastical court", "catchpole" - literally "chase fowl", a tax inspector, who collected poultry in default of money, and "sumner", a petty officer, who summoned people to appear in court.

In monasteries and religious houses, too, French was the preferred mode of address. Accordingly, this led to such distinctions of rank and class as "clerk, cardinal, chaplain, parson, vicar, sexton, friar, hermit", but the Saxon "bishop" and "deacon" remained inviolate. Since the ruling classes took over control of every aspect in the military sphere, there was very soon a surfeit of names associated with chivalry, weapons and armour, and the sport of archery: "bachelor, champion, sergeant, squire, page, templer, arblaster (crossbowman), archer, fletcher, jenner (engineer, designer of war engines), palfreyman (keeper of the saddle horses)". Yet, in these particular categories the traditional Saxon terms more than held their own, as exemplified by "knight, kemp (warrior), rider, arrowsmith, bowyer, bowman, stringer (bow string maker)".

In the agricultural domain, the "farmer", the very epitome of the stolid, down-to-earth English character, ironically started out as a Norman rent collector, an agent who "farmed" out the land and collected the rents from it. But this strange paradox is more than made up for by the survival of the Saxon "fisher, fowler, forman (swineherd), thresher, cowherd, herdman, shepherd, calvert (calf herd)". Indeed, these old native names, along with others such as "baker, miller, roper, weaver, webb, saddler, wheeler" and the ubiquitous "smith" and "wright" plus a mass of compounds, still retain their more homely-sounding qualities in comparison with the more refined aura of the Norman imports "draper, falconer, painter, carpenter, joiner, butcher".

Nowhere is this dichotomy between the Norman and Saxon artisan better illustrated than in the building trade, in the doublet "stonehewer - mason". The Saxon term is a straightforward, no-nonsense explanation of what the Saxon builders did - they actually hewed the stone out of the quarries and shaped the blocks, whilst the Norman word, from Old Central French "maçon" is just a vague description of their superior building skills.

Stonehewer later develops into Stonier, Stanier and Stanyard in north Staffordshire, with Stonier/Stanyer far outnumbering all other variants. In addition, it is the alternative Norman French form "machun" - "mason" - Machin, which ramifies to a remarkable degree across north Staffordshire, pushing its partner Mason into the background. This is the surname, that Arnold Bennett chose for his inspired comic creation Denry Machin in *The Card*, just to add that little bit of extra colour to the narrative. He uses this device to perfection in *Anna of the Five Towns*, when talking of Ephraim Tellwright, a respected Wesleyan Methodist in Bursley, and father of the eponymous Anna. Bennett himself appends a footnote informing the reader that the surname means *"tile-wright, a name especially characteristic of, and possibly originating in, this clay-manufacturing district"*. Meteyard, in Volume 1 of her biography of Josiah Wedgwood, corroborates this derivation, when she says that *"the surname of "Tellwright" or "Tilewright", which, variously spelt, fills a considerable portion of the parish registers of Burslem down to a late period of the eighteenth century, and is still common, is curious evidence of the antiquity of the tilewright's craft in this locality. Every worker in its clays became a tilewright, whether he moulded tiles or formed the homely pipkin or porringer, the slab-like dish or ale vat for the hall"*.

The study of the regional distribution of surnames derived from trades, occupations and offices is fraught with difficulties. Some of the inherent problems have been touched upon in Volume 1 regarding the surnames Biddle, Mayer and Blower(s), where local dialect plays a crucial role. Another important factor is the way in which different names were adopted in certain regions to describe the same occupation. For example, one of the most widespread manufacturing industries during the Middle Ages, when our hereditary surnames were being formed, was the production of cloth. The cloth first had to be scoured and thickened and this was done by treading it out in a trough. In the south west of England, the person employed in this particular process was usually known as a Tucker, in the south and east of England he was known as a Fuller, whereas his counterpart in the West Midlands, north of England and in Scotland bore the name Walker. Walker wins hands down in north Staffordshire with Tucker and Fuller barely making an impact.

The weaving trade also produced a rich crop of surnames, and here, the distribution is very revealing, for they were known as Weavers, Webbs, Webbers or Websters, depending on where they lived originally. The Webbs are concentrated south of a line that connects the Dee with the Wash, one broad belt extending from Somerset in the west, through Wiltshire, the South Midlands and on into East Anglia. In Somerset the Webbs are swelled by the Weavers, but the latter mingle with the Webbers in Devonshire, and then move northwards into Gloucestershire and Worcestershire. Webster reigns supreme in the industrial north. The corresponding situation in our county is: Webber is hardly in the picture, whilst Weaver is fairly common but scattered. By far the two most widely diffused names are Webb and Webster, with Webb holding the upper hand in north Staffordshire.

As far as the tanning trade is concerned, Tanner was the most common name in the southern half of England, whilst Barker claimed precedence in East Anglia, the east Midlands, the north of England and Scotland. The surname Tanner is not frequent at all at any stage in Staffordshire but Barker is extremely prolific from the Middle Ages onwards.

A similar situation arose affecting surnames from milling. Miller was widespread during the medieval period, but not particularly common in any one region, whilst Milner cropped up chiefly in the east Midlands, East Anglia, the north of England and in Scotland. Milward/Millward/Millard on the other hand, became entrenched in the south of England, the south west and the West Midlands. Indeed, it is Milward which prevails in north Staffordshire with Miller concentrated south of Stafford.

Of course, many occupational surnames have always been very common, occurring in virtually every county throughout England with varying concentrations: Baker, Wright, Cooper, Cook, Hunt, Bailey, Ward, Carter, Chapman, Parker, Hall, Fletcher, Glover, Hayward, and so forth. Head and shoulders above all rivals stands Smith, the most numerous and familiar surname in the English speaking world. The main reason for its undisputed dominance is that during the Middle Ages skilled workers in metal were an essential component of any village community. On their craftsmanship depended rich and poor alike for the basic tools in their own jobs - ploughshares, scythes, shears, and so on. The horses needed shoeing, the armourer wanted bright, shining armour, the arrowsmith required iron arrowheads - the list went on and on. Moreover, his name was such a basic, simple Saxon name, that it took hold at the very time when our surnames were sticking fast.

Clark, too, stands very high on the list of our most common occupational surnames, and it is not difficult to see why, for he also possessed rare talents - he could actually read and write in an illiterate age. Consequently he was in great demand, perhaps as a secretary in some great land-owning baron's castle, or he may have been appointed parish clerk in some tiny medieval village church, where he led the responses of the local congregation, or, then again, he could have been a struggling student at one of the emerging Universities.

The high frequency of the surname Taylor is down to the fact that the Normans, with their flair for innovation and eye for detail, soon set new standards in fashion. Up until their arrival, the native English populace had made do with simple, loose-fitting clothes, that hardly needed any "tailoring", but the very word "tailor" is a Norman import, meaning literally "cutter". This immediately conjures up images of a new class of professional cloth workers cutting and designing new outfits, cloaks, capes, gowns, hose, gloves and even shoes, not only for the better off, who could afford them, but also for anyone who desired to follow the new trends.

Apart from these very familiar surnames there is a whole host of lesser known occupational names which are seldom given a proper airing, e.g. Plant, Lymer, Flackett, Copestake, Dresser, Poyser, Gleave, Doorbar, Sherwin, Armitt, Cantrell, Challinor, etc. In this volume, my aim is to explore both sides of the story by travelling back in time to the Middle Ages, when these names first saw the light of day, emerging into a medieval world where Saxon steadfastness and pride of nationality were tempered by Norman passion for law and order and genius for assimilation of new ideas. This method will enable us to analyse them in their proper context, free from modern prejudices. Thereby we may gain a better insight not only into the social and economic milieu in which they flourished, but also into ourselves.

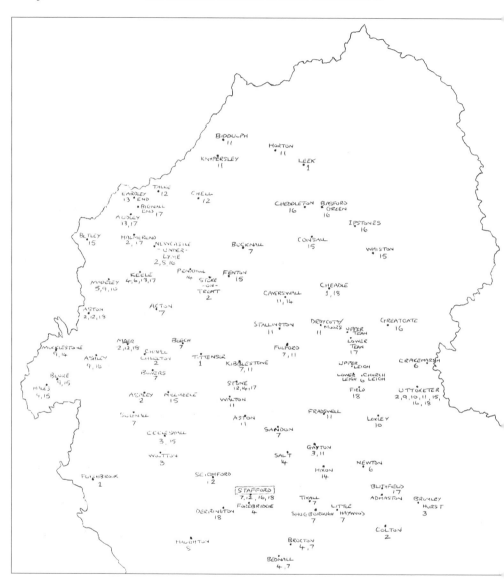

MAP 1   KEY

1. BARBER   5. HALLMARK   9. LIGHTFOOT   13. REEVE(S)   17. SILLITOE
2. BUTLER   6. HAYWARD   10. PAGE   14. SALE   18. SPENCER
3. GROOM(E)   7. LANDER/LAUNDER 11. PORTER   15. SARGEANT/SERGEANT
4. HALFPENNY   8. LEACH/LEECH   12. RATHBONE   16. SHERWIN

SURNAMES AT THE TIME OF THE 1666 HEARTH TAX RETURNS

CHAPTER ONE

KING OF THE CASTLE

In the aftermath of William the Conqueror's victory at Hastings and his subsequent coronation on Christmas Day, 1066, England became subject not only to a new monarch, but also to a new ruling class anticipating rich pickings in the form of lands and high office in Church and State. Indeed, for several generations after the Conquest this is exactly what happened, with nearly all the important positions and great estates monopolised by Normans or men of foreign blood. These mighty Norman barons and their families dominated their individual areas of the country as feudal lords in control of extensive tracts of land and forest, encompassing vast estates and manors.

Their military power, which often rivalled even that of their king, was dependent on their castles. At the outset they were rough-and-ready constructions of earth and wood, mostly of the motte and bailey type, but when the new revolution in building castles out of stone swept Europe in the twelfth century they had a profound effect on the contemporary political scene. Nowhere was this revolutionary technology put to better use than in England by the Normans, whose impregnable castles not only prevented invasion of a region, but also provided effective control over the local population.

Castle owners were thus in an unassailable position. Was it any wonder, therefore, that throughout the Middle Ages, local families like the Audleys at Heleigh Castle, the Staffords at Stafford Castle, the Ferrers at Tutbury and the Verduns and Furnivals at Alton Castle enjoyed power on a scale hitherto unknown? In the shadow of these great fortifications the new aristocratic families commandeered the old Saxon settlements, some of which had been in existence for at least three hundred years. Gradually, Saxon villages everywhere with their distinctive endings such as "-ton" and "-ley" acquired new labels, sometimes preceding the placename, and sometimes after it. Those most affected were common Saxon village names like Weston and Acton. Weston Coyney near Meir got its new tag from John Coyne (Koyne) who held the place in 1242. His name comes from an Anglo French word "coigne" - "a die for stamping money" or "a piece of money". The allusion is to a coiner or minter. In 1310 Richard, abbot of Croxden, sued Robert and William, sons of Richard Coyne of Gledenhurst for trespassing on his land at Dogge Cheadle and allowing their cattle to graze on his pastures. The local sheriff issued an order for their arrest. However the modern surname Coyne can also be an Irish name representing (O') Coyne -"O' Cadhain" - "wild goose", or an abbreviated form of (Mac) Kilcoyne, both prominent in Connacht, cf Ellen Coyne, greengrocer of Liverpool Road, Stoke in 1887.

Coyne

O'Coyne

Trussell

Acton Trussell, west of Cannock Chase, preserves a somewhat similar Norman name, derived from Old French "troussel" - "packet", employed in the Middle Ages for a puncheon or mould involved in the process of stamping coins, hence a maker or user of "trussels". The Trussell family owned land in this region from at least 1342, but at the time of Domesday the place belonged to the Bishop of Chester.

These two Norman baronial families hardly evoke a post-Conquest world of financial wizardry and cut-throat double-dealing, but the truth of the matter is that the Norman Conquest had very little impact on English coinage. The Norman kings continued to issue pennies in their own names, that is, the old silver pennies, introduced three centuries earlier by their Anglo Saxon predecessors. Twelve of these made up a shilling, 160 a mark and 240 a pound, and they were the only coins in circulation until the end of the thirteenth century when Edward I in 1279 issued two new denominations - halfpennies and farthings. The borough mint at Stafford was only of minor importance, and was probably in existence from the time of Athelstan in the early decades of the tenth century until the suppression of most of the local mints in 1180. A certain Colebrant "monetarius" - "minter, moneyer", appears in a pipe roll at Stafford in 1159/1160.

Money

Surnames connected with our coinage are surprisingly fairly common but often difficult to interpret accurately. This applies especially to Money itself, which in fact could turn out to be totally counterfeit with no financial implications at all. Monnai in Orne, south of Normandy, has been proposed as a locative source, reinforced by a nickname from Old French "moigne" - "monk", used for someone with a reclusive nature. In Ireland Money is a variant of Mooney from "moenach" - "dumb" or "maonach" - "wealthy", so Daniel Money, recorded at Betley in 1726,

Mooney

could be traceable to any one of these sources: 1872, Miss Eliza Mooney (Lady

Penny
Penney

Superior) Convent of the Sisters of Mercy, Alton. Penny and Penney are derived from the coin "penny", but the exact sense is vague, although there was a Saxon name "Pening", which might have given rise to the surname: 1851, James Penney, owner of a beerhouse in High Street, Hanley; 1851, Reverend Henry Penny, curate

Pennington
Pinnington

at Cauldon. Pennington and Pinnington are worthy of inclusion here, since they go back to Pennington near Ulverston in Cumbria, Pennington in Lymington, Hampshire, both of which designate a village that had to pay a penny geld, or to Pennington north east of Warrington - "village of Pinna's people". James Pinnington and Elizabeth Day were married at the Church of St. Mary, Swynnerton on April 14th, 1793. 1851, Myles Pennington, goods manager at Stoke Railway Station; 1887, Thomas H. Pennington (tea merchant) of Lamb Street, Hanley.

Newpenny
Bentpenny
Halfpenny

Obsolete compounds include: 1256, Inquisitions post mortem, William Newepeny (of Hanford or Longton) and 1308, Adam Bentpeny, tenant of the Audleys at Audley. Surviving compounds include Halfpenny, which has its origin in some obscure medieval condition of tenure, where tenants were required to contribute a halfpenny towards the cost of repairing some structure like a mill or dyke. Yet there is an archaic northern phrase "to have one hand on a halfpenny", applied to anyone cautious with money or attentive to his or her own interests. If this dates back to the Middle Ages, then this could provide a suitable alternative solution. At Audley in 1729, a vestry meeting compiled a list of poor people who were eligible to receive weekly payments in accordance with their needs. Amongst the inhabitants at Bignall End and Eardley End was widow Halfpenny, aged 70, who was granted one shilling per week to help her get by. On April 21st 1805, Samuel Halfpenny (bachelor) got married to Margaret Perks (widow) at Seighford. Both parties signed the register with a cross, showing that they were illiterate; 1873, Thomas Halfpenny (joiner, builder), Victoria Street, Goldenhill; 1907, Frederick Halfpenny (weighman), Bratt Street, Cobridge.

Of course, throughout recorded history there have always been people protective of their hard-earned cash and some of these misers have been immortalised in literature like Charles Dickens's "Scrooge" and George Eliot's "Silas Marner". Yet others are commemorated by such apposite nicknames as "money grubber", "scrawmer", "scrape good" and "pinch penny", whilst the remainder are brought down to earth by such telling phrases as "he'd skin a gnat for its hide", "he wouldn't part with dirt from under his fingernails" or "he wouldn't give a blind man a light". Anyone intent on a profit was once identified by the nickname Turnpenny, as in the case of John Turnpenny of Handsworth, cited in an Inquisition dated 1291. George Turnpenny was mayor of Walsall in 1698. Henry Monypeny (Manypeny), deceased, cited at the local assizes in 1277, in connection with some disputed rent at Darlaston (Stone), was so obsessed with gain and miserliness, that he literally hoarded "many pennies", giving us the surname Moneypenny. In the Barton-under-Needwood parish registers for 1762, George and Mary Moneypeny had a daughter called Sarah, baptised on April 4th. Cf also the obsolete William Manybaggs of Ellastone (1605).

Winpenny/Wimpenny too was a typical medieval expression for someone who was desirous to "gain a penny": 1907, Stephen Whympenny of Heath Street, Goldenhill; 1907, Frank Winpenny (fitter), Brook Street, Hanley. Another old word for a person too careful with his pence, a niggard or skinflint, is "pennyfather", which survives as Pennyfather and Pennyfeather. In the Eccleshall parish registers (1577-1611) we come across 1577, Thomas Pennifather; 1581, Jocosa Penifather, and 1611, Grace Penyfather of Croxton. Roger Getegod, who is paying three pence per year rent to the Audley family in 1308 for 5 cottages in Betley, may possess a name that means literally "get goods", that is, a hoarder of goods, someone with a mania for collecting things, like a magpie storing up stolen trinkets and such like. But it does not ring true, somehow. On the other hand, Scattergood is for "scatter goods", that is, either a nickname for a person who squandered his money, or conversely for someone who gave money away to help others, a medieval philanthropist. In 1348 a local assize convened to determine whether Henry **Scattergood** Skatergode, along with several other defendants, had dispossessed Henry, son of Richard de la Pole of Hartington (south east of Sheen), of a rent of nineteen shillings and eight pence and the third part of a mill in Alstonefield. On the Thursday after the Feast of the Exaltation of the Holy Cross a jury found the defendants guilty and awarded Henry, son of Richard de la Pole, damages to the tune of 10 marks (£6/13/4d). Clearly, the Henry Skatergode here was living up to the former nickname! Edward Scattergood was buried at Ellastone on March 4th, 1633. The ten marks granted in damages in the above assizes suggests that the surname **Mark(s)** Mark(s) might be a name derived from the coin, but this is too hasty, for these surnames have three origins: the Latin personal name "Marcus", the locative Marck in Pas-de-Calais across the English Channel or a toponymic for a dweller by a boundary: 1907, Arthur Marks (telegraph engineer), Moston Street, Birches Head. **Hallmark Allmark Halmarack Hammock** Hallmark/Allmark/Halmarack/Hammock is plentiful. These stand for "half a mark" and are probably identical in meaning with Halfpenny, that is, a relic of some curious medieval system of tenure or a form of contribution to the upkeep of some mill or dyke. Peter Halmarke was a member of the trained band at Madeley, Betley and Balterley in the 1640 Muster and Joseph Hallmark had a tailoring business along Navigation Road, Burslem in 1851.

The farthing, first issued in 1279 by Edward I, has also given rise to a surname. It means "fourth part", that is, a quarter of a penny, and John Ferthinge and Margery Halpeny were amongst those assessed at Pershore in the 1327 lay **Farthing** subsidy rolls for Worcestershire. Robert Ferthing (Ferthyng), cited for Stafford in inquisitions post mortem for 1336/1337, could be a nickname from the coin, or from the Scandinavian personal name "Farthegn, Farthin". In addition there was an Old English "feorthing" - "fourth part", a measure of land or homestead consisting of a "fourth part", found in fieldnames like "the Ferthings (1570)" in Cannock and "Le Farthyng" (1562) in Handsacre. A surname could have developed from this, denoting someone who cultivated such a piece of land, or who owned the actual homestead. Anne Farthing, an illegitimate child, occurs at Mucklestone in 1635.

During the Middle Ages the royal revenue was obtained from a number of different sources, chief amongst which were the rents from the Crown lands. The principal agent responsible for collecting the crown rents and accounting for them **Sheriff** was the "sheriff" or "shire-reeve", but he had numerous other duties besides, including the collection of fines from litigants in the assize courts or amercements of offenders, imposed by the Royal Justices. He also seized estates that had been forfeited, giving possession to the rightful heirs when they came of age, sat as judge in the county and hundred courts and generally acted as the King's agent. At the outset there was a tendency for the office of "sheriff" to become hereditary in one family or at least to be restricted to the baronial ranks, and there are signs of this in the list of Staffordshire "sheriffs" in the centuries after the Conquest. For example, the Audleys, Staffords, Swynnertons, Bagots, Caverswalls are almost permanent fixtures on the roll of honour until at least the Battle of Agincourt in 1415. Gradually, however, their power and influence waned, and with the rise of the Justices of the Peace and of Quarter Sessions their administrative and judicial potency shrank, and by the time that government had been thoroughly centralised by the House of York, the position of "sheriff" had ceased to carry any weight and had become one of purely honorary distinction.

So what about Richard le Schirreue (Schereve), assessed at Hatton and Gunstone south of Brewood in 1327/1332? He was probably an official at the local

eriff

assize court. Later recordings are: Elizabeth Sheriffe, resident at Milwich in 1590, and George Sheriff, grocer and beer seller of Pratt Street, Fenton in 1875. Shreeve

reeve

shows up now and again: 1872, Daniel Shreeve (farmer) of Fradley near Alrewas. All the money that was collected throughout the country was accounted for at the court of the Exchequer, which derived its name from the great table covered with a chequered cloth on which the accounts were set out and calculated by means of counters. The chancellor and officials sat on one side of the table and the person, whose accounts were being checked, on the other. The chancellor was in fact a secretary, a custodian of writings or records, financial or otherwise, also an usher in

ancellor

a law court: 1685, George Chancellour of Newcastle-under-Lyme.

The accountant or treasurer was known simply as the "counter", "the person

ounter

who counts or reckons", hence the modern Counter. In some cases he might have assisted the sheriff in collecting the county dues. In 1343 Simon de Ruggeleye sued William le Counter of Colton and two accomplices for taking fish from his fisheries at Rugeley to the value of 100 shillings. None of the defendants appeared and the sheriff was ordered to arrest and produce them at the Octaves of Michaelmas.

In the households of the sovereign and the great barons it was the steward

eward

who was entrusted with keeping an accurate record of the accounts, and the lands and rents due from them and he had auditors to help him in these particular tasks. Also he kept track of the actual acreage, produce and livestock on the manors. Often, on the biggest estates there were two stewards, one who managed the estate itself, whilst the other was in charge of the domestic routine. The steward of the estates, who was frequently a knight, was especially busy, since he was obliged to hold the lord's courts, supervise the council of knights and officials who advised the lord, and on occasion to represent the lord at the king's court or to act as his deputy. Consequently some of these stewards were very highly paid and lived a veritable life of luxury. Richard of Havering, steward to Simon de Montfort, held one-fourth of a knight's fee from his lord, plus some other lands and rents. During the barons' revolt against the king in 1265, led by Simon, Richard was put in charge of the garrison at Wallingford Castle.

In Scotland the Lord High Steward was the first officer of the Scottish king in early times with control of the royal household, enjoying great administrative powers and even on occasion given the privilege of leading the army into battle. With the accession of Robert the Steward as Robert II this office fell in to the Crown, thus giving rise to the royal house of Stuart. The Scottish clan Stewart is from the same word, that is, Old English "stiweard" or "stigweard", often interpreted as "sty ward" or "keeper of the pig sty". Rather the first part of the compound refers to some kind of building, not originally confined to pigs. In the main, the surnames Steward, Stewart and Stuart go back to a manorial official, who conducted the local manorial court in the absence of the lord, a man of very high standing who had to know *"....how many acres could be ploughed and how much seed will be needed. He must know all his bailiffs and reeves, how they conduct the lord's business and how they treat the peasants. He must know exactly how many halfpenny loaves can be made from a quarter of corn, or how many cattle each pasture could support. He must forever be on the alert lest any of his lord's franchises lapse or are usurped by others. He must think of his lord's needs both of money and of kind, and see that they are constantly supplied"*.

Steward
Stewart
Stuart

Prior to the Industrial Revolution the main focus of attention of the surname is the southern half of the county, with heavy concentrations around Codsall, Bushbury, Bilston and Wolverhampton. Specimens in our region comprise the following: 1590, Joanna Stewarde of Norton-in-the-Moors; 1669, Nicolas Stuart of Stoke-on-Trent, cited as Nicholas Steward in 1671; 1851, William Steward Esquire, steward to the Duke of Sutherland, Trentham; 1875, Reverend J.C. Stuart (Wesleyan) of Newcastle Street, Burslem; 1875, William Stewart (draper) of King Street, Newcastle-under-Lyme.

One of the most celebrated Stewarts is Frances Stewart (later Duchess of Richmond), the original model for the figure of Britannia, which appeared on our copper coin in 1665, during the reign of Charles II. Nowadays, of course, the term "steward" has taken on a whole range of new meanings. Stewards attend to passengers' needs on ships, trains and aircraft, they organize shows, demonstrations and race meetings, they are responsible for catering arrangements in clubs, colleges, and so on, whilst the shop steward is elected by factory employees to represent them in dealings with management. In the day-to-day running of the medieval manor the steward outranked all other manorial officials. For example, Richard le Styward, assessed for two shillings at High Offley in 1332, stood over all his contemporaries, including the bailiff, reeve, beadle, constable and hayward.

Bailiff
Bailey

The duties of the "bailiff" or "bailey" on the manorial lands covered a wide spectrum. First and foremost, he had to have a sound knowledge of agriculture, so that he did not have to pester the steward constantly for instructions. Indeed his daily tasks were manifold - he had to inspect the crops, meadows, pastures and woods on the lord's domain every morning, checking that the ploughs had been yoked properly and were ready for use, and that the land was marled and manured. He examined all the lord's livestock, including the oxen, cows, heifers and sheep, weeding out the old and weak animals that were unlikely to survive a harsh winter. He kept a close watch on all the agricultural workers such as the threshers, ploughmen, harrowers and sowers, and, according to the season, he supervised harvesting and sheaving, and even the sheep shearing, for he was obliged to sell the wool and skins at the local markets for the best prices.

Since the bailiff was a free man and the mouthpiece of the lord of the manor, living moreover in the manor house at the lord's expense, he was, understandably, regarded with great suspicion and contempt by the villagers and unfree tenants. His unpopularity is summed up in a fourteenth century story which tells of a certain bailiff, who rides to a village to collect rents, accompanied by the Devil in human form. They are confronted by a poverty-stricken widow whose only cow had been confiscated by the bailiff the day before. She falls down on her knees and with outstretched hands, shrieks at the bailiff *"To all the devils of Hell I commend thee!"* Whereupon the Devil exclaims *"To be sure, this is mine, because thus cordially you have been bestowed on me, I am willing to have you"*. And, snatching up the bailiff, he carried him off to Hell.

The word "bailiff" survives in three forms. The basic spelling, as in 1355, Adam le bailiff of Standon, results in surnames such as Bailiff, Baileff, Bayliff(e) and Baylyff. Ursula Bayliff was buried on July 11th, 1699, at the parish church of St. James the Great, Audley. This variant is far less common than Bailey. Old French "baillis" ends up as the modern name Baylis(s), Bayless and Bailess: 1613, Jane Baylys of Shelton-under-Harley; 1851, James Baylis, licensee at the Highgate Inn, Brownhills, Burslem. This form too is rather scarce. By far the most widespread variant is Bailey, Bailie, Baillie, Baily, Baly, Bayley, Baylay, Baylie, Bayly, since these are sometimes to be traced back to Old French "bail(e)" - "the wall of the outer court of a feudal castle, used later of the courts themselves", hence "guardian of the courts or bailey", whilst a lesser contribution comes from the locative Bailey north west of Whalley in Lancashire, as exemplified by Robert de Bayleye, taxed at Newcastle-under-Lyme in the 1327 lay subsidy rolls. In 1374 Henry Bailly of Cauldon, together with several other persons, were attached at the suit of the Abbot of Burton for coming with force and arms to Cauldon and cutting down his trees to the value of £10 on the Monday before the Feast of the Invention of the Holy Cross. This particular incident had occurred some four years previously and the surviving defendants denied the trespass and injury, and appealed for the case to be tried before a jury, which was summoned for the Quindene of Easter. In the 1841 Scriven report on children employed in the Staffordshire Potteries, Thomas Bailey, aged 8 years 3 months, was a mould-turner for Thomas Sergeant at Messrs. Thomas and John Mayor's Earthenware Factory in Longport. He told the commissioners *"I come to work at half past five; light fires, get the ashes out and slack in. I go home at night always, except Monday nights, then I go at six"*. Trade directories list: 1851, Harriet Bailey (matron) at Leek Workhouse; 1875, Samuel

ailiff
aileff
ayliff(e)

aylis(s)
ayless
ailess

ailey
ailie
aillie
aily
aly
ayley
aylay
aylie
ayly

Bailey (tobacco dealer) of Cross Street, Longton; 1887, William Bailey (market gardener) of Trent Vale; 1887, Ann Bayley (pastry cook, confectioner) of High Street, Newcastle-under-Lyme.

Beadle

Certain manorial officials had duties which overlapped and it is often impossible to differentiate the individual terms. The beadle, for instance, could be an under-bailiff, a crier or usher in a law-court, a town crier, a mace bearer, a messenger of justice. At any rate, he was appointed either by the lord of the manor or by his local community. It was his job to make all the summonses ordered by the hallmote (the local manor court where the lord meted out justice to his tenants), to collect the fines, and generally to serve as the village policeman. For instance, in 1349, John le Bedel of Eccleshall, was sued by John de Okovere in a plea *"that he should render to him a reasonable account for the time he was the receiver of his money at Okeover"*.

Beadel Beedle

This spelling ends up as the modern surname Beadel and Beedle. However, the form "budel" as in Simon le Budel, sub-bailiff of William le Botiler (bailiff of Offlow Hundred) in 1360, develops into Buddell and Buddles.

Buddell Buddles

"Budel" in fact, is the Staffordshire dialect form of Old English "bydel" - "beadle", which becomes Biddle in south eastern England. In Staffordshire, we have already seen that the surname Biddle/Biddell is a local pronunciation of the placename Biddulph, as confirmed by 1471 Assizes, John Bidyll of Bidyll, noted as John Bedille (Biddulph) of Biddulph in an earlier lawsuit of 1464.

Biddle Biddell

Beddall Bedall

The modern Bedall and Beddall are most likely variants of "Bedel": 1608, Humphrey Bedall (founder) of Newcastle-under-Lyme; 1875, John Beddall (iron bedstead maker and furniture broker) of Miles Bank, Hanley.

Hayward

One of the most familiar figures in medieval villages was the "hayward", whose main responsibility was to guard - not the hay, despite the first syllable - but the hedges or enclosures round the Lammas lands when they were enclosed for hay. The "hedge" was a dead hedge made out of stakes and brushwood, a moveable hurdle easily erected and carried from field to field, which were shared out in strips and cultivated communally by the villagers. In effect it prevented animals from breaking through into the enclosed strips and trampling down the precious crops. It was the duty of the hayward to impound stray animals and to repair breaches in the hedges. Under certain conditions he had to serve as an officer at the hallmote and was part of the management team on the lord's demesne farm. His badge of office was his horn, which he used to sound a warning that the cattle had strayed into the corn. In the well known nursery rhyme, Little Boy Blue was a hayward. At the Tunstall manor court, held on the Thursday after the Feast of the Apostles Peter and Paul, 25th June, 1326, Richard le Hayward appeared in a plea of transgression against Simon Kelye (sic), most likely for Kelynge, *"for that he had burnt his hedges to his damage which is taxed at 1 penny. And the said Simon came and acknowledged it, therefore in mercy one penny."* In 1461 John Heywarde sued Richard Fernyhalgh of Aston near Stone (yeoman) *"to give up to him a certain pyx*

J. DE TANZIE STEWART,

Teacher of Pianoforte

AND

Patronized by His Grace the DUKE and Her Grace the DUCHESS of SUTHERLAND,
COUNTESS CROMARTI, The Most Noble the MARQUIS and MARCHIONESS
of STAFFORD.

Qualified Practical PIANOFORTE TUNER and MAKER,
from London. Local Examiner to the Royal College of
Music. Tuning promptly attended in Town or Country.

ADDRESS:

PORTLAND VILLAS, BASFORD,

STOKE-ON-TRENT.

Stewart p. 14

KNIGHT & SON,
SOLICITORS,
Telegraphic Address,
"KNIGHT",
NEWCASTLE-UNDER-LYME,

Newcastle under Lyme,

Staffordshire,

April 5ᵗʰ 1887.

Knight p. 22

Leek, *Sept. 18* 189⟨⟩

M *Charles Watson Esq*   *Hill Pottery Fence Burslem*

Dr. to ISAAC BAILEY & SONS,

... TIMBER MERCHANTS. ...

August	17	To 14 Post 9 feet long at 1/9ᵈ		1	8	0
		taking same to Burslem			5	0
				1	13	-

Bailey p. 14

(casket) *containing deeds and writings which he had unjustly detained"*. From time to time there is inevitable confusion with the locative Haywood, which normally goes back to Great and Little Haywood near Shugborough. In the Seighford parish registers, for instance, from the years 1767/1768, Robert Hayward alternates with Robert Haywood. On 16th July, 1636, at Newcastle-under-Lyme, Martine Tomkinson, son of Thomas Tomkinson, cordwainer (shoemaker), was apprenticed to Richard Hayward, freemason for 7 years with *"meat, drink, lodging and apparrell for the sixe laste years to be provided."* In 1851 Henry Hayward ran an eating house in High Street, Longton and William Heyward was licensee at the Four Crosses in Sandon Road, Stafford.

Hayward
Haywood

The similar name Hayman/Hyman could denote a keeper of the enclosure or refer to habitation near some enclosure, or it could be an occupational term for a seller of hay, or a nickname for a high (tall) man. In the 1666 hearth tax returns for the county William Haymon was taxed on one hearth at Bishop's Offley near Croxton, whilst Thomas Hyman is recorded in the Keele parish registers in 1796. 1907, Arthur Hayman (coachman), Normacot Road, Longton.

Hayman
Hyman

Occasionally some animals escaped the vigilance of the herdsman and wandered off into the surrounding forests, where they might mix with other stray animals from neighbouring villages. When these stray beasts had been captured they were brought back to the village and put in a small fenced enclosure called a "pinfold" or "pound" until they were claimed by their owners. The local official in charge of the "pinfold" was the "pinder" or "pinner", and his job complemented nicely that of the hayward and his never-ending struggle with strays on his own patch of territory. Pinder and Pender are the more commonly occurring variants: 1639, Elizabeth Pender (Barton-under-Needwood parish registers); 1851, Thomas Pinder (manufacturer of ironstone, china and earthenware), Swan Bank, Burslem; 1868, Joseph Pinder, elected to the board of trustees for the Endon Well Dressing Festival.

Pinder
Pender

Pinner is much scarcer, but here other sources come into the picture, such as a maker of pins or pegs, wire articles, small needles which were inserted in cards used in the dressing of cloth, or a maker of horn combs, or even a locative from Pinner in Middlesex. Locally, in the Corporation Minutes for Newcastle-under-Lyme, it is reported in 1632, that, at an assembly at the Guildhall *"weare elected and chosen Stephen Halles and Robert Hewitt to bee Pinners for the Towne ffeilds and to drive the Commons and to pinn all the cattell of those whoe overstaint the Commons and to have for every beast the Pinn eight pence a beast and two pence a sheepe ffor their payns takinge"*. John Pinner crops up in the Burslem parish registers for 1666, and in the Alton Vestry Book for June 5th, 1850, William Bailey was appointed as pinner to round up stray animals and to keep them in the pinfold - cf The Pinfold in Essington (1834 Ordnance Survey Map) and The Pinfold in Bloxwich. Directories show: 1872, Daniel Pinfold (farmer, miller), Bishops Offley. Pinfield is a possible variant: 1804, Thomas Pinfield of Brierley Hill, plus Penfold (no examples).

Pinner

Pinfold
Pinfield
Penfold

under
wnder
ynder

Pounder, Powder and Poynder convey the same idea of keeping stray animals in a pound. In 1630 Randulph Pounder and Anne Read were married at Standon, but Robert Pounder, enrolled at Colwich in the 1539 Muster, appears as Robert Pondor in 1532. If the original surname here is Pondor, then this is a toponymic for habitation by a pond. In addition, in the Trentham parish registers,

wner

William Powder (1709), is quoted as William Powner in 1722. Now Powner is usually a weakening of Pownall on the analogy of Tunster for Tunstall, and in this case the derivation is Pownall (Park) in Wilmslow - "nook of Pun or Puna", eg.

wnall

Phoebe Pownall of Stoke-on-Trent (1789) occurs as Phoebe Powner in 1791. In 1851 James Powner (shoemaker) lived in Bury Bank, Darlaston, and in the same

wney
yner

year Edward Powner was mine host at the Swan Inn, Maer. Powney is another later variant: 1690, Matthew Powner of Seighford (1693, Matthew Powney). Poyner, common around Penkridge during the seventeenth and eighteenth centuries, can also be from Old French "poigneor" - "fighter, warrior": 1662, September 4th, Sarah Poyner and William Cooke married at Penkridge.

eve

The "reeve", nominated from among the peasants and mostly chosen by them, was by common consent *"the best husbandman in the village"*. Although of servile origin, he was a man of substance, often holding a yardland (30 acres) or more, and strictly accountable to the lord of the manor for everything to do with the manorial economy. Hutred le reve, for example, of Audley in the 1308 Inquests on the Audley estates, was paying an annual rent of 14 shillings and three halfpence for a messuage (homestead) and land, by far the highest amount in the village. From Lammas to Michaelmas (during the harvest season), he dined at the lord's table in the manor house, and, along with the bailiff or sergeant, he had responsibility for almost every aspect of the management of the lord's demesne farm. It was his duty to see that *"the keepers of all kinds of beasts do not go to fairs, or markets, or wrestling matches, or taverns, whereby the beasts may go astray without guard or do harm to the lord or another, but they must ask leave and put keepers in their places that no harm may happen"*.

Since the reeve was of servile stock, he knew his fellow villeins better than any of the other manorial officials, and hence, this allegiance to his roots, on the one hand, and his obligations to the lord of the manor, on the other hand, must certainly have caused him many a twinge of conscience. Indeed, free tenants always insisted that they be exempt from service as a reeve, since to have been a reeve was clear legal evidence that one was not a free man. Chaucer's "reeve" in the Canterbury Tales, is a classic portrayal of the ambivalence inherent in his character:

> *Well wist he by the drought and by the rain*
> *The yeelding of his seed and of his grain.*
> *His lordes sheep, his neet, his dayerye,*
> *His swine, his horse, his stoor, and his pultrye*
> *Was holly in this reeves governynge.*
> *Ther was ne baylyf, herde ne other hyne*

> *That he ne knewe his sleight and his covyne;*
> *They were adread of him as of the deth.*

(wist = knew; neet = cattle; dayerye = dairy; stoor = stores; pultrye = poultry; holly = wholly; herde = herdsman; hyne = farm servant; sleight = tricks; covyne = cheating; the deth = the plague)

Reeve
Reeves

    On December 12th, 1512, John Reve came to the manor court at Tunstall *"and took seisin* (possession) *of 3 acres and one third of an acre in Bignel Ende which were of his father Hugh Reve to hold, and he gives for ingress three shillings and fourpence"*. George Reeve was curate at Caverswall in 1649. In the 1666 Hearth tax returns the surname is especially common around Audley, and it is in this area where it gains an extra "s" at the end, becoming Reeves: Audley parish registers, 1703, Margaret Reeves, daughter of John Reeve (sic), buried on July 26th. Reeves is usually either for "servant at the reeve's (house)", or, by misdivision, from Middle English "atter evese" - "dweller at the edge or border of a wood or hill". This develops into "atte revese", with the "r" becoming attached to the second word. On the 1844 Tithe Map for Kibblestone, Ann Reeves occupied a house and garden, owned by William Turner, and in 1851 Elizabeth Reeves was proprietor of a shop along Church Street, Stoke that specialised in millinery, including straw hats.

    If the reeve had a male heir, then he would naturally be known as "son of the reeve", as typified by Henry le Revesone, classified amongst the top band of taxpayers at Marston near Whitgreave in 1327, and by Adam Reveson, assessed for two shillings and threepence at Biddulph in the same tax returns. These end up as the modern Reeson, but there could well be some confusion with Reason, Raison,

Reeson
Reason
Rayson
Raisin

Rayson, Raisin. For example, John Resun, resident at Cresswell near Draycott-in-the-Moors in 1327, is probably from Middle English "resoun" - "reason", a nickname for a person of some considerable intelligence, yet later families bearing these surnames could be derived from Old English "raesn" - "beam, block of wood", with reference to an individual who was solidly built or possibly a carpenter who made such beams for the building trade, or a manual worker who actually put the beams in position. Market Rasen in Lincolnshire also contains the same word in the sense of a plank bridge, so there may even be a locative involved.

Grieve(s)

    In northern England and in Scotland the Old English "gerefa", source of "reeve" elsewhere, retains the original "g", resulting in Grieve(s), and in the Danelaw shires Grieve(s) is mostly from the Old Norse "greifi" - "steward". In some English counties there is frequent confusion between Grieves and Greaves/Greeves/Greve(s), but in Staffordshire the latter denote a dweller by some

Greaves
Greeves
Greve(s)

brushwood, a thicket or some grove, as in Walter in the Greve, cited in the 1220 Patent Rolls for the county. However, in the Bucknall cum Bagnall parish registers for 1806, Thomas Greaves signs his name as Graves. James Greaves (collier) lived in Cobden Street, Hanley in 1912. In the main, residence by some grove is indicated by the surname Grove(s): 1703, September 21st, Joseph, son of John and Mary

The reeve keeping an eye on the progress of the reapers (Reeve p. 20)

Beds protected by curtains (Chamberlain p. 25)

Grove(s)

Groves, baptised at Seighford; 1887, Frederick W. Grove (Palissy Works), Chancery Lane, Longton.

Constable

The career of the constable is truly extraordinary. It is another official term that entered our language via the channels of Norman administration. He was originally "comes stabuli" - "the groom in charge of the stable", but by the time the word came over to England with the Normans its equine ancestry had been all but forgotten and it had come to denote anything from the chief officer of the household or court, military officer, governor of a royal fortress to a parish constable. The constables picked by John of Gaunt for his fortresses at Tutbury and Newcastle-under-Lyme were entrusted with the provision of artillery and bows and arrows, the repair of the castle walls, and so on. But in general, the constable was content to be a minor officer of the law, an attendant on the sheriff or bailiff in the manor courts, as in the case of William Cokes, assessed for Knightley, south west of Eccleshall in the 1381 Poll tax returns, who is alternatively styled "constabularius ville" - "constable of the local village". He was probably appointed to "keep the peace" in the neighbourhood. In a lawsuit of 1528, Germaun Pole (armiger), contended that John Constable and his wife Joan had illegally taken possession of a fourth part of a messuage (homestead), 40 acres of land, 8 acres of meadow and 26 acres of pasture in Combridge, near Uttoxeter, belonging to him. John and Joan remitted all right to Germaun and his heirs, for which Germaun gave them twenty pounds sterling. In the 1666 hearth tax returns Henry Cunstable of Alstonefield was exempt from any payment and on March 28th, 1743, Mr. John Constable from Mr. Fitzherbert's was buried at the Church of St. Mary, Swynnerton.

Sergeant

In many ways the functions of the "sergeant" coincide with those of the bailiff of the hundred, since he was employed in issuing summonses and making arrests and enforced the judgments of a tribunal. If anyone in the village was assaulted, it was the sergeant who was called in to deal with the matter. Yet, during the age of chivalry, it could also designate a servant or attendant of a noble or knight, whilst the king's sergeants were tenants by military service under the rank of a knight. A recording such as Thomas Williameserjant Benet of Butterton-on-the-Moors (1338 Assizes), could well denote Thomas, servant or attendant of William Benet. In 1318 Robert le Serjaunt of Slindon, along with a dozen others, was charged in connection with the death of Vivian, son of Vivian de Standon, husband of Alice, at Swinchurch on Thursday in the week of Pentecost, 1317. Robert, who was in the custody of the sheriff, was too infirm to appear in court. The surname survives in several variations, but Sargeant is by far the most prolific form, followed

Sargeant
Sergeant
Sargant
Sarjant

by Sergeant, Sargant and Sarjant. In 1771 Bridget Ashe licensed Hugh Serjeant of Wetley Rocks to dig for lead and copper ore on her land at Mixon Hay for a term of 21 years. 1851, John Sargeant (butcher) of Knenhall, Moddershall; 1887, Frederick William Sergeant (fruiterer), Glebe Street and Richmond Street, Stoke.

At Betley in 1308, Adam the clerk was paying $3^{1/2}$ pence rent per annum for

atchpole

land which had once belonged to Alexander Catchpole, whilst over at Newcastle-under-Lyme in 1370/71, Thomas Cachpolle was 9 shillings in debt to the community chest. On the medieval manor the "catchpole" was one of the most unpopular of all officials. His name means literally "hunt or chase fowl", but in reality he carried off the peasant's prized hen (poule) in lieu of payment to the lord of the manor. In *The Vision of Piers Plowman*, when the two thieves are crucified with the Saviour, we are informed that: *"A cachepol cam forth... And cracked their legges."* In effect he was just a petty officer of justice, whose business it was to show who was boss.

Vagstaff
ongstaff
ardstaff

Surnames such as Wagstaff, Longstaff and Hardstaff are construed by some scholars as nicknames for combatants skilled in the use of the quarterstaff, but they are all more likely to be allied to the name Tipstaff, the medieval law officer who went about the manor carrying a tipped, staff that is, a staff furnished with a silver top or iron spike. One of Chaucer's friars, who had a licence to beg in a particular area *"wente his wey with scrippe and tipped staf"*. Therefore the medieval official in question here would be on a par with the catchpole or beadle. In 1619 Timothy Wagstaffe, armiger and Gervase Hall, gentleman were in dispute with John Offley, knight, over 12 messuages, 12 gardens, 12 orchards, 400 acres of land, 100 acres of meadow, 300 acres of pasture, 30 acres of wood, 200 acres of furze and heath, 200 acres of moor and 10 shillings rent in Over and Nether Elkstone, Swinscoe, Alstonefield, Blore, Okeover and Woodhouses. Henry Wagstaffe submitted tax on one hearth at Heaton near Rushton Spencer in 1666. William Wagstaff was proprietor of a newsagent's and tobacconists along Broad Street, Hanley in 1875. 1907, T.J. Wagstaff (French polisher), Arbour Street, Hanley.

ickerstaff(e)
ickersteth

The surname Bickerstaff(e)/Bickersteth is the odd man out, since this is derived from a locative, stemming in fact from the village of Bickerstaffe near Skelmersdale in Lancashire, from whence came Gilbert de Bickerstath, one of the bailiffs at Newcastle-under-Lyme in 1381. This spelling points to "the landing place of the bee-keepers", or there may be a Saxon personal name involved like "Bicera", associated with the modern "bicker" - "to argue, dispute". Later instances of the surname include: Ellastone parish registers, 1589, Helen, daughter of John Byckerstaffe, baptised on January 2nd, and buried on January 10th; 1626, September 24th, Richard Bickerstaffe, married to Elizabeth Semell, and Newcastle-under-Lyme parish registers, 1798, Ralph Bickerstaff. Here it is interesting to note that Dean Swift, in a satirical pamphlet against Partridge, the Almanac maker, adopted the nom de plume Isaac Bickerstaff. The fascinating point about the surname Bickerstaff is the later interchange between initial "B" and "V", which is

icarstaff
ickerstaff(e)

prevalent from the seventeenth century onwards e.g. 1654, Henry Vicarstaff of Eccleshall; 1801, Ralph Vickerstaff (blacksmith) of Newcastle-under-Lyme; 1851, Thomas Vickerstaff (farmer) of Horsley, near Eccleshall; 1907, F. Vickerstaffe (milliner and dressmaker) of Ford Street, Leek. The difference in articulation between the two consonants is not great - "b" is formed by pressing both lips together, whereas "v" is formed by pressing the lower lip against the upper teeth. Thus it is quite easy to slide from one sound to the other. Intriguingly, the locality Vicarwood in Kedleston near Kirk Langley, Derbyshire, was formerly known as "Bikerwode" in the Middle Ages - "bee keeper wood".

THE HOUSEHOLD

A typical medieval castle was made up of two parts - a courtyard surrounded by a ditch and a wall, and a keep or a tower, usually situated on an artificial mound at one end of the courtyard. In many of the smaller castles the living rooms were situated in the keep, but in the more strongly fortified castles the living quarters formed a separate building standing within the protected area itself. The chief room was the great hall, where the lord of the castle, all the household staff, retainers and military personnel took their meals, passed their spare time, and of course where many of them slept. These halls were often very large, one-roomed structures, aisled like a church, divided lengthwise by rows of wooden posts or stone pillars supporting the timbered roof. In the medieval house, even more so than in the castle, the keypoint of the whole building was the hall. It was a room with a lofty ceiling, usually one and half to twice as long as it was broad. Stretching across one end of the room, sometimes on a raised dais, was the high table, where the master of the house sat, together with his family and guests.

At right angles to the master's table, running lengthwise down the hall, were the tables for the servants of the household. Indeed, it is through employment as a servant at one of these halls that a humble villager might have acquired a surname like Hall in the Middle Ages, as typified by Isolda de le Halle, assessed at 9 pence for Loxley in 1327. Yet Richard del Halle is classified as headborough at Chell in 1363, which indicates, that he was a man of considerable importance in the local village community, since he was head of the frankpledge, that is, a rudimentary police system whereby villagers were made mutually responsible for each other's behaviour. Indeed, the headborough later became virtually synonymous with the petty constable. In some cases, the "man at the hall" could denote a steward who deputised for the knightly owner in his absence. In 1438 William Halle of Kingsley (yeoman) and William Wodecok of Cheddleton (husbandman) were sued by John Lockwood for treading down and consuming his corn and grass at Kingsley with their cattle. The churchwarden's accounts for Tunstall (Stoke-on-Trent) tell us that in 1632, William Hall was given two shillings *"for carryinge the bell wheels from Trenthum"*, whilst at Ellastone, the burial of Thomas Hall (ye aqua vita man) (sic) took place on April 4th, 1643. Zephaniah Hall was gamekeeper at Madeley, near Keele in 1851 and in the same year Reuben Hall is listed as a lustrer and enameller, and resident in Dale Hall, Burslem.

Occasionally Hall is synonymous with Sale(s), as confirmed by William del

Hall

(s)　Halle of Tunstall (1360), recorded as William de la Sale in 1327. Usually the surname Sale(s) is from Old English "s(e)alh" - sallow, willow" with reference to habitation by such a feature, or from Sale in Cheshire. An assize in 1289 attempted to determine whether Alan de la Sale and others had unjustly dispossessed Adam del molyn (mill) of 3 acres of moor in Sandon. 1851, Enoch Sale, owner of a beerhouse in Brunswick Street, Hanley; 1851, Thomas Sales (farmer), Mount Zion, Denstone, Rocester.

Just like the manor or village, the household of the great medieval land-owning barons was a self-contained community with its own ménage of specialists and functionaries, and naturally the size of the staff depended on the wealth of each individual lord. The "chamberlain" had access to the private room or chamber mberlain where his lord slept, assisting him in ordinary, everyday things like getting him dressed, fetching the water for washing, making his bed, generally tidying the room, and performing tasks normally undertaken by a valet or housemaid. As a result of this close contact with the king in a royal household, the chamberlain became one of the most influential persons in the Middle Ages, and even now the Lord Chamberlain remains a highly distinguished title in the royal entourage. But the surname could also have arisen from the "chamberlain" who was in charge of the sleeping accommodation at an inn, that is, an attendant, waiter or chambermaid. In a curious case, heard at the local assizes in 1323, Andrew le Chamberleyn (possibly of Swynnerton), in company with a whole host of unsavoury characters, were charged with being *"common malefactors and disturbers of the peace, riding about armed through the country to the terror of the people, and that they had come with others who were unknown, armed to the County Court held at Stafford on a certain Thursday in the summer of 1312, to the great terror of the people, and had forcibly closed the doors of the hall of the Court and placed guards so that none could depart, and they had threatened to kill Hugh de Croft, the Sheriff and William de Stafford, knight in full County Court, unless the Court was stopped."* This brief reign of terror cost the defendants fines ranging from twenty shillings to ten marks (£6/13/4d). In another case, in 1391, Robert Chaumberlayn of Fulford *"in his own person appeared against Henry atte More of Coton, for breaking "vi et armis"* (by force and arms), *with John Basset of Fulford, into his close at Fulford, and taking his goods and chattels, to the value of £100, and for treading down and consuming his grass with his cattle, to the value of 100 shillings"*. Hearth tax contributors for the county in 1666 include Isaac Chamberlyne on three hearths at Stafford, Christopher and Richard Chamberlin on 3 each at Uttoxeter, with William Chamberlyne exempt at Stone. In 1873 Richard Chamberlain lived at Holden Farm in Ford Green.

Chambers was originally identical in meaning with Chamberlain, but later mbers took on connotations such as chamber attendant, chamber man or chamber maid. In 1326, Richard de la Chaumbre, parson of the church of Leigh, sued John de

Hungerford, parson of the church of Uttoxeter, for breaking into his houses at Flitley and stealing goods and chattels valued at £20, and in 1345, Isolda, daughter of William de la Chaumbre, and Christiana, sister of Isolda, sued John, son of Richard de Delves for five acres of land in Knutton. John prayed a view, and the suit was adjourned to the Morrow of St. Martin. A certain Nicholaus de Chamboure was elected Mayor of Newcastle-under-Lyme in 1374. The parish clerk at Stowe-by-Chartley records that Thomas Chambers, *"a very poore man"*, was buried on January 5th, 1625, whilst Anne Chambers and John Bailey were married at Seighford on May 30th, 1745, the year of the Jacobite Rebellion led by Bonnie Prince Charlie. In 1851, Joseph Chambers was one of the teachers at the Free School at Abbot's Bromley and in 1875 Jane Chambers ran a general dealer's shop along Grove Road, Heron Cross. The Scottish form of Chambers is Chalmers (no examples), but compare 1887, John Charmer, owner of refreshment rooms in Salters Lane, Newcastle-under-Lyme.

Chalmers

The marshall suffers from a split personality. At court or in the medieval households of the sovereign or the great baronial families he was a highly important official, entrusted with the military affairs of his king or a superior kind of usher looking after the seating arrangements for the guests at state banquets or sumptuous feasts. Meanwhile, away from these dizzy heights, lurked his genuine calling, betrayed by the original Latin form "marescallus" - "horse servant". During the Anglo Saxon period horses were not only essential for hunting and fighting, but they were also a much sought after status symbol. Consequently, the honour of looking after the horses was only bestowed on the most loyal and trusted of the king's men. After the Norman conquest the Saxon term "horse thegn" was ousted by the Old French "mareschal". In Norman and Plantagenet times the person who was chiefly responsible for the care of the horses was not the "groom", but the "marshall". His duties entailed buying and selling horses in his charge, shoeing and grooming them, and even diagnosing and treating their diseases. In fact he was a groom, blacksmith and horse doctor all rolled into one. A memorandum from the Standon Manor Court for 1338/1339 states that *"Henry le Mareschal undertook to make the ironwork of one plough belonging to the lord, and of his own iron and at his own furnace, and the fastenings of the same plough, for two heifers, in front and behind for 4/4d, from the Feast of the Ascension to the same feast for one entire year"*.

Marshall

In medieval eyes the "smith" and the "marshall" were craftsman of the same ilk. But the marshall did not have it all his own way, for in 1323, Roger le Marchal and others were robbed of cloth, silver, jewels and other goods as they were returning from the market at Newcastle-under-Lyme. 1689, John Marshall, churchwarden at Ellastone; 1773, December 30th, Ann Marshall and Thomas Carnel, married at the parish church of St. Edward the Confessor, Cheddleton; 1851, Thomas Marshall (fitter), Gas Works, Stone; 1875, Robert Marshall (cab proprietor and beerseller), Vine Street, Hanley. The variants Mascall and Maskell are very

scall
skell

rare, but compare 1623 Feet of Fines, Humphrey Mascall of Clent.

If we look at the magnificent colours and richness of the costume of medieval sovereigns and their aristrocratic entourage, it is at once apparent, that only an expert with an eye for detail and the latest fashions could have been put in charge of the robes and the wearing apparel of the lord or lady of the household. This was the keeper of the wardrobe, who often employed tailors to design the clothing for his superiors, hence such modern surnames as Wardrobe, Wardrop and

rdrobe
-drop
-droper

Wardroper. At the 1339 assizes, Ralph Basset of Drayton, executor of the will of Ralph, son of Ralph Basset of Drayton, appeared by attorney against Richard, son of John de la Wardrobe of Pembrugge (Pembridge in Herefordshire, apparently). Alice del Wardrope is cited in a Tatenhill manor court roll for 1344.

Another highly influential member of the domestic staff in a lord's household was the officer who controlled the buttery, where beverages were kept in butts or bottles. John del Boterie of Abbot's Bromley (1370 assizes), may well have been employed by some local land-owning family in just such a capacity, possibly even by the Ferrers family at Chartley Castle. This same gentleman occurs as John de la Botelerie in 1342, confirmation, that "boterie" - "the place where liquor was stored", was identical with "botelerie" - "wine cellar". However, as far as our county is concerned, the surname Buttery has an alternative local origin - the

ery

locality called Buttery (Farm) near Lilleshall, Shropshire. William de Botereye, taxed at Sheriffhales in 1327, most likely came from this place. The meaning of the placename seems to be "butter island (marsh)", that is, marshy ground near to which there was good pasture for cattle yielding plenty of butter. At Newcastle-under-Lyme in 1517, one of the wardens of the assize of bread was John Botterey, whose duty it was during his term of office to see that the bakers in his local domain did not cheat their customers with poor quality bread or underweight loaves. In 1851 Samuel Buttery (shoemaker) lived in Great Haywood, and in 1907 Edgar Buttery (miner) was resident along Poole Street, Fenton.

The two protagonists in several lawsuits covering the years 1336 and 1337 are Geoffrey de la Botellerie of Tixall and Malcolm Wasteneys (chivaler). In 1337 the aforesaid Geoffrey also appears as Geoffrey le Botiller, sued by Malcolm for

er

cutting down his trees at Tixall to the value of 100 shillings. The butler was in charge of the wine cellar, but he was higher ranking than the servant who looked after the buttery, mainly because he was responsible for the supply and importation of wine. In 1496 William Butlere was prior at the Augustinian abbey of Rocester, and at Newcastle-under-Lyme in 1664/1665 John Butler was granted liberty to erect on the green a barn of three bays, paying a groat a bay and to have a lease for 21 years. In 1851 George Butler of Boothen, worked as an audit clerk at Stoke Station and in the same year Joseph Butler kept the Rose and Crown in Stafford Street, Longton.

In a baronial household supplies of the more expensive foodstuffs like spices

Spencer

had to be carefully monitored and this very important post was filled by the "spencer", the "dispenser" of provisions, a house steward. This lends itself to the suffix in Rushton Spencer north west of Leek, held by Hugh le Despencer (Hugh le Spenser) circa 1265. In the Staffordshire Hundred Rolls of 1275 he occurs as Hugh le Despencer, and he was co-parcener of the manor of Alstonefield with Warine de Vernun and Henry de Audley, but unfortunately all his lands were forfeited by the Crown during the reign of Edward III. Rushton Spencer was one half of Rushton, the other half being Rushton James, which got its addition from James de Audley, land-owner there circa 1250. In the plea rolls for 1306, William le Wodeward of Haughton and William le Despencer of Doxey had stolen a falcon from the Prior of Ronton Abbey and they are described in no uncertain terms *"as common robbers of falcons"*. In 1349 Isabella, formerly wife of John de Myners (chivaler), sued Robert le Spenser (chaplain) for a third part of 40 acres of land in Uttoxeter, which she claimed as dower. At Seighford in 1708 Richard Spencer, carrier to Worston Mill, was killed by a fall from his horse in Coton Lane and was buried on December 23rd, whilst at a public vestry meeting held in the parish church of Cheadle on the 5th November, 1769, George Spencer, one of the churchwardens, agreed to let Mrs. Eliza Wharton *"take James Lord's wench from the workhouse and keep her for four years with sufficient meat, drink, clothes, washing and lodging and to have ten shillings a year for the first 3 years and at the end of the fourth to give her clothes fit to go out to another place"*. 1851, Ann Spencer (wheelwright) of Weston on Trent; 1875, Henry Spencer (wholesale tobacconist), Tontine Street, Hanley.

Spence
Spens

Larder
Lardner

Just as Spencer is a truncated form of Old French "despensier", so Spence/Spens is an aphetic form of "despense" - "larder, a person who was in charge of the larder, or a servant who worked there". Originally it was the place where bacon was stored (French "lard"), hence the names Larder and Lardner: 1273 Inquisitions post mortem, Alan de Lardener (sic) of Salop. William le Spens (sic), taxed at Ashley near Mucklestone in 1327, could have followed either calling. At the turn of the twentieth century the "spence" was still in provincial usage, applied to a safe, a cupboard, a convenient place in a house for keeping provisions, a pantry, or even an eating room in a farmhouse. 1851, Robert Spence (manager, Gas Works), Holehouse, Burslem; 1875, William Spence (registrar), Cemetery Lodge, Hanley. A similar trimming down process affects Old French "despendour" - "steward", which turns into Spender. Cotgrave gives *"a cater, or clarke of a kitchen";* 1327 Lay subsidy rolls, Adam le Spendur of Sutton, near Aqualate Mere. On August 8th, 1811, the marriage took place between Hannah Spender and George Martin at the Church of St. Mary the Virgin, High Offley and in 1851 James Spender was farming land at Greatwood, Eccleshall. So it looks as though the surname Spender has its home in this region of the county.

Spender

Cater
Chater

Cater and Chater are contracted variants of Anglo French "acatour", Old French "achatour" - "buyer", with reference to the official who purchased provisions for a large household. In 1374 Almaric Catour sued John de Solyhull and John Buggyng of Lichfield, for forcibly breaking into his houses and close at Lichfield, and treading down and consuming his growing corn and grass with their cattle. After the charter of incorporation, granted by Queen Elizabeth on 18th May, 1590 for forming and creating the burgesses of Newcastle-under-Lyme, at the first council meeting a regulation was made, that no man should be admitted a burgess until after he had been resident in the borough for a year, so that the town might have trial of his behaviour. In April 1591 the fee fixed for a burgess was £5. One of the burgesses elected in 1615 was John Cater alias Ashmore, who had to pay *"twenty shillings in hand and the rest at twenty shillings per annum"*.

THE KITCHEN

Employees engaged in the preparation of meals in the kitchen are commemorated by such surnames as Kitchen/Kitching and Kitchener, although the latter more often than not alluded to a worker at a kitchen in a monastery. In 1383 John de la Pole, the elder, sued William of the Kychen of Yoxall for leaving his service at Newborough near Hoar Cross without reasonable cause and without his permission. Peter Kitchen was witness to the marriage of James Chadwick and Sarah Barnett at Cheddleton on 7th February, 1772. 1907, Ralph Kitchen (quarry maker), Waterloo View, Porthill. In 1896 Francis Elliott Kitchener, headmaster of Newcastle High School and brother of Lord Kitchener of Khartoum, became the owner of The Old Hall at Oulton near Kibblestone.

The breathless-sounding Panter and the feline-looking Panther are but relics of the household officer who supplied the bread and superintended the pantry, whereas in a monastery the "panter" distributed loaves to the poor of the local villages. In his *Boke of Nurture* (circa 1460), John Russell urges the student:

> The furst yere, my son, thou shalt be pantere or buttilare,
> Thou must have three knyffes kene in pantry, I sey thee, evermare,
> One knyfe the loaves to choppe, another them for to pare,
> The third, sharp and kene, to smothe the trenchers and square.

Henry Jonespaneter Hastang, implicated with several others in the death of Vivian de Standon, husband of Alice, in 1318, probably refers to Henry Paneter in the service of John Hastang. Pantry/Pantrey too survives - officer in charge of the pantry, as in Richard de la Panterie and Joan his wife, called to warranty in 1371 by Roger Straunge (chivaler) and Aline, his wife, in a suit concerning some land in Shenstone given as dower to Isabella, wife of Edmund de Walsyngham.

With Sellars/Sellers there is more than meets the eye. On occasion the surnames are certainly derived from Anglo French "celer", which ultimately goes back to medieval Latin "cel(l)arium" - "cellar, storehouse, storeroom for provisions, a granary, buttery or pantry". From this source comes Simon del Celer, who, in a final concord, dated 8th July, 1272, along with his heirs, was entitled to hold eleven acres and three roods of land in Milwich of William de Acoure (Okeover) and his wife *"for one pair of white gloves or one penny yearly"*. Synonymous with this is "Celerer", as indicated in a 1306 gaol delivery roll, in which Ralph de Bromleye is called *"a conspirator, because he procured himself to be put on a certain inquisition and falsely and maliciously indicted Robert the Celerer of Deulacres for a robbery of which he was afterwards acquitted"*. The "Celerer" was in fact the person responsible for the provision and stores in a monastery, in this case, Dieulacres Abbey. Later it was used of an innkeeper. Other possibilities vie for attention - an occupational name for a saddler, from medieval Latin "sellarius, cellarius", Old French "seller", as in Geoffrey Sellarius (Cellarius) de Stafford in a thirteenth century deed from the Ronton Chartulary or a derivative of Old English "sellan" - to give, hand over, hence a dealer or seller. Dorothye, daughter of Ann Sellers, (father unknown), was baptised at Ellastone on March 6th, 1594. In 1851

Sellers Joseph Sellers (marble stonemason) was resident along Liverpool Road, Stoke and Ann Sellers (stay maker) occupied a shop in Foregate Street, Stafford.

Shutler The very scarce Shutler, as epitomised by Hugh le Scotiler, taxed at six pence for Sheen in the 1327 subsidy rolls, amongst the lowest band of taxpayers in the village, preserves the medieval Latin term "scutellarius" - "a servant having charge of the scullery", or it may be a derivation of Old English "scutel" - "dish" or "platter", hence a scullion or a dealer in crockery, or even from an unrecorded Saxon word "scytel" -"shuttle", an instrument used in weaving. Here the reference would be to a maker of shuttles or a weaver.

THE SERVANTS

Of course such an immense household could not operate smoothly without an experienced staff of servants to back up their superiors. The most basic term for a servant was "man" as opposed to his "master". For instance, John Elmesalesman (1361 assizes), of Alton, was the servant of Hugh de Elmesale. At the Newcastle-under-Lyme manor court in 1379, Roger Smyth accused William Mon of trespassing on his land and destroying grain with his cattle. The spelling "Mon" is the local pronunciation for "Man". In 1466 John Mann, late of Walton near Stone (labourer), was involved in a robbery and breach of the peace, but could not be found. 1851,

Mann Sophia Mann (dyer) of High Street, Burslem; 1907, Frederick Mann (railway brakesman) of Hollings Street, Fenton. Two other compounds are worthy of inclusion here. Matthewman - "servant of Matthew": Agnes Mathewman, buried at

Matthewman Ellastone on July 20th, 1581; 1872, Edward Matthewman (tin plate worker), Eastgate Street, Stafford; and Penkethman, either "servant of a person called

Penkethman Penketh" or "someone who actually came from Penketh", that is Penketh near Warrington - Welsh "pen coed" - "end of the wood": 1907, Joseph Penkethman (carter) of Furlong Lane, Burslem. Arnold Bennett gives this surname to Mrs Penkethman, the widowed headmistress of the Wesleyan Day School in his short story *The Lion's Share* from *The Grim Smile of the Five Towns*.

This theme of servility is perpetuated in many of our surnames. In the Middle Ages "boy" and "lad" were virtually synonymous for a young man (of low birth) or a servant, but today they tend to evoke childhood innocence and youthful exuberance. In an Inquisition at Dudley, dated 1292, it is stated, that Adam de Elmburgh, the king's subescheator in the county, and Stephen de Bosco, his bailiff, with Thomas, the boy of the aforesaid Adam *"very often by night as well as by day, with bows and arrows, harriers and other dogs, took game to the amount of forty at the least, and this for the advantage of the aforesaid Adam de Elmbrugge"*. Here "boy" in the sense of "servant" is one origin of the surname Boy(s)/Boyce/Boice: 1594, John Boy of Perry Barr; 1912, John W. Boyce of Caverswall Lane, Blythe Bridge. Yet also involved is a Saxon name Boia*, a Germanic "Boio" or a toponymic for habitation by a wood, from Old French "bois" - "wood": 1276 Assizes, John del Boys of Bramshall.

"Lad" survives alone in the surname Ladd(s). In 1310, Richard Ladde of Swynnerton, with at least a dozen others, were attached to answer the plea of Vivian de Standon, that they had broken into his park at Fenton on the Vigil of St. Thomas the Martyr (1309), and had chased and taken twenty bucks and does, and for which he claimed £20 as damages. It also occurs in Goodlad, Goodlatte, Goodlet(t) - "good lad, young man, servant", although Geoffrey Godladde, fined 4 fowls at Alrewas in 1273 for carrying off vert (green vegetation) from the lord's wood, had let the side down. The compound Summerlad is a trick, because it is from Old Norse "Sumarlithr" or "Sumarlithi" - "summer warrior", "summer rover, Viking". Summerland is a late corrupted form: 1597, Margaret Somerland of Betley; 1851, William Summerland (farmer), Uttoxeter Wood. Sumbland is also a possible later perversion of the name: 1907, John Sumbland (potter) of King Street, Burslem.

To begin with, Groom, too was just another serving man, a manservant, and only later did it take on the specialised sense of horse attendant. Groom, as in "bridegroom" is from a totally unrelated word - Saxon "guma" - "man", with "r" added in the seventeenth century. In 1282, John, the groom of Edmund de Stafford and eleven others were charged with breaking into the park of William de Rye at Endon and taking from it some wild animals, viz a certain eyrie of hawks. The sheriff was ordered to arrest the defendants and produce them at the Octaves of St. Martin. Richard Groome was assessed on one hearth at Wootton (Eccleshall) in 1666 and William, son of William and Judith Groom was baptised at High Offley on September 14th, 1687. In 1851 James Groom (baker and confectioner) lived in Tean Street, Cheadle and in 1875 George Groom had a grocer's business along Nile Street, Burslem.

Groom is often equated with Page, as exemplified by Thomas Page (grome) of Colton, charged with several others in 1430 with *"breaking into the King's park at Adgresley* (Agardsley), *at Neuburgh* (Newborough), *and chasing and taking his wild animals*". In spite of its low status within the household, it was apparently an office much sought after by the sons of the lower nobility and this may account for its fairly high frequency in our local telephone directories. Edward Page of the parish of Kynson (Kingstone) near Uttoxeter, and Elizabeth Tumkyson (sic) of the parish of Stowe, were married at Stowe-by-Chartley on January 21st, 1605, and in 1875 Thomas Page was proprietor of the Etruria Inn in Lord Street, Etruria.

Paget(t)

The diminutive offshoot Paget is a name borne by the Paget family, to whom Abbot's Bromley was granted at the Dissolution of the Monasteries, hence its alternative name Paget's Bromley, recorded as "Pagettes-Bromlye" circa 1578. One of the most illustrious members of this family was William Paget, who served on the Privy Council under Mary and was appointed Lord Privy Seal in 1556. He acquired monastic lands, and took over a new estate called Beaudesert in Cannock Chase. Padgett is a late variant of the name: Lichfield Cathedral Registers, 1753, March 7th, Benjamin Padget and Mary Langham of Walsall, married.

Padget(t)

Hine(s)
Hyne(s)

Middle English "hine" - "servant, hind" lives on in the names Hine(s) and Hyne(s), but it started out as a clannish term for a member of a family, household or religious house. In 1371, John le Hyne and his wife Joan remitted all right to John de Croftes, vicar of the church of Baswich, for a messuage, some land and 2 acres of meadow in Cowley near Gnosall. They received 10 marks of silver from the vicar; 1851, John Hine (wheelwright) of Sandon. In the north of England especially, the word continued to be used in the form "hind" as a rustic labourer, with no connection whatsoever with "hind" - "female of the deer", but inevitably the two surnames became inextricably intertwined. If the original name was Hind, then the odds are that it was a nickname for someone as timid as a hind. In the Hints parish registers John Hines (1783) is also entered as John Hinds in 1786. Later examples include: 1851, Josiah Edwin Hinds (attorney), Lad Lane, Newcastle-under-Lyme; 1851, George Hind (farmer), Leek Frith; 1875, William Hines (grocer and second hand clothier), New Street, Longton; 1875, Thomas R. Hinde (ropemaker), Houghton Street, Hanley.

Hind(s)
Hinde

Durward
Durrard
Durrad

Servants who kept watch over the outer door of the castle are also much in evidence. Here belongs Durward - "door-keeper, porter". During the Middle Ages the office of door-ward to the king in Scotland was an hereditary one. In Staffordshire it is contracted to Durrard or Durrad: 1871 Census, William Durrard (retired bookseller), High Street, Eccleshall.

Dorman

Dorman is misleading, for it comes from the Saxon personal name "Deormann" - "beloved man" or "brave man": 1907, M. Dorman of Mountford Street, Burslem. The "usher" was either a door-keeper or the person who checked that the guests at table were seated in their proper places. At Newcastle-under-Lyme

Usher

in 1687 John Usher was granted liberty "..*to erect a cottage of one bay of building on the marsh at the end of Thomas Smyth's house*" and in 1732 it was ordered "*tha Thomas Usher's two daughters have necessary clothing and be put into the workhouse"*. Lusher (no examples) retains the French definite article.

Port and Porter are chiefly occupational names for a keeper of the door or gate, but sometimes Port may be a locative from Port-en-Bessin in Calvados (Normandy) or a toponymic for a dweller in a market town or port, whilst Porter may occasionally denote a porter or carrier of burdens. In addition, in Staffordshire, the surname Port can be equivalent to Yate(s) - e.g. 1327 Subsidy Rolls, Henry ad Portam, assessed for Rushton Spencer, is quoted as Henry atte Yate in 1332. In 1471 Richard Porte (yeoman) of Mayer (Maer) was named in a plea of trespass along with several other defendants on the lands of Robert Boughey, possibly in the Whitmore area, and by a deed, dated 1716, John Port of Ilam left a stock of wool to provide an annual distribution of 40 shillings to the poor of Alstonefield township. In 1298, on the Audley estates at Audley, Alan le Porter was paying an annual rent of twenty pence for one messuage and one acre of land. From the list of 50 horses compiled on 14th July, 1640 for carriage of ammunition in the Staffordshire Muster, one of the geldings was provided by Ralphe Porter of Sareley (sic), most likely Saverley near Fulford. He received £5 for the sale. On June 8th 1806, Robert Porter was inducted as rector of the church at Draycott-in-the-Moors and in 1887, Elijah Porter was a dealer in wardrobes in the Shambles, Burslem.

Portman has nothing at all to do with gates or doors. On the contrary, it is a very distinguished official name applied to a townsman, chosen from the body of citizens to administer the affairs of a borough. In 1614 William Portman remitted all right to some tenements, orchards, many acres of land, meadow, pasture, furze and heath to William Brabazon and his heirs in Harlaston, Edingale, Clifton Campville and Haselour. E.B. Portman was one of the witnesses to the marriage between Ayshford Wise (bachelor) of Totnes, Devon, and Mary Whitby (spinster) of Cresswell at Seighford, on June 19th, 1809.

Carrier/Carryer could signify any one of a number of things - a carrier or bearer, a porter or even a carrier of messages, a messenger, cf 1670, Mucklestone parish registers. John Smith of Woore (the letter carrier), buried on April 25th. Ales Carrier was buried on March 6th, 1596 at Stowe-by-Chartley. 1851, Rupert Carryer (pawnbroker), High Street, Newcastle-under-Lyme.

These messengers were the medieval equivalent of the modern postman and parcel post, and they were found in the service not only of the monarch, nobles and sheriffs but also of abbots and bishops. The king employed a dozen messengers on a fixed salary. They followed him on all his travels, ready to be at his beck and call at all times. A good, reliable foot messenger could cover about thirty miles a day, and those in the service of Edward II were allowed four shillings and eight pence a year to buy shoes and received three pence a day when they were on the road. It was a paltry wage but for those who brought good tidings there were often great rewards. Edward III gave forty marks pension for life to the queen's messenger when he announced the birth of the Prince of Wales, the future Black Prince. They were indispensable to any medieval landowner who possessed estates scattered over a large area, such as the great landowning families like the Staffords, Audleys and Giffards. Indeed they did set on full-time messengers to carry letters and writs from manor to manor. Letters were generally written on a sheet of parchment by a scribe from a dictated statement, and then sealed in wax with the master's signet. Yet often the messenger encountered occupational hazards unknown to the modern mailman. Matthew Paris narrates, that Walter de Clifford, a Welsh baron, was convicted in 1250 of having *"in contempt of the king violently and improperly treated his messenger, who bore his royal letters, and of having forced him to eat the same with the seal"*. Walter was fined the huge sum of 1,000 marks.

One official message in writing, which was sometimes delivered was the "brevet", which gives the surname Brevett/Brevitt; 1887, Mary Brevitt (milliner) of Bath Street, Burslem. Messenger itself is pretty infrequent. In an Inquisition, dated 2nd December, 1277, Nicholas le Messager of Admaston rendered three shillings and seven pence yearly as rent to William le Marshall for four plots of meadow, held at farm, and one pence annually for a certain moor, held in fee. Arthur Messenger is noted in the Stafford St. Mary's parish register for 1581.

Passant is from an Old French phrase - "passe avant" - "go on in front", a nickname probably applied to a herald or messenger; 1907, Thomas Passant (miner), Hall Street, Tunstall. Another Old French term in the same context is "galopin", a derivative of "galoper" - "to gallop" with allusion to a galloper, errand boy, messenger or page, but later it designated a turnpit or scullion in a monastery. Either way, these end up as the surname Galpin. In 1322, William Galpyn of Cheadle and seven others were attached to answer the plea of the Abbot of Croxden, that they had illegally taken and impounded the cattle of his plough at "Doggechedle", on the Tuesday before the Feast of St. John the Baptist the previous year. In 1398, Ralph Galpyn, who was clearly related in some way to the aforementioned William Galpyn, was charged with causing damage to some tenements in Dilhorne and Cheadle, including digging and selling marl and clay from two acres of land, pulling down a hall and selling the timber, cutting down forty oaks and sixty ash trees in the local woods, plus twenty pear trees and twenty apple trees in the gardens and selling them all.

The pair of surnames Trott and Trotter normally indicate a person who was wont to trot along the road briskly, hence another soubriquet for a messenger, but Trott is often to be traced back to Anglo French "trote" - "old woman, hag". In 1617 Baptist Trott (gentleman) contested the lawful ownership of 16 acres of wood in Mayfield and Snellsdale with Thomas Cokayne (armiger). Thomas eventually remitted all right of the wood to Baptist and his heirs, for which Baptist handed over £41. In 1907 Robert Trotter (porter) was resident in Riley Street South, Burslem.

One of the most remarkable compounds here is Sherwin, which is a contracted form of "shear wind", meaning literally "cut the wind", a very apt

Brevett
Brevitt

Messenger

Passant

Galpin

Trott
Trotter

Sherwin

A professional messenger p. 33

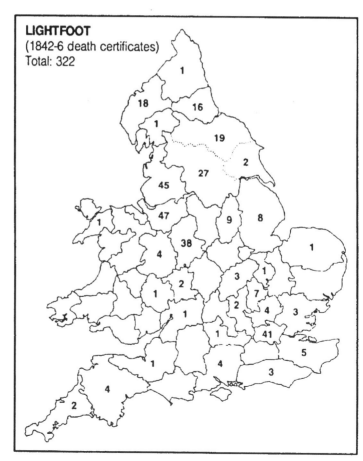

LIGHTFOOT
(1842-6 death certificates)
Total: 322

Lightfoot p. 36

definition of a runner or messenger who was fleet of foot and could run like the wind. Curiously enough, it has a counterpart, not only in French - "Taillevent", but also in German - "Schneidewind". Richard Schirwynd, tenant of the Audleys at Alstonefield in 1308, held a messuage and worked one bovate of land (10 to 18 acres) for an annual rent of three shillings. Sherwin is the usual spelling of the surname, but Sherwen also crops up now and then as in 1564 Feet of Fines, John Sherwen of Burton and Rickerscote. As a result of Archbishop Laud's visitation in 1635, James Sherwin of Ipstones was reprimanded for being *"..a rebellious recusant, affirminge, that he neither cares for church, bishopp, minister or magistrate"*. In 1818 Samuel Sherwin (cheese factor) lived at Longnor in the upper Manifold valley and in 1851 Robert Sherwin (camel hair pencil maker) was resident in Market Street, Hanley. Shearing could be a late variant via Sherring, as in James Sherring, son of Thomas Sherwin at Cheadle in 1666.

Sherwin
Sherwen

Shearing

Lightfoot is a perfect description of a medieval messenger or herald, endowed with a sprightly step or springy gait, but one bearer of this surname, a certain Thomas Lightefote of Whiston near Penkridge, had obviously been led astray, since he was accused in 1398, with several others, of the rape and abduction of Joan, daughter of William Engelton. 1690, April 7th. George Lightfoot and Elizabeth Kelsall, married at Audley; 1851, William Lightfoot, parish clerk at Ashley; 1875, Edward Lightfoot (tailor) of Meir Green. This surname is virtually confined to north west Staffordshire up until the Industrial Revolution, and during this period we also encounter forms such as 1539 Muster, Attewell Layfford (sic) of Bishop's Offley; 1604, George Lafoot (sic) of Madeley near Keele and 1760, Elizabeth Leightfoot of Betley. The modern Layford/Lafford is clearly a variant of Lightfoot because of the local tendency to pronounce "light" as "leyght" and also with the common confusion between "foot" and "ford" - e.g. Newcastle-under-Lyme parish registers, 1771, John Drakeford (joiner). 1779, Martha Drakefoot of Stoke.

Lightfoot

Layford
Lafford

Golightly/Galletly/Galletley conjures up the same picture of a medieval letter-carrier going speedily and safely about his daily task; 1872, Henry Gallatley (shopkeeper), Bridgtown, Cannock. 1907, W. Gallately of Longton Road, Stone.

Golightly
Galletly
Galettley

The unsolved Sillito(e) may also belong here, since the two surnames Lightfoot and Sillito(e) have conquered the same territory in the north western corner of the county, commencing with Audley and Keele in the north, continuing southwards in the direction of Blore and Hales and Mucklestone, and on towards Seighford and Eccleshall. The earliest instance that has been unearthed is Richard Solito (sic), taxed at Almington near Blore Heath in 1327. This looks suspiciously like "Selito", that is, "happy, blissful toe", either comparable to Fulljames, from Old French "fol, jambe" - "foolish, silly leg", not a medieval forerunner of the fielder "silly point", but a nickname for someone with a "useless, maimed leg", the unfortunate consequence of a duel, battle or accident, or a messenger with a happy

Sillito(e)

spring in his step, synonymous with Lightfoot. The latter is an infinitely better proposition. Once upon a time, the adjective "silly" meant "blessed" and alluded to anyone who was utterly without guile or a care in the world. In his English Surnames, Bardsley remarks that Spenser's "silly virgin" was no foolish maiden, but one who was helpless in her innocence, and Shakespeare's "silly women" in Two Gentlemen of Verona were but inoffensive and unprotected females. There was an old proverb - *"Whylst grasse doth growe oft sterves (starves) the seely steede"*. The phrase "silly Suffolk", used to describe one of the counties in East Anglia sounds distinctly disparaging, but the natives take it as a compliment, because it sums up their splendid isolation and individuality. The original sense of "blessed, happy" is preserved in the surname Selman/Sellman/Silman/Sillman - "happy man", someone of a cheerful disposition, content with his lot. But in 1348, Robert Selymon showed the darker side of his nature when he broke into the house of Cecilia, daughter of Thomas de Denston, at Cambridge, beating, wounding and ill-treating her. The name seesaws back and forth with Salmon, for Thomas Selman (1689) appears as Thomas Salmon at Burslem in 1695. If Salmon is the original name, then this is from a Hebrew name from "shalom" - "peace", brought over by the Normans as "Salomon, Salemon". John Selman was bailiff to William Davenport, Esquire at Holmes Farm, Maer in 1851. The Audley parish registers teem with the surname Sillito(e) from the sixteenth century onwards, as shown by the following random specimens: 1540, June 23rd, Helen, daughter of Richard Syllytoe, baptised; 1588, July 23rd, Margery Sillitoe (widow) buried; 1637, June 29th, Richard Sillitoe and Margery Brockes, married, and so on. In 1851 George Sillito was farming land at Huntley near Cheadle, and in 1875 Thomas Sillitoe of Hope Street, East Vale, Longton, was one of the local Board of Health Officers.

The surname Rathbone (Rathband) has not yet been satisfactorily explained. Ideas put forward range from the Irish "Rathbane" - "white fort", and Welsh "Rhathbon" - "stumpy clearing or plain", to the Welsh Ruabon. All early recordings have no preposition and therefore Richard Rathebon, cited for Worcestershire in the 1275 subsidy rolls and 1347 Catalogue of Ancient Deeds. John Rathebon of Cheshire should be discussed with Thomas Rathebon, head of one of the families at Shugborough in 1532 and Richard Ratthbon, member of the Brewood muster in 1539, plus Margaret Raithbone from the Betley parish registers, dated 1543. This latter example, although somewhat late, implies a derivation from Middle English "hrathe (rathe) bon(e)," literally "swift bone", where "bone" refers to the legs, and this would be an ideal nickname for a fast runner or messenger. This should also be compared with 1317 Gaol Delivery Rolls, Robert Rathebayn of Yorkshire, a hybrid of the Saxon "hraeth" and the Old Norse "beinn" - "leg", again a very appropriate description of a speedy herald or errand boy. This, in its turn, is reminiscent of the surnames Raybone and Rabone, which are from Old Norse "ra-bein(n)" or Old English "ra-ban" - "roe-bone", a nickname for a person with legs as fast as those of the roe deer - cf. 1310 Inquisitions, William Rebone (sic) of Ashley near Mucklestone.   But the Old English compound "ra-ban" normally develops into **Roebone Rawbone** Roebone and Rawbone, as typified by 1532, John Rabon of Tixall, noted as John Rawbone in the 1539 Muster.   Yet Rawbone often vacillates with Rathbone, as verified in the Churchwarden's accounts for Tunstall in 1645, where Edward Rawbone is alternatively quoted as Edward Rathbone in the same year.   But this is nothing when set aside James Rathbond of Gnosall (1615), whose name is written down in the registers from 1615 to 1630 as Raborne, Raubonne, Raebone, Rabone and Rawbone, virtually running the whole gamut of variations.   There is even a locality called Rathbone in Cheshire (1842 Ordnance Survey map), situated north east of Newbold Astbury, but whether this has spawned any Rathbones over the centuries is not known.   Spellings such as "Raborne, Raebone" above, could **Raeburn Rayburn** produce the hybrids Raeburn and Rayburn, but these are normally Scottish imports from the old lands of Ryburn in the parish of Dunlop, Ayrshire cf Wolstanton parish registers.   1680, December 13th, Marriage between Margrett Rayburn and Thomas Stanway.   The Corporation minutes for Newcastle-under-Lyme in 1557 report that *"Hugh Rathbone of Stone, one of the kinge and the queens Majesties yeomen ys admitted to be a free burgess of this borow for his lyffe"*.   During the Chartist riots in September, 1842, one of the Sunday school teachers involved in the disturbances was Charles Rathbone, master of St. Edward's Sunday School, Leek, who had marched all the way with the rioters to Burslem.   He expressed regret for his actions, but was suspended for two months without pay.   1875, Joseph Rathband of London Road, Newcastle-under-Lyme; 1887, John Rathbone (family grocer and mechanic) of Church Street, Talke; 1907, Reverend T. Hervey Rabone, surrogate of marriage licences, Waterloo Road, Burslem.

Rabold Raybold Raybould In imitation of the couplet Newbon/Newbold, the surname Rabon(e) is transposed into Rabold/Raybold/Raybould, as evidenced in the parish registers of St Matthew's Church, Walsall, where Thomas Rabone (1615) is quoted as Thomas Rabold in 1612. Rabold in all its variations is more often than not derived from the Germanic personal name "Raginbald, Rainbald, Reinbald" - "might bold", which the Normans brought to this country as "Rainbaut, Raimbaut, Raimbault, Rambaut".   Register of Robert de Stretton, 1384, John Reynbolt of Herdewyk (priest); 1441, John Reybald, vicar of Wolstanton; 1571, Elizabeth Reabolt of Lapley. Another development is Rainbow: Newcastle-under-Lyme parish registers, 1791, William Rainbow (potter) of Stoke, married to Charlotte Bates.

MISCELLANEOUS SERVANTS

In the households of the wealthy there was usually some kind of washstand, or at least a cupboard on which was placed a metal basin and a container for water. People were encouraged to wash their hands and face and clean their teeth every morning, but the subject of baths seems to be the last thing on their minds.   King

John, however, is known to have taken a bath about once every three weeks, in a large tub, protected by a curtain or canopy. Some of the better-class households did employ attendants who prepared the bath for their superiors, often accompanying their masters on expeditions around the country. This is one source of the surname Bath, but also possible is a locative from the cathedral city of Bath in Somerset, whilst in our county the surname is often a variant of Batch/Bach, since Thomas Bath, John and William Bach all occur at Kinver in the 1666 hearth tax returns. At Thursfield in 1625, William Bath, member of the frankpledge, *"presents that Ant. Milnes and Richard Edge broke the assizes"*. Each was fined four pence. In 1907 Frederick Charles Bath (potter's fireman) lived in Brocksford Street, Fenton.

Whether soap was used for personal hygiene has not been definitely ascertained. The soap was made and sold by the Soper/Soaper. Castlechurch parish registers, 1752, Ann Soaper married Samuel Harris on August 16th. But soap or some type of solution containing wood ashes and caustic soda or lye, was resorted to for washing and rinsing sheets, table-cloths, towels etc in a wooden trough. This work was done by the laundress, and it is not difficult to picture Margaret la Lavendere of Endon, tenant of the Audleys at Endon in 1308, toiling away in her cottage, rented for six pence a year from the lord, and then hanging out the day's washing to dry on the croft at the back. This is the meaning of the modern surname Lavender, better known in its abbreviated forms Launder and Lander, and of course in the modern offshoots - "to launder" and the nouns "laundry, laundress, launderette". Apparently, there is no connection at all with the aromatic herb, but surely Margaret, the launderess of Endon would have preferred this association, and then she would have been transported from her steamy, smelly wash-house to a romantic rendezvous under blue medieval skies, exchanging fragrant flowers as love tokens with her sweetheart. Both Launder and Lander ramify strongly across the county from the Reformation onwards and the two spellings often alternate with one another, e.g 1532, Richard Launder of Stafford, quoted as Richard Lander in the 1539 Muster. In 1851 Thomas Lander was farming land at Moddershall and in 1875 George Lander sold tallow candles in his shop in Massey's Square, Burslem. Nowadays the most widespread variant is Lander with Launder and Lavender very sporadic, and a fourth version Landor extremely thin on the ground: 1872, George Lavender and Son (grocer), Heathfield Lane, Darlaston (near Wednesbury); 1872, Robert Landor, Church Street, Rugeley.

Whilst the washerwoman was occupied with her daily chores in the laundry, the feminine presence was also evident whenever anyone in the household fell ill, and the nurse was summoned to tend the unfortunate victim. The word is from Middle English, Old French "norice, nurice", connected with the verb "nourish". In 1402 Egylyn Nurse held a burgage at Abbot's Bromley with an adjacent garden, at the will of the lord, and for an annual rent of two shillings and sixpence. In 1470 Margaret Nurse of Huntley near Cheadle (labourer), in collaboration with three others, broke into Thomas Belet's close at Biddulph and stole five oxen worth 100 shillings. The spelling "norice" has been absorbed by Norris, which normally goes back to Anglo French "nor(r)eis" - "the northerner, the man from the north": 1344, Henry le Norreys of Alstonefield. Samuel Norris was incumbent at St. Margaret's Church, Betley in 1735. Sometimes Norris is reduced to Norr(e)y: 1614, William Norres (Norrey) of Ranton. In 1907 Ernest Norry (potter) lived in Legge Street, Newcastle-under-Lyme.

Norris
Norr(e)y

If the patient's illness proved difficult to diagnose, then the doctor was notified. The medieval general practitioner was known as a "leech", as in Stephen le Leche of Standon (1332 lay subsidy rolls), assessed as Stephen medicus in 1327. This gives the modern surnames Leach/Leech/Leetch/Leitch. The doctor's first task was to find out the natural temperament of the person he was treating by calculating the proportions of the four elements which made up his or her character -"earth, air, fire, water" - the four medieval "humours", denoting whether the patient was sanguine, choleric, phlegmatic or melancholy. Then he decided, whether there was any blood-letting to be carried out, leeches to be applied, or any purges to be administered, and so on. Recommended cures sound loathsome in the extreme and very dangerous to the modern patient. For instance, for anyone suffering from quinsy, the cure advocated was *"Take a fat cat, skin it, draw out the guts and take the grease of a hedgehog and the fat of a bear and fennugreek, and sage, and gum of honeysuckle and virgin wax. All this crumble small and stuff the cat, roast it whole and gather the grease and anoint the patient therewith"*.

Leach
Leech
Leetch
Leitch

In 1354, one of these medieval doctors, John le Leche of Stafford, and his brother Ralph, were two of thirteen defendants accused of beating, wounding and ill-treating Richard de Aldelyme (Audlem), monk of the Priory of St. Thomas the Martyr near Stafford. A jury found nine of the accused not guilty of the injury and trespass, but John le Leche, his brother Ralph and two others were found guilty of the charges and the plaintiff's damages were fixed at 100 shillings. Leach and Leech, together with Letch and Latch(es) are also to be derived from the dialectal "latch, letch, leach" - "stream, bog" as in 1344 Assizes, Ralph de la Lache of Alstonefield, who clearly resided by some boggy stream. This term occurs in the surname Cartledge, discussed in volume 1. In 1700/1701 widow Elizabeth Leeche received 6 pence each week from the overseers of the poor at Newcastle-under-Lyme, and Jane Leech was married to Thomas Seabridge (widower) at Swynnerton on August 6th 1811. Leachman/Leechman, plus the Scottish equivalents Leishman and Lishman refer to the servant of the physician.

Leachman
Leechman
Leishman
Lishman

Old French "mire" - "physician", survives as Myers, but this is a south Staffordshire surname. Mary, daughter of Robert Myers of Oaken Park, was baptised at Codsall on May 20th, 1634. An alternative origin might be Old Norse "myrr" - "marsh", denoting habitation nearby. 1907, S. Myers (tobacconist), Lichfield Street, Hanley.

Myers

In medieval England the "barber" was first and foremost a surgeon, bloodletter and dentist and only rarely a shaver of beards, for that is its true derivation, from Latin "barba" - "beard". It was not until the sixteenth century, that the various guilds of barbers and surgeons were amalgamated into the United Company of Barber-Surgeons, out of which was formed the Royal College of Surgeons in the eighteenth century. In 1293, Henry le Barbur of Newcastle-under-Lyme was arrested for the death of Richard of the Brokhurst, a robber, whom he had beheaded. When a robber or fugitive fled and resisted capture he was killed by his pursuers and his head brought in as a means of identifying him. From Bishop Blythe's visitation in 1518, it emerges, that John Barbour was one of the brethren at Ranton Abbey during the priorship of Thomas Alton. In the 1871 Census returns for Bagnall James Barber is described by the enumerator as aged 27 years, a stone quarryman, born at Leek, and in 1887 Henry Barber (monumental mason) traded from his premises along Newcastle Street, Burslem.

By the beginning of the fourteenth century there were about 750 hospitals of various types throughout the country, many founded by the Church, others established by trade or professional guilds, whilst a few owed their existence to private benefactors. For instance, St. Bartholomew's Hospital in London was founded in 1123 by Rahere, apparently to honour a promise he had made when he was recuperating from a bout of malaria on the island of S. Bartolomeo in Rome on the river Tiber. Some hospitals employed paid attendants and John atte hospital of Enville (1332 Inquisitions) was probably just such an employee, mixing the remedies and potions, keeping the cubicles and day-rooms clean and tidy, and so forth. The name eventually becomes shortened to Spittle, as in Amice atte Spitele, sued for a third of thirty acres at Morfe in 1346, by Matilda, former wife of William de Bermyngham. This surname is characteristic of the southern sector of the county e.g. 1872, Moses Spittal, Midland Hotel, Station Street, Burton-on-Trent; 1872, Mark Spittle, Park Place, Soho Hill, Handsworth.

Chaucer's Doctor
Leech p. 40

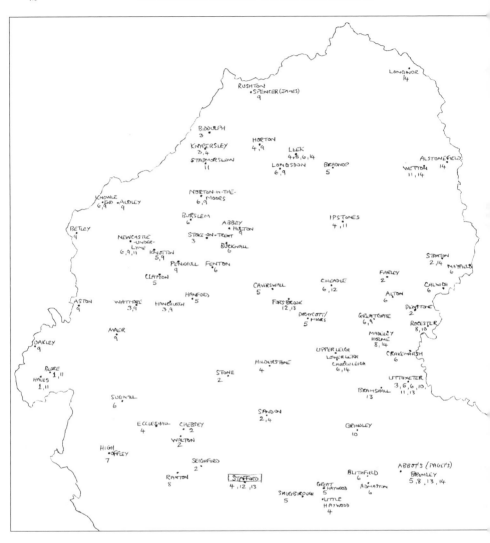

MAP 2 KEY

1. BENBOW   5. FISHER   9. KNIGHT   13 WARNER
2. BILL   6. FOSTER   10. PLIMMER   14 WOODWARD
3. BOWYER   7. FURBER   11. PRINCE
4. FAULKNER   8. KEMP   12. TIPPER

SURNAMES AT THE TIME OF THE 1666 HEARTH TAX RETURNS

CHAPTER TWO
THE AGE OF CHIVALRY

In Anglo Saxon society every free man was liable to follow his lord into battle, whilst the "thanes", roughly equivalent to the later medieval "barons", had to turn out in full armour to serve the king and even to muster a specified number of armed soldiers. In order to attain the status of "thane" the person in question had to be in possession of five hides of land, but this particular tenure of land was not in any way a prerequisite for his military service. This archaic term "thane" survives remarkably as the surname Thain(e)/Thane/Thayne. An assize was convened in 1300 to decide whether Roger le Theyn and William son of Thomas Dadus had unjustly dispossessed Emma, daughter of Thomas Dadus of Podmore of a messuage and a bovate (about 15 acres) of land in Chatcull.

The obsolete "dreng" lives on too - young man, used of a free tenant, especially in ancient Northumbria, holding by a tenure partly military, partly servile, or a personal name - Old Norse "Drengr". In 1227, William Dreng sued Robert Luvel (le Vel), Nicolas de Olregate (Alregat) and Beatrice his wife for two acres in Tamworth, but remitted his claim for half a mark of silver. Lichfield Cathedral Registers, 1702, August 4th, Elizabeth Dring married John Barton of Kingstone near Uttoxeter. Drointon near Blithfield Reservoir preserves the same word - "Drengeton" (1279) - "homestead of the drengs".

In the twelfth century "smallman" is coupled with "thanes" and "drengs" in a way, which seems to show that he was inferior to both in the medieval pecking order, possibly a holder of a small portion of land, and thus on a par with Smallpiece. Thomas Smalman (yeoman) was buried at Stowe-by-Chartley on September 7th, 1599, and the marriage took place at Audley on October 3rd, 1636, between Elizabeth Smalman and Thomas Nickson. 1907, Arthur Smallman (porter) of Charles Street, Hanley.

Under the Normans, however, military tenure was an integral cog in the feudal machine, constituting in fact one of the conditions by which the noble classes held their land. Under this system every foot of land throughout the kingdom belonged by right to the reigning monarch and he could apportion any fraction of it at will to any noble who took the oath of "fealty" - "faithfulness", by which he promised to assemble a force of armed men to come to the defence of the realm in time of a military crisis. In their turn the nobles handed out portions of their own land to under-tenants, who swore "fealty" to them and agreed to render aid to their lords should the need arise. The service required of them was that of a fully armed horseman, or knight, and the land which the knight held was known as a "knight's fee", that is, deemed sufficient to maintain a knight with suitable retinue. In 1297

Robert de Hastang held the Manor of Chebsey for one Knight's Fee, worth £10 yearly in homages.

Thus, the state of being a knight in medieval society, with all its trappings of chivalry, pageantry and obligations, depended on training as a mounted warrior in the lord's cavalry in return for the ownership of some land. Knighthood could also be a great honour and a stepping stone into the ranks of the lesser nobility, but in essence the knight combined the functions of the horseman and servant, since the former idea is perpetuated in western European languages by the words "chevalier, cavaliere, caballero" and "Ritter", whereas the latter lives on in the Saxon "cniht" and the German "Knecht". To the Saxons it meant "youth, boy", then a young servant, and only in the Middle Ages did it take on the sense of a mounted attendant who was fully armed and bound to some lord or noble to serve as a mounted soldier. Consequently, there is no way of knowing whether, in the 1327 Lay subsidy rolls, Richard le Knyght of Longridge near Penkridge was a servant of some military leader, a man at arms, household servant of some lord, or just a common soldier. Assessed at three shillings in the top band of taxpayers, he was certainly of some status thereabouts. Another member of the fraternity, nevertheless, was less fortunate, for in 1307, John le Knyght of Cannock was physically beaten by Richard Austyn of Norton and John, son of Thomas Tromewyne of Cannock, both of whom were paid four shillings by John Knoke to carry out the attack. John Knoke denied the fact, and put himself on the country. A jury found him guilty, and he was committed to gaol. At a session of the Tunstall manor court, held on 9th December, 1512, Richard Stephenson *"makes fine with the lord to have twelve men for twelve pence to enquire whether Thomas Knyght owes John the chaplain the rent of 16 acres at Tunstall which were lately Richard's"*. In 1851 Josiah Knight was farming land at Milwich and in 1905 the Endon Brass Band, consisting mostly of miners, gave a series of concerts in the recently erected Young Men's Christian Association hut on School Bank, Brown Edge under their conductor M. Samuel Knight.

Knight

The Norman pronunciation of "knight" was "knivet", origin of the modern surnames Knivett/Knevet/Knevit/Nevett/Nevitt: 1199 Assizes, Osbert Knivet. In 1572, Thomas Knevett (armiger) remitted all right to Mathew Cradock and William Cradocke, of a tenement, 2 tofts, 100 acres of land, 100 acres of meadow and 100 acres of pasture in Silkmore, Stafford, and of a free fishery in the water of Penk. Thomas was given 200 marks of silver for the transaction. In 1851 Jane Nevitt (milliner and dressmaker) had a shop in Tipping Street, Stafford. 1907, Samuel Nevitt (flour mill man), Wellington Street, Fenton. Newett and Newitt are possible variants: Barton-under-Needwood parish registers, 1730, John Newit, son of John and Anna Newit, baptised on October 18th. In the Welsh border counties all these names are colloquial forms of the Welsh "Ednyfed".

Knivett
Knevet
Knevit
Nevett
Nevitt

Newett
Newitt

The Knights of the Temple or Templars was a military and religious organisation consisting of armed horsemen, chaplains and men at arms, who had taken semi-monastic vows, based on rules drawn from the Augustinian and Benedictine orders of monks. It was founded at Jerusalem about 1115 to protect the Holy Sepulchre and pilgrims to the Holy land but accusations of heresy led to suppression of the Order by the Pope in 1312. The Knights Templar got their name from their occupation on or near the site of the Temple of Solomon in Jerusalem. From this military order come the names Temple, Templer/Templar and Templeman. Robert Temple, and his wife Ann and son Thomas were amongst the inhabitants of Barton-under-Needwood in 1532, and Reverend Robert Temple was curate at St. Mary's, Forebridge, Stafford in 1851. Richard le Templer of Congreve near Penkridge contributed eighteen pence to the local subsidy in 1327, whilst in 1666 Godfree Templer was too poor to donate anything at Alstonefield to the hearth tax collectors. Templeman refers to a person who lived on a manor owned by the Templars. 1907, John Templeman (fish dealer) of Waterloo Road, Burslem.

The Scottish surname Bannerman is popularly believed to have been adopted by some ancestor who held the office of standard bearer to one of the early kings. The name Banner is a similar name, signifying the banner or standard bearer of a knight or a lord in the field of battle, or someone who summons, proclaims or heralds. Another suggestion is that the banner-man took part in the Corpus Christi procession, carrying the ensign of the lord, whose retainer he was. This recalls the annual "beating the bounds ceremony" in pre-Reformation days, when the lord of the manor, accompanied by priests in surplices and parishioners with hand-bells, walked round the parish in a great procession, stopping at wayside crosses, "singing gospels to the corn", and the lord himself holding aloft some appropriate banner. In 1398 Katrine Banner sued John Warylowe and Joan his wife for forcibly breaking into her houses and close at Burton-on-Trent, and taking her goods and chattels to the value of 100 shillings. 1907, Sarah Ellen Banner (newsagent), Bucknall New Road, Hanley; 1907, Ernest Banner (potter's placer), Adelaide Street. Fenton. But in our county, where "shanner" becomes "shonner", Banner develops into Bonner, as in the Tatenhill manor court rolls, where William Banner (1433) crops up as William Boner in 1466. If the original name is Bonner, then the origin is Old French "bonnaire", a contracted form of "debonnaire", a nickname for an individual who had a good, pleasant air or manner. William Boner was taxed to the tune of two shillings for Whitmore and Hanchurch in 1332 and in 1875 James Bonner (solicitor's clerk) had premises in Caroline Street, Longton.

The "rider" too was a mounted warrior, a knight or cavalryman, often with his own attendant or servant, e.g. 1327, Geoffrey le Rideresmon of Brocton by Cannock. Yet the chief forester was also popularly known as "the Rider". He was of knightly rank, in charge of the rangers and other foresters, whose duties corresponded to those of the modern gamekeeper, and his office was hereditary. Some families called Rider or Ryder had ancestors who dwelt by a clearing, from an old Saxon word "ryd" or "ried", but this is not evidenced for Staffordshire. In

1306 Henry, son of William le Rider of Butterton-on-the-Moors was accused of feloniously killing Roger, son of Benedict de Boterdon in Butterton itself, and in 1459 John Crecy (clerk) sued John Ryder of Newcastle-under-Lyme (yeoman) for breaking into his close at Newcastle, stealing 40 shillings in money and depasturing cattle on his grass. Joane Ryder was married to Richard Adhamson at the Church of St. Mary, Swynnerton on June 20th, 1573. In 1666 Thomas Rider was charged on one hearth at Tittesworth, whilst Mary Rider was exempted at Leek. 1851, Samuel Rider (blacksmith) of Thursfield; 1875, David Ryder (coal dealer), Hanover Street, Hanley.

Rideout
Ridout

Rideout/Ridout is simply a nickname for a rider: 1851, James Ridout (silk manufacturer), King Street, Leek; 1907, Charles Ridout (secretary for Chemical Works), Chatterley.

Squire(s)

In the twelfth and thirteenth centuries the chivalric concept was encouraged by the legends surrounding the larger-than-life figures of Charlemagne and King Arthur and the Knights of the Round Table. But the era which deliberately fostered the knightly attitudes and ideals more than any other was the fourteenth century with the victories of Edward III and the Black Prince during the Hundred Years War with France such as Crecy and Poitiers. Inspired by these stupendous triumphs, many young men set their sights on joining the knightly ranks. As a "squire", or knight-aspirant, he started out on his career as a shield bearer for the knight - Old French "escuyer, esquier". Young boys of the knightly class were sent as "pages" to the castle of their father's liege lord at about the age of seven. They graduated to the rank of "squire" at the age of thirteen or fourteen, when they were apprenticed to knights and trained in the knightly pursuits until about the age of twenty or twenty one. Then they were fully fledged knights. In 1292, Alexander the esquire of William de Mere, who entered Dudley Park and took 6 does along with other poachers and brought them to the Castle of Dudley, was most likely a young man of good birth, attendant on a knight. In 1666 Richard Squire was charged on two hearths at Weston upon Trent Constablewick and in 1851 John Squire (manufacturer) lived in South Bank House, Leek. 1887, Arthur Squires (silk mercer), Waterloo Road, Burslem. The northern counterpart is Swire(s), Swiers,

Swire(s)
Swiers
Swyer

Swyer: 1618, Anna, daughter of John Squire, "vulgaritur" John Swyer, of Skipton, north Yorkshire. By the seventeenth century, the "squire" had turned into the "country gentleman", a rather middle-aged, rural pillar of society, far removed from his humble beginnings.

Bachelor
Batchelor
Batcheler
Backler

Sharing the same status as the squire is the "bachelor" - novice in arms, later a knight serving under another's banner. Modern spellings of the surnames include Bachelor, Batchelor, Batcheler and Backler, not all of which are evidenced. Chaucer uses the word in the sense of "university graduate" in the Franklin's Tale: *"His felawe...was that tyme a Bacheler of lawe...."* And in the sense of unmarried man in the Merchant's Tale: *"Bacheleris haue often peyne and wo"*. In 1264 Roger de Miners is dubbed "bachilarius" of Simon de Montfort the younger, that is, young retainer, aspirant for knighthood, and in 1376 in the suit of Richard Bromshulf against William Grislay and others, for breaking into his property at Chartley and Kingstone, and other places, and cutting down his trees, none of the defendants appeared, because most of them, including Henry Bachiler (probably of Loxley), were dead and the rest had vanished into thin air. James Batchelor of Beech was buried at Swynnerton on December 20th, 1705 and Mary Bachelour and William Heath got married at Standon in 1723. F.J. Batchelor was selling mantles and costumes in Piccadilly, Hanley in 1907.

The name Child harks back to Anglo Saxon England, when the "child" enjoyed the same status as the "drengs" of the northern Danelaw, that is free tenants who held land from the lord of the manor in return for performing military service and certain servile duties for him. In the Age of Chivalry, however, it was applied to a young noble awaiting knighthood. But the surname Child(e), Childs, Chiles can also refer to the youngest child or a minor at the time of his parents' death, or it may be a reprimand for someone who was childish or immature, a locative for habitation by some spring, from Old English "celde", as in Honeychild in Kent - "Huna's spring", or even a corrupted form of Giles: Rugeley parish registers, 1617, Henry Child alias Gyles. 1626, Henry Joyles (sic) alias Child. Giles is originally from Greek "aigidion" - "kid", put down in Latin in medieval documents as "Egidius" as in 1227 Assizes, Giles (Egidius) de Erdinton. In 1348 John de Burghton recovered five acres of land in Eccleshall from Walter le Childe of Sugnall, and Alice, his wife. Elizabeth Child was buried at Ellastone on February 20th, 1639. Trade directories: 1851, Peter Child (brick and tile maker) of Ellenhall; 1875, William Child (cabinet maker and upholsterer) of High Street, Longton; 1907, James Child (saggar maker), Etruria Road, Hanley.

Chil(l)man represents either an attendant of a young noble or is traceable to either one of two Saxon personal names - Cildmann, or Ceolmund - "ship guardian", the latter preserved in Cholmondeley in Cheshire. William Childeman appears in a Staffordshire assize, dated 1253, concerning the rightful ownership of some land in Levedale, north west of Penkridge.

Two compounds of interest here are Goodchild - "godchild" or "good child" (no examples) and Fairchild - "beautiful child". At the Standon manor court, held on Monday, the eve of the Feast of St. Chad the Bishop, 1361, William Fairchild was fined two pence for allowing his cattle to stray into the lord's enclosure. An infant called Sarah Fairchild, aged 3 years, was buried at Newcastle-under-Lyme on May 20th, 1805.

As soon as the knights had completed their training and undergone the elaborate dubbing ceremony, by which they became members of the order of chivalry, they had to test their skills by tilting at the quintain. This consisted of a stout post or block of wood mounted on a support, which had to be tilted at with

Tilting at the quintain. (Quinton p. 49)

Novice being knighted and receiving his sword. (Knight p. 44)

lances or poles. Sometimes the quintain was fashioned into a revolving dummy, made of chain mail, covered with a shield, or with a bar, that was weighted down with a sand-bag, which swung round and unseated unskilful horsemen. This could be one source of the modern surname Quinton. In 1414 the vill of Normacot had to forfeit the value of an arrow with which Robert Wilteshire had been feloniously killed by Richard Quynteyne. This amounted to one penny. However, a number of other lines must be investigated, such as the Old French personal name "Quentin", from Latin "Quintinus" - "fifth", common in medieval France on account of the cult of St. Quentin of Amiens. Several locatives, too, are under the microscope, comprising Quinton near Halesowen, Quinton south of Northampton and Quinton in Gloucestershire, all for "the queen's manor", whilst the Normans may have brought the name from Saint-Quentin in La Manche, or Saint-Quentin-en-Tourmont in Somme, cf. Wolverhampton parish registers, 1636, Elnor Saintquinton. Heads of households in 1532 include Thomas Quenton at Rocester and Richard Quenton at Hixon. Rowland Quinton ran a tailor's shop in High Street, Tunstall in 1887.

At the beginning of the fourteenth century the sword was the symbol or badge of rank of a knight, and indeed this particular weapon was regarded almost as exclusive to the nobility. Lessons in the "noble art of self-defence" were given by the fencing master, the "skirmisher", from the Old French verb "eskirmir" - "to fence", hence our "skirmish" and "scrimmage". The "skirmish" was originally a hand-to-hand encounter between two knights or mounted warriors. The surnames derived from this word have been subject to much wear and tear over the years, but the two most common survivals are Scrimgeour and Scrimshaw. Various Skrimshires were sheriffs of Staffordshire during the seventeenth century, eg 1618, Thomas Skrimshire of Johnson Hall near Eccleshall, 1638, John Skrimshire of Norbury, 1651, Gerrard Skrimeshire of Aqualate and 1676, Walter Skrimshaw of Orslow.

Gradually the knights perfected their skills in mock battles and jousting tournaments organized by their overlords and princes. Essentially these were training grounds for the actual business of war itself. In preparation for these public spectacles the knight's armour and weapons had to be thoroughly cleaned and polished by his attendants, but more often than not by the "frobisher" or "furber". Richard le Fourbour of Stafford was on the receiving end of a dastardly assault by Adam de Erbryghton at Stafford in 1306. Elizabeth Furber married George Audley at Audley on May 20th, 1670. In 1851 local farmers included Thomas Furber at Tunstall (Adbaston) and William Furber at Vicarage Farm, Ranton. In 1907 Harry Furber (machine agent) lived in Stanier Street, Fenton. The parish registers for High Offley overflow with the surname Furber from 1659-1812. Apparently Frobisher Hall west of Swynnerton is one of a number of Government establishments built in the area in the early 1940s, named after naval heroes cf Drake Hall and Raleigh Hall near Eccleshall.

The knights on their war-horses (destriers or chargers) formed the backbone of a medieval army, but the knight and his personal retainers only made up one unit of the medieval cavalry. The commanding officers of the troops were the leading members of the aristocracy - the barons, earls, dukes and princes, and the poorer knights without a retinue were demoted to fighting in the ranks. The infantry consisted of 3 categories - heavy infantry, composed of dismounted men-at-arms, medium infantry of partly armoured crossbowmen and spearmen, and light infantry in the form of longbowmen, and spearmen without armour, and the peasantry armed with a whole range of primitive weapons such as cudgels, spades, and slings.

But how did people outside the nobility acquire their "noble" surnames such as Lord, Earl, Baron, Duke, Prince, not to mention King? In placenames the element "king" as in Kingstone near Uttoxeter and Kingsley near Cheadle signifies "royal" or "held by the king". King's Bromley north of Lichfield was owned by the Kings of Mercia and then by William the Conqueror. When we examine the Staffordshire subsidy rolls for 1327 and 1332 and discover entries such as Adam le Kynge at Bucknall, Robert le Kyng at Seighford and William le Kynge at Cheddleton and other inhabitants called "le Kyng(e)" in village after village right across the county, then we are compelled to ask the question - "What is the real reason for this royal obsession?" The solution is simple - the surname King is a relic of the ancient Spring and May Day ceremonies, when it was customary for young people to go out "Maying" very early in the morning on the first day of May. To simple rural folk in medieval England it was a fundamental part of their way of life, culminating in the crowning of the King or Queen of the May, hence all these tax-payers in the subsidy lists boasting the name "King". Nowadays, this role has been usurped by the May Queen.

Nevertheless, some bearers of the name King could trace their ancestry back to the King of the Minstrels, another medieval ceremony, once prevalent at the Tutbury Court of Minstrelsy. Under the Duchy of Lancaster, Tutbury became renowned throughout the kingdom for its princely magnificence and it was soon a magnet for minstrels from far and wide. In order to determine their claims for precedence, one of their own number was appointed and given the title of King of the Minstrels. He in turn had several inferior officers to assist him in the execution of his duties. With regard to the legal status of the King of Minstrels, there can be no doubt, because his power and privileges were outlined in a subsequent charter granted by Richard II and ratified by Henry VI *"in the 21st year of his reign to licence trumpeters and other minstrels"*. King was also used as a personal name before the Conquest.

In 1307, at the local assizes, Adam son of Robert le Kyng of Tunstall, was indicted for the death of John, son of Robert de Chelle. This snippet is ample proof of the genuine origins of the name. Here Robert le Kyng might have got his name on account of his swaggering behaviour or kingly appearance, or from playing the

Kinge(e)
Kings

role of "king" in some pageant or play. Anne Kinge, "a poore woman", was buried at Stowe-by-Chartley on February 28th, 1609, and Mary King was married to John Jonson at Seighford on November 4th, 1689. In 1875 Alexander King (grocer) was trading at Newcastle-under-Lyme Ironmarket and in 1907 Edward King of Hall Street, Burslem was the local market inspector.

Overall, all the surnames derived from the ranks of the nobility, have a touch of irony or mockery about them and came about as nicknames for villeins at the very bottom of the social ladder, who imitated the haughty attitudes and grandiose ways of their superiors, either consciously or otherwise, and tried to get above their station. In the Middle Ages the term "baron" was also applied to freemen in the cities of London and York and the Cinque Ports. The latter in fact had the honour of bearing the canopy over the head of the sovereign on Coronation Day. Circa 1249 Robert Baron was amongst those present at an enquiry concerning the value of Newcastle-under-Lyme and the surrounding manor and in 1286 Simon Cotyn of Madeley withdrew his suit against Nicholas le Baroun of Stafford respecting common pasture in Great Madeley. After the end of the Middle Ages the surname Baron/Barron is not all that common in our county. John Baron was the incumbent at the Church of St. Matthew, Walsall in 1822 and in 1907 Mrs J.Barron was the owner of a grocer's shop in Vessey Street, Newcastle-under-Lyme.

Earl(e), Earll, Earls is just as scarce. The allusion here may be to someone who was employed in an earl's household, but again there are hints of sarcasm for an individual with aristocratic pretensions, or a name from the pageants. William le Erl, taxed at twelve pence for Kinver in 1327, is most likely a nickname. 1851, Henry Earls (boot and shoemaker), Mill Street, Leek; 1875, Emanuel Earl (headmaster), Orme's School, Higherland, Newcastle-under-Lyme.

Duke(s) and variant spellings such as Dooks, Doke, Doak, Duck and Duckes, are very tricky to decipher. Ultimately "duke" goes right back to Latin "dux" - "leader", "chieftain", "head", becoming our "duke" via Old French "duc". In medieval England it was the highest hereditary title of the nobility or a sovereign prince ruling a duchy or small state, as in William the Conqueror, Duke of Normandy. In 1379 there were only two dukes in England - John of Gaunt and John of Brittany. In the Middle Ages, the two words "duke" and "duck" are almost impossible to tell apart - e.g. "duke" occurs as "duc, duk(e), douk, doke", whilst "duck" is written as "duk(ke), duck, doke, dook". Thus, Henry le Duk, assessed at Yarnfield in 1327 is ambiguous, although he may be identical with Henry le Ducke, recorded as paying his subsidy at Swynnerton in 1332. John Dukes of Blithbury, cited in a dispute over a tenement and land in Mavesyn Ridware in 1320 could be a nickname for a person who fancied himself as a leader of men, captain of an army or something along those lines. In 1612 John Dooke was paying four pence rent per annum for his penthouse in Newcastle-under-Lyme. 1851, George Dukes (swine dealer), parish of Stowe-by-Chartley; 1851, William Dukes (butcher), Maybank,

Jukes
Juckes
Jewkes

Wolstanton. There is later fluctuation with Jukes, as in Pelsall parish registers. 1800, John Dukes, noted as John Jukes in 1804. Jukes, Juckes and Jewkes are normally short forms of "Jukel, Jokel", from the Old Breton/Old Cornish personal name "Iudicael". The "D-J" interchange is an echo of Dewsbury-Jewsbury. 1875, Barnaby Jukes (joiner), Blantyre Street, Dresden; 1907, Mrs Annie Elizabeth Juckes (newsagent), Uttoxeter Road, Longton.

Lord

Lord was a title of honour bestowed on monks and persons of superior rank, but in the realm of surnames there may be some remnant of a nickname for the person who presided over the Christmas revels and who was known as the Lord of Misrule. He commenced his Rule on All Hallows Eve and relinquished it on Candlemas Day. In addition there are overtones of a pompous person, full of his own importance, forerunner of the modern Lord Muck of Muck Hall! Strange to think, that this word, of Saxon origin, originally meant "guardian of the loaf" - Old English "hlaf-weard", whilst his lady was "hlaf-dige" - ""kneader of bread". In 1450 Henry Lorde of Cauldon (yeoman), part of a mob from Blore and Ilam, armed and arrayed in manner of war, with bows and arrows, swords, jakkes, palets, daggers and other arms, assaulted Thomas Mane at Mapleton near Ashbourne, in the county of Derbyshire, and the said Thomas was then killed by an arrow that had lodged in his left thigh. 1851, Vernon Lord (coal dealer), Russell Street, Leek; 1907, Charles A. Lord (registrar), Hazeldene, Gladstone Place, Stoke.

Prince

Guppy found that the surname Prince was most typical of our county and the neighbouring counties of Cheshire and Derbyshire. It comes from playing the part of prince in a pageant, from service in a prince's household or a nickname for someone with lordly demeanour. In 1345, Thomas le Prynce and other local inhabitants at Stafford debated the state of a certain fishpond of the King's called "Kyngespol" near Stafford, and they came to the conclusion *"...that it will greatly increase the safety and profit of the defence of the town of the Lord the King of Stafford if the said pool be repaired and raised"*. Reparations were also on the mind of the churchwarden at Tunstall, Stoke-on-Trent in 1641, since eleven shillings was shelled out to Richard Prince for flags and slate for alterations to the porch. Jane Prince of Brund (died 1823), left £5, the income to be distributed to five poor widows of Sheen. 1851, Charles Prince (gamekeeper) of Alstonefield; 1851, Uriah Prince, licensee of the Shoulder of Mutton, Quixhill; 1875, John Prince (milk seller) of Loftus Street, Hanley.

WARFARE, WEAPONS, ARMOUR

Battle
Battell

A medieval army was split up into three divisions, called "Battles", and a soldier was often known as "(man) of the battle array, a warrior". In 1280 Juliana, the widow of Robert de Esyngge, sued Robert Batayle for a third of five acres of land in Alveton (Alton) as her dower, and recovered possession of it by default of Robert. This same Robert occurs as Robert de Bataille in 1316. Another Robert Battell is registered as head of the household at Eccleshall in 1532.

The rare surname Warr(e) literally signifies "man of the war", hence again for "warrior", "soldier": Lichfield Cathedral Registers, 1735, September 19th, Thomas Warr, married to Ann Tranter. The name is common around Brierley Hill during the nineteenth century. The original form "de la Warr" travelled all the way across the Atlantic and became the American state Delaware, named after Thomas West, Lord de la Warr, the English soldier and colonist who was appointed governor of Virginia in 1610.

The native term for a warrior was "cempa", a very old-fashioned word indeed and a much-sought after title by competitors in trials of strength, or wrestling or athletic contests on the village green. In 1356 Roger and Simon Kempe (possibly of Sandon), were amongst eight suspects arrested *"..in consequence of an indictment made before Robert de Aston, the coroner of the county, that on the Thursday after the Feast of St. Barnabas (1355), they had feloniously killed Adam de Chetewynde at Sandon"*. They were brought before the Justices by the Sheriff and pleaded not guilty to the charge. A local jury, sworn in to hear the evidence, stated that they were not guilty and had not fled, and hence they were all acquitted. In the 1539 Muster John Kempe was enrolled at Stafford, and Richard Kempe at Bromley Hurst. 1851, Thomas Kemp (horse breaker) of Rocester; 1874, Lydia Kemp (baby linen warehouse), Paradise Street, Tunstall; 1875, George Kemp (miner), Hot Lane, Burslem.

Kemp also developed into Camp due to the influence of the Old English noun "camp" - "battle", compare Adam de Camp, customary tenant of the Audleys at Chesterton in 1308, renting 18 acres from them at thirteen shillings and one penny per annum. Newcastle-under-Lyme parish registers 1812, Mary Camp, aged 3 days, buried on May 3rd.

Champ also occurs in this same area, as verified by the following specimens: 1875, John Champ (butcher) of Higherland and 1887, Henry Champ (butcher) of London Road, Chesterton. The two names Camp and Champ must be variants of one another, based on the pair Campion/Champion (see below).

Until trial by jury was introduced by Henry II in the twelfth century, in certain criminal cases, the accuser and the defendant opposed each other in the so-called "trial by battle" or "ordeal by battle". They were both bare-headed and bare-legged and wore no armour, although they were armed with a staff furnished with an iron horn (like a small pick) and carried a shield. Ordeal by battle was also resorted to by both parties over arguments about the rightful ownership of land, but here each side sometimes preferred not to fight their own battles but nominated a representative instead, a "champion" to do battle for him. Many of these "champions" were professional swordsmen or duellers, earning considerable amounts of money. The following "champion" was certainly not in this category. William le Champion was arrested in 1293 for the theft of one hundred and forty sheepskins from the house of John Derkyn of Featherstone, north of Wolverhampton. He was put on trial but pleaded that he was a "clericus", that is, a cleric in minor orders, since William de Norton, acting for John the Archbishop of Dublin and Dean of Penkridge, claimed him as being within the jurisdiction of his Deanery of Penkridge. Thus he belonged to the collegiate church at Penkridge, in all probability. Campion is a Norman French variant. In 1388 John Campyon of Engleton appeared in person against John Smyth of Coven, for forcibly treading down and consuming his corn and grass with his cattle at Engleton to the value of forty shillings. Joone Campion and Roger Harison were married at Ellastone on November 20th, 1557. In 1907, Joseph Campion (blacksmith) lived in Salisbury Street, Tunstall.

Campion *(margin)*

WEAPONS, ARCHERY AND BOWMAKING

Under the Plantagenets the bulk of the fighting in any battle was undertaken by the feudal cavalry, supplemented by professional soldiers and archers who used the crossbow. This was a short-range weapon that was not very effective against chain-mail or armour, although its greatest asset was its stunning impact, which slowed down an attack by opposing horsemen. The medieval name for the crossbow was "arbalest", and the soldier who used it was known as an "arblaster", a name also shared by the craftsman who made such a bow. In 1227 Robert le Arbelastir was involved in a suit with Ciprian de Tunstal respecting a tenement in Tunstall (probably Tunstall near Adbaston). This results in modern surnames such as Arblaster, Alabaster, Albisser, e.g. 1351, Adam le Alblaster of Tutbury, noted as Adam le Arblaster in 1357 and Rugeley parish registers, where Henry Alblaster (1618) also appears as Alabaster in 1624 and as Arblaster in 1637. Yet a spelling such as Alabaster may apply to a carver in alabaster, since Tutbury has always been the main centre of the working and extracting of gypsum in Staffordshire. For instance, the alabaster carving on the west doorway of Tutbury Priory church (1160-1170) is reputed to be the earliest known use of this material in Britain. The trade of alabaster carving was established at Burton-on-Trent in 1481, where Robert Bocher and Gilbert Twist were working for a number of religious houses, and this indicates, that it may have been a flourishing trade there in the Middle Ages. Mrs Martha Arblaster of Cheddleton parish, married Edward Phillips Esquire of St. Chad parish, Shrewsbury at Cheddleton on 12th February, 1784. In 1851 John Arblaster owned a beerhouse in Market Place, Stoke and in 1873 Henry Arblaster (cashier, hosier, fancy dealer) was resident in High Street, Tunstall. Apparently the marble called an "alley, ally" is a diminutive of "alabaster".

(margin: Arblaster / Alabaster / Albisser)

The square-headed arrows or bolts for the crossbow were known as "quarrels", giving us the surname Quarrell, a user or maker of such weapons. The rare Quorroll could well be a variant of this surname: 1875, Joseph Quorroll (hosier) of Market Place, Burslem. In a plea roll, dated 1293, the jury presented *"that*

(margin: Quarrell / Quorroll)

certain crossbow men of Gascony were passing through the vill of Longdon, near Rugeley and one of them wounded John de Hundesacre with a "quarrel", so that he died. None of the neighbourhood ventured to pursue the said "balisters" in consequence of their great number".

Robert Bolt is listed as one of the tenants of the Audleys at Audley in 1308, paying an undisclosed annual rent for a messuage (tenement) and four acres of land. This medieval gentleman could have been a maker of crossbow bolts or iron bolts in general, but the surname Bolt(e), Boult is also a nickname for a short, heavily built person or from an Old Norse name "Boltr", preserved in the north Yorkshire village of Boltby north west of Rievaulx Abbey. William Boult was a member of the Eccleshall militia in 1539 and Thomas Bolt was curate at Caverswall in 1569. In 1887 T. Boult was secretary of the Working Man's Loan Company in Pall Mall, Hanley. Bolter and Boulter are either derivatives of Old English "bolt" - again for an artisan who made bolts of any kind, or for a sifter of meal, from Old French "buleteor", as exemplified by Robert le Bultere of Lichfield in a lawsuit of 1320. The marriage between Richard Boulter and Mary Floradine was celebrated at Hints near Weeford on September 25th, 1803.

The crossbow was indeed a deadly weapon in the hands of an experienced bowman, so lethal in fact, that it had been condemned by the Church as barbaric on its introduction in the twelfth century. However, its major fault was its slow rate of fire, and this led to the gradual acceptance of the longbow by the English archers during the reign of Edward I, the first great era of army reform. In the time it took to set up and fire the crossbow at least a dozen longbow shafts could be winging their way towards the enemy ranks. During the Middle Ages England boasted the finest archers in the whole of Europe, and it was the longbowmen who were mainly responsible for the resounding victories against the French during the Hundred Years War, at Crecy, Poitiers and Agincourt. From the time of Edward I archery was the national sport, and in their spare time, at the local archery butts, in pageants or on countless village greens up and down the country, young men practised the skills and techniques that were essential to any good bowman - the sideways stance, becoming accustomed to the weight and strength of the bows, and most important of all, the hand-eye co-ordination in loading and aiming the arrows. It was this proficiency which caused such devastation to the French cavalry during the Hundred Years War. One of the most popular competitions at many a traditional May Day festival was the knocking down of a wooden parrot or "popingay", fixed on the top of a steeple, pole or tall tree. Richard Papejay of Sandon (1348 Inquisition post mortem) obviously won the contest that particular year, and thereby earned himself the name Papigay or Pobjoy.

One medieval exponent of this ancient craft in Staffordshire is Nicholas le Archer, defendant in a case dated 1350, centred on land and tenements in Field near Leigh belonging to Henry de Stanydelf. Ralph Archer, his wife Joan and family lived at Barlaston in 1532 and in 1851 Thomas Archer was taking in boarders at the Shelton Hall Academy in Shelton, Hanley. In 1887 George Archer was innkeeper at the Bridge Inn, West Street, Burslem. The uncommon Larcher retains the original French definite article, as in 1334 Assizes, Nicholas Larcher of Walsall.

Larcher

Another budding marksman by the name of Richard le Boweman was renting one stall from the Audleys at Alstonefield in 1308 at an annual rent of twelve pence. The name is still found at Alstonefield in 1664, for this was the year when Alice, the Quaker wife of Henry Bowman, was put in prison for disturbing the administration of the Sacrament on Easter Sunday. The rare Boman also crops up at Alstonefield in 1532 - Richard Boman, wife Isabel and family, and at Ilam in the same year - Robert Boman, wife Elizabeth and their family. 1851, William Bowman (boot and shoe maker), Stafford Street, Longton; 1907, Alf Bowman (road foreman), Villiers Street, Longton.

Bowman
Boman

Unlike the string of the short bow, which was drawn back only to the chest, the bowstring of the longbow had to be drawn back to the ear. Consequently the extra effort required in obtaining the correct tension gave rise to the nickname Benbow, literally "bend bow". By a curious coincidence, two medieval archers were on opposite sides of the law in 1368 when Richard Bendebowe and five others were sued by Adam le Alblaster for breaking into his close at Hoar Cross and trampling down his growing corn and grass with their cattle and consuming the said crop. In the 1841 Scriven report, John Benbow, aged 32, had been employed for about 17 years in the slip house at Messrs. Minton and Boyle's China Factory, Trentham Road, Stoke. He was suffering from Tubercular disease, brought about by the sudden transition of temperature from the hot slip-kiln to the cold slip-house. 1851, George Benbow (senior collector and parish clerk), Barlaston; 1875, Charles Benbow (brick and tile manufacturer), Lightwood, Longton. In his Dictionary of British Surnames, Professor Reaney adjudges the surname Carnall/Carnell to be an occupational term for an archer posted on the battlement of a castle during a siege in order to repel invaders, from the imported Norman French word "carnel", variant of "crenel". This origin will suffice for some of our local Carnalls and Carnells, but not all, since in the Ellastone parish registers, the name Carnell exists alongside Carlell/Carlill, which is derived from the placename Carlisle in Cumbria. This contains the Welsh "caer" - "city" and a British name which goes back to a personal name "Luguvalos". The most pertinent example at Ellastone concerns Dorothie, daughter of William Carlell, baptised on August 31st, 1587, who is almost certainly identical with Dorothie Carnell, married to Nicholas Hall on February 20th, 1617. A certain Robert de Carliol, monk at Croxden Abbey (1277 feet of fines) obviously hailed from Carlisle and may have given rise to a substantial number of Carlisles and Carnalls. The actual transition from Carlisle to Carlill/Carlell and then to Carnell and eventually to Carnall was set in motion by the weakening of Carlisle to Carlell through lack of stress, as in the American pronunciation "missal" for

Benbow

Carnall
Carnell

Carlisle
Carlill
Carlell

"missile" and in the Shakespearian "stirrell" for "sterile" in the First Folio of *Henry IV, Part 1* and "fertill" for "fertile" in Cavendish's *Life of Cardinal Wolsey*. Then, in order to make the name trip off the tongue more easily, the first "l" was replaced by the nasal "n". In 1532, heads of the household comprised Edmund Carlyll at Waterfall, and Arthur Carlyll at Ipstones, whilst William Carlisle was incumbent at Ipstones in 1789. In 1851 Betsy Carlisle was victualler at the Crown in Horton near Rudyard. 1873, Joseph Carnall, glass and china dealer of May Bank, Wolstanton; 1907, George Henry Carnall (caretaker of schools), Alberta Street, Longton. Carnwell too may be a late variant of Carnell: 1851, Elizabeth Carnwell (farmer) of Dilhorne.

Adam atte Shute, probably of Haughton near Gnosall (1340 lawsuit) was so named because he either lived by a shooting place, where archery practice was regularly carried out or dwelt by some steep hill. His descendants live on in the surname Shut(e), Shutt(s) and possible Shott cf Agnes, formerly wife of Robert de la Shote of Dilhorne, who sued Richard Aleyn in 1341 for a third of a messuage and 20 acres of land in Dilhorne as her dower. In 1666 Walter Shutt was charged on one hearth at Blithfield and Admaston; 1851, Samuel Shutt (butcher), Paradise Street, Tunstall. The extended name Shutter, Shotter and Shooter denotes an archer or bowman with a good aim. In 1403 Thomas Shoter of Alton was summoned to appear at the local assizes by William Vykers of Caverswall for mayhem and breach of the peace.

Traditionally the stave of the English longbow was made from yew, maple or oak, but if these woods were in short supply, then the bowmakers had to make do with hazel, ash or elm. In a long, drawn-out assize of 1314, involving the killing of Robert de Esnyngton (Essington) at Essington, there are several references to the actual weapons which delivered the fatal blows to the deceased, including *"...a bow of Spanish yew, two ells in length (about seven feet six inches), and of the thickness of four men's thumbs......", "...a bow of Irish yew...", "...a bow called Turkeys of Spanish yew, one and a half ell in length (about five feet eight inches), and a bow made of elm"*. Such great bows as these were crafted by the "bowyer", like John le Bowyer who was received unto his liberties at Newcastle-under-Lyme in 1369 and paid forty shillings for the privilege. In his *History of the Borough of Stoke-upon-Trent*, Ward mentions that the Bowyers of Knypersley, who eventually became allied with the Gresleys of Drakelow and the Heathcotes of Longton, were originally from Newcastle-under-Lyme, and probably exercised the "Bowyer's craft" there. Hugh le Bowier, the father of Thomas, who married Katherine the heiress of Knypersley, together with William de Brompton, had a grant from John of Gaunt of 40 acres of his demesne of Castle Cliff in 1365. In 1379 William de Morton of Congleton and his wife Margery remitted all right to a third part of two parts of the manor of Knypersley to Thomas Bowyer and Katherine, from whom they received 100 marks of silver. This same Thomas is cited as Thomas le Bower

ARMS AND WARFARE IN THE 14TH CENTURY

ARMS AND WARFARE IN THE 14TH CENTURY

in 1386, hence the variants Bowyer and Bower, but see also the surname Bowers in Volume 1. During the Civil War, despite the establishment of a royal garrison at Biddulph, the Moorlands area was controlled for the Parliamentarians by Sir John Bowyer of Knypersley. Another development is Boyer, as verified by John Boyer of Maer (1532), enrolled in the Muster of 1539 as John Bowyer. In the Kingsley parish registers, covering the years 1730 to 1737, Job Boyer also appears as Boor, Bore, Boar and Booyer. If the original surname is Boar, Bore or Boor, then we are looking at a nickname for someone as wild and aggressive as a boar. John Boyer of Butterton-on-the-Moors married Joan Goodwin at the parish church of St. Edward the Confessor, Cheddleton on 16th April, 1732. In 1841 Ralph Bowyer, aged 38, worked in the dipping house at Mr William Ridgeway's Earthenware Factory in Charles Street, Hanley. He had been a potter for 31 years apart from three years as a publican and licensed victualler. 1907, Henry Bowyer (telephone man), Trafalgar Street, Hanley.

Boyer *(margin)*

The bowstrings of hemp, flax, linen or silk were the domain of the "stringer". They were waxed with beeswax to ensure a quick release of the arrow. In 1379 Geoffrey le Stryngere of Newcastle-under-Lyme and his wife Agnes had taken unlawful possession of three tenements and ten acres of land in Newcastle-under-Lyme, Knutton and Great Clayton. They acknowledged the rightful owner to be Henry de Delves, who then granted them to Geoffrey and Agnes for their lives at a rent of a rose yearly, with reversion to Henry and his heirs for ever. It is surely more than coincidence that these two surnames Bowyer and Stringer occur side by side at Newcastle in the Middle Ages, since these two crafts are so closely connected, demanding intricate workmanship. Robert Strynger was prior at the Augustinian Priory of Trentham circa 1501, and he died in 1530. 1851, Charles Stringer (miller), Biddulph Steam Mill; 1851, James Stringer (cheese skin maker), Bridge Street, Uttoxeter; 1875. John Stringer (organ builder), Mill Street, Hanley.

Stringer *(margin)*

But it was the making of the arrow which called for the most expert eye and the most delicate handiwork. Usually the arrows were constructed from birch, ash or oak and some had strange names like *"a barbed arrow called a Doggearewe"*, *"...a barbed arrow called a Wolfearewe"*, mentioned in the same assize of 1314 concerning the death of Robert de Esnyngton (Essington). They were of two types - lightweight flight arrows for distance, and heavy sheaf arrows for piercing armour at close range. The most important artisan engaged in the craft of arrow-making was the "arrowsmith". One of the tenants of the Audleys at Betley in 1298, John le Arwesmyth, would certainly have known all the trade secrets. George, son of Richard Arrowsmythe, was baptised at Audley on August 21, 1594. In 1875 Thomas Arrowsmith was manager of William Boulton's Engineers (Iron Foundry) in Navigation Road, Burslem. Harrowsmith also appears now and again :1722, Thomas Harrowsmith of Ranton, written down in the register as Thomas Harrysmith in 1766.

Arrowsmith *(margin)*

Harrowsmith *(margin)*

A Statute of the Realm, dated 1405, criticised the "arrowsmiths" for making faulty heads for arrows and quarrels for crossbows, and recommended that in future all these heads were to be boiled or braised and hardened at the points with steel. In reality this was a task normally assigned to the "tipper", for it was he who fitted metal tips to the ends of the arrows, as in the case of William le Tippere, assessed at two shillings and sixpence at Abbot's Bromley in the 1327 lay subsidy rolls. A year earlier, John le Tipper (Parson of the Church of Swynnerton) and seven others had been sued by John de Kynardesleye for taking his goods and chattels to the value of ten pounds from "Shortelyme". At the Staffordshire Assizes, Daniel Tipper, aged 22, John Lovatt, aged 21, and James Smith aged 23, were tried for assaulting William Gould on the Highway leading from Leek to Macclesfield on the 26th December, 1832, and stealing from his person a gun, a watch, three sovereigns and thirteen shillings. Tipper and Lovatt were sentenced to death. On the 11th of September, 1845, the Commissioners responsible for the allotment of pews in Cheadle church awarded one sitting to George Tipper in pew 9, north side of the middle aisle, and one sitting to Sarah Tipper in pew 10. In 1851, Mary Tipper was the licensee of the Flint Tavern in Stafford Street, Longton and in the same year Samuel Tipper (wheelwright) lived in Colton near Blithfield Reservoir.

The "fletcher" busied himself with fixing the flights to the arrows, using duck, goose or peacock feathers. Again, from the same assize roll of 1314, one of the attackers who shot Robert, husband of Margaret, in the back, was armed "...*with a bow made of elm, and with a barbed arrow called a Scotisehe arewe, which was made of a wood called in Romanis "Boul", an ell in length, and feathered with the red feathers of a peacock....*" In 1298 Roger le Fleccher was a customary tenant of the Audleys at Horton near Rudyard, paying an annual rent of fifteen pence for a tenement and four acres of land. In 1415, Thomas Fleccher of Betley was robbed of a sum of forty shillings by Thomas Overton of Madeley Holme in the parish of Checkley, who surrendered and produced a general pardon. Included in the impressed band for Totmonslow Hundred in the 1640 Muster was William Fletcher of Cheddleton. 1851, James Fletcher (fruit and vegetable dealer), High Street, Tunstall; 1851, Joseph Fletcher (mining agent), Norton-in-the-Moors; 1875, Sarah Fletcher (dressmaker) of Windsor Street, Hanley.

Feathers and plumes have bequeathed some other pretty obvious surnames, such as Feather(s): Lichfleld Cathedral Registers, 1750, May 13th, Ann Feather of Shenstone, married to Robert Tedd. The name signifies either a dealer in feathers or it may be a nickname for a feather-brained person, someone prone to silly behaviour. Spellings like 1532, William Plome of Walsall and 1583, Thomas Plume of Eccleshall are most likely for traders who sold plumes or feathers, but with the extended name Plumer or Plomer we must be wary. Usually they are derivatives of "plume", as in William le Plomere of Lichfield (1327 lay subsidies), but also common in the Lichfield area are forms such as William le Plummer (1361) and

William Plummere (plummer) (1415), which refer to a plumber. Hence the confusion between the two names. Plummer itself often fluctuates with Plimmer as in the Rocester parish registers, where James Plummer (1652), is put down as James Plimmer in 1629. Hannah Plummer ran a private boarding house in Horton, near Rudyard in 1888. 1907, Peter Plummer (lodgeman), High Lane, Burslem; 1907. Priscilla Plimmer of Garner Street, Longton; 1907. John Plumb (bricklayer), Victoria Street, Stoke.

Plummer
Plimmer

Plumb

WEAPONS AND ARMOUR

If it were the archers and cavalry who grabbed most of the glory at the historic battles of Crecy, Poitiers and Agincourt, then no small credit must also go to the dismounted men-at-arms and the infantrymen who bore the brunt of many of the enemy assaults. The Statute of Winchester (1285) stipulated, that every freeman between the ages of 15 and 60 was liable to serve in the national defence, and to provide his own equipment in accordance with the annual value of his lands and goods. This meant that the poorest infantrymen often had to resort to the most basic weapons in hand to hand combat, such as cudgels, clubs and maces. Before the main battle got under way, the slingers often went into action, creating a hail of missiles with their lead bullets and stones, but such tactics as these were most suited to sieges rather than open warfare. Thomas Slynge was one of the guardians of the Lamp of the Blessed Mary in the Chapel of Keele in 1354. He may have got his name from using a staff sling which hurled larger projectiles or from an Old Norse name "Slengr", whilst there might even be a building term implicated, that is, an occupational name for a workman who operated the "sling", a stout rope or ropes hitched round large blocks of stone and over a hook as a means of lifting them up on to the scaffolding surrounding a building. This would be synonymous with the surname Slinger.

Slynge

Sling
Slinger

    In 1437 Walter Kibbulle, late of Ashby, Leicestershire (gentleman) and two of his friends were sued by Richard Harecourt for taking by force from Dudley a horse belonging to him, which was worth £10. This is perhaps from an Old Saxon word "cybbel", Middle English "kibble" - "cudgel", hence a maker of cudgels, or, better still, a soldier who used such an implement in the heat of battle, or a nickname for an individual who was stout and heavy like a cudgel. This survives as the surname Kibble, Keeble, Keble: 1666, Richard Kibble, taxed on one hearth at Cowley and Coton Constablewick near Gnosall; 1730, January 14th, Ann Kibble and John Ward, married at Blymhill.

Kibble
Keeble
Keble

    One weapon much favoured by the rank-and-file infantryman was the mace, a heavy staff or club, made entirely of metal or having a metal head, often spiked. The modern mace, the sceptre or staff of office and symbol of the Speaker's authority in the House of Commons, is a reminder of this primitive implement, which could cause havoc in the opposing forces of cavalry. It could be one origin of the surname Mace, but we are also dealing with a variant of "Meys", the local pronunciation of Coldmeece or Millmeece, as in 1370 Assizes, Philip Willesone Hobbesone de Meys (Millmeece), a double patronymic, that is mainly confined to the northern counties in medieval times. Robert de Mees was assessed for eighteen pence for Slindon and Aspley in the 1327 lay subsidies. Therefore, the modern names Mees, Meese, plus Mays, Mayes and Meys are probably from either source, but there is a third possibility, represented by Juliana le Mey(s) or Juliana le Meyes of Apeton south west of Stafford in a plea roll of 1301. These stand for Juliana, servant of someone called May, where May is a pet form of Mayhew, the Norman counterpart of Matthew. In this horrific case, heard before the Sheriff on the Thursday before the Feast of the Epiphany, 1301, Agnes, formerly wife of Geoffrey de Wolaston appealed to Juliana le Meyes of Apeton for feloniously and against the King's peace on the Sunday before the Feast of St. Edith the Virgin (1299), holding Geoffrey her husband in her arms whilst Hugh de Mutton, the husband of the said Juliana feloniously killed the said Geoffrey with a knife. The outcome of the case is an illuminating insight into the processes of the ancient County Court in a criminal appeal - Juliana was found not guilty, since Geoffrey was killed by an infuriated husband, who found him in the arms of his wife. By way of contrast Agnes was adjudged to have brought the appeal out of malice, and, being poor and a mendicant, she did not even have *"sufficient to make restitution according to the statute"*. Margery Mayse and John Jenkes were married on February 3rd, 1565 at Church Eaton. In 1851 Edward Mace was farming land at Winnothdale near Croxden and in 1907 Arthur Mace of Paynter Street, Fenton was a coal dealer.

French "martel" - "hammer", was employed as a nickname for a hammer or mace bearer, but also possible for the surname Martel is a pet form of the classical personal name Martin, borne by St. Martin, who lived in the fourth century A.D. The father of monasticism in Gaul, he originally served in the Roman army until his conversion to Christianity. In 1262 Martin Martel and his wife Sibilla disputed the rightful claim of Reginald, son of Roger de Sadington, to half a messuage, 48 acres of land, and twenty eight shillings rent in Blithbury.

Dagger is from Old French "dague" - "dagger", plus the suffix "ard": 1912, Reverend J.H.J. Dagger, Archbury, Whiston, Kingsley, whilst Daggett/Daggott is a diminutive form of the same word, and both names refer to a soldier or knight equipped with a dagger for piercing the chain-mail or armour of the opponent. The marriage between John Daggott and Mary Tresom (both of Rushton Grange), was solemnized at Burslem on January 21st, 1653, and in 1666 John Dagott was paying tax on three hearths in Eastgate Ward, Stafford. The very scarce Bodkin comes from Middle English "bodkin" - a sharp, pointed weapon, a dagger, hence a user, maker or seller of such implements. Elline, daughter of John Bodkine was buried at Gnosall on November 19th, 1626. Mary Bodkin and Thomas Broadhurst (potter), both of Stoke, were married at Newcastle-under-Lyme on December 5th, 1796.

Some of the most prolific surnames in this category are those which can be traced back to the more offensive weapons such as swords, lances, spears and pikes. The basic Sword is simply for a maker of swords: 1907, Sword and Sons, solicitors and commissioners for oaths, Cheapside, Hanley. The compound Brownsword is a local variant of Brownsett, as outlined in Volume 1.

Sword

Trenchard is a derivative of Old French "trenchier" - "to cut", possibly a nickname conferred on a combatant renowned for his swordsmanship. In 1618 Thomas Trenchard (knight) and his wife Elizabeth were embroiled in a heated dispute over tenements, land, gardens, orchards, and the right to dig peat and turf in Fole, Checkley, Upper and Lower Nobut, Leigh, Withington, Dodsley and Middleton Green. The one fictional Trenchard who always springs to mind is John Trenchard, the young hero of John Meade Falkner's adventure novel, Moonfleet, set amid the rugged scenery of Dorset.

Trenchard

Lance itself is misleading, for it is a survival of the Germanic personal name "Lanzo", a pet form of personal names beginning with the theme "Land-" such as "Lanbert, Lambert" - "land bright". In 1382 William Launce and several other local inhabitants were sued by Walter de Wrottesley for treading down and consuming his wheat and grass at The Wergs in Tettenhall with their cattle, to the value of ten pounds. In 1851 Captain William Henry Lance of Compton, Leek, was superintendent of police and inspector of weights and measures. Lancelot is a double diminutive of "Lanzo", that is, "Lanz-el-ot", and bequeaths the modern surnames Lancelot(te), Lanslet. In 1424, Richard Gerveys and Agnes his wife, executrix of the will of Launcelot de Swynnerton, brought a writ of debt against William Wyrley of Adbaston (husbandman), executor of the will of Richard Halle and two others. However, with the non-appearance of any of the parties to prosecute their case, the suit was dismissed. In the 1666 Hearth tax returns for the county, William Lancelett was deemed ineligible for any charge at Leek. 1907, John R. Lancelott (saddler), Selwyn Street, Stoke. Whether that famous symbol of knighthood, Lancelot, who eventually betrayed King Arthur by his guilty love for Queen Guinevere, shares the same Germanic name, is open to serious doubt, since it is more than likely of Celtic origin, just like all the other names in the Arthurian legends.

Lance

Lancelot(te)
Lanslet

Shaft, Spear and Staff are all surnames in their own right. John Staffe, enrolled at Bishop's Offley in the 1539 Muster, probably boasted ancestors who acquired their name for being as lean as a staff, a nickname reminiscent of the modern "thin as a rake". On the other hand, Roger Schaft, assessed at two shillings in the 1327 lay subsidy rolls for Pelsall, could have been a maker of (arrow) shafts or spear handles. Spear(e)s, Speer(s) refers to an infantryman who was skilled in the use of the spear or lance: Abraham Speare, son of Abraham and Jonne was baptised at Stowe-by-Chartley on February 10th, 1634; 1851, Reverend James Speers (Presbyterian), Mount Street, Stafford; 1873, Jemima Spear (draper),

Staff

Shaft

Spear(e)s
Speer(s)

-man Heathcote Street, Kidsgrove. Spearman, too, denotes a spearman or lance man, who supported the cavalry and missile throwers in the early stages of a battle: John Spermon, taxed at two shillings and eight pence for the vill of Penkhull in the 1332 subsidies, and Hugh Spermon and his wife Johanna, who contributed two shillings at Morton and Wilbrighton near Aqualate in the 1381 Poll Tax returns.

-point
-int   There are some intriguing compounds to excite the imagination here. Spearpoint is simply a variant of Pierpoint with the addition of initial "S" after the fashion of the couplet Pilsbury-Spilsbury: Madeley parish registers, 1708, James Spearpoint of Onneley and Sarah Mallaby married on November 4th; 1887, John Pierpoint (hairdresser), St. John's Square, Burslem. The names go back to any one of several localities called Pierrepont in Seine Inferieure or Calvados or from two places in La Manche, Saint-Nicholas-de-Pierrepont or Saint-Sauveur-de-Pierrepont. The only Englishman ever to have become Pope, Nicholas Breakspear (Adrian IV): 1154-1159, was born at Abbot's Langley near St. Albans. His other great distinction was crowning Frederick Barbarossa as Holy Roman Emperor in 1155. The most

-speare famous compound of all is undoubtedly Shakespeare, borne by our greatest dramatist and playwright. It has attracted a good deal of attention from surname scholars and some fantastic theories concerning its meaning have been propounded over the years. Ewen, especially, in his *History of British Surnames*, devotes a ten-page essay to the subject, attempting to prove, that such a surname cannot possibly be a nickname. But that is just what it is - a name for a spearman or soldier who had a tendency to shake or wave his spear or lance about in the air before releasing it at his enemy. In fact, he proffers an exhausting list of instances, which he discovered relating to Staffordshire, such as Thomas Schakesper (debtor) of Newcastle-under-Lyme, 1335 and Alice Schakespere (trespasser), 1352, also of Newcastle-under-Lyme. Eventually his deductions are, that the name is either from some lost placename or a fictitious Saxon personal name. But the award for the most ludicrous explanation of all must go to Baring-Gould in *Family Names and Their History*. He derives Shakespeare from "Schalkesboer" - "knave's farm", whilst poor old Nicholas Breakspear came from some mythological village known as "Bragisboer" - "farm of Bragi". Of course, all this is pure moonshine, but amusing all the same! My own recordings for Newcastle-under-Lyme are as follows. In 1379 William Shakespere was on the committee of six who inquired about the cutting down of a crab-tree at Wolstanton, which was growing on some land belonging to Agnes de Fulford. They decided, that she had cut the tree down lawfully and was not liable to any charges. After John Shakespere died in 1412, for his copyhold land a heriot of one mare with a foal, worth two shillings, was due to the lord of the manor. Trade directories: David Shakespeare (gamekeeper) of Ebon Ash, Horsley, near Eccleshall in 1851.

-shaft
-sheff   Virtually synonymous with Shakespeare is Shakeshaft (variant Shakesheff): 1789, Betley parish registers, Elizabeth, daughter of John and Betty Shakeshaft,

born on April 23rd and baptised June 14th; 1851, Richard Shakeshaft (butcher) of Trent Vale; 1875, Robert Shakeshaft (bricklayer, clogger) North West Terrace, Smallthorne.

Winspear
Winsper
Winspur

One final compound of dubious origin is Winspear, Winsper, Winspur. Bardsley gives Mary Winspeare married to John Swanwick at Canterbury in 1668, whilst locally, John Winspurre was a member of the impressed band in the 1640 Muster for the districts of Tipton, Darlaston, Bentley, Wednesfield and Willenhall. 1872, Mrs Mary Winsper (carpet bag lockmaker and beer retailer), Green Croft, Bilston. The ending of the name is either "spur" or "spear", and, taken as a whole, there is some latent allusion to "winning one's spurs", that is, to be accepted into the knighthood. When a man was knighted, the person who had the honour of dubbing him, presented the new knight with a pair of gilt spurs. But, if the original spelling is Winspear, then this could designate the winner of a race, in which a spear was set up as a winning post and handed over as a prize.

Gleave(s)
Glave(s)

A similar name is Gleave(s), Glave(s), from Old French "glaive, gleive", Middle English "gleyve, gleve" - a type of lance with a broad, single-edged blade rather like a large knife blade, mounted on a 5 foot shaft. This was often placed in a strategic spot and claimed by the victor in a race of some kind: Audley parish registers, 1701, Baptism of Joshua son of Matthew Gleave on February 8th; 1851, Samuel Gleaves (boot and shoe maker), Market Place, Burslem; 1887, George Gleaves (coal dealer), Booth Street, Tunstall; 1887, Frederick Gleaves (potter), Watlands View, Wolstanton.

Burdon
Burden

Old French "bourdon", Middle English "burdoun" referred to a stout staff, club or cudgel, sometimes a spear or spear shaft, or even a pilgrim's staff or lance, hence a maker of, or dealer in such items or possibly for the person who employed them offensively. This is preserved in Burdon/Burden, but these are also to be traced to a diminutive of the Germanic name "Burdo", or a locative from Great Burdon near Darlington in Durham, Burdon Head in the West Riding of Yorkshire, Burden near Harewood (also in the West Riding) - all for "hill with a fort", or from an unidentified Burdon in Durham - "valley with a byre". Thomas Burdoun of Hamstall Ridware feloniously killed William Burdoun and his wife Juliana at Hamstall Ridware on the Feast of St. Peter ad Vincula, 1316. The actual relationship between the assailant and victims in this tragic incident is not on record. 1907, Edward Burden (collier), Toll Street, Hanley; 1907, James Burdon (grocer), London Road, Stoke.

Bill(s)
Billes

Biller

One of the most formidable weapons of war used by the medieval infantryman was the agricultural bill-hook on a long haft, used in a similar fashion to a bayonet for a full frontal attack or charge or simply as a static hedge of spear-points. With a hook added to the spike this became the "bill", one source of the modern surname Bill(s), Billes. Yet the name can also be equivalent to Biller - a maker of bills, billhooks or halberds, or from a Saxon personal name "Bil" from

FRANCIS FIGGINS,

Auctioneer, ✦ Appraiser

AND

GENERAL AGENT.

Bills of Sale & Rent Warrants Promptly Executed.

Sales by Auction of Property, Furniture and Stock-in-Trade
conducted on the most reasonable terms.

Agent for the Atlas Fire and Life Assurance Company, and the
Lancashire and Yorkshire Accident Insurance Company.

RENTS COLLECTED.   PROMPT SETTLEMENTS.

REFERENCES.

Offices—18 LIVERPOOL ROAD,
NEWCASTLE-UNDER-LYME,

Figgins p. 70

27, Market Place, Burslem ; 11, Church Street, Stoke ;
and 7, Market Street, Longton.

2/9/03

Sept 1 Aug 190 *3*

Mr. ....

Bought of James Boult,

TAILOR, CLOTHIER AND HATTER.

Largest Stock in the Potteries to select from.   Lowest Prices.

*Dear Sir will you kindly
send me the
particulars of farms to be
sold on the 10th inst*

Boult p. 55

"bil" - "sword", or from the Old Norse name "Bildr". Distinct forms of "bills" evolved during the sixteenth and seventeenth centuries and were painted or varnished in different colours, hence the various "blackbills" and "brownbills". In 1469 John Somerford sued Robert Bille of Walton near Chebsey (yeoman), for a tenement, 12 acres of land, 6 acres of meadow and 8 acres of pasture in Somerford, near Brewood. Robert appeared by attorney, and asked for an adjournment to the Octaves of St. Hillary, which was granted. Five years later, Robert, who must have harboured some grudge against John, broke into the latter's close at Somerford and stole 4 mares, 4 oxen, 12 cows, 6 calves, 2 colts and 2 sows worth 20 marks. On this occasion Robert had gone into hiding. The surname Bill is extremely common around Chebsey, Eccleshall, Walton and Seighford from the mid-sixteenth century onwards, and some of these families may even be descendants of this same Robert, who so tormented John Somerford a couple of generations earlier. Before the Industrial Revolution the water-mills of the Moddershall valley were used for grinding corn or fulling cloth for the wool trade, but in 1726 Thomas Benson was granted the first patent for grinding flints in water, using water power to drive the machinery supplied by the Moddershall water-mills by Scotch Brook. In 1772 William Bill went into partnership with a certain Mr Harvey *"to work mills to supply the pottery industry"* with ground flint, and the restored Wetmore Mill, where William originally undertook his work, was known for a time as "Bill's Mill". In 1798, when rumours were rife of an imminent invasion of England by Napoleon, Volunteer Corps were set up in various parts of the country to take the place of the militia and regular troops, should they be called upon to confront the intruders. The patriotism of north Staffordshire was soon evident by the formation of the Pottery Troop, an independent force, equipped at their own expense. Their Captain was Josiah Spode, and one of the sergeants was Robert Bill. 1887, Mary J. Bills (baby linen and ladies' underclothing warehouse), Liverpool Road, Stoke; 1907, Harold Bill (milkman) of Ford Street, Longton. Incidentally, any notions of a pet form of William are somewhat premature, because Bill is a modern invention, although its exact first appearance on the scene is not known.

Pike
Pyke

Massed ranks of pikemen, armed with pikes with shafts of fifteen feet, created an almost impenetrable barrier for any cavalry onslaught. Thomas Pyke, resident at Fradswell in 1532, may have had some ancestor, a pikeman, who regularly participated in a defensive manoeuvre of this type. However, the name Pike/Pyke is not so simple. Other alternatives comprise a maker or seller of pikes, a fishmonger, who specialised in the sale of pike, two nicknames - either for a person who was as tall and as thin as a pike or spike, or from Old French "pic" - "woodpecker" - an individual who was as noisy or as gaudy as a woodpecker, whilst a toponymic is also to be weighed up, for habitation by some point, peak or hill, as demonstrated by Richard del Pike in a thirteenth century deed from the Trentham Cartulary.

Pickman, too, as in Matthew Pickman, charged on one hearth at Knowle End, Audley in 1666, can designate a pikeman, a seller of pike, a person who lived by a peak, or a nickname for a tall, slender person. In the Betley parish registers, Pickman spellings compete with Pitman - e.g 1632 Edward Pittman; 1713, Penelope Pickman. Pitman is usually for residence by a pit or in some hollow. In addition, there might even be some clash with the surname Pick: 1327 subsidy rolls, Robert Picke, contributing fifteen pence at Leigh, near Uttoxeter. This is either a shortened version of Pike, or an occupational term for a maker or seller of pickaxes.

Another similar surname, that is especially plentiful around the Audley area from the 1540s onwards is Piggot, also spelt Piggott, Pigot(t), with variants such as Picot, Pikett and Pickett very much on the periphery. The very early example - Picot, under-tenant of the Bishop of Chester at Hixon near Stafford in the Domesday survey, has a name derived from an Old French personal name "Pic", to which has been added the suffix "-ot". But also to be taken into account is Old French "picot" - "point, pointed object", probably a nickname for someone lean and lanky, and thus akin to the juvenile "lamp-post" or "walking telegraph pole". In 1306, William Pigod of Coton killed his brother Richard somewhere in the vicinity of Gnosall and hastily departed from the scene of the crime. Members of the Staffordshire muster in 1539 included William Piggott at Audley and Thomas Pygot at Eccleshall. In 1851, Samuel Piggott of New Road, Talke-on-the-Hill, is listed as a plumber and painter and in 1873 George Herbert Pigott ran a chemist's shop in Market Square, Tunstall.

Old French "fiche" - "iron point" is the basis of a number of surnames, some of which are very tricky to unravel. The principal idea, inherent in all these names, however, is that they are all in some way to do with iron-pointed weapons or implements used in warfare or by skilled craftsmen with a knowledge of sharply pointed tools. The usual thesis that such surnames as Fitch and Fitchett are provincial nicknames for the "polecat", is not borne out by the early recordings from the twelfth century for Northumberland, Dorset, Yorkshire and Suffolk, where spellings like "Fiche" and "Fichet" are common. The polecat is from Old French "fissell", and this does not exhibit forms such as "fechet" and "fichat" until the sixteenth and seventeenth centuries. Robert Fichet occurs circa 1257 in the Okeover deeds and in 1451 John Fychet of Throwley near Wetton appeared before Sampson Meverell (knight), Justice of the Peace at Stafford, along with two other defendants, charged with stealing 12 oxen worth £8 and 12 cows worth £6 at Blore, of the goods and chattels of Ralph Basset (armiger). In the Wolstanton parish registers there are a whole range of corrupted forms, such as John Fitchard (1793), written down as John Fitchat in 1788 and as John Fitchett in 1799. Eventually these transpose into Fitchford: 1802, Samuel Fitchford, who may be identical with Samuel, son of John and Elizabeth Fitchat, born on July 31st, 1774. Fitcher could then be a simple reduction of Fitchard: 1907, Mrs Mary Ann Fitcher of Queen Anne

Street, Shelton, Hanley. Other examples of the names are: 1887, James T. Fitchford (teacher of Music), Maybank, Wolstanton; 1907, William Fitchett (railway drayman), Brook Street, Fenton.

Fick
Fickett
Feaks
Feek(s)
Feakes

Besides "Fiche" and "Fichet" there was the Norman "Fiquet", from which we get Fickett and the contracted variant Fick: *Catalogue of Ancient Deeds for Staffordshire*, 14th Century, Ficka. This, in turn, evolves into other names like Feakes, Feaks and Feek(s): Seighford parish registers, 1654, Margaret, daughter of William Feakes and Alice, buried on March 22nd. Fick is then hardened to Figg Before the Feast of the Translation of St. Edmund the Archbishop (1269), Gervase de Levedale, his servant John Fige and William Hod entered Teddesley Hay in the Forest of Cannock, found a dead doe there, and took it in a covered cart to the house of the said William, where they skinned it and divided it among themselves. Renold

Figg
Figgins
Figgitt
Figgett
Fidgett

Fyge, member of the Fulford and Great Fenton militia in the 1539 muster, was equipped with a bill. Figgins is a later offshoot. Francis Figgins, land surveyor and engineer, lived at Stockton Brook in 1842, and Mrs Ann Figgins was resident in Foregate Street, Stafford in 1851. Undocumented variants also include Figgitt Figgett and Fidgett.

Armer
Armor
Armour
Larmer
Larmour

Protection against this array of lethal weaponry was afforded by armour made by the "armourer". In 1457 several inhabitants of Hilton near Featherstone including Robert Armerer (labourer) trespassed on the land of John and William Harecourt (armigers), John Walker and Richard Coton at Bushbury and helped themselves to 4 oxen, valued at 4 marks. At Penkridge, Mr. Edward Armourer had a son John baptised on August 25th, 1696, and a daughter Mary baptised on July 16th 1700. The modern forms of the surnames are usually Armer, Armor and Armour, or Larmer and Larmour with retention of the original definite article "le".

Shield

Shields, too, of all shapes and sizes, parried many a glancing blow in close combat. William de Chatculne (Chatcull) and his wife Alice, and Roger de Neupor and his wife Edelina, recovered possession of two tenements in Stafford in a suit versus Henry Schelde and his wife Petronilla in 1295. In 1875 James Shield was a shopkeeper in Upper Green, Newcastle-under-Lyme.

Basnett

The surname Basnett is very late on the scene and its actual meaning remains very much in the balance. The immediate reaction is to ascribe it to the medieval helmet known as "bacinet, bascinet, basnett" etc, a conical steel cap, sometimes fitted with a neck-piece of mail or of plate. It had a moveable visor, pierced with holes, which could be pulled down to cover the face. Yet our sights must also be set on a possible locative derivation, however tenuous, that is, Bassenthwaite north west of Keswick in Cumbria - "Bastun's clearing (glade)". This place may have

Postlethwaite

been converted into Basnett by analogy with Postlethwaite in Millom (also in Cumberland), which is pronounced colloquially as "Poslet" and develops later into

Posnett

"Posnett" - Rugeley parish registers, 1598, Jane Postlette buried on April 5th, and 1872, John Posnett (shopkeeper) of Hednesford. In 1854 James Basnett was the owner/occupier of a stone quarry at Endon Edge, and a brick kiln at Stoneywood and Daniel Basnett was farming land at Bagnall in 1871. In 1907 Thomas Basnett (miner) lived at Stanfield, Burslem.

Laying siege to a castle or a fortified town in the Middle Ages was a very expensive and tedious undertaking, involving many kinds of siege engines, each with their own distinctive method of propulsion. The "espringale" or "springald" was a contraption resembling a giant catapult or crossbow, that fired iron shafts or javelins, although it could also be adapted for hurling stones. The person who was in charge of such an ancient military engine would thus acquire a name like Springall, Springle or Springett - e.g. *Great White Book of Lichfield Cathedral,* circa 1274, Robert Springold. But the names are also from Middle English "springal(d)", a derivative of "spring" in the sense of a young man, youth or stripling. In 1272, Roger, son of Emma Springhalt of Lilleshall, Shropshire, sued Hugh, son of Henry de Knitchton (sic), for a tenement and some land in Knighton. Which Knighton is not specified - it is either Knighton near Mucklestone or Knighton near Adbaston. In Staffordshire, where many of the locatives ending in "-well and "-wall" are weakened to "-ell", "-all", there may be some connection with Springwall in Teddesley Hay, Cannock (1841 Tithe Awards) - "copse or young plantation with a stream". This could easily be contracted to Springall.

Another type of catapult was the "mangonel", which could project stones 300 pounds in weight for distances up to about a quarter of a mile, pounding a castle's walls to rubble with well-aimed shots. Here we have one source for the surnames Mangnall, Manknell and Mangold. In 1227, Walter Mangunel was one of nine defendants who had unjustly expropriated some pasture in Brineton near Weston-under-Lizard from Richard de Onne (High Onn). Lancashire families bearing any one of these names trace them back to Mankinholes near Todmorden, recorded as "Magnolles, Manknell" in the sixteenth and seventeenth centuries. The man who designed these war engines and had a hand in their construction was the "engineer", which was shortened to the more amenable "ginner, genner, jenner": Alrewas Manor Court Rolls, 1338, William le Giner (chaplain), brother of Ralph le Giner (benefactor of St Mary's Chantry). At a session of the Court of Star Chamber in 1500, regarding a dispute over the rightful ownership of some land in Prestwood, contested by John Madeley and John Fitzherbert Esquire, one witness called to give evidence was Richard Jenner, aged 80 of Quixhill.

In the sixteenth and seventeenth centuries, the names Gynder, Ginder(s), Jender and Gender are well established in this same region of the county - e.g. Ellastone parish registers, 1589, Roger Gynder; 1604, Richarde Gynders; 1628, November 23rd, William Ginder of Quicksell married Janne Buxtons etc. In the 1666 hearth tax returns at Quixhill, John Ginder is assessed for one hearth whilst William Ginder is charged on three. In addition, Richard Jender is paying tax on two hearths at Madeley Holme. In 1726, Henry and William Ginder (two Papists) lived at Alton.   The Ginner- Ginder, Jenner-Jender pairings would thus ape the couplets Warriner-Warrinder and Mulliner-Mullinder.   The accepted derivation for Ginder(s) and Gender(s) is the French "Gendre, Legendre", a surname of relationship, which became a family name when a son-in-law inherited the house of a father-in-law, but in view of the above specimens the forms with intrusive "d" seem infinitely more probable.

To return momentarily to the name Jenner, it is certainly ironic, that this medieval surname, born out of the chaos of warfare, should have been made famous all over the world by Edward Jenner, the Father of Immunology, who discovered the smallpox vaccine, that subsequently saved so many lives.

FORESTS AND HUNTING

Prior to the arrival of the Normans, the Saxons and Vikings had reserved large areas of land for the purpose of hunting, but it was the Normans with their flair for administration, who incorporated these reserves into their own medieval forests, increased and enlarged them, and devised a complete new system of forest laws, that remained in force for many generations to come. *The Anglo-Saxon Chronicle's* sobering account of the new "status quo" cuts through like a knife:

"He (William the Conqueror) set apart a vast deer preserve and imposed laws concerning it. Whoever slew a hart or a hind was to be blinded. He forbade the killing of boars even as the killing of harts. For he loved the stags as dearly as though he had been their father".

The word "forest", introduced by the Normans, is ultimately from late Latin "forestis silva" - "wood outside the walls of a park, not fenced in", and this is exactly what the medieval forest was - an area of unenclosed land, formed by boundaries such as rivers, streams, valleys, bridges, fords, and the forests inside these boundaries invariably belonged to the king and his nobles.   The surname

Forest
Forrest

Forest/Forrest refers to a dweller by some forest, or more likely, to a worker there: 1617, June 8th, Alice Forreste and John Mottershed, married at Audley; 1715, Thomas, son of Steven and Ann Forrest, christened at Standon; 1912, Harry Forrest (ovenman), Cobden Street, Longton.

By the time of the signing of the Magna Carta in 1215, there were three royal forests in Staffordshire - Cannock, Kinver and Brewood, and on these no one but the king and those authorized by him could hunt the red deer, the fallow deer (introduced from the Continent in the 12th century), the roe and the wild boar. The latter was, reputedly, the favourite quarry of Henry I and King John. If the poor were forbidden by law to hunt the deer, then they poached them for food, and if they were caught killing game in the royal forests, then this was known as being "in bloody hand", that is, caught "red-handed", having the blood or blood stains of the newly slain beast on their hands or clothing. A popular belief is that the courts meted out barbaric sentences to the unfortunate poachers, but in reality fines were the norm, as in a case from the Staffordshire Pleas of the Forest for the year 1271:

"It was presented, that Walter le Bere of Swindon (in Seisdon Hundred), and Walter Petit of the same, took a hind in the said forest (of Kinver) on the Saturday before the Feast of Pentecost, which was in front of the dogs of the king, and carried it away secretly. And they appeared, and being convicted thereof, are detained in prison. And Walter le Petyt is pardoned because he is weak-headed. Walter le Bere is afterwards released for the fine of a mark."

To prevent poaching, to guard against trespass and all other offences contrary to forest law, a whole army of officials was recruited. In 1238, England was split up into two regions or provinces, so that the process of implementing these laws by the officers was made somewhat easier. The river Trent was chosen as the boundary between these two areas, which were known, not unreasonably as "north of the Trent" and "south of the Trent".

One of the most important officers in this complex hierarchy was the "verderer", who was chosen by the freeholders of the county, and who was responsible for prosecuting cases of "trespass against the vert" - damage to vegetation by grazing or woodcutting, and cases of "trespass against the venison" - "poaching the king's deer". This results in the modern surname Varder/Verdier (no examples). In 1262, the verderers at Cannock were Ralph de Coven, Richard de Grendon, Robert de Esington and Thomas de Tamehorn. Next in line was the "forester", whose duties and functions corresponded roughly to the modern gamekeeper. In the Domesday survey, Ricardus Forestarius - Richard, the forester, the king's sub-tenant, whose estates incorporated the then wild area of northern Pirehill Hundred at Thursfield, Dimsdale, Knutton, Clayton, Hanford, Hanchurch, Whitmore and Normacot, and further south around Rodbaston and Huntington close to Cannock Forest, has been identified as the same Richard Chenvin, appointed by William the Conqueror as forest ranger at Cannock and holding 3 hides of land from the King at Codsall in 1086. Some foresters were not averse to abusing their position. In 1286 Richard Murel of Norton (probably Norton Canes), appeared before the Forest Court, having shot a doe during the time he was a forester in Gailey Hay in Cannock Forest. He had carried the venison to his house at Rodbaston, which he had constructed out of wood he had taken from the said Hay. He was committed to prison, but later the sentence was commuted to a fine of one mark.

In the suit of Geva, formerly wife of William Russel of Bradwell, brought against Thomas le Forester of Newcastle-under-Lyme for dower in 1303, Thomas called to warranty Thomas the son and heir of Nicholas de Aldytheleye (Audley), who was under age and in ward to Hugh le Dispenser, and whose lands were in the custody of Amadeus, Count of Savoy. He produced a deed of the said Nicholas,

granting the tenements to him and his heirs with a clause of warranty. Thomas le
Forester was mayor of Newcastle-under-Lyme in 1316.

Forester
Forrester
Forrister

By the advent of the Industrial Revolution the surname Forester, Forrester
Forrister is extremely widespread across the county: 1691, June 2nd, Isabel Forester
and William Bagnall married at Cheddleton; 1783, December 28th, Thomas
Forrister and Mary Tumpkin, married at Swynnerton; 1851, John Forrister
(engraver) of Cobridge; 1875, Richard Forrester (marine store dealer, Regent Street,
Burslem; 1875, Martin Forrester (colliery manager and proprietor), Meir Green,
Meir.

Forster

But the name Forester is often contracted to Forster, as testified by 1360
Assizes. William le Forester of Alrewas, cited as William le Forster for Fradley a

Foster

year later. Forster in its turn is reduced further to Foster: Norton-in-the-Moors
parish register, 1800, John Forster signs his own name as John Foster. However, the
high incidence of the surname Foster is attributable to the fact, that there are a
number of other valid sources. It may be a variant of Anglo French "fuster" - a
maker of saddle bows (the wooden framework of the saddle). This origin would
certainly apply to the south of the county, particularly around Walsall and environs,
by dint of its association with the manufacture of saddles and bridles. In addition
the name Foster is a slightly altered form of Old French "forcetier" - a maker of
scissors, a shearer or cutler, or it may designate a foster parent or nurse: 1731, 12th
August, Susanna Forster married William Cooper at Cheddleton; 1851, William
Forster (tailor), Navigation Road, Burslem. In 1853, Oulton Retreat, Kibblestone
described in 1851 as *"a large and well conducted private Lunatic Asylum"*, was
sold to a Benedictine Order of Nuns. The First Lady Abbess was Miss Alice Forster.
The surname Foster outscores both these names after the Reformation; 1539, John
Foster, servant of John Clarke senior at Abbot's Bromley; Ellastone parish registers,
April 1st 1612, William Foster, coachman and horsekeeper, buried; Churchwarden's
accounts for Tunstall (Stoke-on-Trent), 1641, Paid Roger Ffoster the carpenter
10/6d for sawing; 1733, September 24th, Edward Foster and Elizabeth Sillito,
married at Seighford; 1841, George Foster, aged 10, mould runner for Charles
Hammersley at Mr Burton's Earthenware Factory, Hanley; 1871, Census, Edward
Foster (police constable), Stafford Street, Eccleshall.

Inside the royal forests the king's own demesne lands often made up but a
fraction of the forest as a whole and so a substantial area of the woodland belonged
to individual private landowners. Of course, they were subject to forest law, and, if
any timber had to be felled, charcoal to be burnt, or buildings to be erected on these
private lands, then a special licence had to be obtained from the king. In fact, by
law, these private landowners were obliged to employ officers known as

Woodward(s)

"woodwards", whose duties included, not only the surveillance of the landowners'
woods, but also the protection of the "vert" and "venison" owned by the king.
Indeed, the woodwards had to swear an oath before the chief justice of the forest,
that they would defend and safeguard the interests of the king at all times. One

woodward, who fell foul of the law during the reign of Edward II, was William le Wodeward of Blithfield, who killed William de Gayton (miller) at Blithfield on the Feast of Easter, 1319. On the other hand the more law-abiding forest employees dutifully paid their subsidies on time in 1327 - e.g. Henry le Wodeward (two shillings at Chartley), and Adam le Wodeward (two shillings and sixpence) at Whitgreave near Stafford. By the time of the compilation of the Hearth tax returns in 1666 the surname Woodward has ramified to a great extent in the north eastern sector of the county, particularly around Leek, Longnor, Alstonefield, Wetton, Madeley Holme and Leigh near Uttoxeter. 1851 recordings include: Thomas Woodward and Company (Limeburners), Bank Farm, Hanley and Samuel Woodward (blacksmith and wheelwright) of Checkley. In the Corporation Minutes for Newcastle-under-Lyme, Thomas Woodwarde, son of Henry Wooddwarde (sic), 1608, is also known as Thomas son of Henry Woodworth in 1624. In 1851, John Woodworth (wheelwright) was licensed victualler of the Red Cow, Willslock, Woodlands, Uttoxeter; 1887, Benjamin Woodworth (engineer) of Grove Road, Fenton. There is a locative in Cheshire - Woodworth Green in Lower Bunbury, which might be involved in some of the Woodworths. In the Barton-under-Needwood parish registers, Francis Woodward (1639), occurs as Francis Woodard in 1645. If the original surname happens to be Woodard, then this is either an occupational term for "wood-herd", that is, a person who tended animals that fed in a wood, probably a swineherd, or from an old Saxon personal name "Wuduheard". 1295 Assizes, John Wodard of Warwickshire, one of many knights summoned by the King from the counties of Staffordshire, Shropshire, Worcestershire and Warwickshire, to determine the bounds between the King's manor of Claverley (Salop) and John de Tresel's land in Trysull.

In the past, Woodruff, Woodroff(e) and variants have been linked with "wood-reeve", another forest officer, but the real meaning is far more attractive. They go back to Old English "wudu-rofe" - "woodruff", a small, inconspicuous plant which has sweet-scented leaves. It was probably used during the Middle Ages as an air freshener to dispel obnoxious odours drifting into rooms from the streets outside, although there may also have been a nickname for a woman who habitually doused herself with such a fragrance, or in the case of a man who used it, an ironic allusion to his effeminate nature. In 1413 Henry Woderove with three accomplices, namely, John Walter of Coton (fleccher), John Lord (chaplain) and William Gretebache, broke into the park of Humfrey Stafford the younger (chivaler) at Bramshall, and harassed and took away some of his game. James Woodrooffe and Ellen Walker got married at Ellastone on November 11th, 1547. In 1851 Edward Woodroffe was farming land at Bromley Marsh, Abbot's Bromley and in 1875 David and John Woodroffe (general drapers) were trading in Market Square, Hanley. Woodrow may be a variant of Woodrough - 1644. Richard Woodrough of Dunstall near Tatenhill, based on the couplet "enough-enow".

Since Norman barons were not permitted to hunt in the royal forests without the king's approval, they often enclosed large tracts of land with a fence or wall in the vicinity of their own castles, called "parks". This was known as "imparking" and the fence which was erected around the park was usually constructed out of

Palliser
Pallister
Palser

pales or palings, and the workman who put up the fence was a Palliser, Pallister or Palser. Richard Palicer (labourer) of Brewood and district, assessed in the 1381 Poll Tax returns, for two shillings may well have been responsible for carrying out such a task for a member of the nobility in his own neighbourhood. Sometimes, if the king was in a generous frame of mind, he often gave deer to his nobles to stock their own parks. In 1222 the Crown made a grant of ten hinds taken from Cannock Forest to Henry de Audley for stocking his park at Heighley.

Parker

These "parks" were patrolled by the park-keeper or "parker", as he was more familiarly dubbed. At the Great and Little Court of Tunstall, Stoke-on-Trent held on the 29th April, 1326, the Tuesday before the Feast of the Apostles, Peter and James, Lucy, daughter of William le Parkere was obliged to give the lord of the manor eighteen pence to have licence to marry (the dreaded "merchet", one of the banes of the medieval villein's life). In 1473, Sampson Parker, late of Little Haywood (yeoman) was sued by Thomas Wolseley for insulting, wounding and ill-treating the latter's servant, Thomas Hille. Robert Parker was one of the body of Augustinian canons at Ranton Abbey in 1532, five years before its demise. In the churchwarden's accounts for Tunstall, Stoke-on-Trent (1654), there is a record of payment, made out to Mr Richard Parker (high constable) for seven shillings and dated for the year ending April 23rd, 1655. This is entered as *"maimed soldiers money"*, that is, a rate imposed by the Quarter Sessions on every parish to relieve soldiers and sailors incapacitated in the service of the State. The average payment was not to exceed sixpence a week per parish. Another gentleman named Richard Parker was given the unenviable job of cleaning the streets of Newcastle-under-Lyme in 1708, although he did have one consolation - he received a halfpenny for every load of muck he carted away! 1851, Charles Sampson Parker (organ builder) Salter's Street, Stafford; 1875, Edward Parker (fishmonger) of Lord Street, Etruria 1887, James Parker (engraver) of Newcastle Road, Hanley. The original "Nosey Parker", a person forever poking his nose into other people's business, is said to be based on Matthew Parker, chaplain to Henry VIII and Archbishop of Canterbury in 1559. He was notorious for making detailed enquiries into church affairs which did not concern him. But the medieval "parker" was a stickler for nosing out poachers and the name could have arisen then.

Park(e)

Park and Parke are generally synonymous with Parker, with reference to a "park-keeper", but a toponymic is also possible for a dweller in or near some park or enclosure. However, all these types of surnames are far more characteristic of the southern half of the county than the northern sector, as in 1327, Walter del Park of Wolgarston near Penkridge and 1327, William atte Park of Sedgley. There are vestiges of this preposition still remaining in 1539 - e.g. Thomas a Parke of Sedgley. This trio of specimens naturally survive as the singular form Park(e): 1851, George Park (silk throwster), Upper Hulme, Leek Frith; 1875, John Park, proprietor of the New Belle Vue Inn, Basford, Wolstanton.

With the plural forms Parks and Parkes it is altogether a different story, beset with problems. Apparently the trail begins with Richard Purchas of Dudley in an inquisition post mortem of 1292. This is from Old French "purchas" - "pursuit, pillage", which was eventually applied to couriers or messengers. The upshot of this is the modern surname Purchase: 1907, John H. Purchase (postman), Riley Street South, Burslem. The "ch" sound in this word is often hardened to "k", since the same Richard Purchas occurs as Richard Purcuz in 1273, that is "Purkuz", forerunner of surnames such as Purkess, Purkis(s), Pirkis(s), Porkiss and Porcas. When "er" developed into "ar" as in "clerk - clark", the spelling "ur" would naturally be associated with "er", and thus we get a form like 1406 Assizes, Richard Parkehouse of Dudley. This is normally taken as a toponymic for a dweller at a house in the park. The development here is modelled on the dialectal "coalus" for "coalhouse". Parkehouse itself later turns up with medial "s" as in 1614 Feet of Fines, Adam Parkeshowse of Trysull, who is alternatively known as Adam Parsehouse in 1622. Again, with the fluctuation between "ar" and "er", this ends up as Pershouse, as typified by 1583 Feet of Fines. Oliver Parshouse of Brierley, recorded as Oliver Persehowse in 1594. The modern spelling is Pursehouse: 1872, Peter Pursehouse (shopkeeper), Bilston Street, Hallfields, Bradley, Bilston; 1872, William Henry Purshouse, Red Cow, Churchbridge, Cannock. Bardsley proffers an officer or purser in charge of the counting house, where the accounts of the lord of the manor were received and paid. Furthermore, Richard Parsehowse of Rowley Regis (1594 Feet of Fines) has the alias Parkes, and so by the most circuitous of routes the latter is just a very late version of Purkess. Yet the matter does not end there, for we are also dealing with a pet form of Peter, because in the lay subsidy rolls for Lutley near Enville, we come across Richard Perkys in 1327 and Ralph Perkynes in 1332. These are from "Per (Peres)", Old French "Piers", plus the diminutive suffix "-kin", and the "n" is sometimes lost as in 1362 Assizes. John Wylkyns of Darlaston near Wednesbury, found as John Wilkys in 1361. Perkyns and Perkys spellings also switch back and forth around Wolverhampton, Tettenhall and The Wergs during the fourteenth and fifteenth centuries. Perkys too could have developed into Perkehouse, Perkeshouse: 1441 Assizes, John Perkeshouse of Sedgley, whilst Parkys would have resulted in Parkehouse, Parkeshouse: 1532, William Parkyshows of Woodsetton (Sedgley). At Sedgley in the 1666 hearth tax returns, this surname appears in a wide range of forms, including Parkshouse, Perkshouse, Pars(e)house, Pearshouse and Persehouse. Here the vacillation between "Per-, Par-" is reminiscent of the locative Perton-Parton. Perks and Parks, reduced forms of Perkins and Parkins, crop up in the Ronton parish registers, where

Thomas Perks (1714), is written down as Thomas Parks in 1746. In 1887 Edward Perks was steward of the Conservative Workingmen's Club in High Street, Tunstall.

In the Middle Ages the term "warren" denoted either the right to hunt and take certain wild animals or the actual land over which such a right was exercised. Provided that this land was not under forest law or subject to stringent hunting regulations imposed by the king, then any member of the general public could hunt game there. At first sight, the surname Warren seems to be connected with this ancient right, but this is illusory, for the name was imported from La Varenne in Normandy, recorded as "Warenne" in the Domesday survey: 1532, Robert Waren, householder at Stafford Green, Castlechurch; 1637, John Warren vulgarly called Pedley of Endon, buried at Leek; 1851, James Warren (mill manager), Church Mayfield; 1887, John Warren (coal dealer), Jubilee Terrace, Tunstall. There is, however, some overlap with Waring, Wareing, which goes back to the Germanic personal name "Warin": Domesday survey, Warin, under-tenant of Robert de Stafford at Blymhill and Brineton near Weston-under-Lizard; 1327, Roger Waryn, assessed for two shillings at Mayfield; 1610, August 24th, Richard Waringe and Margaret Pearson, married at Audley; 1887, Edwin Waring (hairdresser and perfumer), Church Street, Chesterton; 1887, James Wearing (auctioneers), High Street, Tunstall. In the Trentham parish registers, Edward Waring of Cocknage (1720), is alternatively entered in the register as Edward Warren in 1718.

The official who was engaged in the protection of a "warren" and enforcing its laws was the "warriner", a French term just like "forester" and "parker": 1303 Assizes, Richard le Warrener of Weeford. In 1378, at Tunstall, Stoke-on-Trent, Thomas Veatrer (sic), warrener of Audley, was paid 32 shillings and four pence wages for 48 weeks work. These become the modern Warrener and Warriner: 1716, Nathaniell Wariner, buried at Church Eaton on August 14th. An extra "d" creeps in occasionally, as in Blymhill parish registers, 1741, William Warrener, who appears as William Warrender in 1745. In 1907 George Warrinder (engine driver), lived in Garner Street, Stoke. The name also undergoes contraction to Warner, as exemplified by 1332 Assizes, Ithel le Warner of Cheadle who is identical with Ithel le Wariner, juror for Totmonslow Hundred in 1307. But Warner has an alternative scenario - the Germanic name "Warinhar(i)", brought over by the Normans as "Warnier": 1199 Assizes, Warnerus son of Brunie. The surname Warner is well established across north Staffordshire by the advent of the Industrial Revolution: 1559, December 2nd, Thomas Warner and Margaret Harison, married at Ellastone; 1666, Thomas Warner, exempt from hearth tax at Stafford; 1785, Elizabeth, daughter of Thomas and Ann Warner, baptised at Seighford on April 17th; 1851, Mary Warner (brick and tile maker), Trent Vale; 1851, Henry Warner (farmer) of Maer.

The central French version of the personal name "Warnier" was "Garnier, Guarnier", one origin of Garner, but also to be considered is Old French "gerner,

Warren (margin)

Waring / **Wareing** (margin)

Warrener / **Warriner** / **Warrinder** (margin)

Warner (margin)

Garner (margin)

gernier" - "storehouse for corn (granary)", with reference to the keeper of the granary. In 1308, one of the poorest tenants of the Audleys at Betley was Richard Garner, who was paying an annual rent of one penny for one plot of meadow. Garner is also a late form of Gardener: Swynnerton parish registers, Thomas Gardiner of Nowall (1765), recorded as Thomas Garner of Nowall in 1767. Trade directories: 1851, James Garner, owner of a beerhouse in Tinkersclough, Hanley; 1851, Francis Garner (shopkeeper and parish clerk) of Colton, Blithfield; 1875. Samuel Garner (horsekeeper) of Dale Street, Burslem; 1875, John Garner (hosier) of High Street, Hanley.

Another forest officer or gamekeeper was the "ranger", but normally it was an official title for a custodian of the royal parks. In 1371, for example, the king appointed a ranger for the forest of Cannock to hold office during the royal pleasure. A ranger - also sometimes known as "ranger and bow bearer" - continued to be appointed by the Crown, either for life or during pleasure, until the reign of Elizabeth I. The last recorded holder of the office was Henry, Lord Stafford in 1560, who was given the post for life, together with all the usual profits except for a fee of six pence per day. 1873, Joseph Ranger (grocer) of May Bank, Wolstanton; 1875, Samuel Ranger (greengrocer), Lord Street, Etruria; 1907, Ralph Rainger (potter's fireman), Knutton Road, Wolstanton.

Two compounds of similar formation are relevant here - Warboys and Mortiboys, both of which contain the Old French element "bois" - "wood". Warboys means literally "guard wood", as in 1207 Pipe Rolls. Richard Wardebois, a nickname for a forester, but the name is also derived from Warboys near Ramsey Abbey, Cambridgeshire (of disputed meaning). John Warboys was Abbot of Ramsey in 1510. Mortiboys stands for "dead wood", which sounds totally meaningless as a name, but when we realise, that dead wood was used widely during the Middle Ages for fuel, not only by charcoal burners and villagers, then a nickname may have arisen, whose actual meaning has been lost in the mists of time. Milwich parish registers, 1646, Isabella Morteboy, married to James Bordman on December 17th; Weston-under-Lizard parish registers, 1789, John Mortiboys and Jane Northwood, wed on May 4th; 1907, Job Mortiboy (engine driver), Mill Street, Fenton; 1907, Mrs Julia Mortiboy (grocer), Challinor Street, Tunstall.

HUNTING

Hunting as a way of life in the Middle Ages was not just a sport indulged in by the king and his barons, but also by poachers throughout his realm, for the poorer classes needed fresh meat to supplement their meagre meals of bread, cheese, vegetable broth and a mug of ale. Despite the tight controls on hunting, it is a most remarkable fact, that the native Saxon terms for "hunter" - Hunt and Hunter lived to fight another day, and positively flourished, with Hunt far outstripping its companion Hunter. In 1299 William le Hunte of Hanford and Agnes his wife, together with a number of other local residents, were accused of unjustly taking away eighty acres of heath and moor in Trentham from the Prior of Trentham. The defendants denied any injury to the Prior, and stated, that Thomas, Earl of Lancaster held the tenement at the date that the Prior had sued out his writ (viz. 21st June 1298), and that the tenement was not in Trentham, but in Hanford. Moreover, one Roger de Honefort held the tenement together with William le Hunte and the other defendants, but this gentleman was not named in the writ. Therefore, they pleaded that the Prior never was in possession of the tenement. The suit was adjourned through lack of evidence. In the 1539 Muster, John Hunt was enrolled at Knutton Geffrey Hunte at Abbey Hulton and William Hunte at Stone. 1851, Samuel Hunt (baker, flour dealer), Mill Street, Leek; 1887, Maria Hunt (spur and stilt maker) Liverpool Road, Burslem; 1907, Jesse Hunt (guard on the North Staffordshire Railway), Neville Street, Stoke; 1907, Robert Hunt (dipper), Rathbone Street Tunstall.

Hunter

On the other hand, the surname Hunter is comparatively late in making its debut. In 1459 William Wolryche sued William Leek of Whitgreave (harper), for breaking into his close and houses at Whitgreave and insulting and beating Joan Hunter, his servant. On December 3rd. 1553, John Hunter and Agnes Dale were married at the parish church of St. James the Great, Audley, and in 1663 Anne Hunter of Newcastle-under-Lyme was allowed five shillings per annum *"if she leave the almshouses and keep unmarried"*. This poor woman is surely to be identified with Anne Hunter, ineligible for any hearth tax at Newcastle in 1666 1873, George Hunter (underground bailiff), Talke Cottage, Talke; 1907, Maria J Hunter (beer retailer), Bridge Street, Fenton.

Venner
Venour
Venor

The Norman equivalent of the Saxon "hunt" was "veneur", as in William le Hunt, who held a burgage at Betley on the Audley estates in 1298 for sixteen pence per annum, entered by a Norman scribe as William le Venor in 1308. The modern survivals are Venner, Venour, Venor. The two contrasting surnames occur side by side in an assize of 1303, where Adam le Hunte is one of the sureties of Robert le Venur of Uttoxeter, who withdrew his writ against Theobald de Verdun, senior and Philip de Barenton respecting common pasture in Crakemarsh.

Gravenor
Gravener
Grosvenor

This Norman word "veneur" is the basis of Gravenor/Gravener and Grosvenor, the former representing "grand veneur" - "great huntsman", whilst the latter stands for "gros veneur" - "chief huntsman". They are virtually interchangeable, since a lawsuit of 1573 cites Walter Grosvenor (otherwise Gravener) of Bushbury, and in the 1581 Feet of Fines, Jonas Gravener of Bushbury is alternatively quoted as Jonas Grosvenor. The two forms also occur at Alstonefield in the Middle Ages. In 1293 Robert le Grant Venur was amongst those summoned by the Sheriff of the local assizes, to show by what warrant they claimed free warren, fair, and market in Alstonefield. Fifty years later, in 1343, Ralph de Vernor of Shibbrok (chivaler) sued Robert, son of Robert le Grovenour for a sixth part of the manor of Alstonefield. On top of these examples, there is an interesting assize, dated 1462, in which Thomas Gravenor of Gravenor, county Salop (husbandman), was sued by Thomas Broke and Robert Bradmedowe for breaking into their close and houses at Clareley. Here Gravenor could well be an abbreviated local form of Gravenhunger near Woore - "slope covered with brushwood", or for High Grovenor near Claverley, east of Bridgnorth (1833 Ordnance Survey Map). In 1666 George Gravener was excused from paying any hearth tax by the Constable at Uttoxeter by reason of his poverty. Edward Gravener, too, was in the same boat at Okeover, Ilam and Castern. William Grosvenor, licensed to practise as a physician and surgeon at Leek in 1697, was described as an apothecary in 1705. 1873, John Grosvenor (builder, joiner, stonemason), Alfred Street, Tunstall; 1851, George Fox Grosvenor (ironfounder, boiler maker), Eagle Foundry, New Hall Street, Hanley.

There are all kinds of roundabout ways of defining a medieval hunter. Some of the more inventive names include phrases or expressions containing the Norman words "Pass(e)" or "Perce", in which "Pass(e)" refers to passing over or crossing some obstacle or other, whilst compounds in "Perce-" allude to piercing or going through terrain difficult to negotiate. Passmore/Pasmore, for instance, has been explained as from Old French "passe mer" - "cross the sea", a nickname for a seafarer or sailor, but surely more to the point is a hunter, with the base being Old French "passe mere" - "cross pool (lake)". This derivation is certainly strengthened by John Passemere of Uttoxeter (1419 assizes), who is also known as "forster", a forester, who would obviously have crossed many local pools or lakes as he patrolled his home territory in pursuit of poachers, or checking for fallen trees, and so on. In 1266 William de Mungomeri appeared by attorney against Walter Passemore and twenty others for burning his manor of Cowley and breaking into his parks at Cowley and Marchington, and carrying away his animals. Edward Pasmer, who was vicar at Brewood from 1614 until his death in 1629, also occurs as Edward Pasmor in 1623. In 1666 another Edward Pasmore was paying tax on two hearths at Kingswinford, whilst Francis Pasmore was excused payment at the same place.

Paslow, too, is held to be synonymous with Passmore, that is, from Old French "passelewe" - "cross the water", a nickname for a sailor, but other sources favour a holy water sprinkler. Again, a more accessible origin is a name for a hunter who habitually waded through water whilst stalking deer etc. as evidenced by 1276, Henry de Barton (alias Passelewe), vicar of Rugeley. At least in this particular case, the holy water sprinkler suggestion would be very apt. Later on the name develops into some very curious forms, including Parslow, Parsloe, Parsley, Pasley, Pashley and Pashler, not all of which are in evidence for our county. 1907, George Pashley (stoker) of Clarence Street, Stoke; 1907, Bert Pashley (engine driver) of South Street, Fenton. But Pashley also goes back to the locative Pashley in Ticehurst, Sussex. There may even be some overlap with surnames such as Purslow and Pursley, on the analogy of Parsehouse-Persehouse (Pursehouse). In the main, these are to be traced to Purslow a few miles west of Stokesay Castle in Shropshire - "Pussa's burial mound (barrow)": 1556 Feet of Fines, Nicholas Purslowe of Little Sandon. In 1666 neither John Pursley nor widdow Pursley was required to submit any hearth tax at Brewood.

Pursglove

Bardsley's assumption that the Derbyshire surname Pursglove is a corruption of Purslow is just a shot in the dark. Cottle adds little to the debate with his simplistic "glove with a purse in it". It is indeed a Derbyshire name with fieldnames like Pursglove Croft in Brampton near Chesterfield, Pursglove Plantation in Middleton and Smerrill Grange near Youlgreave and the modern Purseglove Drive and Purseglove Street in Tideswell. William Pursgloves, vicar of Tideswell, was involved in two Staffordshire assizes. In 1444 he was one of several defendants sued by Ralph Basset (armiger) for treading down and consuming his hay at Throwley in stacks with their cattle, and in 1448 he was charged with depasturing cattle on the same Ralph Basset's corn and grass at Grindon and Musden. The surname Pursglove is as yet a mystery, but there is one clue which is worth going into, and that is Peersclough Farm, north east of Rawtenstall, Lancashire. This looks very much as though it could be for "pierce clough", that is, a hunter who penetrated a valley whilst on the trail of some wild animal. The initial element of the name Peersclough would easily fluctuate with "Purs(e)" as in Pearsehouse - Purshouse. At any rate, it would be an ideal name for a county like Derbyshire with its magnificent valleys and gorges. Moreover, it would thus be a hybrid on a par with Perceval/Percival - literally "pierce valley" - Old French "perce val", a hunter who trudged through the valley in his quest for game: 1280 Assizes, John Percevall. The names are also from either of two places called Perceval in Calvados (Normandy): 1203 Assizes, Richard de Percevill or from a personal name, borne by Perceval de Somery of Warwickshire, who sold William de Burmingham a suit of mail and an iron gorget (armour to protect the throat) for £10 at Aspley (1294). William Percevall was buried at Ellastone in February, 1542 and Edward Percival got married to Elizabeth Smith at Seighford on February 23rd, 1693. In 1851 Thomasin Percival was a schoolmistress at Mayfield and in 1907 Walter Percival (deputy borough surveyor), was based at Longton Court House, Commerce Street. The most tragic Perceval of all is Spencer Perceval, the Prime Minister, who was assassinated by a madman in the lobby of the House of Commons in 1812.

Perceval
Percival

One of the justices of the assize at Lichfield in 1370 was a certain Henry Percehay, who boasts an Old French name "perce-haie" - "pierce hedge", a nickname applied either to a poacher who regularly trespassed through a hedge that protected some forest or enclosure, or possibly there may be a hint of a military name for a fearless warrior who could penetrate the defences of the enemy. These lines of enquiry lead us to the modern surnames Pearcy, Pearcey, Piercey and Piercy. In 1666 John Pearcy was charged on one hearth at Bednall Constablewick near Cannock Chase, and in 1875 J. Beaumont Piercy was Secretary of the Staffordshire

Pearcy
Pearcey
Piercey
Piercy

Potteries Water Works Company, Hanley. But there is inevitable confusion with Percy, which goes back to Percy in La Manche, or any one of three places in Calvados, including Percy-en-Auge, from where William de Perci took his name, companion of William the Conqueror and ancestor of the Percies, dukes of Northumberland. The most famous of this line is Sir Henry Percy (1364-1403), known as Henry Hotspur on account of his hot temper and his reckless feats of horsemanship. He was immortalised by Shakespeare in Henry IV, Part 1, and he also appears in the ballads of "Chevy Chace" and "Otterburn". Locally, we find that William de Persi was assessed for twelve pence at Uttoxeter in the 1327 lay subsidies, whilst in the Abbot's Bromley rental roll of 1402 David Percy was in tenure of a messuage for an undisclosed annual rent. James Percy and Margaret Cumberbatch were married at Stoke-on-Trent on April 27th, 1636 and Mary Percy was resident in High Street, Goldenhill in 1907.

One perplexing surname in this category needs to be addressed, and that is Cashmore. Recordings are unfortunately very late, and consequently any attempt to solve the puzzle must be speculative, to say the least. Nevertheless, in the West Bromwich parish registers for the seventeenth century we come across 1614, Thomas Cashmore, noted as Thomas Cassmore in 1613 and as Thomas Casmore in 1621. The latter pair of spellings could represent Old French "casse mere" - "break pool (lake)", and, by analogy with Passmore, q.v., would denote a hunter, more likely a fisherman, who traversed some local pool or lake, and literally "broke" the surface of the water with his boat or some such water craft. There is a place called Cashmoor, north east of Blandford Forum in Dorset, not far from Cranborne Chase, but whether it is of any consequence here is not determined. The burial of William Cashmore took place at Ellenhall on May 26th, 1588. Trade directories: 1875, William Cashmore (grocer) of Bleak Street, Burslem; 1907, Moses Cashmore (engineman) of Heron Street, Fenton; 1907, Mrs Elena Cashmore (fried fish dealer), Borough Market, Market Lane, Longton; 1907, Percy Cashmore (miner), George Street, Longton.

Fewtrell/Fewtrill too is obscure. In Staffordshire Customs, Superstitions and Folklore, Hackwood cites from the registers of St. Leonard's Church, Bilston a Mr John Fewtrill of Easthope, Shropshire for July 20th, 1699. The name also occurs in the Penn parish registers; 1736, Ann Fewtrel, and at Pattingham, where Richard Fewtrel married Ann Light on November 13th, 1777. The surname is very rare in north Staffordshire, but William Fewtrell (contractor) was resident in South Street, Fenton in 1907. It might be connected with the medieval "fewterer" in whose charge were the greyhounds, used in hunting and coursing. Cottle concedes, that it is a surname typical of Shropshire.

To improve their chances of catching game in the forests or on the vast acres of rolling countryside, some hunters and poachers relied on tried and trusted methods of setting traps and snares. The surname Trapp(e) fits into this category,

Thorp(e)

from a Saxon word "traeppe" - "trap, gin, snare", with reference to the hunter who set the trap. But locally it can be a variant of the locative Thorpe, as in the Tunstall manor court rolls, where 1603, Ralph Thorpe (Throppe) is recorded as Ralph Trappe in 1601. "Thorp" is a Danish word, introduced by the Scandinavians in the ninth century and refers to a hamlet or outlying farm. It occurs in the Staffordshire locality Thorpe Constantine north east of Tamworth, which is probably the major source of the surname in our county, but contributions must also come from the village of Thorpe north west of Ashbourne, close by the place where the rivers Manifold and Dove intersect on the Derbyshire side of Dovedale, plus other Thorpes in the Danelaw counties, containing various suffixes. John de Thorp was assessed at Mayfield, south east of Ilam in the 1327 lay subsidies. Later the letter "r" tends to drift about, as in the Tunstall specimens, and also results in the rare Tharp: 1671 Katherine Tharpe of Mucklestone. Thorp(e), however is the regular modern spelling: 1699, September 14th, Gabriel, son of Henry and Ann Thorp, buried at Swynnerton; 1707, William Thorpe (apothecary) died at Leek; 1907, David Thorp (labourer) of Trafalgar Street, Hanley.

Trainer
Trainor
Treanor
Traynor
Triner
Tryner

Another hunter well versed in the art of laying a trap or lure for wild animals was the "trainer", which lives on in the names Trainer, Trainor, Treanor, Traynor Triner and Tryner. Mucklestone parish registers, 1640, Katherine (sic), daughter of John and Elizabeth Triner, baptised on March 7th; Madeley parish registers, 1701 Edward Triner and Mary Mottershed (both of Audley), married on January 25th 1907, F. Trainer (carter), Ronald Street, Longton; 1907, Joseph Tryner (potter's printer), Gibson Street, Burslem.

Stalker
Stark(e)y
Stoker

On the other hand, the "stalker" preferred to pursue his quarry by walking stealthily: 1640 Muster, Robert Stalker, member of the pressed band at Newborough and Hoar Cross. Yet families called Stalker, Stauker, Staulker, Stawker, Stoaker Stoker, Starky and Starkey proliferate around the Stafford, Weston-on-Trent Seighford, Haughton and Gnosall areas in the 1500s, 1600s and 1700s and must be variants of one another, although concrete proof is lacking. The pairing Stalker - Stoker would imitate the dialectal "toke" for "talk", whilst Starkey, a nickname for a strong person, could fluctuate with Stalker/Stawker by analogy with Archard - Orchard, where the sound "or" is often spelt "aw", as in "shaw - shore". The terminal "ey" is easily transformed into "er", as we have already witnessed in Pashler-Pashley from Passelowe. 1615 Feet of Fines, William Starkye of Haughton near Gnosall, compared with Thomas Stoker in the Haughton parish registers for 1664, and St. Chad's parish register, Stafford. 1687, John Stalker, contrasting with John Starkey, charged on one hearth at Derrington near Stafford in 1666. One cunning ploy often resorted to by hunters for creeping up on their prey and capturing it unawares was the "stalking-horse". It was either a real horse, that was trained to allow the hunter to conceal himself behind it or under its coverings, or it was an artificial, portable contraption, that is, a screen made of canvas or some other light material, built in the shape of a horse. This was an especial favourite of the "fowler" in his pursuit of wild birds. Nowadays, the word "fowl" is generally restricted to domestic birds reared for food, but in the Middle Ages it referred to any kind of wild fowl or bird, and at this particular time, small birds as well as large were limed and netted in large numbers both by the peasantry and by the sporting gentry. In addition to the normal fare on the menu like pheasant, partridge and grouse, our medieval ancestors also had a taste for larks, wrens, finches, thrushes, swans, geese, teal, mallard, woodcock, egret, snipe, pigeons and stork. So the "fowler" had a lot to do to keep his family or lord of the manor happy. In 1311 Roger le Foulere of Bagot's Bromley was sued by Thomas de Rideware to render to him a reasonable account for the time he was bailiff in Hamstall Ridware. Roger did not appear, and the Sheriff was ordered to arrest him and produce him at Easter Term. In 1332 Adam le Fouler of Swynnerton handed over his twenty pence subsidy to the tax collectors. Robert Fowler was vicar of Leek in 1652. In the eighteenth century the boys of poor parents were put out as apprentices, and it was formerly a common practice to draw lots to decide to whom each boy should be apprenticed. William Fowler was one of those present on the 3rd November, 1771, at a vestry meeting, held in the parish church at Cheadle, where it was agreed to put out as apprentices all the poor children of the parish, and tickets were to be drawn on the 15th November. 1851, Joseph Staniland Fowler, town crier at Stafford; 1875, John Fowler (butcher) of Marsh Street, Longton.

With the stringent controls on all types of hunting and because fresh meat was unobtainable for a large part of the year and fast days were numerous, fish was an essential item in the diet of the nation. It was this dependence on fish which made the "fisher" such an invaluable member of any self-supporting community. It is all too easy to conjure up an idyllic rural scene where Adam le Fisschere of Fradswell (1327 Subsidies) idled away his leisure hours by the riverside in the morning sunshine, waiting patiently for a roach or bream to take the bait. But this picture would be totally false, for in reality, the medieval "fisher" was no casual angler - on the contrary, he was a seasoned professional, often employed by the lord of the manor to set sophisticated traps and nets on the local rivers, ponds and fens, besides his day-to-day business of catching fish with rod and line. Centuries before drainage and land reclamation schemes were even thought of, and before the insidious pollution of local rivers by modern chemicals, our ancestral fisherman was thoroughly at home with all the various aspects of his craft. The importance of fish in medieval Staffordshire is patently obvious from an assize of 1344, in which John, son of Juliana de Colton and John Stykkebukke were sued by Simon de Ruggeleye for taking fish from his fish-pond at Rugeley, including pike, bream, roach, tench and eels worth 100 shillings. Simon was awarded the full damages of 100 shillings for the theft. In 1408 Richard Fissher of Colwich actually stole some fish from Humfrey de Haloughton's (Haughton's) fishery at Silkmore to the value of ten pounds. Of course, the "fisher" sometimes set up his own stall at the local market, where he sold his hard-won catch: 1465 Assizes, William Fysshe (fysshmonger) of Lichfield. In the 1640 Muster Edward Fisher was a member of the trained band at Tean and Draycott-in-the-Moors. In 1851 the Reverend Samuel Fisher was the incumbent at Hope Church, Northwood, Hanley and in the same year William Fisher was the licensee at the Black Swan in the Sheepmarket, Leek.

Fish

Fish in its own right as a surname probably denotes a catcher and seller of fish: 1666, William Fish, chargeable on two hearths at Uttoxeter; 1851, Richard Fish (farmer) of Loxley.

Wyles
Wiles
While
Wile

Wild(e)

Eels were a particular delicacy, and the "fisher" set up wicker traps or "wyles" to catch them: Rydeware Chartulary, 1270, Geoffrey de la Wyle, hence names like Wyles, Wiles and While or Wile, but some of these may denote a person of many wiles: 1851, Joseph Wile (ironmonger), Gaolgate Street, Stafford. At Rugeley there is some fluctuation with Wild, as in 1591, William Wilde alias Wyles. If Wilde is the original form, then this is a nickname for an untamed spirit, an undisciplined individual: 1851, Isaac Wild (owner of a beerhouse), Willow Cottage Longton; 1875, Joseph Wild (auctioneer, furniture broker), Bridge Street Newcastle-under-Lyme.

Kiddle
Kiddell
Kidwell

A "kiddle" was a dam, weir or barrier that had an opening in it, fitted with nets or other appliances for catching fish as they attempted to swim through. Hence someone like Ralph Kydel of Lichfield (1362 Calendar of Charters) would probably be the keeper of the weir, and his descendants are with us now in the guise of Kiddle or Kiddell, or possibly Kidwell, by analogy with Biddle (Biddulph)- Bidwell, since in a Star Chamber proceeding, dated 1547, Richard Byddell of Biddulph is alternatively written down on the record as Mr Bydwell (Biddulph). In 1875 Moses Kidwell (shopkeeper), was resident along Fenton Road, Hanley. Kidwell and Kiddle, however, are typical of the county of Somerset, where they are corrupt forms of Cadwall - "cold well".

Weir
Wear(e)
Wears

The more obvious surnames for a fisherman who was in charge of the weir are Weir, Wear(e) and Wears: Alrewas Manor Court Rolls, 1272, Robert atte Were. Cassandra Weere and Richard Cooke were married at Swynnerton on November 20th, 1574 and in 1851 William Weir was one of the masters at the National School at Alton. In 1907 Charles Weare (labourer) lived in Florence Street, Newcastle under-Lyme.

Falconer

Of all the forms of hunting in the Middle Ages the one that was most entirely aristocratic was the pursuit of falconry, for every king, member of the nobility and every lord of the manor had his falcons, and it was the "falconer" who looked after them for his master and trained them. The office of State falconer was valued so highly in Norman England, that the Domesday survey records four different tenants in-chief for the counties of Hampshire, Berkshire and Norfolk, each of which is designated as "accipitrarius" - "falconer". Indeed, up until the reign of King John

Fishermen hauling in nets 15th
century. (Fisher p. 85)

Water mill with eel traps.
(Wyles p. 86)

Selling fish at a stall,
13th century. (Fish p. 86)

Falconers cooling down their birds. p. 86

Falconers. p. 89

only those of the highest rank in society were permitted to keep hawks, but in the thirteenth century Edward I decreed that every freeman could have eyries of hawks, sparrowhawks, falcons and eagles in his own wood. Edward III went a step further with a statute, passed in 1361, which stated that anyone who found a stray hawk was to take it to the sheriff of the county, who was then to proclaim the discovery in the neighbouring towns. However, if the person who found the stray bird, concealed it for his own use, then he was liable to a prison sentence of two years. In 1227 an assize convened to find out, whether Robert le Noreis, father of Nicholas le Noreis was in possession of half a virgate of land in Hilderstone, now held by Henry le Falconer and Ralph le Falconer. The defendants did not appear, and the assize was conducted in their absence. In 1435 John Fauconer of Froghall (smythyman) and several other inhabitants of Froghall and Ipstones were sued by Hugh Erdeswyke for breaking into his close at Kingsley, digging in his soil, cutting down his trees, and carrying away timber and earth and stone, to the value of 50 marks, and also for depasturing cattle on his corn and grass. Nowadays, the spelling Falconer plays second fiddle to Faulkner. James Falconer, rector at Standon in 1763, resigned in 1765. In 1851 John Faulkner (cutlery and hardware dealer) traded in Greyfriars, Stafford and Samuel Faulkner ran a shop in Checkley.

Triner p. 84

MAP 3 KEY

1. ARMITT/ARNETT   5. FROST   9. POPE
2. BISHOP   6. MAIDEN/MEADEN/MEADON   10. PROCTOR/PROCTER/PROCKTE
3. CANTRELL/CANTRILL   7. MORT   11. SANT/SAINT/SAUNT
4. DEAN(E)   8. PARSONS   12. SNOW
                                                       13. VICKERS/VICARS/VICCAR

SURNAMES AT THE TIME OF THE 1666 HEARTH TAX RETURNS

CHAPTER THREE

THE CHURCH AND RELIGION

At the time of the Norman Conquest England had been Christian for almost four hundred years and its saints and scholars were famous all over Europe. Charlemagne, the most powerful figure in Christendom during the ninth century, had even employed an English missionary, Alcuin (Aelhwine), a product of the cathedral school of York, as tutor to his sons. Until the landing of Augustine on English soil in 597 AD pagan gods were worshipped all over England. With the exception of the kingdom of Essex, all the Anglo Saxon dynasties claimed a descent from Woden, the God of the dead. His name is not only preserved in Wednesday, but also in the Staffordshire placenames Wednesbury and Wednesfield in the heart of Mercia. These places have long been pronounced as "Wedgbury" and "Wedgfield". The former in fact still exists as a surname.

gfield

The task which lay ahead for Augustine and his little band of about forty monks was a formidable one, for their new faith, based on the teachings of the New Testament, stood in sharp contrast to the religion and mythology of the Anglo-Saxons. Their way of life was based on loyalty to family or clan chieftain and laid emphasis on avenging any wrong done to destroy these bonds. In Germanic philosophy physical courage and bravery were extolled and independence fiercely guarded. Augustine, on the other hand, preached the Christian ideals of meekness and humility, patience and virtue, and forgiving one's enemies. Yet, by the time of Augustine's death seven years later, the kingdom of Kent had become wholly Christian, and, within a hundred years of his arrival on our shores, all England had been converted to Christianity.

Despite this wholesale conversion to the new faith, the Anglo Saxons shied away from the use of Biblical names, partly because they preferred to coin home-made names from their own language and partly out of respect for holy names. In the years leading up to the Norman Conquest even the bishops of Lichfield and Coventry bore Anglo Saxon names. The Anglo Saxon Chronicle reports, that in 1052 Wulfsige, bishop of Lichfield passed away, and Leofwine, abbot of Coventry, succeeded to the bishopric. Clearly, the pagan customs of name-giving were too deeply entrenched to be modified by Christian ethics or well-intentioned religious institutions.

This same veneration for the Bible held sway right across Europe and was perpetuated by the Popes, who for the first five centuries of Christianity refrained from using names of persons connected with the life of Christ. Instead they stuck to artificial concoctions such as Pious and Innocent. The Normans, however, unlike the Saxons, once they had been converted to Christianity, had few inhibitions when

Bible

it came to religion and names from the Bible. Incidentally, the surname Bible is a trick - it stands for "Bib-el", a diminutive of "Bibb", a pet name of Isabel. 1875 Richard Bible (miner) of Liverpool Road, Burslem.

Without any hesitation they gave monasteries they built in England sacred names like "Gracedieu" in Leicestershire - "grace of God", and "Dieulacres" near Leek - "may God increase it". The story goes, that Ranulph de Blundeville, the founder of the Cistercian abbey of Dieulacres in 1214, was visited in his sleep by the spirit of his grandfather, who advised him to transfer the Cistercians of Poulton in Cheshire, where the monks there were being persistently threatened by Welsh raiders, to the new site at Leek. When Ranulph related this dream to his wife, she being of French descent, exclaimed "Deulencres" - "May God grant it increase".

Many of the Normans' favourite expressions and sayings had religious significance, and a substantial number of them contained this element "Dieu". In 1306 William de Halsheye of Churleye feloniously killed Thomas Deu Vos Garde of Hammerwich at Churleye (Chorley), whilst in the 1379 Poll Tax returns, Agnes Dieugard was assessed for twelve pence at Lichfield. These early spellings are

Dugard

transposed later into Dugard, e.g. Samuel Dugard and Ester Vyse, married a Standon in 1718. The literal meaning of the name is "May God protect you". In the West Bromwich parish registers John Duger (1646) could be a reduced form of the name. This same gentleman occurs as John Duker in 1629, which might survive as

Ducker

the modern Ducker: 1851, Thomas Ducker (farmer) of Mucklestone.

Fido(e)
Fiddy

In 1688/89 Henry Fidoe, a noted ironmonger in the Wednesbury area, was purchasing his iron from the Stour valley forges, because the output of the Tame forges was insufficient for his purposes; Elizabeth Fidoe was a witness to the marriage of John Russell and Mary Hall, which took place at Hints on February 22nd, 1773; 1872, Thomas Fidoe (general dealer), Swan Village, West Bromwich. These names may sound as if they have been invented on the spur of the moment by some fanatical dog-lover, but they are in actual fact from French "fitz Deu" - "son of God", most likely an utterance to which someone was partial in the Middle Ages, when the name came into being.

A common expression in medieval England, much resorted to by Chaucer, is "pardee": *"I have a wyf, pardee, as wel as thow"*. This is an oath derived from

Pardew
Pardey
Pardy
Pardoe
Perdue

French "par Dieu", perhaps a shortened version of "de par Dieu" - "in God's name" as borne by the French actor Gerard Depardieu. It survives as Pardew, Pardey, Pardy, Pardoe and Perdue: Rydeware Chartulary, Temp. Edward III, Walter Perdu, Lichfield Cathedral Registers, 1743, Thomas Pardoe and Mary Harris of Brewood married on January 9th; 1907, Jos. Pardoe (compositor), Hulme Street, Burslem. 1907, Madam Pardoe (palmist), John Street, Hanley. A very similar name is Purdey.

Purdey
Purdie
Purdy(e)

Purdie, Purdy(e) - French "pour Dieu" - "for the grace of God": Thomas Perdy paying 14 pence subsidy for Lutley near Enville in 1327, is assessed at two shillings and sixpence at the same vill in 1332, but written on the tax list as Thomas Purdy.

In Volume 1 I took the surname Maydew/Madew as a variant of Meadow, but now I am not so sure, for there is an isolated John Mundewe at Marston-by-Stafford in the 1482 Assize rolls. This also suggests something like "(par) mon Dieu", but this on its own is inconclusive. In addition, we must also consider "Madeu", a form of Matthew found in the Massif Central region and Le Midi in France. This may have been brought over by French immigrants during the Middle Ages. The unexplained Ingledew could also belong here, with allusion to the "angel of God", since Henry Angel-Dei occurs in the 1273 Hundred Rolls for Lincolnshire. In the Bushbury parish registers Thomas Ingledew widower married Ann Oakley on August 24th, 1792.

Purefoy represents Anglo French "par fei", central French "par foi" - "by (my) faith". An assize of 1227 cites Henry Parfey, uncle of Dionisia, who was in possession of half the manor of "Burh" at his death, but was now held by Norman Pantof. The modern spelling Purefoy - "pure faith" - came about when "per, par, pur" fell together in pronunciation, as in Persehouse, Parsehouse, Pursehouse. William Purefoy was a member of the committee for regulating markets at Cheadle in 1652, which decided to alter market day from Thursday to Friday after a petition to that effect was submitted by the inhabitants of the town.

The native Saxon population responded to the Norman "Dieu" by invoking the assistance of their own "God", as in Godhelp - "may God help me". John Godhelp of Leek (yeoman) would certainly have appreciated some divine intervention in 1457, after he entered the park of John, the Earl of Shrewsbury at Alton, with Ralph Madeley of Denstone (gentleman), John Prestwode of Denstone (yeoman), John in Doowe (sic) of Leek (gentleman), and chased and took the lord's game. In 1532 Richard and Ralph Godhelp with their respective families were settled at Alton, whilst John Godhelp, wife Elizabeth and their children resided at Ellastone. Entries from the 1532 list, such as John that God sendhus at Wetton and Alice that God send at Colclough near Tunstall are either bastards or foundlings.

The very rare Godbehear, Godbehere could stand for "may God be in this house", or "may there be good in this house". Vincent Godbeheare was one of the 5 burgesses elected at Newcastle-under-Lyme in 1572, and in 1851 Anthony Godbehere ran a butcher's stall at Uttoxeter Sheepmarket. In 1873 Hannah Godbehere (grocer, draper) traded along High Street, Silverdale. These names are contracted to Godbeer, Godbear or Godber: James Godbeere, taxed on one hearth at Wall near Lichfield in 1666. But these are usually for a brewer of good beer.

Thomas Godsalve, chapter clerk at Lichfield Cathedral (1480-1510), has a particularly appropriate appellation, in total accord with his chosen vocation, for it comes from Middle English "on (a) Godes half" - "in God's name" or "for God's sake". It survives as Godsalve, Godsave and Godsafe.

These phrases and exclamations are the very personification of this spiritual period in our history, the so-called "Age of Faith", when there was only one form

Pope

of religion throughout Western Europe - that taught by the Catholic church, at whose head was the Pope. Thus, his position in the ecclesiastical hierarchy was inviolate, and so, when we come across someone like Richard le Pope of Wrottesley, involved in a local dispute of 1302 over some deeds and William le Pope of Tamworth, cited in an inquisition post mortem of 1341, concerning Geoffrey le Scrope and all the lands and tenements which he held from the King at his death, then we are obviously dealing with the same medieval sense of irony exhibited by the surnames of noble rank in Chapter 2. The name may have applied to a pompous person, or a fellow of austere appearance, or even a nickname for anyone who played the part of "Pope" in a medieval pageant. Thomas Pope, who was chaplain at Salt in 1404, must have borne the brunt of endless jokes about his lowly status in the local clergy. 1851 William Wilson Pope (copper plate printer, bookseller and bookbinder), Piccadilly Hanley; 1851, Amelia Pope, National School mistress of Colwich; 1851, Ellen Pope (stone and marble masons), Navigation Road, Burslem.

Bishop

Prior to the Conquest the words "Pope" and "Pape" had been used to describe the Bishops of Rome, but the surname Bishop was mainly a nickname for a person who had the bearing or appearance of a bishop or came from the ceremony of electing a "boy bishop" on the Feast of St. Nicholas. In 1367 the chapter register at York Cathedral required future "bishops" to be boys who had served the longest and proved most useful in the cathedral. The office was much sought after, for it was a very remunerative one. For example, Robert de Holme, who was "boy bishop" in 1369, received £3/15/1 1/2d from the choirmaster, John Gisson, who acted as his treasurer. There are inventories detailing the custom of "boy bishop" at Lichfield Cathedral for 1345 and the fifteenth century. During his term of office the newly elected "bishop" was paraded through the streets, dressed in his regalia of mitre with silvered and gilt plates and gems, cheveril gloves to match, and blood coloured, velvet cope embroidered in gold. It would be a day which the lucky recipient would remember for the rest of his life, and of course, it may have been commemorated by his own name. In the 1332 lay subsidies William Bysshop was assessed for eleven pence at Bishton and Wolseley, whilst at Brockton, Baden Hall and Ankerton near Eccleshall, Stephen Bysshop handed over twelve pence and Robert Bysshop twenty pence. Clearly the surnames in the two latter cases were already hereditary. At the Standon manor court of 1444, it was presented by the jurors, that *"William Bysshopp allows his grange to be badly roofed, and the said grange to be without a door, and the east end thereof to be almost fallen down"* Under a penalty of 3/4d. William promised faithfully, that he would undertake the repairs himself before the next session of the manor court. Directories list: 1851 Elizabeth Bishop (milliner, dressmaker), Pool Head, Newcastle-under-Lyme; 1851 John Bishop and Co (grocers, provision dealers, hop merchants), Gaolgate Street Stafford; 1875, William Bishop (butter, cheese and bacon factor), High Street Hanley.

It is generally accepted, that surnames derived from ecclesiastical sources such as Bishop and others like Parsons, Vickers etc are all either nicknames or are in some way to do with playing such roles in some medieval pageant or play, since the canon law, imposed by the Norman archbishops after the Conquest, forbade the marriage of ordained priests and thereby prevented the foundation of families bearing their surname. There was also the vow of celibacy taken by the monastic orders. However, it was common knowledge in the Middle Ages, that many members of the clergy did marry and had families, who were quite willingly accepted by society. Immorality and adultery were rife. Chaucer's friar married off many a young woman at his own expense, probably because he had already made them pregnant, and in 1330 a London synod forbade priests to use church funds to buy houses for their mistresses. According to the Hereford visitation of 1397, the vicar of Eardisley was a common usurer, and regularly slept with the maid servants.

The documentary evidence for this fathering of children by members of the clergy is irrefutable. How else to account for William filius capellani (son of the chaplain), taxed at two shillings and nine pence for Clifton and Haunton in 1327, and Hugh filius capellani (son of the chaplain), paying sixteen pence at Parva Ridware in 1332? John le Frereson (*1335 Catalogue of Ancient Deeds for Staffordshire*) is for "son of the friar" and lives on in the name Frearson, Fryerson. In 1583 Henry Fryerson and his wife Alice remitted all right to some meadow and pasture in Acton (Swynnerton) to Humphrey Beardemore. Directories: 1907, John Frearson (engine smith), Basford Road, Wolstanton.

Henry le Denesone of Stramshall (1295 assizes) represents "son of the dean", a senior clergyman (after the bishop) in a cathedral chapter or diocese, or possibly the head of some faculty in an educational establishment. This gives the modern names Denson and Densem, but see also Denstone in Volume 1. Parsonson, Parsison and Parsizon stand for "son of the parson", as exemplified by Richard son of John le Personesone of Milwich and Mary his wife, who were sued in 1312 by Richard son of William de Puyz of Rugeley for a virgate of land and half a messuage in Milwich. In 1368 Ralph le Prestesone (son of the priest) was charged by John de Draycote (chivaler) with breaking into his close at Caverswall and maliciously killing his dogs, and beating, wounding and ill-treating his servants and men, so that he lost their services for a length of time. This name is easily absorbed later on by Preston via a form such as Presson, as in Gregory Presson, enrolled in the 1539 muster at Stafford. A contemporary historian, Giraldus Cambrensis, never one to mince his words about the debauchery of the clergy and the bad example they were setting for their parishioners, satirised the parish priest thus: *"He kept a hearth-girl in his house who kindled his fire but extinguished his virtue, and kept his miserable house cluttered up with small infants, midwives and nurses"*.

Of course, the natural result of all these illicit liaisons was a surfeit of illegitimate offspring or "bastards", but during the Middle Ages, being a bastard was not always considered a stigma. In official documents William the Conqueror was sometimes called William the Bastard, because his mother was his father's mistress, Herleva (pet-name Arlette), daughter of Fulbert, a tanner of Falaise. Herleva herself eventually married Herluin, viscount of Conteville, by whom she had two sons, Odo of Bayeux and Robert of Mortain, who were amongst the most prominent and influential of the Normans who made their fortune in England after

Bastard
Barsted
Barstead

the Conquest. In 1365, one of these local "bastards" called William Bastard of Badnall (Baden Hall) near Eccleshall, was in dispute with Roger le Warde over a messuage, two virgates of land, 12 acres of meadow and ten acres of pasture in the neighbourhood. In 1873 Richard B. Bastard was agent for the Shropshire Union Railway and Canal Company, whose offices were situated in Wharf Street, Stoke. Barsted and Barstead could well be disguised variants of the name. 1907, George Barsted (miner), Hamil Road, Burslem; 1907, John Barstead (carter), Clanway Street, Tunstall.

It may be argued, that these illegitimate children were sons of fathers who were not actually parsons, priests, friars, deans, chaplains and so on, but fathers who bore some passing resemblance in appearance or character to a parson, priest, friar, dean or chaplain in the local community. Whichever point of view is adopted, the "bastard", just like any other newly born infant, had to be baptised at the village church. Since our medieval ancestors believed that the souls of infants who died without undergoing the ritual of baptism would be cast down into hell, it was the custom for a child to be given the sacrament of baptism at the earliest opportunity, usually the day after its birth. The church, where the child was baptised, was the focal point of village life, and it was normally built by the lord of the manor. Consequently it was he, who reserved the right to appoint the priest most suited to serve the local community. In 1366 John de Knyghteleye appeared against three

Priest
Preest
Prest

defendants, one of whom was William le Prest of Ronton, in a plea, that, whereas they had been retained by him in his service at Mutton (probably Mitton south east of Church Eaton), they had relinquished it without his leave and without reasonable cause. Which John de Knyghteleye is alluded to in the above extract is open to conjecture, since there were three of this name during the fourteenth century, and all were keepers and justices of the peace, John de Knyghteleye the elder in 1378, John son of Robert de Knyghteleye in 1380 and 1382, and John de Knyghteleye of Wirlegh (Wyrley) in 1386. Hence, William le Prest, mentioned in the suit, could well be an actual priest in his own right. The priest, living as he did in the world (in seculo), belonged to the secular clergy and often came from peasant stock, working his way up the ecclesiastical ladder by learning a smattering of Latin at some grammar school, and assisting the parson as a "holy water clerk". In 1423 Robert Brid of Eccleshall (halywatyrclerk) discovered that his son John had been involved in the theft of some fish from the local fishery, valued at £20, and belonging to William Heyworth, the Bishop of Coventry and Lichfield. Many priests were poor and were forced to work on the land alongside the parishioners or, like the priest in Piers Plowman, obliged to go from village to village, *"singing for silver"*, offering services which they were licensed to perform to anyone who could afford them. Yet on the other side of the coin, the peasants relied on the priest for their religious instruction, for in those dark days there were no printed books or compulsory religious education to guide them.

This is where the priest was really in his element, for, if he were a good orator and preacher, he could express himself in vivid, emotional language to impress his listeners. Many phrases and proverbs have come down to us from these medieval sermons - *"enough is good as a feast"*, *"many hands make light work"*, *"to run with the hare and hunt with the hounds"*, *"to grease someone's palm"*, and so on. Out of his yearly earnings on his glebe, the priest had to keep the village church in repair, assist the poor and show hospitality to visitors. The money came chiefly from "tithes", an early Christian custom of setting apart a tenth part of their goods - crops, cattle, profits from trading - for the service of God.

The surname Priest, Preest, Prest is not especially common in any region of the county at any point. Thomas and William Prest were members of the Great Haywood militia in 1539, Thomas Priest was buried at Standon in 1706, and Richard Priest (potter) was resident along Shelton New Road, Stoke in 1907. Other variants occur, such as Press(e), as in Richard Presse, head of a household in Bore Street, Lichfield in 1532, and there is some interchange with Price: Church Eaton parish registers, 1798, Ann, daughter of Matthew and Mary Priest alias Price, baptised on December 13th. Price is normally for Welsh "ap Rhys" - "son of Rhys (ardour)": 1596, John ap Rice (alias Welchman) of Gnosall; 1851, John Price (watch and clock maker), Wellington Street, Burslem; 1851, James Price (china, glass dealer), Market Street, Longton. Priestman and Pressman denote "servant of the priest". In 1340 Isabella, formerly wife of Henry le Prestesmon, sued John, son of John de Brumpton, for a third of a messuage, a carucate of land, twenty acres of meadow, and twenty acres of pasture in Church Eaton as her dower, of the dotation of Henry, her former husband.

The "parson" was the chief "person" in the village, for both words are derived from Latin "persona", which was originally an actor's mask or a costumed character or "dramatis persona". Chaucer's parson in the *Prologue to The Canterbury Tales* is introduced thus: *"A good man was ther of religioun, and was a poure person of a toun..."* Spellings in medieval documents also fluctuate between the two forms, as typified by Dieulacres Cartulary, circa 1250, David persona (parsona) de Dodleston. The singular Parson is either an official title for a parson, as in the example just quoted or a nickname for someone who aped the parson's mannerisms. In 1347 John William of Stanshope sued Henry de Narudale for a messuage and twenty acres of land in Alstonefield, of which William le Persone, his great-grandfather was in possession when he died during the reign of Henry III, and he gave the following pedigree:

William le Persone

|

William

|

Henry

|

John, the plaintiff

In the 1532 List of Families in the Archdeaconry of Stafford, we find Thoma Parson living at Rushton Spencer, Thomas Parson at Dunston, and Nicholas Parso at Baswich. John Parson (miner) was resident in Sideway Road, Stoke in 1907. B in the 1532 list, spellings such as Person and Pereson are bracketed together, an hence we are also dealing with the patronymic Pearson(s), Peirson, Pierson - "so of Piers" - Old French "Piers", nominative of "Pierre" - "Peter": Eccleshall pari registers, 1589, Maria Pearson or Person. This extends to the plural form Parso as well: West Bromwich parish registers, 1636, Edward Pearsons, cited as Edwa Parsons in 1637. Parsons has several possible derivations. It can be an ellipt phrase for a person who lived or worked at the parson's house or parsonage as Henry atte Persouns, killed by Richard de Swynnerton, probably at Penkridge 1314. Also to be taken into account is an elliptic genitive for "the parson's servant as exemplified by Jenkyn le Persones, taxed at sixteen pence for Swynnerton 1327. However, the medieval parson was a notorious adulterer, and so the ma origin could well be for "son of the parson": 1332 Lay subsidies, John Personesone, whose contribution amounted to sixteen pence for the vill of Cheadl Specimens of all these surnames are as follows: 1851, Joseph Parson (nail maker Commercial Street, Burslem; 1851, David Pearson (fruit and vegetable deale High Street, Tunstall; 1875, John Pearson (clothier), Red Lion Square, Newcastl under-Lyme; 1907, Frederick Parsons (clerk), Ivy House Road, Hanley. Parsona simply means what it says - a worker or servant at the parsonage: Lichfie Cathedral Registers, 1697, Jacob Parsonage and Mary Berwick married September 21st.

In some parishes a vicar or "substitute" - from Latin "vicarius" - w appointed, who acted as parish priest in place of the priest or parson. Dieulacr Chartulary, 1241, Thomas .Vicarius de Lech (Leek). The plural form Vica Viccars, Vickars, Vickers denoted a servant who was employed at the vicar's hous 1327, William del Vikers, assessed at eighteen pence for Loxley. Ralph Vyke (yeoman) of Milwich, together with several other yeomen and servants of Hu Erdeswyk of Sandon, conspired to kill Henry and Walter Gilbert at Marchington 1409. Hugh had, in fact, given the conspirators shelter after they had committed t said felony. Compare 1359 Assizes, William le Vykeresman of Alrewas - "serva of the vicar", source of Vickerman. After the Industrial Revolution the surnam

Margin notes:

Person
Pereson

Pearson(s)
Peirson
Pierson

Parsons

Parsonage

Vicars
Viccars
Vickars
Vickers

Vickerman

Vickers becomes well established in the north western sector of the county, particularly around Keele, Audley, Halmerend and Newcastle-under-Lyme. From the 1842 report on children working in Staffordshire mines, it emerges, that John Vickers, aged 17, was employed at Thomas Kinnersley's coal and stone pits and iron blast furnace, Kidsgrove. His job was to haul the coal from the pit-head, after it had been brought up to the surface from the "delph". His wage was eleven shillings per week. 1851, William Vickers (carrier) from the Fox and George, Stafford to Cannock (Saturday afternoons); 1907, George Vicars (potter), Princess Street, Tunstall; 1907, Arthur R. Vickers (professor of music), Lily Street, Wolstanton (organist at Fenton Parish Church).

In the same way that Vickerstaff and Viggarstaff are alternative spellings for Bickerstaff, so Vickers see-saws back and forth with Viggars: Nicholas Vicarrs, exempt from paying hearth tax at Audley in 1666, occurs as Nicholas Viggors in the Audley parish registers for 1671. If Vigars, Viggars is the original surname in this particular case, then this is a nickname derived from Anglo French "vigrus" - "hardy, lusty, strong". In 1451 William Vigorys, late of Musden north west of Ilam, was one of several conspirators, who had caused Sampson Meverell, late of Tideswell (knight), to be indicted for the robbery of John Southworth, vicar of Ilam, of 8 marks, and later to be arrested and lodged in the prison of the Marshalsea. 1851, Thomas Vigers (station-master), Longport; 1851, Jabez Viggers (shopkeeper), Alsager's Bank, Halmerend. 1861, William Henry Vigrass (silk glosser) at William Hammersley's Dye Works, Mill Street.Leek. Vicary, Vickery is either a modification of "vicarius": 1381 Poll Tax, Agnes Vicary souster (sempstress) of Brewood, or from "Vikerhey" (1398) in High Whitley near Antrobus in Cheshire - "enclosure belonging to the vicar". This would be smoothed to Vickery at some point in the proceedings.

At first sight the surname Deacon, Deakan, Deakin(s) looks innocent enough - a plain, matter-of-fact reference to some medieval deacon, from Greek "diakonos" - "servant, messenger", hence an official of the Christian Church, who was appointed as the servant of the minister or priest in administrative, pastoral and financial affairs. In Episcopal churches the deacon was a member of the third order of ministry ranking below bishops and priests, and his duties included helping the priest in divine service, especially in the celebration of the Eucharist and visiting the sick in the local community. Early instances from medieval charters, such as Ranulf diaconus of Stone in a twelfth century deed from the Staffordshire Chartulary, and William diaconus de Lek, cited in the Dieulacres Cartulary for the thirteenth century, clearly indicate the office of deacon. Yet William le Dekon, assessed for sixteen pence at Bagot's Bromley in 1332 might apply either to his official capacity as a deacon or it may be an ironic nickname because William was accustomed to putting on the sanctimonious bearing of a deacon. In 1358 Richard Dekene and others unjustly dispossessed John de Knyghteleye of a rent of twenty shillings and of the rent of a robe worth twenty shillings at Chebsey.

Problems begin to accumulate during the fifteenth century, when in the same assize roll of 1413 Henry Dekyn of Tettenhall is also mentioned as Henry Deykyr and as Henry Dikyng. The latter spelling is usually derived from "Dic-un", a diminutive form of Dick, from the Germanic personal name Richard: in 130? Stephen Dicun and Hugh le Pestur (baker) were sued by Agnes, former wife of Adam Hanselyn for the third of three acres in Yoxall as dower. "Dicun" also

Dicken(s)
Dickin(s)
Dickings
Dickons
Dykins
Dekin
Dekiss

develops later into the modern surnames Dicken(s), Dickin(s), Dickings, Dickons Dykins, Dekin and Dekiss, e.g. 1532, Hugh Dekyn of Bobbington, enrolled as Hugh Dykyns in the 1539 Muster, whilst Deakins Grave in Cannock goes by the name of Dickins Grave on the 1821 map of the county. To complicate matters even further in the Norton-in-the-Moors parish registers for June 6th, 1814, Jonathan Deakin

Dakin(s)
Dawkin(s)

who marries Sarah Proctor, signs his own name as Dakin. Dakin(s) is more often than not a variant of Dawkin(s) and both mean "little David": Stoke-on-Trent parish registers, 1716. Thomas Dawkin (1719, Thomas Dakin). Nicholas Daykin was paying tax on two hearths at Highfield (Fawfield Head) in 1666. Nowadays, the Deakin(s) forms far outnumber the original Deacon(s). 1736, April 28th. John Swan of Charlton (sic), parish of Eccleshall and Mary Deacon of Hatton, married at the Church of St. Mary, Swynnerton; 1851, George Deakin (joiner, builder), Cana Yard, Stone; 1851, Joseph Deakin (farmer) of Drointon; 1851, Samuel Deakin (cooper), Derby Street, Leek. Dakin(s) specimens are: 1887, William Dakin (grocer), Windy Harbour, Talke; 1887, George Dakins (headmaster of the High School), King Street, Newcastle-under-Lyme. Recordings for Dickin, Dicken(s) include: 1851, Charles Dickin (brazier, tinner), Market Street, Hanley; 1851 Thomas Dicken (farmer), St. Stephen's Hill, Blithfield; 1875, Mary Dickens (baby linen depot), Broad Street, Hanley.

The sequence Deakin-Daykin-Dykin is reproduced in Dean-Dain (Dayne)

Dean(e)
Deanes
Deans
Deen
Dene

Dine (Dyne). The surname Dean(e), Deanes, Deans, Deen, Dene is principally occupational in origin, referring to the head of the chapter or body of canons of a collegiate or cathedral church, as in Richard de Swynnerton, Dean of the Church of St. Chad, of Salop, who was sued by Thomas de Swynnerton (chivaler) in 1345 for a debt of £25/6/8d. The original Latin form "decanus", from which it is derived, as in Alexander decanus de Stanes (Stone), circa 1180, stood for the head or president of ten monks in a monastery. But as with nearly all surnames of this nature an ironic nickname is always lurking in the background or there may even be a servile connotation for someone employed in a dean's household. A locative from Old English "denu" - "valley" is also to be considered, either for a dweller by or in some valley, or from a place called Dean(e), as in Deane in Greater Manchester, recorded as "Dene" in 1292 - "valley", and a whole host of other localities called Dean in many counties. John de Dene was taxed for two shillings at Pipe near Lichfield in 1327. Later on there is frequent interchange between Dean and Dain: Newcastle under-Lyme parish registers, 1781, Samuel Dean (1789, Samuel Dane, 1794, Samuel Daine); Ellenhall parish registers, 1798, William Dean, noted as William Dain in 1799. Names such as Dain(e), Daines, Dayne(s), Deyns, Dines and Dyne(s) are chiefly from Middle English "dain(e)" - "haughty, reserved", or Middle English "digne, deyn(e)" - "worthy, honourable". In the 1532 List of Families in the Archdeaconry of Stafford, all the spellings Dane, Danes, Dayne and Deyne are indexed together. For example: John Deyne canon at Calwich Priory, Christopher Deyne of Audley, John Deyne of Great Bridgeford, John Deyne of Leek, George Dane canon of Rocester Abbey, plus John Dynes of Uttoxeter. The Constable's Accounts for Uttoxeter in March 1646, at the height of the Civil War, reveal that five shillings was paid to Mary Dynes for her cart and horses, so that Colonel Watson could be transported to Alton. In 1610 Robert Deane was the tenant of a mill at Back Brook, upstream from Hulme mill in Leek Frith. In the 18th century the mill was known as Deans mill (later Danes or Dains mill). Apparently it ceased operations circa 1946. In the records of the Leek Poor Law Union for the year 1838, John Dean, aged seventy four of Endon is described as *"a mole catcher, very lame, earns a little. His wife, Patience, aged seventy three but infirm, and earns nothing"*. They were allowed eight pounds of bread and two shillings and sixpence. In 1887, Ralph Dain, architect and surveyor, had premises in Cheapside, Hanley. 1851, William Dean (policeman), Weston-upon-Trent; 1875, Meshach Dean (potter's manager), Hall Street, Burslem.

Generally speaking, the chaplain was a priest, clergyman or minister, who was in charge of a chapel, but he was also permitted to conduct religious services in the private chapel of the sovereign, some great lord or high officer of state, or in the household of a person of high rank or nobility. In an inquisition made before the King's Escheator at Newcastle-under-Lyme on the 28th July, 1317, it was put to some local jurors to decide whether the King should allow William son of Thomas of Newcastle-under-Lyme to appoint *".... a certain chaplain to perform Divine service, for the soul of the same William and all his ancestors, and all the faithful deceased, in the chapel of St. Katherine of Newcastle-under-Lyme, every day, five messuages and an annual rent of 13/4d, with appurtenances in the vill of Newcastle; to have and to hold to the same chaplain and his successors, chaplains performing Divine service there daily for ever"*. In 1387 Robert Chapeleyn of Keele and several accomplices were brought before the local assize judges, accused by Henry de Delves of breaking into his pigeon cote at Whitmore and carrying away four hundred pigeons, worth forty shillings. Pigeons and doves were very valuable commodities during the Middle Ages, in spite of the damage they caused to the peasant's crops, for they provided extra meals for hungry mouths and also precious dung for fertiliser. Neither form of the surname - Chaplain nor Chaplin - makes much impression on our nomenclature. At the Tunstall manor court in 1369 Henry Chaplain was fined three pence for digging the lord's land and making a dam in the waters of the lord. Widdow Chaplin paid tax on one hearth at Leigh near Checkley in 1666, Chaplin and Horne (carriers) were based at Longport in 1873, and John Chaplain (machinist) was resident in Copeland Street, Stoke, in 1887.

Chappell(s)
Chaple
Chappel(l)

Chappell, Chaple, Chappel(l), Chappells is either a toponymic for a dweller near some chapel or an occupational name for a person who was employed at a chapel in some capacity. In 1348, Richard, son of Robert, son of Ralph de Huntyndon (Huntington near Cannock), was attached to answer the plea of William, son of Adam atte Chapel, also of Huntington, that he had beaten, and wounded, and ill-treated him at Penkridge, on the Thursday after the Feast of St. Michael, 1334 (sic), and had taken from him a pix, in which was contained a deed, by which Robert de Huntyngdon had given to William atte Chapel of Huntyngdon, and to the heirs of his body, a messuage and a virgate of land in Huntyngdon, and for which he claimed £10 as damages. Ellen, wife of Henry Chappell was buried at Alstonefield on April 6th, 1569, and the marriage of Moses Chappell and Mary Tunnicliff was celebrated at the same locality on September 21st, 1764. Joseph Chappells was farming land at Leek Frith in 1851.

Capel(l)
Caple
Cappel(l)

In some instances the Old Norman French variant "capele" - "chapel" - gives rise to names such as Capel(l), Caple, Cappel(l), again for habitation near some chapel or for employment there, but occasionally several locatives enter the fray, such as Capel near Tunbridge Wells, Capel le Ferne near Folkstone, Capel St. Andrew north east of Felixstowe, Capel St. Mary south west of Ipswich, and How Caple and King's Caple not far from Hereford. All contain the same word "capel" - "chapel". However, regarding the north Staffordshire Capels etc another approach is called for, and the solution turns out to be the placename Capewell, an ancient spring or well in Bakewell, recorded as "Capwelle, Cappewalle" in the fourteenth century and as "Cappwell or St. Maries Well" in 1606, namely, a holy well with a covering like a cap, dedicated to the Virgin Mary. This is the obvious parent of the Capewell offspring: 1851, James Capewell (farmer) of Dog Lane, Fradswell; 1851

Capewell

William Capewell, publican of the Cross Keys, Custard Street, Leek; 1875, Edmund Capewell (grocer) of Lichfield Street, Hanley. The surname is modified further to

Capell
Caper
Capie
Capey

Capell, Caper, Capie and Capey, and all the relevant variations are well illustrated in the parish registers at Norton-in-the-Moors, e.g. 1641, Margaret Capell, 1657 David Capewell, noted as David Caper in 1662 and as David Capie in 1664, 1678 James Capye. On July 21st, 1651, Maria Capel and John Floud were married at Burslem. 1875, William Capey (rent collector) for the Burslem district, Mount Street, Tunstall; 1875, Charles Capey (pikelet seller), Paradise Street, Tunstall; 1907, George Capey (stationer and newsagent), Waterloo Road, Cobridge. At this period the Capeys were certainly concentrated around the Tunstall, Burslem Cobridge area. A very rare origin of the surname Capel is a nickname from "capel - "a nag (horse)", perhaps for a person of haggard appearance.

The Old French word "chapele" is ultimately derived from Latin "capella" diminutive of "cappa" - "cloak", since the first chapel was a sanctuary in which St. Martin's sacred cloak was preserved. On the other hand, the Saxon "cirice, circe" - "church", came into our language via medieval Greek "kurikon" from "kuriakon (doma)" - "Lord's (house)". This was the one place in the entire village, which the medieval peasant could call his own, even though it may have been just a simple, cramped building with a rush-covered floor. Here it was his duty to attend Mass every Sunday and on feast-days throughout the year, away from the drudgery on the manor, and it was here where people from miles around in the numerous scattered vills and hamlets would congregate, exchange the latest gossip and jokes, reinforcing the sense of community. Some of the more fervently religious villagers might join in the Latin words of the Lord's Prayer, the "Paternoster". In the Middle Ages this was used in the sense of a bead in a rosary, or for the rosary itself, and Richard Paternoster, taxed at six shillings for Sheriffhales in 1327, could well have been a maker of paternosters, rosaries or chaplets.

The surname Church designated habitation near some church, or the verger or sexton who was connected with the local church. In 1592, during the reign of Queen Elizabeth, Ralphe Churche was one of the complainants, to whom Robert Cowper and his wife Jane remitted all right to some tenements, woodland, gardens, meadow and pasture in Ravenshall and Betley. The "churchman" was the custodian or the keeper of the church: Keele parish registers, 1667, December 24th, Ann Churchman married Samuel Betson; 1907, George Churchman (house painter), Lonsdale Street, Stoke. Some medieval churches were built on prominent hills, and this was how the surname Churchill came into being, either from the placename itself or from residence near some church by or on a hill. An assize of 1286 was convened to decide whether John Giffard of Chillington near Brewood, together with his brothers Ralph and Robert, and Geoffrey de la Cherchehull, had unjustly dispossessed Thomas de la Hide of reasonable estovers in the wood of Chillington, viz. in husbote and haybote, and an oak fit for timber, and fifty cartloads of wood for burning and eight for fencing annually [estovers - rights to take timber for necessary repairs, haybote - for fencing repairs, husbote - for repairs to dwellings]. In 1907 Henry J. Churchill is listed as a park gardener, resident in Hamil Road, Burslem.

Long before the Saxon and Norman invasions of our islands, the native British population had their own organized Christian worship, which revolved around the "egles" - their own church, which survives as the modern Eccles, west of Salford, Greater Manchester, home of the famous cakes, two localities called Eccles in Norfolk (one near Attleborough, the other, Eccles-on-Sea, north of Hickling Broad) and two locations in the Derbyshire High Peak district, Eccles House in Chapel-en-le-Frith and Eccles House in Hope. All must be highlighted as possible sources for the surname Eccles. Scottish families of this name chiefly derive from Eccles in Berwickshire or Eccles in Dumfriesshire, whilst down south the focus is on Eccles north of Maidstone in Kent, but this is not a "church" name at all, since the place refers to an original "oak pasture". At an assembly in Newcastle-under-Lyme Guildhall on 18th November, 1637, it was agreed that *".....William Eccles shall be admitted to ye liberties of this burroughe, paying five pounds ten shillings, which hee gave security to doe. And in regard thereof William Eccles and James Eccles his sonne, borne before his admittance, shall be likewise admitted and made free burgess and thereuppon William Eccles took his oath"*. On June 16th, 1787, Bowyer Eccles (joiner) of Newcastle-under-Lyme married Mary Ravenscroft. Trade directories: 1907, Albert Eccles (potter's printer) of Edge Street Burslem; 1907, Frank Eccles (labourer) of Norfolk Street, Hanley.

Eccleston
Ecclestone

The element "ecles" occurs initially in our own Eccleshall (see Volume 1) and in the compound Eccleston - "hamlet with a church", as in Eccleston near St Helens, Eccleston west of Chorley, Great Eccleston and Little Eccleston on the river Wyre in the parish of St. Michael's on Wyre (all in Lancashire), not forgetting the isolated Eccleston south of Chester. Any one of these could have spawned families named Eccleston or Ecclestone: 1851, John Eccleston, owner of a beerhouse in Castlechurch, Stafford; 1907, Charles Ecclestone (fireman) of Heron Street, Fenton.

Kirk(e)
Kerk
Kyrke

With the Scandinavian colonisation of the Danelaw from the eighth century onwards, the Saxon "church" was in competition with the Old Norse "kirkja", which gave our language the word "kirk" and the surname Kirk(e), Kerk, Kyrke - a dweller by the church. In 1298 Thomas Kyrk was sued by Philippa, formerly wife of Richard de Berdemore, for a third of six acres in Cauldon, which she claimed as dower. 1616 Feet of Fines, Henry Kyrke of Spot Acre (Hilderstone); 1696, May 23rd, George Kirke, buried at Seighford; 1772, January 13th, David Kirk and Ellen Tatton, married at Cheddleton; 1851, Christopher Kirk (millwright) of Etruria; 1875, George Kirk (ironfounder), Shelton Boiler Works, Etruria; 1907, Richard Kirk (iron dresser) of Lower Hadderidge, Burslem.

Kirkman
Kirman
Kerman

The extended name Kirkman, Kirman, Kerman alludes to the custodian of the church and is therefore the Scandinavian equivalent of the Saxon Churchman. At the Great Court of John Audeley (knight), Lord of Audley, held at Betley on the Feast of the Apostles Simon and Jude, October 28th, 1513, Henry Kyrkemon of Betley was fined two pence for breaking the assize of bread. He was a baker and had probably baked some underweight loaves or charged exorbitant prices at his stall in the market. The burial of Elizabeth Kirkeman took place at Audley on June 20th, 1555, whilst Luce Kirkman enjoyed better days, when she got married to Robert Marten at Seighford on April 21st, 1674.

Kirkby
Kirkham
Kirkland
Kirby
Kerby

The element "kirk" forms the initial constituent of three very common surnames - Kirkby, Kirkham and Kirkland. The locatives Kirkby and their simplified companion Kirby - "village or farm with its own church" - are scattered all across the Danelaw districts of the north and east Anglia, especially in the Yorkshire Ridings, Lincolnshire and Leicestershire, and are far too numerous to detail here. The only exceptions to the aforementioned derivation are Kirby Muxloe near Leicester and Cold Kirby not far from Rievaulx in the north Riding of Yorkshire. These refer to "village of Kaerir", an Old Danish personal name. Kirby is far and away the most popular spelling of the surname nowadays, with Kirkby and Kerby very much out in the cold. 1572, August 20th, Robert Kerbye, baptised at Swynnerton; 1609, August 25th, Thomas Kyrkebey, *"a poore laboringe man"*, buried at Ellastone; 1666, Edward and Isaac Kirby, exempt from hearth tax at Adbaston Constablewick; 1868, Thomas Kirkby, figure painter at Minton's, Stoke, who was earning an artist's salary of £156 per annum; 1875, Richard Kirby (greengrocer) of Ford Street, East Vale, Longton. Kirkham, Kirkam, Kerkham are to be traced to Kirkham north of the river Ribble and west of Preston, Lancashire, or to Kirkham south east of Castle Howard in Yorkshire. Both of these locations represent Scandinavianised forms of the Saxon "ciric-ham" - "village with a church": 1631, Bennit Kirkam of Rocester, daughter of Bennit Kirkam, baptised January 22nd; 1748, Thomas Kircum, overseer of the poor at Betley; 1851, Thomas Kirkham (hairdresser) of Paradise Street, Tunstall; 1875, Esther Kirkham (beerseller) of Pleasant Street, Burslem; 1887, Josiah Kirkham (fruit merchant and potato salesman) of Station Buildings, Etruria Road, Hanley; 1907, Harry Kirkham (flint miller), Pitt Street East, Burslem.

The final member of this trio is Kirkland, which goes back to Kirkland north west of Ennerdale Water in the Lake District, Kirkland east of Penrith, Kirkland near Wigton and Kirkland Guards at Blennerhasset (all in Cumbria). All denote land belonging to a church. The Lancashire Kirklands are mainly derived from Kirkland Hall and Kirkland Hall Farm near Garstang, situated west of the place where the rivers Calder and Wyre intersect. The second element of this particular locative is the Scandinavian "lundr", since the place is recorded as "Kirkelund" in the thirteenth century, hence "church wood". Scottish families called Kirkland get their name from places known as Kirkland in Ayrshire, Dumfries or Lanarkshire. Locally, the surname Kirkland is nowhere near as prolific as Kirby or Kirkham: Ellastone parish registers, 1758, Elizabeth, daughter of William and Elizabeth Kirtland (sic), baptised on May 28th; Mary Kirkland and Thomas Scragg (cratemaker), both of Stoke, married at Newcastle-under-Lyme on April 8th, 1793; 1907, Albert Kirkland (potter) of Meir Road, Longton.

The Saxon "stow" originally indicated quite mundanely some place of assembly or inhabited place, but later it often had the specialised meaning of "holy place", as in Stowe north east of Lichfield, found as *"that sacred spot called Stowe"* in the thirteenth century. According to some historians it was here where St. Chad set up a hermitage in the 7th century. Reputedly, Stow Heath near Wolverhampton, points to the site of an earlier minster church than the one which was founded by Wulfrun. Whether Stowe-by-Chartley has any religious significance is open to conjecture. Walter de Stowe (husbandman) was assessed for twelve pence at

Stretton near Brewood in the 1381 Poll Tax returns. When Dorothy Stowe of Wootton (Eccleshall) died in 1686, the pitiful state of her existence was evident from the few items that were found in her possession at the time of her death, namely, a pair of bedsteads, a straw-bed, one pair of sheets, two blankets, an iron pot and kettle, valued at twenty shillings. Samuel Stow (furniture remover) of Wood Street, Longton in 1907, would not have taken very long to dispose of Dorothy's worldly goods.

MINOR CHURCH OFFICIALS AND RELIGIOUS NAMES

The village church was the place not only where the villagers worshipped, but also where they were married, got baptised and were given the last rites. It was also a meeting place, where business matters were discussed. The most familiar sound was the peal of bells summoning the faithful to prayers on Sundays or announcing the seasonal demands throughout the agricultural year, such as the right time to plant beans or to prune apple trees. Yet the medieval villagers were also aware, that if the bells had been christened and blessed by a bishop, their ringing drove away demons and thunderstorms. The surname Bell can often refer to the bellringer himself, to a person who dwelt by the church bell, or town bell, or who resided by the bellhouse, or who lived at the sign of the bell: 1332 Lay subsidies, Elienor de Belle, charged eighteen pence at Engleton near Brewood and Penkridge parish registers; 1629, Alice Attabell, base childe of Margaret Attabell of Dreyton, buried on November 5th. The latter recording must be compared with Richard Bell, also of Drayton near Penkridge in the 1532 List of Families in the Archdeaconry of Stafford.

A nickname for someone who was beautiful or handsome - Old French "belle" - is an attractive option: 1301 Inquisition post mortem, William Belle of Ashley, paying two shillings and eight pence rent to John de Eyton for one messuage and nine strips of land. In addition, 1294 Inquisition, William Bel atte echeles of Wolverhampton might be for Old French "bel" - "fair, beautiful" or a pet form of Isabel.

There is a memorandum in the register of Stoke *"...that the Minister and Churchwardens of Stoke-upon-Trent, on the 29th day of August, 1687, gave unto John Bell, of Cobbrage Yate, a certificate under their hands and seals, in order to his obtaining of His Majesty's sacred touch for his son, Samuel Bell, for the healing of the disease called King's Evil"*. This is a reference to "scrofula" - enlargement and degeneration of the lymphatic glands - which was supposedly cured by the royal touch. Ceremonial touching was introduced by Henry VII and the sufferers were presented with gold coins. The custom was last practised by Queen Anne, who touched Dr Johnson in 1712, without apparently affecting a cure. One gruesome incident came to light on 20th April, 1693, when William Bell and Stephen Delves were fined twelve pence at Tunstall manor court for throwing corpses and carrion into the King's highway to the injury of the neighbourhood. On a lighter note, the

Stow

Bell

Bronte sisters, Anne, Charlotte and Emily wrote their novels under the assumed names of Acton, Currer and Ellis Bell. Trade directories: 1851, Reverend W. Bell (curate), Swynnerton; 1875, Frederick Bell (plumber, glazier, newsagent), Brunswick Street, Hanley; 1887, Herbert Bell (painter, decorator), Liverpool Road, Newcastle-under-Lyme.

Bellman/Belman designates either a bellringer or a town crier: Tamworth parish registers, 1608, Elizabeth, daughter of Richard Belman, baptised on October 30th. Bellhouse, Bellas normally denote residence near a detached bell-house or bell-tower: 1873, George H. Bellhouse (schoolmaster) of Church Lane, Goldenhill, Tunstall, but this name is easily mixed up with Bellow(s), Billows, which is an occupational name for a bellows blower in a forge or smithy, whilst there may be occasional overlap with Bellis(s), since "bellies" was the regular form of "bellows" until the sixteenth century. In Wales and the counties on the Welsh borders, such as Shropshire, Herefordshire and Cheshire, Bellis is most likely a patronymic for "ap(ab) Ellis" - "son of Ellis", the Greek form of the Hebrew name Elijah. Mary Bellis married Joseph Peters at Newcastle-under-Lyme on January 17th, 1779; 1875, Jane Bellis (shopkeeper), Church Street, Hanley.

The modern "sexton" has to be content with ringing bells and digging graves, as immortalised by Hood in his famous punning of 1826: *"They went and told the sexton and the sexton toll'd the bell"*. But in days gone by he was once a highly respected member of the religious hierarchy, preoccupied with looking after the sacred vessels and vestments in a church belonging to some religious order. In actual fact, "sexton" is a doublet of "sacristan", as embodied by John le Secresteyn, paying four shillings subsidy at Rugeley in 1327, and 1532, William Sekerston of Stafford. The letter "t" goes missing, resulting in Sackerson and Seckerson: 1539 Muster, Thomas Saccarson, enrolled at Stafford; 1745, February 19th, Widow Sackerson, buried at Swynnerton; 1851, Reverend Edward Barlow Seckerson (MA), vicar at High Offley; 1907, Thomas Sackerson (potter), Prospect Street, Burslem. The Sexton forms are not very common: Lichfield Cathedral Registers, 1736, June 14th, Joseph Sexton and Sarah Holt married. But there is some clash with Saxton and Saxon. Ostensibly the surname Saxon is an echo of England's tribal past, but the truth is more prosaic, since Ralph Saxton senior, who is paying tax on four hearths at Betley in 1666, occurs as Ralph Saxon in 1638. The fuller form Saxton is normally to be traced to Saxton in Yorkshire, not far from the village of Towton, where the bloodiest battle of the Wars of the Roses was fought in 1461, or to Saxton in Cambridgeshire (now known as Saxon Street). Both localities stand for "hamlet of the Saxons". However, two of the tenants of the Audleys at Betley in 1308 comprised Peter Saxi and Peter Saxi junior, and so we may be dealing with a patronymic - "son of Saxi", where "Saxi" is a contracted form of the Old Norse personal name "Saxbiorn". The surnames Saxon and Saxton are certainly more concentrated around the Betley, Audley, Madeley, Keele area than anywhere else.

Billiter

The bells were cast by the bell-founder, the "belleyeter": 1327 Lay subsidies, William le Belleyetere of Stafford, which gives us the surname Billiter (no examples). The parish clerk at Ellastone makes an interesting observation in the register for October 5th, 1614: *"Richard Dowley (the firste buriall after the casting of our fourth bell of Ellaston)"*. If the metal was not in a sufficiently fluid state during the casting process, then it had to be recast, and this actually happened to Henry Michel in 1313, when he was forced to recast the great bell at Croxden Abbey. During the Middle Ages some bell-founders travelled from manor to manor and set up their temporary foundries in the fields near to some church. These were known as "bellfields", and a toponymic could have arisen for habitation by such a field, bequeathing the surname Belfield, Bellfield. But these are principally to be derived from Belfield, a small settlement in Butterworth township, south west of Clegg, Lancashire, which refers to some open land by the river Beal. The surname is already in evidence at Elkstone near Warslow in 1532, where Christopher Belfeld his wife Joan and their five children are amongst the householders. Isaac Belfield who lived at Barrow Moor near Oakenclough Hall on the Longnor Road in 1772 seems also to have dealt in small wares. In 1851 George Belfield was master of the workhouse at Leek and Emanuel Belfield was listed as a grocer and draper at Warslow. Bellfield is far less common as a surname, e.g. 1851, Thomas Bellfield owner of a beerhouse in Mill Street, Hanley.

Belfield
Bellfield

In the Placenames of Staffordshire, Oakden gives a fieldname in Forton near Aqualate Mere - "Chaunterells medowe" (1487) - which he derives from the surname Cantrell. Yet these two names are quite distinct. Chantrell and Chantrill are from Old French "chanterelle" - "a small bell", probably applied to a bellman or a diminutive of Anglo French "chantour" - "magician, enchanter", later "singer, chorister, precentor (person who leads the singing in a cathedral or monastery)". On the other hand, Cantrell, Cantrill are diminutives of Anglo French "caunter" "singer". However, they may be variants of one another, due to the fact, that in certain words, northern French had initial "C" instead of the "Ch", characteristic of central French. Despite all this, the surname Chantrell, Chantrill is conspicuous by its absence, whilst Cantrell, Cantrill is extremely prolific in the Staffordshire Moorlands and contiguous regions. The earliest instance of the name is Philip Canterel, who appears in an assize of 1203, but a recording such as John Cantrell or Cantrell (sic) indicates a locative source. This gentleman, together with Ralph Wodeward of Calton, John Beale of Alstonefield and three others, cut down some trees and underwood at Throwley in 1438, belonging to John Meverell (armiger). These were valued at 100 shillings. Reaney gives Cantrell in Devon, home of Robert de Canterhulle in 1330, which looks like "hill of the singer", but this is surely too far-fetched to apply to an isolated region like north eastern Staffordshire especially during the fifteenth century. George, son of William Cantrill and Dority Whitgreve, was baptised at Stowe-by-Chartley on December 15th, 1623 and Henry

Chantrell
Chantrill

Cantrell
Cantrill

ell   Cantrell and Elizabeth Buxton were married at Seighford on August 8th, 1644. Trade directories: 1851, Richard Cantrell (blacksmith) of Bradnop; 1907, George Cantrell (miner), Wellington Street, Burslem; 1907, Ralph Cantrell (potter), Goddard Street East, Longton.

          Canter/Cantor and Cant, both of which denote a person who led the singing in a cathedral or monastery, are in short supply. Radulfus cantor is cited in a thirteenth century deed from the Rydeware Chartulary. In the Newcastle-under-Lyme parish registers, Ellena, daughter of Francis Cant, was baptised on February 3rd, 1611, and Alexander Cant was witness to the marriage between Thomas Harper of the parish of Edgmond, Shropshire and Diane Parton of the parish of High Offley at High Offley on March 28th, 1780.

          Old French "chanterie" originally meant "singing or chanting of the mass", and later on took on the additional meaning of the endowment of a priest to sing mass. Later still it was applied to the priests themselves, and finally the chapel where they officiated. Consequently the name Chantrey, Chantry applies either to the chantry priest or his servant. William Chantrie got married to Margeret (sic) Bennet at Baswich on July 25th, 1601.

          The extremely rare Dixey, Dixie is a survival of the Latin "dixi" - "I have spoken", which was used in an identical fashion to the French "Dixi", applied to a chorister on account of the words at the beginning of a psalm: Lichfield Cathedral Registers, 1728, Beawnall Dixie and Elizabeth Corbet, wed on November 7th.

          In the list of the most common surnames in Staffordshire, derived from trades, occupations and offices, as compiled from the 1666 Hearth tax returns, Clark(e) is ranked seventh behind Smith, Taylor, Turner, Wright, Walker and Cooper. This high frequency is due to two main factors. The original sense of the Latin word from which it comes - "clericus" - which became the Saxon and Old French "clerc" - was "a man in a religious order, a cleric or clergyman", and the surname is fairly common during the Middle Ages for someone who had taken only minor orders. Beside this, since all writing in business houses and in legal and State offices, and secretarial work in general was carried out by the clergy, the term gradually came to mean a scholar, secretary, recorder or penman. These functions are now fulfilled by educated laymen. Except those in minor orders, clerks were expected not to marry, but immediately this notion is nipped in the bud by the abundance of the medieval "clerksons, clerkesons", e.g. 1332 Lay subsidies, Adam filius Richard le Clerke, assessed at sixteen pence for High Offley, cited as Adam le Clerkessone for the same vill in 1327, but this time taxed at two shillings. Randulph Clerkeson was in possession of some kind of shop at Newcastle-under-Lyme in 1375 (possibly a butchery). Clarkson is by far the most familiar modern survival of the name, with Clarson sneaking in at the last minute: 1666 Hearth tax returns, Mountfort Clarson, charged on three hearths at Stafford; 1851, Samuel Clarkson (butcher) of Werrington, owner of a stall in Burslem Market; 1907, George

Clarkson (bootmaker), Balfour Street, Hanley.

Clever boys, born to serfdom, whose ambition was to make a career out of the Church, were educated as priests or clerks in reading, writing and Latin at one of the small grammar schools dotted about the country. These establishments were generally under the control of monasteries or cathedrals, hospitals, guilds or chantries, and the masters in charge were members of the secular clergy. The noun "clerk" was pronounced "clark", but still spelt as "clerk" because of its derivation from the Latin "clericus". Up until the beginning of the sixteenth century the surname is invariably written down as Clerk(e), e.g. in 1266 Richard le Clerk and thirty one others were named in an appeal of mayhem and robbery, beating and insulting Adam de Upton in the highroad of the town of Newcastle-under-Lyme, and robbing him of ten marks. In 1391 William Clerk, parson of the church of Colton and John Clerk were charged with breaking into the free warren of John de Gresseley at Colton two years previously, and stealing sixty hares, one hundred rabbits, one hundred pheasants and two hundred partridges. The fluctuation between Clerk(e) and Clark(e) is exhibited by John Clarke, resident at Penkridge in 1532, who is called to arms as John Clerke in the 1539 Muster. From this point on **Clark(e)** the Clark(e) spellings gradually supplant the Clerk(e) forms, until, by the 1660s the Clark(e)s rule the roost. Trade directories list: 1851, Thomas Clarke (sign and heraldic painter), Foregate Street, Stafford; 1851, William Clark (plumber, glazier) Market Street, Hanley; 1875, John Clark (silk linen manufacturer), Jasper Street Hanley; 1887, Adam Clarke (blacksmith and wheelwright), Elder Road, Burslem.

Walter Mauclerc, Bishop of Carlisle (1275 Hundred Rolls) had a name which meant literally "bad cleric", and this must be taken with 1311 Assize **Manclark** William Malclerk. These result in such modern surnames as Manclark, Moakle **Moakler** Mockler and Marklew: Stoke-on-Trent parish registers, 1804, December 9th **Mockler** Elizabeth Marklew, married to James Smith (cordwainer) of Newcastle. Warslow **Marklew** Hall, north of Warslow village, was built by Sir George Crewe in 1830, mainly for the use of Richard Manclark, the agent of his Alstonefield estate. After Manclark death in 1850 Sir John Harpur Crewe used the house as a shooting lodge. In 185 Richard Marklew was selling groceries and provisions in his shop along Greengat Street, Stafford.

"Bad" clerics such as Walter Mauclerc and William Malclerk may have committed some misdemeanour or other, but if a clerk in minor orders was charge with theft or murder, he could plead benefit of the clergy and thus be tried in a ecclesiastical court. The official who served the summons to appear in court wa the "summoner", who was often a clerk in minor orders himself. Yet he was one of **Sumner(s)** the most reviled of all medieval officials, given to bribery and blackmail and spying on his friends and neighbours. One such character who sounds as though he migh easily have fitted into this category is Richard le Somenour, tenant of a messuage Stafford, owned by Robert, the Prior of St. Thomas the Martyr. He was brought book by the Prior in 1360 for paying no rent for two years on this particular holding, although the actual outcome is not on record. The regular developments of the medieval form are Sumner and Sumners: Ellastone parish registers, Helen Sumner and Thomas Bull, married on July 13th, 1584; Barton-under-Needwood parish registers, 1739, November 6th, Sarah Sumners of Barton married to Thomas Alkins of Burton-upon-Trent; 1851, John Sumner (cabinet maker) of Stafford Street, Longton; 1875, Joseph Sumner (grocer, baker), Hope Street, Hanley. Other modern variants are Simnor, Simner: 1730, Ann Simnor of Audley, and probably Sumnall, by analogy with the doublet Tunster-Tunstall: 1887, Samuel Sumnal (grocer), Apedale Road, Chesterton; 1907, Henry Sumnall (manager), Boughey Road, Shelton (Hanley).

The attorney in a spiritual court was known as a "proctor", a contracted form of Latin "procurator", which is connected with the word "procure" in its original sense of "to take care of, to manage (the affairs of others)". But the "proctor" could also be the official steward of some medieval guild or chantry, the head of lay brothers in a Carthusian house or someone who was licensed to collect alms for lepers or enclosed anchorites. In 1465 John Proketour was one of the four mediators called in to settle a dispute between William Warner of Dilhorne (yeoman) and Henry Adderley, in which the latter accused the former of taking by force four oxen belonging to him, valued at 60 shillings. The argument was still unsettled four years later. The surname survives in three varieties - Proctor, Procter and Prockter. In 1506 John Proctor was elected one of the guardians of the church at Newcastle-under-Lyme and in 1648 the accounts of the churchwarden at Stoke-on-Trent, Lawrence Brassington, include a payment of ten shillings *"...of widowe Procter for her husband's buriall in ye church"*. 1851, George Proctor (brickmaker), Copshurst, Normacot; 1851, Daniel Proctor (blacksmith) of Leycett; 1851, Ralph Procter (whitesmith) of Bignall Hill, Bignall End; 1875, John B. Prockter (tobacco and cigar merchant), Piccadilly, Hanley.

Following the introduction of Christianity into Britain in 597, Latin remained the universal vehicle of speech and writing of the learned world, of the church and of the law for many centuries. It was the language of the grammar schools, since it was the fundamental requirement for any student wishing to study grammar, rhetoric, dialectic, music, arithmetic, geometry and astronomy, or the higher professions of divinity, law and medicine. Hence, anyone who was skilled in speaking or writing the Latin language was known as a "latimarus, latinarius", which give us our Latimers, Lattimers and Lattimores. In 1378 Thomas Latymer and his wife Anne were summoned to appear at the local court to explain by what right they claimed certain amounts of land in the manors of Ashley, and Longnor (near Wheaton Aston) and also five marks of rent in the manor of Water Eaton. Occasionally there is some overlap with Latner - "worker in brass or plate-tin", as in 1553 Feet of Fines, John Latimer otherwise Latner of Wolverhampton. Some surname writers have propounded Latimer near Amersham in Buckinghamshire as a locative source, but the jury is still out on this one. 1875, Jos. Latimer (beerseller) Pleasant Street, Burslem; 1907, John Latimer (boat builder), Slater Street Middleport. During the reign of Mary I (Bloody Mary), Hugh Latimer, Bishop of Worcester, was burned at the stake for heresy in 1555.

Some clerks wrote or copied books and manuscripts. In these cases the operative word is Old French "escrivain, escrivein" - "writer", origin of Scriven(s), Scrivins, Scrivings and the extended names Scrivener and Scrivenor. On one night in 1306 Thomas le Screvayn of Newcastle-under-Lyme broke into the house of William Coly in Newcastle, took a cloak worth six shillings, a clasp of silver worth three shillings, and ravished Licoricia, the daughter of the said William. Ann daughter of John and Ann Scriven, was baptised at Seighford on March 9th, 161? and the marriage took place at Swynnerton on October 30th, 1809 between William Scrivens (widower) and Mary Machin (spinster). In 1907 Timothy Scriven (labourer) was resident in Albert Street, Northwood, Hanley. The locality called Scriven near Knaresborough in the North Riding of Yorkshire could provide an alternative source in some instances. It denotes a place at a cave or hollow. The name Scrivener is more sporadic in its distribution. Anna Scrivener and John Blore got married at Audley on November 20th, 1608. A chapel for the Society of New Connexion Methodists, designed by Robert Scrivener of Hanley, was opened in 1862 at the corner of Ball Haye Street and Queen Street, Leek, and a billposter named C.H. Scrivener, dwelt in Keeling's Road, Northwood, Hanley in 1907.

Scriven(s)
Scrivins
Scrivings
Scrivener
Scrivenor

The medieval Latin "notarius" alluded to a notary, secretary, scribe or writer 1380 Poll Tax returns, Geoffrey Heywode (notarius) of Lichfield, and his wife Alice, assessed at five shillings. The Saxon equivalent was "notere", as embodied by Adam le Notyere of Talke in an assize of 1293, apprehended for a robbery and taken before William Bagod and his fellow Justices. Adam turned informer and accused William Budde (also of Talke), of having assisted him in robbing two merchants in the park at Audley. The assize continues: *"....and the said William before the Justices offered to defend himself by his body against the said Adam, and a duel was waged and fought between them and the said William conquered the approver Adam, who was immediately hanged"*. Adam's name lives on as Nutter The Lancashire Nutters derive their name from an occupational term for "nowtherd" - a cowherd, and in the same county the surname fluctuates with Nuttall The origins here are Nuttall between Summerseat and Ramsbottom - "hill where nuts were gathered", and Nuthall near Nottingham - "nook or water meadow where nuts were obtained". In our county there is a locality known as Knotwall End in Tatenhill, which is corrupted to Nottle (Nuttal) End in the 1837 Tithe Awards, plus Nothill Farm and Wood, west of Combridge, found as "The Notel" in 1770. Both must be regarded as subsidiary sources of the surname Nuttall. The Nutter-Nuttall couplet recalls the Sumner-Sumnall interchange earlier. Mary, daughter of Ann

Nutter
Nuttall

Nuttall (a bastard child) was baptised at Ellastone on December 16th, 1683 and Walter Nuttall was proprietor of a tobacconist's shop along Stafford Street, Hanley in 1887.

MONASTIC LIFE

Christian monasticism in its most basic form was a way of life adopted by solitary ascetics or anchorites, such as St. Antony (c.251-356), the religious hermit, who was born in Upper Egypt and who spent twenty years in the desert, where he withstood a famous series of temptations. In the Middle Ages hermits tended to avoid the solitude and isolation of out-of-the-way places, preferring to live instead in cottages or small habitations alongside country roads, begging from the wayfarers and travellers.   Moreover, they were classed in the Statutes alongside beggars, wandering labourers and vagabonds of all kinds. The exceptions were the approved hermits, who were actual men of religion, sanctioned by bishops, that is, possessing "testimonial letters from the ordinary". In the same way that the original "clerk" competed with "clark" until the Reformation, so the medieval "hermite", ermite" vied for recognition with "armite, armet(t)". For instance, Nicolas Armet, who is paying rent to Dieulacres Abbey in 1543, is recorded as Nicolas Ermett, member of the Leek Frith militia in 1539. As with the Clark(e) forms, the Armett, Armit(t) spellings win the day. According to her will, proved in 1688, Joan Armett of Thorneyleigh Hall Farm in Leek Frith, left a rent of £2/13/4d. charged on land at Leek Frith, to be distributed on Christmas Eve to the poor of Leek town, with priority given to those resident in Mill Street. At the end of the eighteenth century Methodism, based on the teachings of John Wesley, was firmly established in north Staffordshire, and in 1817 Joseph Armett of Dunwood, Endon, permitted his house to be used as a preaching place for Primitive Methodists. In 1851 Charles Armitt owned a beerhouse in Horton near Rudyard and Amos Armett traded as a tailor in Clerk's Bank, Leek. As is only too clear from these specimens, north eastern Staffordshire is the true home of this surname. Hermit too survives, but instances are not available. This goes for Hermitage as well, which has to give way for Armitage, as in Armitage near Mavesyn Ridware, recorded as "Le Hermytage" in 1413. There was a hermitage here in the thirteenth century. Armitage near Rocester appears as "The Hermitage" on the 1836 Ordnance Survey map for the county, whilst "The Hermitage" is recorded circa 1530 between Ellenhall and Ranton, and in the Tutbury Cartulary (1192-1247), there is a reference to *"ermitagium de Adgaresleg"*, which would be in the vicinity of Agardsley Park. In 1306 Robert son of Ralph de Pype and his wife Emma sued John del Ermytage (chaplain), for coming with others unknown on the Vigil of the Epiphany (1304), to the vill of Pipe Ridware, to the house of the said Emma and ejecting her from it and taking her goods and chattels to the value of forty shillings and extorting from her a sum of five marks before he would permit her to re-enter the house. Armitage is now the

Hermit 14th century. (Hermit p. 113)

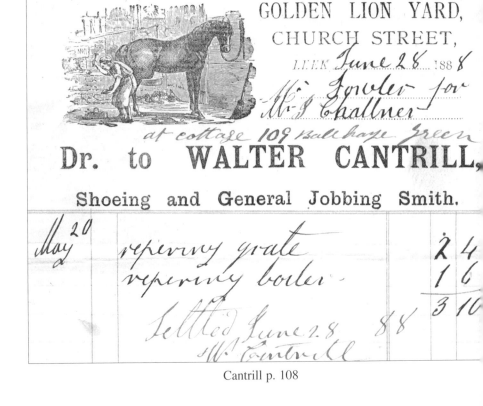

Cantrill p. 108

preferred spelling of the name.   1614, Stephen Armitage of Cheadle; 1875, Reverend George Armitage, The Vicarage, Silverdale.

Anchor, Anker(s), Ankier and Annaker are usually taken as being from the Old French personal name "Anchier".   Nevertheless, we must not ignore the old Saxon "ancre" - "anchorite", a hermit, recluse, as in the "ancres and hermytes", cited in the Prologue to Langland's *Piers Plowman*.   This surname is typical of Cheshire.   On May 5th, 1546, William Anckars married Joone Hethe at Ellastone, whilst there is a very curious entry in the Newcastle-under-Lyme Corporation Minutes for 1681/1682, where Allen Ancres was *"...appointed a common nightwalker and common scavenger to clean the streets"*.   The marriage between Maria Ancker and John Furber was celebrated at Seighford on June 24th, 1810, and in the 1871 Census Charles Ankers is registered as a shoe manufacturer, resident in High Street, Eccleshall.

The other, more familiar form of Christian monasticism was the organized community of monks, who lived in monasteries following a common regime, and devoting themselves to a life of prayer and meditation.   The earliest and most important monastic order in western Europe was that founded in 529 by the Italian abbot St. Benedict of Nursia, who envisaged the monastery as a self-supporting community, separated from the world, directed by an elected abbot and bound together by the three vows of poverty - no monk to possess property of his own, chastity - none might marry, and obedience - to their superiors and to the rule of their order.   It was the Rule of Benedict which St. Augustine introduced into England in 597 with the foundation of the Benedictine monastery at Canterbury and there was no monastery other than Benedictine in England until the order of Cluny established a priory at Lewes in 1077.   The name Benedict is from Latin "benedictus" - "blessed".

At the beginning of the eleventh century Wulfric Spot founded the Benedictine abbey at Burton-upon-Trent.   This century also saw the foundation of two Benedictine priories, one at Lapley, a dependency of the abbey of St. Remigius at Rheims, and one at Tutbury, established by Henry de Ferrers not far from his castle.   But it was during the twelfth century when the monastic movement rapidly gained momentum with the building of two Benedictine houses for monks at Canwell and Sandwell, and three for nuns at Brewood, Farewell and Blithbury. Chaucer's monk in the Prologue to the Canterbury Tales followed *"..the rule of Saint Maure or of Saint Beneit..."* where the latter was one of the medieval forms of Benedict.   Another pronunciation of the name was "Benet", as confirmed by William son of Benedict de Boturdon (Butterton-on-the-Moors), who had unjustly dispossessed Robert Boule of half an acre of land in Butterton in 1330.   This same defendant appears in a later assize of 1338 as William Benet of Butterton.   In another assize, dated 1404, the King (Henry IV) pardoned Thomas Benet of Saverley for the death of his brother William Benet, killed at Saverley within the

Bennet(t)
Bennette
Bennetts
Bennitt(s)

Liberty of Fulford (1401). The prolific surname Bennet(t), Bennette, Bennetts Bennitt(s) can also be derived from the feminine form "Benedicta": 1417 Assizes Benedicta late wife of Henry de Blorton, or from Latin "benedicite" - "bless (you)" probably a nickname from a favourite saying; 1327 Lay subsidies, William Benedicite, rated at two shillings at Wychnor. From the Middle Ages onwards, the surname is not concentrated in any specific zone, but crops up in isolated clusters By the time of the compilation of the 1666 hearth tax returns, there are Bennitts Bennetts around Croxton, Eccleshall and Fulford in Pirehill Hundred and in Uttoxeter, Alstonefield, Beresford (south of Sheen) and Highfield (Fawfield Head) in Totmonslow Hundred. The benefactor of the parish church of Burslem, dedicated to St John the Baptist, and of the bells, which were cast in 1720, was Luke Bennett In 1842 the commission set up to inquire into the employment of children in North Staffordshire mines reported that John Bennett, aged 14, had been working at Mr Hugh Williamson's Pinnox Colliery, Burslem for about five years, drawing slack and coals, because there were no horses. Remarkably, he also told the examiners that before this he had run moulds for nearly twelve months at Eli Hawley's in Burslem, and prior to the latter job he had been a mould runner and jigger turner for two years at Enrick Wood's factory. His working life had commenced at the ripe old age of 6! 1851, Joseph Bennett, farmer and cattle dealer, Meir Heath; 1851, Joe and William Bennett (besom makers) of Mucklestone; 1871 Census, Catherine Bennett (charwoman) of Castle Street, Eccleshall; 1887, Charles Bennett (innkeeper), Black Horse, Paradise Street, Tunstall.

Bennison
Benson

    The popularity of the name Benedict at the height of the surname period resulted in two patronymics - Bennison - "son of Bennet" and Benson - "son of Benn (contracted form of Bennet)". At Bradnop in 1666 Randel Benisson is charged tax on one hearth whereas Randle Benison is exempt at the same constablewick. Eighteenth century marriages at the parish church of St. Edward the Confessor, Cheddleton comprise Rebecca Bennison to Richard Heath on September 27th, 1739 and Hannah Benison to John Millward on December 27th in

Venison

the same year. The surname Venison also occurs in the Cheddleton area, as indicated by William Venison of Cheddleton (farmer), who signed his name as Benison in the Stoke-on-Trent parish registers (1772). The couplet Benison Venison mimics Bickerstaff-Vickerstaff. Beniston(e) is another corrupted form

Beniston(e)

Trentham parish registers, 1770, William Benniston (1774, William Bennison Trade directories: 1875, Arthur Bennison (rockingham ware manufacturer) Lichfield Street, Hanley; 1887, Alfred Bennison (gilder) of Victoria Road Newcastle-under-Lyme.

Benson

    Benson is also local in origin, and to be traced to Benson near Wallingford in Oxfordshire - "settlement of the Benesingas". Members of the Staffordshire Muster in 1539 included Ralph Benson for Trentham and George Benson for Shugborough In the 1720s a miniature industrial revolution was set in motion centred on the water mills of the Moddershall valley. For centuries these mills had been used for the fulling of cloth and grinding corn, but, thanks to a revolutionary new process of grinding flint, discovered by a potter by the name of Astbury, the mills were now converted to accommodate the new trends. The first patent for grinding flints in water, using water power to drive the machinery was granted to Thomas Benson of Newcastle in 1726. William Alphonsus Benson (mining engineer) resided at The Cottage, Silverdale in 1887.

The Saxon counterpart of the Latin "benedictus" - "blessed" was the past participle "iblescede" - "blessed", "made sacred", found as "blessed" in the Middle Ages, as exemplified by John le Blessed, rated at twelve pence for Hilderstone in 1327, and by Richard le Blessede, assessed at eighteen pence for Wootton-under-Weaver in 1332. However, by this time, all religious significance had been lost and the name had come to mean an individual who was happy-go-lucky or just fortunate. Modern spellings of the surname are Blessed, Blessitt, Blest, Blissitt, Blezard, Blizard and Blizzard. The fluctuation in forms is based on recordings such as 1532. Roger Blyst of Pershall, quoted as Roger Blest in the 1539 militia for the same vill. In a probate inventory, dated 1688, Ralph Blest of Eccleshall, owned a herd of cattle, numbering 34 beasts. 1872, Edward Blizzard, Pierio Terrace, Finch Street, Handsworth.

The Benedictines and allied branches constituted what is known as "cloistered" Orders, since their members were confined to the precincts of their cloister or monastery. The brethren were called "monks", hence the surname Monk, Monck, Munk, Munck, either designating the office of monk or an ironic nickname for anyone who deliberately chose an austere life style, yet there is even a hint of a religious man gone to seed after the manner of Chaucer's monk, whose passion was hunting and who wore expensive clothes, sleeves edged in fur, his hood fastened under his chin with a gold pin in the shape of a love-knot - *"He was not pale as a forpined (wasted) ghost, a fat swan loved he best of any rost"*. Of course, the devout monks walked the cloisters, tended their gardens and copied their manuscripts, embellishing them with beautiful illuminations, for many monasteries were seats of learning and centres of art. Fulcher monachus and Joseph monachus de Deulacres in thirteenth century deeds from the Cartulary of Dieulacres Abbey are clearly monks who lived out their lives there, but John le Monk in an inquisition post mortem, dated 1356, made at Stourton, near Kinver, is most likely a nickname. Elizabeth, daughter of John Morris of Brereton near Rugeley, was baptised in 1612 and married to William Munke in 1630. Her 6 children from this marriage were baptised between 1633 and 1649. William Munke died in 1658, and she, as widow Muncke, was paying tax on one hearth at Brereton in 1666. John Monk of Little Onn was buried at the church of St. Editha, Church Eaton on October 31st, 1717.

The plural Monks, Munks is applied either to the servant of the monk or a worker at a monastery. In 1608 Lawrence Monckes won his case against Lawrence

Rope (gentleman) for the rightful ownership of a messuage, a garden, an orchard, 60 acres of land, 20 acres of meadow, 60 acres of pasture, 10 acres of wood and 100 acres of furze and heath in Radwood and Maer. The settlement was agreed at 130 marks. In 1907 George Moncks (miner) lived in George Street, Longton.

Monkman
Munkman

Monkman, Munkman (unattested) refer to the servant of the monks, whilst

Monkhouse

Monkhouse is for someone employed at the monks' house. Jane Muncas and John Cartlich were married at the church of St. James the Great, Audley on April 28th,

Munn(s)
Moon(e)

1656. Munn(s) and Moon(e) are derived either from Anglo French "moun, mun" - "monk" or from Moyon in La Manche: 1907, Charles Moon (manager), Heron Street, Fenton; 1907, Joseph Munn (bricklayer), Gate Street, Hanley. The

Mountford
Mountfort
Montford
Mumford

widespread compound Mountford is generally supposed to be an import from some French locality called Montfort, such as Montfort-sur-Risle in Eure cf. Okeover Deeds, 1257, Peter de Monte Forti. But, as the Middle Ages proceeds, the surname diffuses so rapidly across north Staffordshire, diverging simultaneously into so many odd forms, that other sources closer to home are clearly at work. The surname is particularly common in the neighbourhood of Leek and Cheddleton, and here the most obvious origin is a locality recorded as "Monckesford, Munecford, Munksford, Mouncford, Munkford" during the thirteenth century in the Cheddleton area. Robert de Munkeford is assessed for two shillings at Cheddleton in the 1327 lay subsidy rolls. The reference is most likely to a ford which was used by the monks from the Cistercian Abbey of Dieulacres. The transition to Mountford is apparent from 1567 Feet of Fines, Thomas Munkeford (Mounford) of Cheddleton who is noted as Thomas Mountforde in 1607. John Mountford, who had been indicted before the Justices of the Peace for feloniously stealing a bay horse and a cow, together with 24 shillings of the goods and chattels of Richard Sherard of Ranache (sic) in 1410, surrendered and produced Letters Patent, dated 21st January 1414, by which the King pardoned him for all felonies. Also to be weighed up are two other native locatives - Montford near Shrewsbury, on the river Severn "Manna's ford" or "the men's ford", perhaps in contradistinction to "a maiden's ford", and Mundford in Norfolk, by Thetford Forest Park - "Munda's ford". The modern variant Mumford is heralded by John Mountforde alias Mumforde, who was churchwarden at Stoke-on-Trent in 1678. In 1841, at Wedgwood's Earthenware Factory in Burslem, John Bateman, aged 12, was a mould-runner for Joseph Mumford and in 1851 Harriet Mountford of Drury Street, Longton specialised in millinery and dressmaking.

Under the Rules of St. Benedict the internal organization and daily life of the monastery were directed by a spiritual father, the abbot, who was to be elected by the brethren. In the words of St. Benedict, he *"took Christ's place in the house"* Geoffrey de Mala Terra abbas Burtoniae (deposed 1094 A.D) is undoubtedly his

Abbot(t)
Abbotts

official title as Abbot of Burton Abbey. Conversely, Robert Abbot, rated at twenty pence for High Onn near Church Eaton in 1327, and Agnes Abbot servien (servant), paying the paltry sum of two pence at Alrewas or some nearby vill in the 1380 Poll Tax returns, are obviously nicknames, containing some long forgotten private joke. Amongst those enrolled in the 1539 Muster for the county were John Abbott of Slindon and John Abbot of Ronton, and Andrew Abbott married Sarah Pilsbury at Cheddleton on August 7th, 1785. 1851, William Abbot (rope, twine maker), Lower Street, Newcastle-under-Lyme; 1851, Jesse Abbott (baker, flour dealer), Clerk's Bank, Leek; 1875, Mary Ann Abbotts (grocer), North Road, Burslem.

Second in command to the abbot in an abbey or priory was the "prior", who was appointed by the abbot to maintain discipline and to look after the monastery during his absence. Some peasants must have actually seen this imposing figure, especially if they were employed on the local monastic lands belonging to a priory, and inevitably, as in the case of Abbot, a nickname would have been invented by the quick-witted medieval villagers, the actual content depending on the temperament or physical appearance of the prior in their midst. A certain Roger was Prior at Trentham Priory from 1242 until 1255. In 1343 Henry de Knotton brought a writ of "Mordancestor" against Stephen Priour respecting some tenements in Newcastle-under-Lyme. (This protected an heir from wrongfully being kept out of his inheritance). Margaret, daughter of Henry Pryor, was baptised at Ellastone on December 21st, 1561, and in 1851 Reverend John Prior (B.A.) was curate at Barlaston, an appointment which no doubt provoked as many witticisms as his medieval forebears. In 1907 William Prior (railway foreman) resided in King Street, Fenton.

In contrast to the Benedictines, the houses of the Augustinian Order belonged to a religious order of priests, which followed a Rule, based on the monastic writings of St. Augustine of Hippo, born in Numidia (modern Tunisia) in 354 AD. In North Staffordshire, this Order was responsible for the foundation of six religious houses, at Ranton, Trentham, Rocester, Calwich, Stone and St. Thomas (Stafford), all during the twelfth century. As a surname, Augustin, from Latin "augustus" - "venerable, consecrated" - does not make much impact at all. Augustin is recorded by the Domesday clerks as holding half a hide of land in Barlaston at the time of Edward the Confessor. He was also a free man. In a 1293 assize Augustine de Bokenale (Bucknall) is involved in a complicated suit concerning two acres of land in Clayton Griffiths, but that is all. The name is far more familiar in its vernacular form "Austin", as in the Augustinian Priory of Trentham, alternatively known as the Austin Priory in the Middle Ages. In the 1332 lay subsidy rolls, there are two taxpayers called John Austyn for the vills of Fenton Vivian, Longton and Hanley, one rated at twelve pence, the other at two shillings and six pence. They may be related to the Augustine de Bokenale, quoted in the 1293 assize. By the close of the seventeenth century the surname Austin, Austen has ramified to an extraordinary degree in North Staffordshire and is far less

common elsewhere. In the parish registers for Bucknall cum Bagnall in 1766 Joh
Austen signs his own name as John Austin. 1851, Timothy Austin (boot and sho
maker), Chapel Street, Tunstall; 1875, Leonard Austin (school board officer) c
Spring Garden Road, Longton.

    The religious life in these Augustinian establishments was virtually run alon
the same lines as that in the Benedictine houses, with one exception - the brethre
were called not monks, but canons, and the communities were small by monasti
standards, normally consisting of about twelve canons and a prior. The moder
Canon
Cannon(s)
Channon
surname survives either as Canon, Cannon(s), based on the Old Norman Frenc
pronunciation, or as Channon from the central Old French equivalent, e.g. Nichola
le Chanone, rated at two shillings and two pence for Great Saredon near Cannoc
in the 1332 lay subsidies and 1907. Thomas Cannon (potter's placer) of Bagna
Street, Stoke.

    In spite of the well-known medieval proverb *"This is a friar and therefore
liar"*, the friar, at the outset of the Middle Ages, was virtually the only religiou
Friar
Fryer
figure to court popularity amongst the common people. There were four mai
orders - the Carmelites or "White Friars", named after the colour of their mantle
originating from the Hermits of Mount Carmel in Israel trying to emulate the wa
of life of the prophet Elijah; the Franciscans or "Grey Friars", founded by S
Francis of Assisi in the early 13th century, the Dominicans or "Black Friars"
founded by St. Dominic in 1216 in Italy and the Austin or Augustinian Friars, wh
followed the monastic teaching of St. Augustine of Hippo. Unlike the monks, the
did not care much for cloistered life, and instead, they went about the countrysic
and in the towns, mixing with the common folk, preaching the word of Go
listening to confessions and dealing with the sick. But by the later medieval peric
this missionary zeal had all but disappeared, and all the main orders had acquire
riches beyond their wildest dreams from generous patrons, especially successiv
reigning monarchs. By Chaucer's time, the friar, who rode alongside the priore
on the pilgrimage to Canterbury, was described as *"a wanton and a merry man"* ar
when he sang for his fellow travellers and played his harp *"his eyes twinkled in h
head like stars on a frosty night"*. In 1390 Thomas le Frere of Crowborough ne
Biddulph had his house broken into by Thomas Maynwaryng, his brother Ralph a
John Savage (servant of Thomas), who stole 100 shillings in money, one hors
worth 13/4d and other goods and chattels to the value of 66/8d. Ralph wa
acquitted, Thomas was delivered up to the bishop's prison at Eccleshall and Joh
was sentenced to be hanged. Richard Frere was one of the jurors at Standon man
court for the years 1435/1436. Trade directories: 1851, George Fryer, owner of
beerhouse in Hardings Wood, Talke-on-the-Hill; 1907, Samuel Friar (iron worke
Twemlow Street, Hanley; 1907, Nehemiah Fryer (miner), Cornwallis Street, Stok

Houseman
Housman
    All major authorities are in agreement, that the surname Housema
Housman refers to a servant or someone employed at a religious house or conve

In north Staffordshire these are variants of the locative Wolstenholme, an ancient manor in Spotland, north west of Belfield in Lancashire, a combination of the Saxon name "Wulfstan" (wolf stone), found in our own Wolstanton, and the Scandinavian "holmr" - "river flat" or "island in a fen". Heads of households in 1532 comprise James Wolstonholme at Cheddleton, William Wolstonholme at Horton near Rudyard and Roger Wolstonholme at Colwich. However, as with a good many of the migrant families with unfamiliar surnames, the local parish clerks struggled in vain to write them down correctly in their registers, baffled no doubt by the strange admixture of dialects which bombarded their eardrums on all sides. Consequently this tricky situation gives rise to some bizarre distortions. For example, Thomas Wolsenhome of Cheddleton (1537), occurs as Thomas Wolsnam in 1541 and as Thomas Wolstman in 1531, demonstrating the switch between final "-nam" and "-man" witnessed in Swetnam-Swetman, from Swettenham, east of Holmes Chapel in Cheshire - "Sweta's village", e.g. Croxden parish registers, William Swetnam (1692), noted as William Swetman in 1685. Moreover, James Wolstonholme of Cheddleton, mentioned for 1532 above, is found as James Wolsnam in 1530 and as James Ulseman a year earlier.

The latter spelling, with loss of initial "W" lives on as Oulsnam: 1770, Ann Oulsnam of Ipstones, married to William Wilshaw of Cheddleton on 22nd May; 1887, Joseph H. Oulsnam (cratemaker) of Greenfields, Tunstall. Oulsnam often loses the "l", becoming Ousnam or Ousman: 1589, Margaret Owsnam widow of Norton-in-the-Moors; 1851, William Ousman (gardener) of Sugnall Magna; 1887, Joel Ousman (grocer) of Beresford Street, Hanley. Ousman, of course, is one step removed from Houseman, Housman with the introduction of the initial aspirate "H": 1699, William Housman of Betley; 1907, Annie Houseman (laundress) of Heron Street, Fenton.

Whilst monks came from all walks of life, the nuns, until well into the Middle Ages, were almost exclusively selected from the wealthier families. Not all of these by any means chose the convent life of their own accord, for some daughters were sent to nunneries because they were illegitimate, of unsound mind or simply in poor health. The singular form of the surname - Nunn - is either from the office of being a nun, but when applied to a man, a derogatory nickname for someone who was as meek and as demure as a nun. The plural form Nunns designates a servant at the nuns or a worker at the house of the nuns. The wooded ground on the west side of Rudyard reservoir was landscaped with walks and seats by William Nunns, a Leek gardener in 1851. His nursery was at Barngates in 1849, when plants, rhubarb and cabbages were stolen from it. 1851, Isaac Nunns and Co. (dyers), Tontine Street, Hanley. Noon(e), Noons may belong here too by analogy with Moon(e)-Munn, but these are normally of Irish origin, for (O) Noone - "O Nuadhain", possibly from "Nuadha", the name of an ancient sea-god. 1851, Henry Noon (tailor, draper), Market Place, Burslem.

PILGRIMS AND CRUSADES

Adventurous and warlike by nature, the Normans revelled in crusades and pilgrimages, and in 1096, with the cross as their emblem, they took up arms against the Arabs and Turks, who threatened their Christian faith, vowing to free the Holy Places of the Ancient East for the worship of the Christian pilgrims. Between 1096 and 1270 eight crusading armies, comprising large contingents of warriors of all ranks in the feudal hierarchy, set out to do battle with the Muslims on the eastern shores of the Mediterranean. The most famous of these Crusades is the third (1189-1192), in which Richard the First, otherwise known as Coeur de Lion (Lionheart), captured Cyprus from the Greeks and offered his sister to Saladin, the Muslim leader.

Cross

The "cross" of course was the principal symbol of Christianity, but it is actually a word, adopted by the Saxons, either from Old Irish "cros" or Old Norse "kross", all of which go back to Latin "crux". The medieval records are replete with names like 1321 Feet of Fines, Adam atte cros of Stone; 1327 lay subsidies, Richard atte cros of High Offley; 1380 Poll Tax, Simon atte cros of King's Bromley, and so forth. They allude to habitation near some market cross or better, some wayside cross, that is a wooden cross erected by the roadside on some well-frequented highway, possibly on the outskirts of some vill or town, where penitents were accustomed to stand for an appointed number of hours, their punishment for offending against canonical law. According to tradition, a cross of this sort stood at Weeping Cross near Stafford in the reign of Edward VI and it was always one of the stopping places during the Beating the Bounds ceremony. Residence by some boundary cross is not to be eliminated, since it has been conjectured, that the cross at Hoar Cross, east of Abbot's Bromley, may refer to an old boundary marker between the parishes of Yoxall and Ridware. The association between markets and crosses goes back to the time when most preaching was done out of doors, perhaps in the market place itself, and a stone cross was often put up at such a spot, as at Eyam in Derbyshire. Appropriately, Edmund Crosse was one of the brethren at Dieulacres Abbey six years before its closure in 1538. In 1601 Ralph Crosse was fined four pence for encroaching on the lord's waste at Chatterley, and the parish clerk at Newcastle-under-Lyme informs us that Bryan Cross was killed by a fall from a ladder at John Lightfoot's house on August 20th, 1723. Directories: 1851, Theodore Cross, licensed victualler at the Vine, Vine Street, Hanley; 1875, Henry Cross (printer and picture framer), Newcastle Street, Burslem.

Crosier
Crozier
Croser

Crosier, Crozier, Croser also applied to a dweller by a cross, but additional meanings include a seller of crosses or an official name for the "crosier" who bore the bishop's crook or pastoral staff. John Crosyare was a member of the militia at Coton and Hopwas near Tamworth in 1539.

Gee

Gee Cross in Stockport parish, Cheshire was once the site of a stone cross at a crossroads, associated with Dicon Gee (1494). Whether this locality is the base for the surname Gee has not yet been evaluated with any conviction. One of the householders at Rocester in 1532 was Hugh Gee and Ellen Gee married Thomas Chedle at Audley on June 29th, 1670. In the 1666 Hearth tax returns John Gee is exempt from payment at Tean, and likewise Alice Gee at Draycott-in-the-Moors.

The region around Shallcross Hall Farm and Shallcross Wood by the river Goyt south of Whaley Bridge, Derbyshire, is the most likely place where the surname Shallcross/Shawcross saw the light of day. It appears as "Schakelcros(s)" in 1235 and as "Shawcross" on Saxton's map of 1577 and refers to a cross to which a shackle or fetter was attached, that is, a wayside cross to which pilgrims were fettered as a form of penance. In fact there are the remains of a cross just off Elnor Lane south of Shallcross Road. There is another Shacklecross in Borrowash, east of Derby, plus Shawcross near Nether Alderley, Cheshire. These, too, may be involved in some of the families bearing the names. In 1455 Margery Shalcrasse, widow, sued Hugh Sherard of Shendon (yeoman), Isabella Bentlye of Brokhous (widow), and John Bentlye of Brokhous (husbandman), for breaking into her close and that of John Shalcrosse at Brodcooke (sic) and cutting down their trees and taking goods and chattels belonging to them to the value of 100 shillings. In 1648 William Shalcrosse paid one shilling and four pence arrears in church lunes (church rates levied by the parish) to the churchwarden at Stoke-on-Trent. 1777, June 2nd. Ann Shallcross and William Walker, married at Cheddleton; 1907, Reuben Shallcross (miner) of Bond Street, Tunstall.

Some glades had religious significance, as personified by Crossley north east of Buglawton close by the river Dane - "clearing with a cross", which is to be discussed alongside "Crosseley" (1560) in Preston-on-the-Hill near Runcorn, "Crosselegh" (1620) in Disley and Stanley near Lyme Park Country Park and Cross Lee in the West Riding of Yorkshire. 1539 Muster, John Crosseley, recruited at Ronton; 1851, Richard Crossley (tailor), Thursfield, Newchapel; 1907, Joseph William Crossley (butcher), Hanley Market, Tontine Street.

The Saxon word "cruc", pronounced almost like "crooch" - "cross" - survives as Crouch, Crowch, Crotch and Crutch, and refers again to a dweller by some wayside or market cross. In a lawsuit, dated 1303, Thomas atte Cruche of Tamworth is also quoted as a clerk and in 1851 Walter Crutch (shoemaker) lived at Pershall, Eccleshall, whilst Henry Crouch (joiner) was resident in Hassall Street, Newcastle-under-Lyme in 1875. The Crutched or Crouched Friars, also known as Friars of the Holy Cross, were a minor order of friars, and were so called from the cross of scarlet cloth they wore on the breast of their habit.

For the soldiers of Christ, who fought for the defence of Christendom and the church during the Holy Wars, the touch-stone of their faith was Jesus Christ, whose name is a Greek translation of the Hebrew Joshua Messiah (the anointed one). Nonetheless the surname Christian is not a summing up of the original bearer's religious beliefs, for it is either from the masculine name "Christianus", or more commonly from its feminine equivalent "Christiana", shortened to "Christian", e.g. 1532, Christian Pedley, wife of Thomas Pedley of Leekfrith, and Christian Olyver, wife of Thomas Olyver at Longnor in the upper Manifold valley. In 1329 several tenants at Edingale near Harlaston were ordered by the Sheriff to appear at the local assizes, to acknowledge their tenancies. Amongst those tenants summoned were Simon Christian of Bromley (which Bromley is not mentioned) and his son John, in possession of a messuage and half a virgate of land (about 1 acres).   1565, Thomas Christian, son of Thomas Christian, a beggar, buried February 8th, at Alstonefield.

Pagan

Paine
Payne

Anyone who was not a soldier of Christ - a member of His militant church - from the Latin "miles" - was known as "paganus" - "non-militant, civilian" originally "villager, rustic". In the sense of "heathen" or "pagan" it was bestowed on the Turks, Saracens and Muslims throughout the conflict in the Middle East. As a font name, however, parents chose the form "Payne" or "Paine", probably unaware of its more sinister overtones. In 1298 Thomas Payn, tenant of the Audley at Betley, was paying four pence rent per annum on one plot of land. John Payn enrolled at Derrington near Stafford in the 1539 Muster. During the Civil War, the parish clerk at Ellastone makes the following entry in his register: *1643, June 16th Thomas Paine, who was killed at Wootton Lodge, comming with other souldier from Leeke, buried.* On the other hand, the career of Matthew Payne went from strength to strength under Cromwell's Republic, for he was appointed overseer of the poor in 1651 at Newcastle-under-Lyme, bailiff of the borough in 1657 and churchwarden in 1658. In 1851 James Payne was the licensee at the Bowling Green in Beech Lane, Burslem and in the 1871 Census Thomas Payne of High Street Eccleshall, is registered as a maltster.

Sarson(s)

The Saracen's Head has been a popular inn sign since the exploits of Richard the Lionheart, and the curious fascination with the Saracen lurks in a surname such as Sarson(s), which often camouflages an earlier Old French "Sarrazin" - a Saracen also used as a nickname for someone with a swarthy appearance: 1281 Assizes Stephen called Saracen, Cheshire.   More accessible, though, are two names in "son", that is "son of Sara(h)" - Hebrew for "princess", or "son of Saer (Sayer)" which could represent the Old High German name "Sigiheri", a variant of Sawyer a maker or seller of say (silk) or an assayer of metals. Richard filius Sare paid his two shillings subsidy at Cowley near Gnosall in 1332 and Wylliam Sarson enrolled for Weeford in the 1539 Muster.

In addition to the host of committed Christians, the Crusading armies were a motley collection of kings and barons (often with their wives), knights, squires men-at-arms, grooms, chaplains and the usual desperadoes and hangers-on.   With this continual flow of men from west to east for two centuries, it was inevitable, that the whole new experience would have a more profound effect on some more than others.   Just like the modern tourist abroad, these medieval adventurers brought

Friar p. 120

AN ENGLISH PILGRIM.
(*From the MS.* 17 *C.* xxxviii.)

Pilgrim p. 126

back souvenirs from the eastern Mediterranean, including genuine palm leaves fror
the deserts of Palestine or North Africa. It was the custom of all pilgrims wh
visited the Holy Land to bring back a palm branch to convince their disbelievir
friends back home that they had actually undertaken the hazardous journey to tl
Middle East, whence the modern surname Palmer. The consecrated palm branc

Palmer

was laid on the altar of the local parish church on their return. In the 1327 la
subsidy returns contributions by "palmers" in North Staffordshire vills comprise
three shillings from William le Palmere at Waterfall, twelve pence from Henry
Palmere at Hixon and eighteen pence from John le Palmere at Walton near Ston
There is clearly some discrepancy here, reflecting the social status of the individu
taxpayers. In 1360 William Palmer of Loxley near Uttoxeter, in company wi
seven others, broke into the close of Henry Hardyng at Loxley, trampled down ar
consumed his corn (sic), valued at 100 shillings. In 1640 Humfrey Palmer was
member of the trained band at Marston and Whitgreave. Trade directories a
crammed with the name: 1851, Enoch Palmer (grocer, tea dealer) of High Stree
Longton; 1851, William Palmer (registrar), Queen Street, Hanley; 1887, Charl
Palmer (picture framer), Hanley Market Hall and Bucknall New Road; 1887, Eli:
Palmer (registry office for servants), Stafford Street, Longton.

Whether all the subscribers in the 1327 tax returns had indeed been to tl
Holy Land is impossible to prove now, but an instance from the 1271 Pleas of tl
Forest is unimpeachable, for in that year *"it is presented, that Robert de Staundc
and many others, who are now dead, came with Ralph Basset, who is likewise dea
on Wednesday before Christmas Day, 1264, and took ten does and three bucks, tv
hinds and a fecon* (fawn) *without warrant and carried the venison to the house
the said Ralph at Drayton....and the said William Wodekock* (not previous
mentioned by name) *and Robert de Staundon are in the Holy Land, therefore let
be respited as against them"*.

**Pilgrim
Pegram
Pigrome**

In another case, dated 1262, Walter Pelerinus (the pilgrim) and others ha
taken two hinds without warrant in the Forest of Kinver. How Walter had come t
the attribute of "pilgrim" is not known, but it is quite conceivable, that he too ha
actually made the arduous trek to the Holy Land, or, failing that, had travelled alo
the "Palmers' Way" to the sanctuary of Our Lady of Walsingham or the shrine
Thomas a Becket at Canterbury. These were the two main centres of pilgrima;
during the Middle Ages, when hero worship was confined entirely to the sphere
religion. People from every walk of life were so obsessed with the lives of holy me
and women, that they stopped at nothing to obtain an object which had one
belonged to their hero or heroine. This was the driving force behind the pilgrima;
to Canterbury, where offerings were made in memory of Thomas a Becket, who ha
been murdered in the Cathedral by four knights on the evening of the 29
December, 1170, or to Walsingham where the miraculous statue of the Virgin Ma
was smothered with jewels and precious gifts, or to Glastonbury, where St. Jose;

of Arimathea had reputedly deposited the chalice of the Last Supper and where the Glastonbury Thorn had sprung up from his staff. Pilgrimages were also made to the shrine of St. Chad at Lichfield, and these may well have contributed to the early growth and prosperity of the city. The registers of the Cathedral Church of St. Mary and St Chad, Lichfield, record that Eluathan Pilgrim and Mary Choice were married on June 27th, 1688. In 1851 John Pilgrim (smallware dealer) lived in Derby Street, Leek. One rare variant is Pegram: 1912, E. Pegram (hairdresser) of Old Road, Stone. Another variant - Pigrome - is missing locally.

Some pilgrims embarked on journeys to these famous shrines in expiation of their sins, often barefooted, as Chaucer's parson remarks in his sermon : "*Common penaunce is that prestes enjoynen men comunly in certeyn caas, as for to goon, peradventure, naked in pilgrimage or barfot*". William Barfote, who beat and wounded Roger de Swynnerton at Stafford in 1306, obviously needed forgiveness for his sins. In 1907 James Barfoot was one of the inhabitants in Chapel Street, Kidsgrove.

SEASONS, FESTIVALS AND PAGEANTS

In medieval England, where the sun was the peasant's clock and the seasons his calendar, his holidays were associated with the church, since they were in fact the "holy-days" or festivals of the saints, some of which were the feast-days of the saint to whom the local village church was dedicated. It was normal practice for many countryfolk to commemorate the birth of their children by naming them after this special "holy-day", on which they were born, hence the surname Haliday, Halladay, Halliday, Holladay, Holliday, Holyday. For instance, Robert Haliday, taxed at sixteen pence for Tittensor in 1327, must have been reminded many times by his parents, especially by his mother, about the time he came into the world on some such "holy-day" long ago. In 1382 Adam Halyday and John, son of Richard Reynald of Alrewas entered the free warren of Margaret Griffith at Wychnor, and took away some rabbits, hares, pheasants and partridges. John, son of John Hall and Alice Holiday, was baptised at Ellastone on January 5th, 1564, whilst Richard Hollyday was recruited for the trained band at Alstonefield in the 1640 Muster. 1875, George Halliday (artist), Mount Pleasant, Newcastle-under-Lyme; 1887, Joseph Halliday (travelling draper), Gladstone Place, Hanley.

Sometimes the day of the week itself was sufficient to identify the child in question, as in Monday, Mondy. Penn parish registers, 1753, Joseph Monday, a name for a person born on Monday ("day of the moon"), or perhaps for someone whose tenure of land was dependent on his working for the lord of the manor on Mondays. Yet there must be some confusion here with Mundy, Munday, from the Old Norse name "Mundi". 1851, William Mundey (boot and shoe maker), Oulton Road, Stone; 1907, John Munday (tobacconist and cigar merchant), High Street, Tunstall.

Loveday
Lodey
Lody
Lowdey

The link between "love-day" and religion is tenuous, to say the least, for
was a day set aside by dissenting parties for the settlement of their feuds, with fria
often acting as arbiters. John Loveday was fined one penny *"...for contempt mad
in the court of the lord"* at Tunstall in 1326, and in 1378, on the death of Hen
Loveday, his heir had to hand over one ox to the lord as "heriot". Loveday also go
back to the female Saxon name "Leofdaeg" - "dear (beloved) day". Whatever th
origin, the name is often modified to Lowdey, Lodey or Lody, e.g. Richard Loveda
who brewed contrary to the assize of beer at Tunstall in 1353, occurs as Richa
Loweday in 1360. Keele parish registers, 1595, William Loveday; 1912, Jam
Lodey (miner) of Clarence Street, Stoke.

Christmas
Midwinter

In the fiercely religious epoch after the Norman Conquest few days in th
peasants' calendar were more emotionally charged than Christmas. This was th
time of the year for festivities celebrating the successful consummation of the ye
and the imminent return of the sun. The surname Christmas or Midwinter was ofte
bestowed on anyone born at this time of the year. At first glance, howeve
Midwinter seems too vague a term to have spawned any progeny, but in Ang
Saxon England and well into the Middle Ages Midwinter was just another name fd
Christmas. 1872, George Christmas (brass founder), Lewis Street, Wolverhampto
It occurs as a Christian name thus: Ellastone parish registers, 1549, Christem
Fletewoode, buried on April 15th. The family of Fleetwood came from Hesketh
Lancashire, and John Fletewood (knight) bought the manor of Ellastone fro
Nicholas Longford in 1571. The surname Midwinter is in somewhat healthie
condition: 1875, Messrs. Chas. Midwinter and Company (wine and spir
merchants), Market Place, Burslem; 1907, Robert Midwinter (china ware etchen
Lorne Street, Burslem.

Noel
Nowell
Nowill

The French term for Christmas - "noel", origin of Noel, Nowell, Nowill,
early and fairly common. The Augustinian priory at Ranton was founded circa 115
by Robert, son of Noel (Lord of Ellenhall), who is quoted as Robert filius Noel
the 1166 Black Book of the Exchequer. In the 1539 Muster Jamys Nowe
(gentleman) was equipped with horse and harness at Chebsey and at Eccleshall Joh
Nowell was armed with a salet (flat crowned helmet falling low behind on to th
neck) and a sword. In 1907 Frederick Nowell (kiln fireman) lived in Bath Stree
Hanley.

Youle(s)
Youll
Youel(s)
Yoell
Yule

The old Saxon word for December was "yole", when the peasants burned th
"yole stok" or "yule log" and lit fires to keep demons at bay. Henry Youe
empanelled to serve on the jury at the local assize at Stafford in 1320, bea
testimony to this ancient word, which has given us the modern surname Youle(s
Youll, Youel(s), Yoell, Yule.

Winter(s)
Wynter(s)
Wintour

In certain circumstances the bleakness of the winter landscape at the tin
when a child was born, may account for names such as Winter, Snow and Frost. A
a rule, however, the surname Winter(s), Wynter(s), Wintour is a personal name, a

borne by a tenant called Winter in the twelfth century surveys of Burton Abbey. Also to be taken into account is a nickname for anyone who hated the harshness, cold and lack of sunlight of the long winter months, as characterised by the modern SAD syndrome - seasonal affective disorder. This kind of depressive state of mind is summed up in a story concerning Edward Fitz Otho, keeper of the King's works at Westminster during the reign of Henry III. He was ordered to paint the mantel in the King's chamber and decorate it with a *"figure of Winter, which by its sad countenance, and by other miserable contortions of the body may be deservedly likened to Winter itself"*. At Stafford in 1666 Thomas Winter was paying tax on two hearths in Eastgate Ward, whilst Serjeant Winter was assessed on three hearths in Gaolgate Ward. In 1775 Henry Winter was witness to the marriage between William Mallpas (widower) and Ann Pepper (spinster), which was solemnised at the Church of St. Mary, Swynnerton on December 28th. 1851, Mrs Sophia Winter (housekeeper), Alton Towers; 1907, Thomas Winter (fitter) of Weston Coyney Road, Longton.

Observations about the vagaries of the English climate are always ideal topics for conversation whenever friends get together, and such meteorological data are often prominent in parish registers. In the Alrewas registers for 1607, the clerk reports: *"This yeare, their was a great froste and snowe, the which begane the fyfte day of December, and so continued until the fouretenth daye of February, being Valentine daye, all of which time all our rivers weare frozen and in moste partes they would beare horse and man loaded...."* Some infants may have been baptised Snow or Frost when snow lay thick on the ground, or if there was a skittering of frost, but more credibly these are nicknames for people with snow-white or silvery grey hair or perhaps for individuals endowed with ice-cool personalities, who did not wilt under pressure, or, better still, for anyone lacking in warmth or feeling for others. Inquisitions post mortem, 1337, Hugh Frost of Stafford, and 1356, Henry Snowe of Ellastone. Both of these surnames are far more typical of north Staffordshire than the southern half of the county. 1539 Muster, George Snowe, enlisted at Little Haywood; 1680, John Snowe, a capital burgess at Newcastle-under-Lyme, was fined 40 shillings for absurd and abusive expressions offered to Mr Mayor in the execution of his office. He submitted and paid the fine, whereupon the Mayor returned 20 shillings of the fine to him; 1768, James Snow of Creswell and Mary Griffiss of Seighford, married at Seighford on August 8th; 1851, Robert Snow (blacksmith) of Foxt; 1875, John Snow, licensee of the Jug Inn, Broad Street, Hanley. 1539 Muster, William Froste, enrolled at Seighford, Homfrey Froste and William Frost, likewise at Aston and Doxey; 1620, Margaret Frost alias Brody, adulterine daughter of William Frost of Mole (Mow Cop); 1842, Mary Frost, aged twenty three, of Brown Edge, a single servant and pregnant, allowed two shillings by the Poor Law Guardians of Leek Union; 1875, Eli Frost (assistant borough surveyor), Bagnall Square, Hanley; 1875, William Frost (plumber, glazier, gas fitter,

Snowball

painter) of Greendock, Longton. The quaint name Roger Snowbald, owned by villager at Leek in 1327, taxed at thirteen pence in the lay subsidies, survives as th surname Snowball. It is a graphic description of a snow-white bald patch o Roger's head, which would be very conspicuous if he had dark coloured hair.

Spring

The three remaining seasons - Spring, Summer and Autumn - are absent fror our surnames, despite claims to the contrary. Spring (not evidenced for our county has been taken as a nickname for an active, nimble individual, from Middle Englis "spring", the season when young shoots spring or rise from the ground. There is n proof of any topographical origin, that is, for a dweller at some spring or othe Autumn, that "season of mists and mellow fruitfulness", does not feature at all i our nomenclature, probably because the year was in its death throes and there wer too many superstitions associated with such a time. Some authors accept

Summer(s)
Sommer(s)
Somer(s)

nickname origin for the surname Summer(s), Sommer(s), Somer(s), applied t anyone with a sunny, out-going personality, whilst others tend to go for an ancier Saxon personal name "Sumor", which occurs in placenames such as Somers: Herbert in Derbyshire, just over the county boundary from Uttoxeter - "Sumor nook or valley". The most favoured derivation is an occupational term from Ol French "somier" - "sumpter, driver of a pack horse", found as "somer" in Scotlan 1425 Feet of Fines, Henry Somer of High Offley; Audley parish registers, 165' Marie, daughter of Thomas Sumers, buried on September 9th; 1707, Thomas, sc of John Somers, baptised at Seighford on September 24th; 1842, Thomas Gree aged 10, turned jigger from the age of 7 at Messrs. Meller, Venables, Pinder ar Co's Earthenware Factory, Burslem, first for Thomas Sergeant, then for Thoma Summers, then for William Taylor.

Although peasants' lives during the Middle Ages were governed by t seasons and the unpredictable English climate, it was natural phenomena lil thunderstorms and raging gales which aroused the most conflicting emotions.] 1085, The Anglo Saxon Chronicle reports : *"It is difficult for anyone to realize wh great misfortune was caused by the weather: so violent was the thunder ar lightning that many were killed. Things steadily went from bad to worse f everybody. May God Almighty remedy it when it shall be His will!"*. In the Croxd Abbey charters for 1299 the monks observed that *"...on the day of Saints Fabi and Sebastian a violent wind blew from the south and blew down a wall near Leh for 60 feet in length...."* In the Ellastone parish registers for 1593, one entry read *"The 21st daye of Marche, beinge Thursday, was a terrible wynde wiche ble down houses and trees and did verye muche harme in Englande"*. Such terrifyi

Storm
Tempest

experiences may well be at the root of surnames like Storm and Tempest, for if mother was giving birth in some remote medieval barn or farmhouse, with t thunder crashing and lightning flashing overhead, then the birth would for ever i indelibly imprinted on her mind. Whether the mother actually christened her chi Storm or Tempest as a result of such a traumatic ordeal is another matter. I a inclined to believe, that such surnames are more likely to be nicknames for people prone to tempestuous outbursts: Penkridge parish registers, 1610. Francis Storme, wife of Thomas Storme, buried on May 11th; 1907, Joshua Tempest (potter) of Granville Street, Cobridge; 1907, William Tempest (potter) of Eagle Street, Hanley.

weather   At the other extreme is the sublime optimism, the sunny disposition and beaming smile of anyone blessed with the surname Merryweather. In the Coventry Mysteries one of the female characters goes by the name of Megge Merywedyr, whose "joie de vivre" infected all those around her. This is offset by Henry Muryweder, who belied his name, when he was indicted in 1359 for stealing a gold "formale" - "clasp, brooch or buckle" - worth 20 shillings from William Adames of Stretton, at Brewood in 1357.

Besides Christmas, the other great religious festival in the Middle Ages was Easter, named after the Germanic pagan goddess "Eostre" - "East" or "dawn", whose festival was in early Spring. Nevertheless, most of the customs associated with the Easter period are Christian, with festivities based on the joy of the coming of Spring and the renewal of life, symbolised by lambs and eggs, as verified in an Inquisition post mortem of 1273, where 6 tenants of Geoffrey de Bromleye at Winnington each rendered 40 eggs worth one penny at Easter. However, there is no evidence that the Germanic Easter was ever given as a font name for a child born at Easter time. Rather, the surname Easter is local in origin, and to be traced back to Good Easter or High Easter north west of Chelmsford, Essex. Both localities refer to an ancient sheepfold. Easter occasionally crops up as a form of the female name Esther: Ronton parish registers, 1719, Ester Machin (1724, Easter Machin), and this implies, that the surname might be derived from the Old Testament "Esther", cousin and foster daughter of the Jew, Mordecai, who became the wife of the Persian king Ahasuerus. But there is no proof of this, either. Inevitably, it is the Normans who popularised all the surnames connected with the Easter festival and the resurrection of Christ after his crucifixion. These names ultimately go back to the Hebrew "pesakh" - "a passing over", that is, the annual Jewish festival of the Passover, when God passed over the houses of the Israelites whose door-posts were marked with the blood of a lamb and killed the first-born of the Egyptians. It was latinized as "pascha", hence such medieval variants as "pasch, paisch, pash, passe, pache, pasques, paske, paque" etc. In the north of England, Easter eggs are still called "pace, pasch, pash" or "paste" eggs, whilst young lads or poor adults in Scotland used to beg for "peace" or "paiss" eggs. In the not too distant past these eggs were boiled hard, dyed in bright colours and rolled down grassy slopes as part of the custom of "pace-egging", which also involved parading through the villages, disguised in various get-ups and strange costumes, with the whole charade culminating in the Pace-Egg Play, the Easter version of the Christmas Mumming Play. The fieldname "Pace meadowe" (1657) in Penkridge is perhaps a relic of this ancient village tradition in our county. The surnames Pace, Paice, Pays, Payze and

BURIED.

1593,	Mar.	29.	Geor., s. of Willi. Burne.
,,	May	2.	Jane, bast. of Willi. Chatterley, Gent.
,,	May	25.	Joan, d. of Willi. Thursfield.
,,	June	14.	Eliz., d. of Jocosa fford.
,,	June	26.	Margrett, w. of Tho. Parker.
,,	July	30.	Willi. Unwine.
,,	Aug.	18.	Joan, d. of John Burne.
,,	Nov.	20.	John Holme.
,,	Jan.	30.	Rich. Swinnerton, widdower.
,,	Mar.	1.	Agnes Bomford.
,,	Mar.	17.	John, s. of John Addams.

BAPTIZED.

1594,	May	4.	Eliz., d. of Nicolas Addams.
,,	June	8.	Ralph, s. of Willi. Ffletcher.
,,	Aug.	6.	An., d. of Willi. Bourne.
,,	Sept.	8.	Rich., s. of Willi. Hall.
,,	Nov.	7.	John, s. of John Bourne.
,,	Dec.	26.	John, s. of Rich. Parker.
,,	Jan.	5.	Willi., s. of John Addams.
,,	Jan.	30.	John, s. of Willi. Smith.
,,	Feb.	6.	Rich., s. of Robt. Daniell.
,,	Feb.	25.	Rich., s. of Tho. Addams.

MARRIED.

1594,	Oct.	20.	Tho. Addams & Jane Burslem.
,,	Nov.	30.	Willi. Coxon & Joan Lee.
,,	Feb.	2.	Roger Handley & Jocosa Fford.

BURIED.

1594,	Apr.	16.	Tho. Heath.
,,	May	27.	Petronella Turner.
,,	Jan.	19.	An. Neild.
,,	Mar.	22.	Ellen Crockett, widd.

BAPTIZED.

1595,	May	18.	Ellen, d. of Rich. Daniell.
,,	July	18.	Rich., s. of Robert Simpson.

Copied from Burslem Parish Register

Peace certainly are. The Peace-Pace couplet reflects the dialectal "peyce" for "piece", although Peace can also go back to Middle English "pais", pes(e)", Old French "pais" - "peace, concord", a nickname for a lover of peace or a peacemaker, the latter synonymous with Makepeace, as in Thomas Makepays, tenant of Thomas de Halughton (Haughton near Gnosall), chivaler, and his wife Margaret, at Haughton in 1340. Robson R. Makepeace (colliery manager) lived in Talke o' the Hill, Kidsgrove in 1907. In the 1273 Hundred Rolls Alan Pes was bailiff of John de Verdun, Lord of Alton and in 1456 Ralph Pace of Kingstone near Uttoxeter and several others were attached at the suit of Robert Cuny (Coyney) armiger, for trespassing on his property at Dilhorne, armed to the teeth with swords and bows and arrows, and taking away 5 of his oxen, for which he claimed £20 as damages. Hearth tax contributors in 1666 included Thomas Pace, charged on one hearth at Forsbrook. Trade directories: 1873, George Peace (plumber) of Bath Street, Stoke; 1907, William Pace (pickle works manager), Windmill Street, Tunstall.

Pacey, Pacy and Passey are misleading, for these surnames are locatives introduced by the Normans from Pacy-sur-Eure in Normandy: Dieulacres Chartulary, 13th century, Hugo de Paci (Pascy, Paschy); Alstonefield parish registers, 1678, Passcey Ashton (female) of Basford; Blymhill parish registers, 1786, William Pacey. Patch and Patchett are from Middle English "pache" a variant of "pasches" - "Easter": 1484 Assizes, John Pacche (Pache) lorymer of Walsall. In 1311 Richard Pachet and ten others were accused by Richard de Dockeseye of breaking into his close at Billington on the Monday after the Feast of St. Luke (1309) and cutting down his trees valued at 100 shillings and causing other damage estimated at £20. The very similar Pack and Packett are from Old French "Paque", another word for Easter: 1313/1314 Minister's Accounts, Roger Paket of Tatenhill. In 1620 Packet Woodbourne was fined three shillings and four pence at Standon manor court for not repairing the hedges between "le Bent" and the large town meadow at Bowers. 1907, Clement Packett (potter) of Bond Street, Burslem; James Pack (brewer's drayman) of Albion Street, Burslem.

Yet some care must be taken here, because spellings such as Packett, Patchett and Paget occur alongside one another at Amblecote and Arley in the 1666 Hearth tax returns, and all three may be just for the name Paget. The French name "Pascal", borne by a ninth century pope and saint and the seventeenth century French scholar and scientist Blaise Pascal is derived from the Latin "paschalis" - "pertaining to Easter", and recalls the Paschal candle lit during the all-night vigil in church on Easter Eve. This is the source of the surname Pascall, Paskell and Pasquill in our country too. At Hints in 1580, a foundling was baptized as Pascall, the son of the earth on August 19th, whilst Weekley in his book on Christian Names, entitled *Jack and Jill*, cites the remarkable Paschal Lamb who was rector of Ellington near Huntingdon (1885-1897). Locally we find: 1887, Edward Bailey Pascall (innkeeper), Park Inn, Bucknall New Road, Hanley, and 1907, Thomas

Pascoe

Pascall of Fernlea, Marsh Road, Wolstanton. In Cornwall Pascall is converted int∎ Pascoe.

Pass(e)

Pass(e) is either a pet form of Pascal or from "Passe", another medieval form of "pascha" - "Easter": Tutbury Charters, 1291, Henry Passe of Mayfield Newcastle-under-Lyme parish registers, 1783, Richard Pass; 1851, Simeon Pas∎ (shopkeeper) of Gillow Heath, Biddulph; 1907, Arthur Pass (potter's placer∎ Oldfield Street, Fenton.

Paskin(s)

Paskin(s) may look like a diminutive of "Pask" from "pasque" - "Easter" bu∎ it is in fact from Latin "Pascentius", which survives in Old Welsh as "Paskent" an∎ in Middle Welsh as "Pascen": St. Thomas's Chartulary, circa 1275, Ralph Pasken d∎ Stafford: Barton-under- Needwood parish registers, 1797, John Paskin of Alrewa∎ married Sarah Riley of Barton on June 8th, Witnesses, Mary Paskin and Thoma∎ Riley.

Pankhurst

Surprisingly, Pentecost is still with us, disguised as Pankhurst. This festiv∎ day in the Christian calendar is some 50 days after the death and resurrection ∎ Jesus and commemorates the event in Acts 2 when the Holy Spirit was said to hav∎ come upon Jesus's disciples in Jerusalem, thus enabling them to *"speak in othe∎ tongues"* to those present. In Acts 2.1. this took place on the Jewish feast ∎ Pentecost. In the English church, this day is sometimes called "Whit Sunday∎ Pankhurst in Surrey is named from John Pentecost, tenant there in 1332, and th∎ place occurs as *"Pentecost alias Panchurst"* in 1605. 1851, James Willia∎ Pankhurst (china and earthenware manufacturer, toy and ornament maker), Old Ha∎ Street, Hanley; 1887, Mary Pankhurst (fishmonger), Merriall Street, Newcastl∎ under-Lyme; 1907, Arthur Pankhurst (engineer), Shaw Street, Burslem. In th∎ opening decades of the twentieth century one burning issue of the day was wheth∎ or not women should get the vote. At the forefront of this whole emancipatio∎ controversy was the Women's Social and Political Union, formed in Manchester ∎ 1903 and led by Mrs Emmeline Pankhurst and her daughters Christabel and Sylvi∎ who were known as "Suffragettes", because they demanded the suffrage or right ∎ vote.

Lent

The forty days of fasting known as Lent, were instituted by the Christia∎ church to teach men self-discipline and abstinence, to mark the forty days ∎ Christ's fasting in the wilderness in preparation for His ministry on earth. B∎ whether this period of prayer and penance still exists as the surname Lent ∎ extremely doubtful. In 1875 Henry Lent (tobacconist and draper) traded alor∎ North Road, Burslem. The whole question remains open to debate.

March

Months of the year, too, came in handy as surnames as a last resort. B∎ appearances can be very deceptive. March is a variant of Marsh: Ellastone pari∎ registers, 1606, Margerie Marshe (1626, Margerie March) - "dweller by the marsh∎ or from Old French "marche", denoting habitation by some boundary: 1333, Rog∎ atte merch of Cannock. Of all the months of the year May has always been a speci∎

May

favourite for proverbs, celebrations, games and sports. May is the "growing month", when nature awakens from its winter slumbers, and flowers burst into bloom and trees blossom. Dancing around the May-pole on May-day, electing a May Queen and lighting bonfires are all ancient relics of nature worship. With so many positive aspects in its favour, you would expect a surname to evolve from the month, but no, there is no real basis for this notion at all. On the contrary, the surname May is either from Middle English "may" - "young lad or girl" - a nickname for a virgin or a coy youth, or a shortening of Mayhew, a common Norman form of the Hebrew "Matthew". Henry le May, assessed in 1332 for two shillings and nine pence at Wigginton near Tamworth would probably have acquired his nickname from being shy and awkward in the company of young ladies. Later on the name interchanges with Mea (Mee) and finally crystallizes into Meigh, on the analogy of Lee-Leigh; Alrewas, 1609, Thomas Mee (May); Mucklestone parish registers, 1688, Richard Mea (1691, Richard May); Burslem parish registers, 1768, September 21st, Job Mee of Newcastle-under-Lyme, married to Margaret Malpas of Burslem, signs his name as Job Meigh; 1851, John Mee (newsagent), Sneyd Street, Tunstall; 1875, John Aynsley Meigh, Portland Hotel, Church Street, Longton; 1875, Harry May (surgeon), Trentham Road, Longton. As far as Irish families called Mee are concerned, Mee in Roscommon and Mea in Mayo are traceable to "O Miadhaigh" from "miadhach" - "honourable", whilst in south Down, Mee is used occasionally as a synonym for Meehan as well as MacNamee.

Quite unexpectedly, the month of April has pride of place in our county's nomenclature, not in its native form "April", but in its Old French equivalent "Averill". In 1332 Richard Averil, accompanied by William Benedicite, William de Draycote and Philip de Somerville were accused by Walter de Montegomery of taking by force three of his horses worth £10 from Edingale and driving them to Alrewas, about three miles away, where the beasts were impounded. The surname Averill is probably a nickname for a person whose moods fluctuated like the April weather, rather than a simple statement of fact, that a child was born and christened in that particular month. Before the advent of the Industrial Revolution the heart of the Averill territory is the eastern region of the county, especially around Alrewas, Barton-under-Needwood, Longdon, Newborough, Colton, Hixon and Yoxall. The plot thickens later on, however, since Richard Everhill marries Anne Gaunt at Penkridge on June 18th, 1724, and it is here in 1532, where Henry Averell was lord of the manor. In addition, in the Burslem parish registers, Thomas Everill of Burslem (potter), married to Elizabeth Barnitt of Stoke (singlewoman) on March 31st, 1777, signs his name in the register as Thomas Averill. This is ample proof that these two surnames are one and the same, although Everill, Everhill and Everall have been traced back by some authors to the old Saxon female name "Eoforhild" or its Germanic soul-mate "Eburhilt", both meaning "boar battle". But these are less attractive as possible sources, despite being not uncommon in the Middle Ages.

In any case, in our county, where "ash" is nearly always "ess" and names like Aspley and Asprey often interchange with Espley and Esprey, then a doublet such as Averill-Everill is inevitable.   Interestingly, Horovitz in his *Placenames of Staffordshire* cites the locality known as Averill Side, two and a half miles west of Hulme End, recorded as "Averellsyde, Overelsyde" in 1527, which he takes as "over-hill side".   Other variants also vie for inclusion here, e.g. in the West

Avery
Avory
Averey

Bromwich parish registers Averill alternates with Avery (Avory): 1642, Henry Averil, noted as Avory in 1654.   Normally the surname Avery, Avory represents French pronunciation of the Saxon "Alfred".   Aberell, Abrill, Ebrill also crop up

Aberell
Abrill
Ebrill

now and again: 1539 Muster, Edward Aberell of Penkridge; 1711, Anne Abrill of Ellenhall, and 1907, Uriah Ebrill (boiler maker) of Church Lane, Goldenhill. This is the "b-v" switch, which is a constant theme in the county's surnames. The most

Averill
Everill
Everall

widespread modern forms of the surname are Averill, Everill and Everall: 1691 Thomas Everall of Betley; 1851, Catherine Averill (farmer), Ashley Heath, Mucklestone; 1875, Henry Everill (beerseller), High Street, Hanley; 1875, Alfred Averill (assistant surgeon to Dr Weaver), Bank House, Church Street, Longton.

Of all the devices which the medieval church employed to drive home its Christian message, none made a deeper impression on the illiterate peasant population than the Miracle plays performed throughout the county by various guilds.   Some of these plays were so involved, that they often started at dawn and went on until sunset, commencing with the fall of Lucifer and ending with the Last Judgement.   Lucifer was the name of Satan before his fall from heaven, that is, the Devil, and hence anyone who played this particular role in the epic might have assumed a nickname "the Devil", which would be his surname for the rest of his life and passed on to his descendants. John Devyle, rated at twenty pence in the 1332 lay subsidies at Tean, probably got his name this way.   However, the surname

Deville
Deavill(e)
Deavall
Devall

Deville, Deavill(e), Deavall and Devall were also introduced by Norman immigrants from Déville in Seine Inferieure, as exemplified by Walter de Deville in a thirteenth century deed from the Dieulacres Cartulary, but sometimes this may be split up incorrectly, resulting in Thomas de Eyvill (1280 Assizes) - the modern Evill. In the 1543 Rent Roll of Dieulacres Abbey John Devell was paying an annual rent of 8 shillings to the monks for an unspecified amount of land in Tittesworth; 1723 September 21st, Elizabeth Devell and James Cope, married at Cheddleton; 1851 James Deavell (cabinet maker), Tipping Street, Stafford; 1907, John Deavill (tobacconist) of Heron Street, Fenton; 1912, Thomas Davall (carter), Leek Road,

Davall

Hanley.

Another name that has been deliberately mutilated is Death, divided up into

Death
De Ath
D'Eath

De Ath or D'Eath, as though it were a toponymic from Ath in Belgium, that is, "de Ath" - "the immigrant from Ath".   Of course, this origin is quite feasible, but an additional source is the figure of Death, portrayed in the Chester plays.   William Death was charged on three hearths at Crakemarsh in the 1666 hearth tax returns.

According to Bardsley, there was a firm called Death and Dyson in Cambridge, which was unkindly pronounced by the locals as Death and Dy-soon! The surname Mort/Mart may also belong here, with the Saxon "Death" replaced by the Norman equivalent "Mort", again symbolizing Death in the pageants or Mystery plays. Other derivations are worthy of examination, including an ancient hunting expression - "to blow a morte" - used when a hunter sounded certain notes on his horn to announce the imminent death or killing of a deer, whilst a personal name also comes into the picture - "Mort", found in Mosterton in Dorset, "Mortestorne" in Domesday Book, "Mort's thorn bush". This name is related to dialectal "mort" - "young salmon" or "murt" - "a small person". Gervase Mort was reader at Sheen chapel in 1607 and John Mort ran a carrier service from Wetton to Leek in 1851. In 1887 Frederick Mart (artist in china) lived in Regent Street, Stoke.

The various guilds who put on these dramatic plays, brought the Biblical stories to life for their peasant audiences - the building of Noah's ark and the great flood, the legend of Jonah and the whale, the miraculous birth of Jesus in the manger, the slaughter of the innocents, the Last Supper and the horrific death of Christ on the Cross, and so on. They went to great lengths to construct realistic back-drops and to devise appropriate sound effects with the devil making a spectacular appearance, enveloped in clouds of sulphurous smoke and God and the heavenly host of angels descending on to the stage suspended by an assortment of wires and cranes concealed in makeshift clouds. The surname Angel(l) could easily have arisen from playing the part of an angel in one of these vivid performances, but a sarcastic nickname was never far away. One has only to think of the modern irony of "she's no angel" to comprehend something of the medieval mind and the way it worked. Anna Angel of Hixon was buried at Stowe-by-Chartley on March 19th, 1672. Trade directories: 1907, Thomas Angel of Malkin Street, Burslem; 1907, C.P. Angell (caretaker) of Greville Street, Hanley. Angel was often used as a Christian name, as in Angell Marten, wife of William Marten at Stowe-by-Chartley in 1618, and in the more famous Angel Clare, lover of the doomed Tess in Hardy's *Tess of the D'Urbervilles*. There may be some overlap with the surname Angle(s), although this usually designates habitation in some nook or secluded spot, as in 1277 Inquisition post mortem. John in the Angle of Longnor in Alstonefield parish. 1907, William Angle (potter) of Leek Road, Hanley. The mysterious Ainge/Hainge might be derived from the Anglo Norman "aunge" - "angel" with all the senses inherent in the name Angel, but this remains to be seen: 1851, S.J. Ainge (British Guarantee Fire and Life Office agent), Gaol Square, Stafford.

Virgin and its latinized variant Virgo are either names assigned to someone who had played the part of the Virgin Mary in some Miracle play or a cruel joke intended to denigrate the character of some gentleman: 1887, James Virgo (furniture remover), Boothen, Stoke; 1912, Isaac Virgo (dipper) of Ward Street, Hanley. These notions of being naive, innocent, inexperienced or even somewhat effeminate are also inherent in a name like Maiden/Mayden, especially in the case of Adam le Maiden, quoted in the 1279 Hundred Rolls for Cambridgeshire. In 1633, William Hill, one of the churchwardens at Stoke-on-Trent, paid one shilling on the 8th October to *"Roger Mayden for seats in ye Schoolehouse"*, and in 1666 Thomas

Maiden
Mayden
Meadon
Meaden
Maden

Maiden was exempt from hearth tax at Forsbrook. Trade directories: 1851, Joseph Maiden (huntsman to W. Davenport, Esquire), Wolstanton; 1851, William Mayden (farmer), Heaton, Rushton Spencer; 1875, Thomas Maiden (veterinary surgeon), Newcastle Street, Burslem. The plural form Maidens signifies "the servant of the maiden" or "the maiden's servant". In 1345 William, son of Thomas del Maydene of Waterfall, sued Adam de Grendon (the elder) for a messuage and seven acres of land in Waterfall, which William Pouterell had given to Agnes, daughter of William Pouterell and the heirs of her body, and which, after the death of Agnes, should descend to him as her son and heir. From the 1600s onwards these names diverge into a number of other common forms: 1603, Richard Meaden and Joan Rosse married at Seighford on November 21st; 1669, William Meadon and Anne Boone wed at Standon; 1764, Thomas, son of Thomas and Catherine Meddings, baptised on July 23rd at Church Eaton; 1851, George Meadon (bricklayer) of London Road, Newcastle-under-Lyme; 1851. Richard Meddins (saddler) of Stafford Street, Longton. The isolated John Maden of Betley, who marries Mary Mather (also of Betley) at Seighford on July 21st, 1706, is perhaps another late variant of Maiden based on the word "made", often spelt "maid" or "mayde" in the 16th century.

The re-enactment of the crucial episodes in the life of Jesus called for an number of would-be actors willing to take on the role of "apostle" or "prophet".

Postle(s)
Postill
Possell

The former survives as Postle(s), Postill, Possell: 1386 Assizes, Richard Postel Dean of Wolverhampton; Stowe-by-Chartley parish registers, 1594, James Whitgreve alias Possell, baptised on December 24th; Wolstanton parish registers, 1648, William Postle; Stoke-on-Trent parish registers, 1812, James Yardley an Hannah Possell, married on December 28th. There may even be a hint of hypocrisy attached to the surname, recalling Bunyan's *"a saint abroad and a devil at home"*

Saint(s)
Sant
Saunt

and this would immediately bring in the surname Saint(s), Sant, Saunt, a nickname for an individual with a holier-than-thou attitude: 1666 Hearth tax returns, John Saint charged on one hearth at Grindon, and widdow Saint likewise at Ellastone 1907, Isaac Sant (saggar maker), Howard Street, Burslem; 1907, Elijah Sant (joiner), Selwyn Street, Shelton, Hanley.

Profit(t)
Proffit(t)
Prophet(t)

The surname Profit(t), Proffit(t), Prophet(t) is more than likely a nickname for someone who was skilled at telling people's fortunes, an extremely useful gift at a time, when superstitions abounded. Wolstanton parish registers, 1790, John Prophett, noted as John Proffitt in 1792; Stoke-on-Trent parish registers, 1807 Samuel Prophett (joiner) of Burslem, married to Ann Crompton on September 14th 1851, Joseph Prophett (tailor) of Audley; 1907, John Proffitt (general and coal dealer), Broom Street, Hanley.

One tradition dating back to the ancient fertility cults is the legendary medieval figure known as the Green Man or Jack in the Green, who was actually a man inside a small house made of flowers and evergreens, who carried it in the procession of the sweeps on May-day morning. He was literally a walking bush, but since he was clad in leaves and flowers, he was in direct physical contact with the fertilization spirit of the pagan god of the woods and fields. This was the primal belief in a supernatural power that organized and animated the material universe, endowing plants and natural phenomena with a living soul. Modern surnames such as Greenleaf, Greenleaves and Greenlees perpetuate this very ancient pagan custom. In 1433 Thomas Grenelef of Horninglow (labourer), together with Henry Touneshende, also of Horninglow, (husbandman), and William Walton of Burton-on-Trent (butcher), trespassed on the land of William Howeton at Horninglow, reaped his beans, peas and oats, cut down his grass and carried away his crops, valued at £10. Half a century later, during the first year of the reign of Richard III (1483), Reginald Greneleffe of Rugeley (yeoman) with more than a score of other yeomen, husbandmen, gentlemen and one clerk, from Great Haywood, Bishton, Colwich and Shugborough, broke into Ralph Wolseley's close at Wolseley in the Trent Valley, cut down his underwood and carried it off in 100 cartloads. Ralph put in a claim for £100 damages. Francis Greenleafe was assessed for one hearth at Stretton near Horninglow in 1666. In the Telephone Directory for Stoke-on-Trent, Stafford and Crewe (1987), the surname Greenlees was still extant in the Rugeley area. Scottish interest here is focussed on East and West Greenlees near Cambuslang, Lanarkshire.

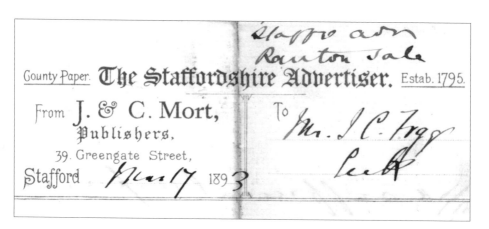

Mort p. 137

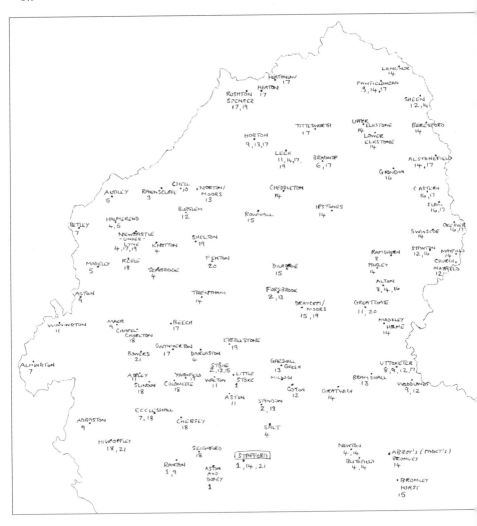

MAP 4 KEY

1. BACKHOUSE
2. BOARDMAN
3. BOWLER
4. BURGESS
5. BUTTER(S)

6. CALVERT
7. CORNES
8. FORMAN
9. GARDNER
10. GATER

11. GOODALL/GOUDALE
12. HURD(E)
13. HORNE
14. MILWARD/MILLWARD
15. PAKEMAN

16. PEACH
17. PLANT
18. STEADMAN/STEEDMAN
19. STODDARD/STODDERT
20. TABBERNER
21. YEOMANS

SURNAMES AT THE TIME OF THE 1666 HEARTH TAX RETURNS

CHAPTER FOUR
RURAL SOCIETY

1. WORKERS ON THE LAND

VILLEINS AND SERFS

"Feudalism", the term given by historians to the dominant form of society in the Middle Ages, was at a very rudimentary stage in England before the arrival of the Normans. But to them it was the social and political form they were accustomed to in their homeland of Normandy, where it was already well developed in all its aspects. The feudal system of land tenure was based on the sworn agreement between two parties, namely the lord and his vassal, dependent on their control of the principal form of wealth of that time - land. Theoretically it was the lord (the king or baron) who was in possession of the land, which was handed over to the vassal for his own use provided the latter performed certain services, primarily military. However, the vassal did not work his own portion of land himself, but employed a varied assortment of peasants to do the work for him.

On the one hand, the menial or servile status of those who had to work on the land for their living - the serfs, villeins, cottars - was described as unfree. They were "adscripti glebae", bound by birth and by possession of Saxon blood to the lord of the manor, and for all intents and purposes their rights of work, movement and marriage were all controlled by their masters. The exact position in society of the medieval villein is well illustrated in a sitting of the Manor Court at Alrewas on Wednesday, June 11th, 1259, when all the land of Robert, son of Reginald was taken into the hands of the lord of the manor with all the crops thereupon as security for a fine. Only after Robert had paid his fine of three pence was the land restored to him. This harks back two centuries to the time when William the Conqueror decreed that any man who had fought against him at Hastings should be a serf for ever.

By contrast, those who had to serve the king or lord by fighting were protected by the king in the royal courts and thus were described as free. This sharp divergence between two extreme types of tenure in medieval feudal society is abundantly clear from the surnames connected with the scale of rank, covered in previous chapters. At the opposite end of the social ladder was the villein, a word ultimately from the Latin "villanus" - "a person attached to a villa, a farmer". He was so completely at the mercy of the lord of the manor and held in such contempt, that the word has now come to mean a thoroughly evil, scheming good-for-nothing, as typified by Alexander Riley, *"....who was murdered by villains in his own house"* at Penkridge on August 13th, 1685. A name borne by Monsire William Boutevileyn, one of the officers in charge of the perambulation of the Forest of Kinver on 11th June, 1300, only added insult to injury, for it denotes literally "hustle the churl", that

Butlin
Bucklin

is, squeeze the last ounce of work out of the poor devil. It survives a Butlin/Bucklin, where the first variant was made famous by Sir William "Billy Butlin, the holiday camp pioneer. Yet I have a sneaking suspicion, that some of ou North Staffordshire Butlins and Bucklins are but slightly modified forms o Butland/Buckland, where the initial element reflects the dialectal "buttle" fo "buckle". The pairs Butlin-Butland and Bucklin-Buckland would then be analogou to Franklin-Frankland (see later). Christopher Bucklin (a Yorkshireman) was burie at Newcastle-under-Lyme on October 30th, 1755.

Neighbour(s)
Naybour

The degeneration in meaning of the word "villein" is mirrored by "boor" which originally referred to a farmer, but now of course it signifies anyone of a rud or ill-mannered disposition. This word forms the second element of ou "neighbour", that is "nigh boor" - "the farmer near at hand", and the surnam Neighbour(s), Naybour: 1341 Inquisition post mortem, Roger Neighbor o Bushbury; Newcastle-under-Lyme parish registers, 1794, John, son of Joh Nighbour, baptised on March 14th.

The rural population of Staffordshire recorded in the Domesday surve consisted mainly of "villani" - "villeins", "bordarii" - "bordars" and "cotarii" "serfs". It is not known how much land each of them farmed but in Eccleshall the end of the thirteenth century the villeins were probably farming virgates of abou twenty acres and in return they worked for two, or even three days a week on th Bishop of Lichfield's demesne lands. Apart from this, they did extra work for th bishop during the most demanding seasons of the agricultural year, such as helpin out with the ploughing in autumn and spring, and assisting with the hay-making an reaping in summer.

Boarder
Border(s)

The "bordar" was allocated some land for subsistence, probably smallholding of five or six acres with a cottage, and, as part of his side of th bargain, worked for one day a week on the bishop's home farm, in addition to th seasonal obligations outlined above. This is one origin of the surnam Boarder/Border(s): Burton Abbey Charters, Twelfth century, Ailwin bordarius o Stretton near Horninglow; 1532, George Border and his wife Maud, resident Haughton west of Stafford; 1672, Margaret Boarder and Joseph Walter, married Lapley on May 23rd. Also pertinent is a carpenter who made boards or planks o even wooden tiles for roofing - compare William le Bordhewere, rated at 15 penc for Uttoxeter in the 1327 lay subsidies, or the Norman import "bordeor" - "jeste buffoon", synonymous with Latin "joculator", as in Burton Abbey Charters, Twelf century, ----- joculator of Whiston near Penkridge (no first name given). The allie

Board
Boardman

names Board and Boardman probably contain all the above senses except "jester Wolstanton parish registers, 1548, Andrew Borde (rector); 1666, John Boar charged on one hearth at Thickbroom near Weeford. At the Great Court of Tunsta held on the Tuesday after the finding of the Holy Cross (4th May, 1378), Thom Bordman of Burslem was fined 2 pence, possibly for some illegal digging on th land of the Abbot of Hulton and the land of the lord. In 1803 Hugh Bourne, who was at that time a Wesleyan, visited Brown Edge every Tuesday and held religious meetings there. On August 24th his brother James was preaching in John Sarjant's house in Woodhouse Lane, and had a talk with William Boardman, who, according to Hugh Bourne's account *"...is seting (sic) out for Heaven"*. William Boardman resided at "Woodhouse", a thatched seventeenth century property now known as "Boardman's Bank". In the early nineteenth century the Boardmans farmed 26 acres of land in Brown Edge, and a William Boardman had been warden at Norton Parish Church. The surname Boardman persists in Brown Edge in association with Wesleyan Methodism until the latter decades of the nineteenth century. 1907, John Boardman (potter's presser), Fenton Road, Hanley. At Burslem George Boardman (1718) also occurs as George Boardmore in 1720, and this fluctuation in the ending between "-man" and "-more" imitates the couplet Swetnam (Swetman)-Swetmore, Sweetmore.

The "cottar" was a villein who held a cot or cote, a primitive cottage or shelter for man and beast, and he or she often owned no land at all, sometimes being forced to hire themselves out to their lord and master. This male-female distinction is expressed thus in the 1381 Poll tax returns, where Richard atte Ook "cotarius" is assessed for 12 pence at Penkridge, as opposed to Alice Blakemere "cotaria", who is paying an identical amount at Rugeley. But it is the Old French "cotier", as in Petronilla de Ipstones "cotier" of Church Eaton (same returns), which gives us Cottier/Cotter. 1851, James M. Cotter (revenue officer) of Waterfall. From this comes the diminutive offshoot "coterel" - "cottager", origin of the familiar names Cottrell, Cottrill, Cotterell and Cotterill: *Great White Book of Lichfield Cathedral*, circa 1280, Ralph Coterel. At Wollaston and Shredicote near Church Eaton, the contribution made by Richard Coterelle and his wife Avicia towards the Poll tax of 1381 amounted to two shillings and four pence. In 1532 James Cotrell and family were settled at Foxt near Ipstones, whilst Geoffray Cottrell and Ann Greaves were married at Ellastone on October 14th, 1593. Elizabeth, daughter of George and Elizabeth Cottrell was buried at Stowe-by-Chartley on December 19th, 1617. Trade directories: 1851, Jonathan Cottrell (farmer), White Moor, Biddulph; 1875, Arthur Cotterill (hosier and haberdasher), Piccadilly, Hanley; 1887, James P. Cottrell (master), St. Thomas's National School, Mow Cop; 1887, Richard John Cotterill (innkeeper), Staffordshire Knot, Cross Street, Fenton. Cottrell is also a late variant of Catherall, from Catterall on the river Calder, south of Garstang, Lancashire. The meaning of the locality has long been the subject of much heated debate, with one ingenious theory linking it with Katterall in Norway. This is derived from Old Scandinavian "kattar-hali" - "cat's tail", signifying a farm, situated on some land, shaped like a cat's tail - elongated but uneven. Baines, in his *History of Lancashire*, gives Richard de Caterhale, who held land in 1257/58 at "Gosenhar" - Goosnargh and "Katerale" - Catterall, among other places. Locally, in the Ellenhall parish

registers for 1730, Jane Catherall is mentioned as coming from Stone. Th
transposition from Catherall to Cottrill is proved by this statement from Pape
Newcastle-under-Lyme in Tudor and Early Stuart Times: *"When he, that is, Phili
Sherwin, became mayor in 1637, he was no doubt instrumental in admitting, in th
month after the mayoral election, Francis Catherall or Cottrill (as the name soo
became) to his burgess rights"*. In the same paragraph William Catherall (1636)
noted as William Cottrill. Both were local pioneers in the pipemaking industry.

Yet the very early specimen William Katerel in a Staffordshire assize rol
dated 1203, also points to a pet form of Catherine, a name borne by the virgin marty
of Alexandria, patron saint of wheel-wrights, who was torn to pieces on a spike
wheel. The actual rounding "Cat-" to "Cot-" at the beginning of the names is merel
a reflection of the dialectal "rot" for "rat".

Bond

Before the Conquest "bond" was simply another name for a peasant wh
tilled the soil, but after 1066 it was applied to a serf or unfree tenant. An inquisitio
of 1249, concerning the value of the royal domain of Newcastle-under-Lym
belonging to Henry III, conducted by Lord Vivian de Standon and other high
ranking members of the local hierarchy, discovered that *"....the men of Penchul hor
8 bovates of bondsmen lands for 20 shillings and eight pence ....and also th
bondmen of the same vill* (Wolstanton) *hold 4 bovates of land and render therefor
by the year 8 shillings"*. (A "bovate" could be anything from 10 to 18 acres). Th
Ferrers family of Tutbury parcelled out their demesnes around Marchingto
Uttoxeter, Rolleston and Barton-under-Needwood to bond tenants, who wer
obliged to mow the grass in the meadows, make the hay and carry it to Tutbur
castle, to work on the arable land by ploughing it, sowing, reaping, mowing ar
carting the crops to the castle and manor house. In 1308 Adam le Bonde paid
pence rent per annum to the Audleys for 3 acres of land without a messuage
Horton near Rudyard, and Thomas Bonde was charged 4/9^{1}/2d annually for one pl
of land at Talke. The surname Bond is also traceable to a personal name: 131
Great White Book of Lichfield Cathedral, Bonde de Moniasch (Monyash west
Bakewell). 1851, Benjamin Bond (land agent and surveyor), Draycott-in-th
Moors; 1851, Thomas Bond (brick and tile maker), Moss House Bridg
Shallowford, Chebsey.

Bondy
Bundy

The equivalent Scandinavian "bondi" survives as Bondy/Bundy: 1327 La
subsidies, Roger Bondy, rated at 2 shillings for Weston-on-Trent and Amerto
1875, Thomas Bundy (ironmonger), Piccadilly, Hanley. Bound(s) is rare: 132

Bound(s)

Adam le Bonde of Cold Norton, quoted as Adam le Bounde in 1332; 1907, Samu
Bound (potter), Arthur Street, Longton.

Bownd
Boon(e)
Bown(e)
Bone

The modern locality known as Boon Hill in Audley appears as Bound Hill
the 1833 Ordnance Survey map. Furthermore, at Standon, Andrew Bound (1608
is variously entered in the parish registers as Andrew Boond in 1594, Andrew Boor
in 1595 and as Andrewe Bownd(e) in 1616. Normally Boon(e), Bown(e) and Bo

are derived from Bohon in La Manche. Bohun's Hall in Essex, the seat of the great Earls in that county, occurs as "Boneshall, Bowneshall" in the sixteenth and seventeenth centuries, and is now pronounced Boon's Hall. The local spellings such as Bownd/Bound for Audley and Standon have developed from Boon/Bown because of the tendency in north Staffordshire to pronounce words like "drown, show" as "drownd, shownd". In addition, the surnames could be a nickname for someone with a bone deformity - again, on account of the dialectal "boon" for "bone", but Bone, together with Bonn and Bunn are generally from Old French "bon" - "good": 1644, Edward, son of Robert and Isabel Bunne, baptised on June 16th at Seighford; 1907, Edward Bone (potter), High Street, Sandyford; 1907, Margaret Bowne (widow) of Shaw Street, Burslem; 1907, Harriet Boon (stationer, confectioner), Market Street, Fenton. Bond is also unrounded to Band: Stowe-by-Chartley parish registers. 1615, Richard Bonde (1622, Richard Bande).

The word "bond" continued in general use as a common noun, and formed the second syllable of several compounds, including "husband" - "bond (farmer) with a house", "householder, husbandman". In 1408 John Housband of Whitmore sued Thomas Swynnerton, Thomas Hare and Henry de Borghstone, for beating, wounding and illtreating him at Whitmore, so that his life was despaired of. John Husband was curate at Hints from 1681 until 1721 and Joan Husbands got married to Walter Brooks at Penkridge on December 8th, 1709. Younghusband, denoted the "young farmer". In 1298 John, son of Robert le Yungehusebonde, together with his brothers Peter and Gerard, was in dispute with Alan, son of Simon de Acton over the third of 9 acres in Acton Trussell. In the Middle Ages the term "husband" signified first and foremost a man of a certain social class, who farmed from 10 to 40 acres. It was one of the brutal facts of life in medieval England, that a man could survive by hiring himself out as a farm labourer, but he had no chance of keeping his wife or family unless he held some land. It was the "husband", who was in possession of the land and who was responsible for the day-to-day running of the household.

Another compound of "bond" is Lightbound, Lightbown, Lightband, as exemplified by John Lightboun ("Seynour" - lord or senior), who was sued for a debt of 10 marks in 1395 by Henry Delves, John Grene and Margaret, formerly wife of John, son of Henry Delves, executors of the will of John, son of Henry Delves. This refers to a little husbandman or a husbandman who was active. It may also have developed later into Lightburn, Lightbourn(e), eg John Lightbourne and Elizabeth Homersley, married *"ye 9th of June"*, 1581 at Standon. Yet these might also represent "active or little child", or go back to Lightburne in Ulverston, Cumbria. 1873, Thomas Lightbourne (licensee), Roebuck, Winton Terrace, Stoke.

Swain immediately conjures up images of a long-lost rural England, inhabited by love-lorn farm labourers wooing innocent young maidens, but this world only exists in poetry. The truth is, that it was an occupational term for a boy or servant, a swineherd or a peasant, and any of these descriptions could apply Richard le Sweyn, taxed at 12 pence for Ashley near Mucklestone in 1332, and Hugh le Sweyn, assessed at 22 pence for Wootton-under-Weaver in the sam returns. A subsidiary source for the surname Swain(e), Swayn(e) is the Old Nor personal name "Sveinn", recorded in the Domesday survey as "Suain, Suuain" f Madeley (near Keele), Meaford, Milwich, Derrington, Forsbrook, Wootton-und Weaver and High Onn. It was also anglicised as "Suan, Swan" as in Ront Charters. Thirteenth century, Swanus de Flotesbroc (Flashbrook). However, t Saxon "swan" - "swineherd, peasant" became "swon" later on, thereby clashi with "swan, swon" - "swan". With its snow-white elegance this is a nickname f a pure, innocent person when applied to a woman: 1357 Assizes, Alice le Swon Stafford, who was tragically killed by William, son of Elen Cubbok at Stafford son 11 years previously. But when used for a man it probably carried overtones passion and rage, reminiscent of the male swan, who is very aggressive during t breeding season: 1327 Lay subsidies, William le Swon of Crakemarsh, rated at shillings. At Alrewas, on July 26th, 1645, Humphrey Swayne was buried after *" was bitten with a mad doge in the hand upon the third day of the same month thereabout, and that was the cause of his death"*. Richard Swain was one of t witnesses to the marriage of Ralph Fenton and Mary Lovatt, which took place Cheddleton on 14th April, 1765. 1907, Percy Swain (assistant cashier), King Terrace, Stoke; 1907, William Swain (miner) of Vernon Square, Burslem. Lat specimens of Swan(n) comprise: 1851, John Swan (hairdresser), Mount Pleasa Street, Burslem; 1851, William Swann (maltster and tallow chandler) of Mark Lane, Newcastle-under-Lyme.

Swan(n)

Swaines
Swailes
Swale(s)
Swayll(s)

Swain and Swaines also fluctuate with Swayll(s), e.g. Penn parish registe 1611, Fraunces Swayll (1614, Ffrances Swayles; 1616, Ffrances Swaylls; 162 Frances Swaines). Mrs Anne Swaile was chargeable on two hearths Wolverhampton in 1666. Swale and Swales are additional modern variants of t name.

Swainson

The corresponding patronymic Swainson refers either to "son of Sveinn" "son of the swain": 1227 Assizes, Robert son of Swane of Stanton near the Weav Hills and Edricus filius Swayne of Stafford in a thirteenth century deed from t charters of St. Thomas's Priory, Stafford. However, apart from the isolated Richa Sweynson in the Tatenhill manor court rolls for 1517, the surname is spelt Swinson or Swenson during the sixteenth and seventeenth centuries, e.g. 15 Thomas Swenson of Tixall; 1593, Margerye Swinson, married to Thomas Smyth Stowe-by-Chartley on November 19th; 1666, William Swinson, paying tax on o hearth at Cheadle and Robert Swinson, charged on three hearths at Croxden. T latter appears as Robert Swenston in 1646, when he was listed amongst t benefactors *"...in Greetyate towards the relief of Stafford, visited by God's hea judgement of the plague"*. His own personal contribution was six pence. In t

Swinson
Swenson

Ellastone parish registers Samuel Swinson (1807) is cited as Samuel Swainson in 1810; 1907, Charles Swinson (fireman), South Street, Fenton; 1907, Annie Swinson, Alton Castle Inn, Cheadle; 1916 (Kelly's Directory). Lieutenant E. Swainson of Penkhull New Road, Penkhull.

Occasionally, anyone who held, occupied, owned or possessed a chunk of land in the Middle Ages was known quite simply as a "holder", hence the name Holder/Houlder. John le Holdere, assessed for seven pence at Broughton near Charnes in 1327, would have been recognised in the local community as an owner of land. 1875, William Holder (painter, glazier) of Caroline Street, Longton; 1907, John Holder (potter), Upper Normacot Road, Longton. Holding and Houlding may hint at some similar tenure of land, but they are nothing of the sort, for they are alternative forms of Holden/Houlden: Leek parish registers, 1653, John Holden, noted as John Holding in 1654. This, in turn, fluctuates with Howden: Cheadle parish registers, 1632, Richard Houldin, who occurs as Richard Howden a year later. The Holdings in Rudheath Lordship, Cheshire was originally "Holdene" in the Middle Ages - "deep valley", and hence is synonymous with Holden Vale in Haslingden chapelry, Holden Gate near Todmorden, Holden in Bolton by Bowland (all in Lancashire), Holden (or Howden) Clough in the West Riding of Yorkshire and Howden in Northumberland. But Howden north of Goole denotes a head (chief) valley. 1851, William Houlding (farmer) of Madeley (Keele); 1851, John Holden (colour manufacturer), Barnfield Buildings, Burslem; 1875, John Holding (tea dealer), Church Street, Silverdale; 1887, Mary Holden (milliner) of Liverpool Road, Stoke.

The medieval "tenant" too was a holder or possessor of some land and his descendants live on in the modern-day Tennant and Tennent: 1875, Frederick Tennant (wine and spirit merchant), Market Place, St. John's Square and Church Street, Burslem; 1887, Edmund Tennant (registrar), County Court, Hanley.

FREEMEN

The very nature of villeinage differed from manor to manor, and some peasants succeeded in buying their freedom from the lord of the manor. In a final concord, dated 3rd July, 1272, relating to the *"nativity"* of Hugh de Leye of Whystone (probably Whiston near Penkridge), that is, *"the condition of being a serf"*, Robert de Acton and his wife Margery admitted Hugh to be a freeman, for which Hugh gave them 20 shillings. In the accounts of the Borough of Newcastle-under-Lyme for 1383/1384 John Walshe owed 1/6d for his freedom and in 1378 Roger Gray was to retain his liberty as long as he remained unmarried. A woman could escape bondage by marrying a freeman, but even here there were snags at every turn, for she reverted to bondage on the death of her husband. A man could become free by proving himself a bastard, hence the survival of the surname Bastard, discussed in Chapter 3. If a man failed to convince his local manor court of his illegitimacy,

then, as a last resort he ran away to a chartered town or to a royal demesne, and i
he lived there the statutory year and a day, then he automatically gained his freedom
joining the growing ranks of "freemen" like John le Fremon of Chebsey (1327 La

Fremon

subsidies) and Richard le Fremon of Alton, rated at twelve pence in the 1332 lists
Now these "freemen" could hold their heads up high, for they were able to cultivat
their own land and had the right to sell it if they so desired. All they owed the lor
of the manor in return was regular attendance at the manor court, as in the case c

Freeman

William Freeman of Standon, who gave 6 pence for suit of court at Standon in 1338
But Freeman is essentially a South Staffordshire surname and in fact it
exceptionally scarce in the north of the county prior to the Industrial Revolution
Henry Freeman was deemed ineligible for any hearth tax at Adbaston in 1666 an
Thomas Freeman got married to Margaret Trubshaw at Seighford on February 20th
1683. In 1841 Walter Freeman, aged 12 (figure maker), worked for Edward Oxle
at Messrs Allerton, Brough and Green's China, Lustre and Earthenware Factor
Longton; 1851, Selina Freeman (milliner, dressmaker), Gate Street, Longton; 187
George Freeman, gardener to Mrs Hitchman, Fenton House, Fenton.

Free
Fry

With his newly acquired status, a man may have simply been called "th
free": 1731, Mary, wife of William Free, buried at Rushall near Walsall on Octobe
4th. The variant Fry is far more widespread: 1607, Thomas Frye married Margre
(sic) Lythegoe at Eccleshall on September 21st (both employed as servants by Lo
Gerrard of Gerrard's Bromley). 1851, Robert Fry (licensed victualler), proprietor c
the Red Lion, Weston-on-Trent. One of the most distinguished bearers of th
surname is Elizabeth Fry, the prison and asylum reformer (1780-1845).

Frank(s)
Franck(s)
Frankham
Francome
Francombe
Franklin
Franklyn
Frankland

The two French equivalents, Franklin/Franklyn and Frankham/Francom
Francombe are far less common than Freeman, but, together with Frank(s), all a
more typical of the southern half of the county. Robert le Frank of Wootton ne
Eccleshall (1351 Inquisition post mortem) was either a Frank (Frenchman)
"free", that is, neither a serf nor a slave, but the modern names Frank(s) a
Franck(s) are also to be traced to the Germanic name "Franco" - "a Frank". 188
Edward Franks of Newcastle Street, Burslem; 1907, George Franks (potte
placer), Victoria Road, Fenton; 1907, William Franks (ironworker), Chapel Stre
Tunstall.

Frankham
Francome
Francombe

Frankham and variants is a compound of "franc" and "homme" - "free mar
The Turton family of West Bromwich, who were established as nail-masters in t
Oldbury area by the second half of the sixteenth century, traded in nail rod a
finished nails. One member of this family - William (born 1607) - married Elean

Franklin
Franklyn
Frankland

Francombe in 1634. The social standing of the medieval "franklins" was high, f
they were landowners of free but not noble birth, ranking just outside the gentry b
within reach of the knights, squires and sergeants at law. Their privileges includ
exemption from all or most labour services, participation in the Hundred courts a
attendance at the king's justices in eyre, whenever they sat in the neighbourhoc

Reaping (Mower p. 154)

Boardman p. 142

Chaucer's "franklin" cut a prosperous figure, who loved nothing more than a cake in wine sauce in the morning, and he always had a fat partridge in a cage and carp and pike in his private fish-pond. In 1443 several inhabitants from Leek including Robert Frankelyn (yeoman) were sued by John Holand (knight) for taking his goods and chattels worth £40 from his property at Leek. 1851, Charles Franklin (plumber) of Great Haywood; 1873, Robert Franklin (baker) of Rathbone Street, Tunstall; 1907, Elizabeth Franklin (fish dealer) of Heathcote Road, Longton. Frankland is a late corruption, as verified by the Trentham parish registers, where Peter Frankli (1657) is cited as Peter Frankland in 1662.

Frankland

The "yeoman" started out during the Saxon period as "young man", then, at the beginning of the Middle Ages he became a servant or attendant in a royal or noble household - compare 1381 Poll Tax returns, Thomas le Yomon (serviens) of Isabella Meygnille vidua (widow) at Weston Jones near Norbury. He was ranked between a sergeant and a groom, or a squire and a page. By the later Middle Age he had settled down as a freeholder under the rank of a gentleman. Thomas Yeoman enrolled at Norbury in the 1539 Muster is most likely a descendant of the Thomas quoted above. The marriage between John Yeoman and Margaret Johnson took place at the parish church of St. James the Great, Audley on June 25th, 1618. Sleigh cites Henry Yeomans (buttonman), resident at Leek in 1780. Trade directories 1887, William Yeomans (printer), Church Street, Hanley; 1907, Reuben Yeoman (carter), King William Street, Tunstall.

Yeoman(s)

If a villein could escape into a town or borough which had full municipal rights and remain there for a year and a day without being claimed by his master then he became known as a "burgess", granted freeman status, freedom from manorial dues and the right to transfer property. Newcastle-under-Lyme mentioned as a royal borough in the Pipe Rolls of 1172/1173, and by 1212 there were 160 burgesses in the town. On the other side of the county, Uttoxeter, founded by the Ferrers family in 1252, soon boasted a total of 145 burgesses. The same family also established a new town in 1101 by the woodland village of Agardsl near Needwood Forest. It soon changed its name to Newborough with 1 burgesses each paying 1/6d a year. In 1365 Richard Burgeyse stood surety Thomas de Weston at Standon manor court, when the latter was accused of letti his colt stray on to the lord's corn. John Burges junior was one of the mill-reev appointed at Newcastle in 1679 to look after the horse mill for grinding m towards the maintenance of the poor of the borough. 1851, Charles Burgess (r collector) of Goodfellow Street, Tunstall; 1875, Samuel Burgess (fruit deale Railway Terrace East, East Vale, Longton; 1887, Ralph Burgess (butcher) Congleton Road, Talke.

Burgess

During the fourteenth century the status of the labouring classes stead improved and fixed money payments were often substituted for the days' work d to the lord of the manor, bringing the villein's status more in line with the f tenants. There was now more incentive to individual effort and more opportunity for the adventurous to reap the rewards of their own enterprise. Ironically, it took an appalling event like the Black Death to accelerate these profound social changes, for, in its aftermath, there was a serious shortage of labour on farms and estates all over the county, and local bailiffs were forced to compete with each other to hire workers. The peasant seized his chance by demanding higher wages, a privilege hitherto reserved for the free man. Many survivors of the catastrophe wandered from village to village after a job, eventually drifting into large towns, where whole areas lay deserted. Soon this vacuum was filled by ambitious peasants, eager to climb the social ladder, but first they had to conceal their true identity from their new employer just in case the lord of the manor was still on the lookout for them. Thus, William, who had been a shepherd, say, in his home village, probably possessing the name Shepherd, might be known as "the newman, the newcomer" or "the stranger" in his adopted town. The three basic names involved here are New, Newman and Newcome/Newcomb(e): 1665, August 10th, Margaret New of Brewood and Thomas Fletcher of Haughton, married at Lapley; 1673, February 28th, Anne, wife of John New of Alstone, buried at Church Eaton. Henry Newcome conducted and witnessed marriages at Leek for the years 1654 and 1655; 1887, Percy Newcombe (local agent for the Midland Railway Company), Glebe Buildings, Stoke. In 1430 John Neweman of Gunstone (husbandman) and several other local inhabitants were sued by Richard Pyry for breaking into his close at Gunstone and depasturing cattle, by force, on his grass. 1851, Thomas Newman (lock and white smith) of Eastgate Street, Stafford; 1907, James Newman (fireman) of Darnley Street, Hanley; 1907, George Newman (cycle maker and repairer) of Victoria Street, Stoke. Based on the couplet Swetman-Swetnam, the name also interchanges with Newnam (Newnham): Weston-under-Lizard parish registers, 1695, Sarah, illegitimate child of Mary Newman and John Blackmore, known as Sara Blakemore alias Newnam in 1717. If the original surname is Newnam (Newnham), then this is to be derived from any one of a number of locatives called Newnham in several counties - "new homestead", e.g. Register of Robert de Stretton. 1384, William de Newenham (rector or vicar at Wolstanton); 1907, George Newnham of Victoria Street, Silverdale. Newnham near Knighton-on-Teme, Worcestershire might be of major relevance here, together with King's Newnham near Rugby and Newnham Paddox west of Lutterworth.

New arrivals from some unknown village were also distinguished by names such as Strange and Guest, although Strange may have been applied in certain cases to "foreigners", that is, immigrants from Normandy or any region of France. Elizabeth Guest (widow) and William Wild were married at High Offley on May 23rd, 1745. In 1841 George Guest, aged 11, worked for John Moss at Messrs Meller, Venables, Pindar and Company's Earthenware Factory, Burslem, running moulds to and fro from the stove to the jigger-box. For this work he received three

shillings a week.   1851, Lewis Guest (foreman) of Vale Street, Stoke; 159
Margery, daughter of Hugh Strange, buried at Audley on May 25th; 1912, Morr
Strange (labourer) of Chatterley; 1912, Mrs Strange, Peel Street, Longbridge Haye

AGRICULTURAL OCCUPATIONS

Although the Saxon villeins and bondmen answered to their lord and master (wl
spoke French), they continued to speak their own native language, English.   In
well-known passage (circa 1300), Robert of Gloucester discussed the relative stat
of the two languages: *"Thus England came into Normandy's hand, and the Norma*
at that time could speak only their own language, and spoke French just as they d
at home, and had their children taught in the same manner, so that people of ra
in this country who came of their blood all stick to the same language that th
received of them, for if a man knows no French people will think little of him.   B
the lower classes still stick to English and to their own language....."

Indeed, the Saxon peasants still "tilled" the Saxon "acres" and "ground" wi
Saxon "ploughs" and most of the everyday tools they worked with were Saxon
origin - "spade, harrow, hook, fork" and the "crops" they "sowed, reape
harvested" such as "corn, rye, wheat, oats, barley" were all Germanic words.   Tl
archetypal common man in medieval England was Langland's Piers Plowma
steering his heavy iron-shod plough in long narrow strips of "ridge and furrow

Furlong

The modern surname Furlong is testimony to the ploughman's toil, for it mea
literally "a furrow long", that is, a length of field ploughed by him.   Later on it w
used in the sense of a course for footraces, and so the surname is either f
habitation by a furlong or for a runner who competed in the "furlong" - cf. 12(
Pleas of the Forest, Robert de Blakefurlong of Otherton near Rodbaston.   Neith

Plowman
Plowright

Plowman nor Plowright (maker of ploughs) is recorded as a surname for the count
but in an assize of 1418 Robert Forest of Bilston is described as a "ploman", whil
Robart Woode (ploweright) was buried at Seighford on September 26th, 1624.

After the land had been ploughed and the corn sown, the ground had to l
covered by harrowing.   The harrow itself was a heavy grid or lattice of oaken bai
furnished with rows of iron teeth pointing downwards.   This was attached behind
horse or oxen, which dragged it slowly across the field, breaking up the cloc
clearing away the weeds, and bedding down the seeds.   This very importa

Harrower

procedure was supervised by the "harrower": Madeley parish registers, 1587, Ai
Harrower, buried on July 1st.

Despite the lack of scientific knowledge during the Middle Ages, agricultur
technology was not entirely primitive.   The husbandman, for instance, resorted
three chief methods to restore and improve the soil - by letting a field lie fallow f
one year, by marling (spreading a clay containing carbonate of lime), or by usi
cattle or sheep manure.   William le Marlehewere, taxed at 2 shillings for Hi;
Offley in 1327, would have known all about the fertilising properties of the marl

Agricultural workers: reaper, sower, tiller, mower. p. 152 and 154.

Marler
Marlor

Marlow
Marley

quarried - the name means "hewer or quarrier of marl" - the modern Marler/Marlo
Swynnerton parish registers, 1801, John Marler of Beech.   However, there i
interchange, not only with Marlow, as in Weeford parish registers, 1656, An
Marlor, daughter of Thomas Marlow, but also with Marley, as in Barton-unde
Needwood parish registers, 1602, Thomas Marlar, entered as Thomas Marlow i
1604 and as Thomas Marly in 1599.   The locatives of consequence here includ
Marlow near High Wycombe, Buckinghamshire - "village at some spot where a lak
had been drained", Marlow in Leintwardine (Herefordshire), of unknown derivatio
- cf. Nicholas de Merlowe, taxed at Wolgarston in 1327.   On the other hand, th
Marley spellings may go back to a locality in Weston-under-Lizard, found a
"Marleye" in the thirteenth century and as "Marleyhay" in 1330 - probably "glad
by an enclosure where marl was extracted", with outside assistance from Marle
Green south west of Nantwich (of obscure meaning), Marley Hill near Gateshea
(Tyne and Wear) - "boundary glade", Marley near Bingley in the West Riding c
Yorkshire - "glade frequented by weasels", and either of two places in Kent - Marle
near Canterbury or Marley near Deal, both denoting a pleasant glade.   In 188
William Marlow lived in Brickhouse Street, Burslem and in 1907 Frederick Marlo
(potter) was resident in Birks Street, Cobridge.

Tiller

A high percentage of surnames associated with the basic agricultural task
are Saxon in origin.   The ancestors of William Tiller, charged on one hearth a
Croxton in 1666 were farm labourers or husbandmen who tilled the soil, but in th
same tax returns, Richard Tyler was assessed on one hearth at the same place, s
there is evidently some overlap with the name Tiler (see Chapter 5).   Reaping an
harvesting the crops were the domain of the "cropper": 1575, Peter Cropper an
Elizabeth Humfray, married at Newcastle-under-Lyme on May 26th; Norton-in-th

Cropper

Crapper

Moors parish register, 1595, Johanna Hytchcocke alias Cropper (Croop).   Crappe
is an unrounded variant, based on the couplet Croft-Craft.   In 1412 Henry Crappe
and three others killed Roger Kyng of Wolverhampton at Sedgley, and it was state
before the Justices of the Peace that *"they were common robbers, lying in wait a
highways and fields and that Adam Deykyn had knowingly received them a
Tetenhale on the Thursday after the Feast of the Conception...."*   1875, John
Crapper and Company (dental surgeons), White House, Broad Street, Hanley.

Mower
Mawer

The "mower" cut the crops down with his scythe: William le Mower, rate
at 12 pence for Cauldon in 1332; 1408 Assizes, William Mawer of Crakemars
1550, Robert Mower and Joone Radcliffe, married at Ellastone on May 6th.   Mow
is also a local pronunciation for Moor(e): Thomas Mower, member of the Gayto
militia in 1539, is noted as Thomas More in 1532.

Mather(s)

Another term for a "mower" or "reaper" was Old English "maethere", sourc
of Mather(s): 1532, Dominus Matthew Mather, curate at Colwich; 1674, Ma
Mathers of Milwich; 1851, James Mather, manager of Alton paper mills.   There

Madder(s)

frequent alternation with Madder(s): Betley parish registers, 1795, John Mather cited as John Madder in 1793; 1851, Jas. Madders (butcher) of Puddle Dock (sic), Halmerend. If the actual surname is Madder(s), then this comes from the Saxon "maedere" - "madder", a red dye stuff prepared from the plant of the same name, and hence the reference would be to a dyer with madder or to a person who sold it.

The job of separating the grain from the corn by beating was entrusted to the "thresher". In 1298 Nicholas le Threshere rented one messuage and one acre of land from the Audleys at Betley for 16 pence per annum. Thrasher is the preferred form in north Staffordshire: 1851, John Thrasher, owner of a beerhouse in Wharf Street, Stoke; 1907, John Thrasher (joiner) of Mulgrave Street, Hanley.

The Norman "tasker" threshed the corn with a flail as a task or piece work, as exemplified by Fylkyn le Taskere, paying his 16 pence subsidy at Fenton Vivian in 1327. In the 1539 Muster Richard Tasker of Great Sugnall was equipped with a bow, and the burial of Dorothie Tasker took place at Haughton near Gnosall on January 5th, 1611.

The corn was sifted in a coarse, wire-meshed sieve by someone like Laurence le Siuiger (1308 Gaol delivery rolls) - the modern Sivyer, Sevyer (no examples), whilst the actual sieve was made by the "sievewright": 1872, Miss Mary Jane Sivewright (warehouse for fancy goods), High Street, Tutbury. The Saxon word for a sieve - "hriddel" survives as Riddler, Ridler, a sifter of corn: 1381 Poll tax returns, John Rideler (taillour), assessed at 12 pence and William Rideler and his wife Alice rated at 2 shillings (all for Church Eaton); Lichfield Cathedral Registers, 1713, Richard Ridler and Elizabeth Marshall, married on January 14th. The surname Riddle(s), Riddell, Riddall is normally a nickname from Old French "ridel" - "a small hill", although its exact significance is veiled in mystery, or a locative, traceable to Rydal near Windermere in the Lake District - "valley where rye was grown", or to Ryedale in the West Riding of Yorkshire, which is probably identical in meaning. John Ridel paid 18 pence subsidy at Moreton near Colwich in 1327. Yet these names could occasionally be occupational for a sifter of corn: 1851, James Riddle (manufacturer) of Longton, residence in Barker Street; 1907, Harry Riddell (miner) of Blantyre Street, Longton; 1907. Frank Riddle (engine driver) of Keary Street, Stoke.

After sifting, the corn was stored in a barn, granary or grange (originally a barn where grain was kept): Kniveton Deeds, 1272, William de la Grange de Gayton (near Salt). Rushton Grange near Cobridge and Normacot Grange were model farms set up by the Cistercian monks of Hulton Abbey, for the development of new agricultural techniques, clearing and draining woodlands and sheep-rearing. 1532, John Grange, his wife Agnes and children Richard and Elizabeth were settled at Madeley near Keele; 1907, John Grange (miner) of Biddulph Road, Pittshill; 1907, Mrs. Eliza Grange of The Marsh, Wolstanton.

The "granger" was the farm bailiff, whose time was taken up looking after the grange or granary. In 1380 Ralph le Graunger and numerous others were sued

by Henry de Braylesford (chivaler) for treading down and consuming his grass wit
their cattle at Grindon-on-the-Moors, valued at 40 shillings. Prior to the Industria
Granger
Grainger
Revolution the surname Granger/Grainger makes its home in the southern half o
our county, hardly ever straying north of Stafford. Marie, daughter of John Grange
was baptised at Seighford on March 26th, 1591; 1875, John Grainger (shopkeeper
of Normacot Road, Longton; 1912, Ephraim Granger (plasterer), Hanover Stree
Hanley; 1912, Joseph Granger (potter), Podmore Street, Burslem.

Binne
Binns
Binnes
Bins for the corn, meal or bread were made by the Binner, or someone wit
the name Binne, Binns or Binnes, but the Saxon "binn" - "bin, manger" was als
used in a topographical sense for habitation by the hollows, whilst Yorkshir
families called Binns trace their name back to Binns in Southowram near Halifa
In 1549 Agnes Byns (widow) remitted all right to Thomas Chatwyn and his hei
regarding a messuage, 60 acres of land, 40 acres of meadow and 20 acres of pastu
in Salt. The settlement was agreed at £40. Richard Bynns (Binns) was rector a
Cheadle in 1704; 1887, George Binns (decorator) of Pyenest Street, Hanley; 190
Frederick Binns (coach trimmer) of Croft Street, Burslem.

Bushell
Bushill
Bussell
Bissell
A similar name is Bushell, Bushill, Bussell, Bissell, which is derived from
Old French "buissiel", Middle English "busshel" - "bushel", probably applied to
person who measured out corn, etc. in bushels, or to anyone who made bush
vessels (baskets). A less common alternative source is Old French "bucel" - "sma
barrel" with reference to a maker of such containers. In 1279 Richard Buissel an
others were charged "in absentia" of unjustly dispossessing William de Audythe
(Audley) of a place in Thursfield. William was awarded 20 shillings damages. Joh
Bussell was curate at the Church of St. Editha, Church Eaton in 1550 and Margare
daughter of Thomas Bissell received her baptism at Barlaston on July 16th, 160
In 1666 Henry Bushell paid tax on one hearth at Hopwas near Tamworth.

Cocker
Coker
At harvest-time, the hay, after mowing, was tossed, spread, left to dry an
then put up into "cocks" by the "cocker". Adam le Kockere, assessed at 18 penc
for Croxton in the 1327 lay subsidies, may well have been a farm labourer, engage
in this very task - the modern surname Cocker, Coker. Yet these are also a derivativ
of the verb "cocken" - "to fight", applied to a fighter, wrangler or wrestler, whil
later migrants could have brought the name from East, West and North Coker nea
Yeovil in Somerset, which are situated on the stream at Coker (the crooked stream
In 1308 Richard Coker rented a cottage on the Audley estates at Endon for 8 penc
per annum. 1873, W. Coker (shopkeeper), High Street, Silverdale; 1875, Edw
Cocker (haberdasher), Trent Terrace, Fenton. The phrase *"according to Cocker"*
"by or in accordance with strict rule or calculation", is attributed to Edward Cock
(1631-75), mathematician and reputed author of a very popular work entitle
Arithmetick.

On some manors the serf was not even allowed to grind his own corn exce
at the lord of the manor's mill. This is well illustrated by the case of Geoffrey, so

of Alice de Frodele (Fradley) at the Alrewas manor court in 1272, who was fined 6 pence because he did not have his corn ground at the Alrewas mill to which he was tied. In medieval Staffordshire the right of a lord to compel his tenants to bring their corn to be ground at his mill was a profitable source of income. Consequently, anyone who could grind the corn in his own mill, which he rented from the lord of the manor, held a position of unrivalled supremacy in the small, tightly-knit communities dotted about the countryside. Indeed, the medieval miller was one of the most prosperous of all craftsmen, but at the same time, he was also one of the least popular, since he frequently cheated on weight as he measured the grain, substituting bad grain for good. A medieval riddle posed the question : *"What is the boldest thing in the world?"*, and the answer came back - *"A miller's shirt, for it clasps a thief by the throat daily"*. Chaucer's miller had *"a thumb of gold"*, that is, the thumb might turn yellow from sampling the grain, but otherwise it might also be used to add extra weight to the scales.

The miller's craft has bequeathed several very familiar surnames. The basic Saxon word for a "mill" was "mylen", and this gives the modern name Miln(e), Milln(s), Mylne: 1348 Inquisition, Henry atte mulne of Sandon - a worker at or dweller near a mill. Robert Mylnes was elected burgess at Newcastle-under-Lyme in 1520, whilst Joone, daughter of William and Ellen Milnes was baptised at Ellastone on June 9th, 1644. In 1907 Alfred Ernest Milne was manager of the Home and Colonial Branch Shop in Stamer Terrace, Stamer Street, Stoke.

This was simplified to "mill", as in Elena Mille, late wife of John atte Mille of Cheadle (widow), who was sued in 1432 by Robert Moton (knight) for a debt of £17 and 22 shillings. Besides denoting a mill-worker the singular form Mill is occasionally a shortening of Millicent or a variant of Miles: Alrewas Court Rolls, 1273, Mille Potter, whereas the plural Mills, Milles often fluctuates with Milnes: Tunstall manor court rolls, 1622, John Millns, Mylnes (Mills), or stands for Miles, as in a thirteenth century deed from the Staffordshire Chartulary, where we find Milo or Milles de Padewic. This is the Germanic name "Milo", brought over by the Normans as "Milon, Miles". Contributions to the Defence of the Nation Subscription Fund in 1798 during the Revolutionary Wars with France included five shillings from Ralph Mills of Oulton near Kibblestone. 1851, William Mills (wheelwright) of Blythe Marsh, Forsbrook; 1875, Sidney Miles (manager) of the street railway, Trinity Street, Hanley; 1875, Edward Mills (artist), Meir Road, Normacot; 1907, H. Mill (baker), Model Bakery, Uttoxeter Road, Longton.

Workers at the millhouse left descendants such as Niclys Mylhouse, member of the Tutbury muster in 1539 and another Nicholas Milhous, rated at six hearths in the 1666 tax returns, for the vill of Ellastone. The imported French equivalent for "mill" - "moulin", as in the famous "Moulin Rouge" in Paris, immortalised by the artist Toulouse-Lautrec, survives in the modern surnames Mullin(s), Mullen(s), Mullings, Molins. In 1289 Adam del Molyn of Sandon was unjustly dispossessed

of three acres of moor by William Trumwyne, his son William, Henry de Horseleg
and Alan de la Sale. Trentham parish registers, 1773, Thomas Mullins; 1907, Joh

Mulliner
Mullinar
Mullener
Mulliner

Mullin (labourer) of East View, Middleport. The extended form is Mulline
Mullinar, as in Thomas le Molyner, assessed at 16 pence for Salt and Enstone in th
1332 lay subsidies. Eccleshall parish registers, 1610, John Cocke alias Mullener,
bastard, supposed son of William Mullener of Coottes; 1875, John Mulline
(bootmaker) of Brewery Street, Hanley; 1907, William Mulliner (mechanic), Wilso
Street, Newcastle-under-Lyme.   Modelled on the couplet Warriner-Warrinde

Mullender
Mullinder

Mulliner transposes into Mullinder: John, son of Thomas Mullender of Yarnfield
baptised at the Church of St. Mary, Swynnerton on May 28th, 1744. Mullinder the

Mullington

turns into Mullington: Betley parish registers, 1676, Philip Mullinder (1678, Phili
Mullington).   Another import from France is the name Molineux, Molyneux

Molineux
Molyneux
Mullineux
Mullineaux
Mullinex

Mullineux, Mullineaux, Mullinex, which is derived from "moulineaux" - "th
mills", a locative occurring umpteen times on French soil. George Mollineux wa
churchwarden at Ellastone in 1607 and William Mullineux got married to Elizabet
Massey (spinster) at Swynnerton on December 29th, 1805; 1907, Jesse J. Molyneu
(miner) of Sneyd Street, Cobridge; 1907, Alfred David Mollineux (cratemaker) c
Queen Street, Fenton.

Miller
Millar

The basic surname Miller is common enough during most periods in i
evolution. At Tunstall manor court, held on the Tuesday after the Feast of Trinit
1326, John le miller was one of the pledges for John Rost, who surrenderd 4 acre
of land into the hands of the lord of the manor. Ralph Myller, his wife Joan an
family were amongst the inhabitants at Bishton near Colwich in 1532, and An
Miller was charged on two hearths at Endon in 1666. 1851, Henry Samuel Mille
(canal inspector), Boat Yard, Stone; 1851, Thomas Miller (parish clerk), Caverswal
Millar is essentially a Scottish variant but it does crop up in our county now an
again: Nathaniell Millar, son of John Millar, baptised at Penkridge on March 19t
1671.

Sometimes Miller overlaps with Mellor on account of the local tendency t
pronounce a word such as "shilling" as "shelling", e.g. 1702, William Miller c
Alstonefield, found as William Mellor in 1705.   If the original surname

Mellor
Meller

Mellor/Meller, then two locatives come into the equation - Mellor, about four mile
south of Mottram-in-Longdendale, transferred to Cheshire from Derbyshire in 193
and Mellor in Blackburn parish, Lancashire, both of which denote a "bare hill"
James Mellour of Hope, near Alstonefield (yeoman) and over 50 others wei
attached at the suit of Ralph Basset in 1450, for breaking into his close at Blore, c
the Thursday before the Feast of All Saints, and burning 40 cartloads of peas, 2
cartloads of hay, to the value of £10, and taking 2 "armulasas" (cloaks) of a blac
colour, 2 bows and 1,000 arrows worth £20, and for beating and wounding h
servant Adam Baxtondene, so that he lost his services for a length of time. Edg
Top Farm on Hollinsclough Moor, dated 1787, was built for Micah Mellor, a loca

hawker. When Samuel Mellor of Alstonefield, owner of the George Inn, was declared bankrupt in 1826, he was also described as a cheese factor, dealer and chapman.

Just as Mills seesaws back and forth with Milnes, so Miller follows suit by becoming Milner, Millner, although in the Danelaw counties, a derivation from Old Norse "mylnari" is to be preferred. Two local millers who were at loggerheads in 1398, were John Milner of Alton and John Milward of Waterfall. The former, together with Adam de Beresford and Richard de Gritton, was sued by John Milward for breaking into the dwelling house of his mill at Grendon (Grindon) and taking goods and chattels belonging to him to the value of 100 shillings. John Meller (milner) was buried at Ellastone on April 12th, 1605. Susannah Milner, aged 12, was employed in 1841 as a paper-cutter at John Goodwin's Earthenware Factory, Longton. She had nine brothers and sisters, some of whom were married with families of their own. Her mother was out of work, but she had no father. Susannah's working day began at six in the morning and went on until six or eight in the evening. Her wage was 3 shillings per week. 1851, Jacob Milner (corn miller) of Lower Tean; 1875, Isaac Milner (fruit dealer) Ford Street, East Vale, Longton.

John Milward, quoted in the extract above, boasts the most characteristic of all Staffordshire surnames for a "miller" - literally "guardian, custodian of the mill". In the Middle Ages it often appears in its West Midland guise - "muleward", which, in the past, has been wrongly interpreted as "keeper of the mules". In 1360 Richard le Muleward was fined 6 pence by the aletesters at Tunstall (Stoke-on-Trent) for breaking the assize of beer, by brewing poor quality ale apparently. In 1413 John Milleward (chaplain) of Salt, was charged with ravishing Agnes de Berton at Salt, and breaking into the free warrens of Richard Chetewynd at Salt and Ingestre, and stealing 12 pike, 40 chevin (a type of chub), 20 barbel, 40 trout and 200 roach, worth 40 shillings and 20 rabbits worth 40 pence. In her will, dated 1601, Elizabeth Copestake of Alton bequeathed to Elizabeth Milward *"my worse* (probably *"worsted") petticoate, red petticoate and a worse kercheve and a mufler"*. 1851, John Millward (turner, chair maker), Castle Street, Eccleshall; 1851, John Milward, licensee at the Waggon and Horses, Woodhead, Cheadle. Several other variants also survive. Millard is a reduced form: 1646 Probate Inventory, John Milward of Penn, alternatively cited as John Millard, whilst Millard is corrupted further to Mallard: Hints parish register, 1776, James Millard (Mallard). Milward, in addition is altered to Mullard: Brierley Hill parish registers, 1805, Thomas Milward (1808, Thomas Mullard). Mellard is another possible corruption, although it is more likely to be an extended form of Mellor - compare Standon manor court rolls, 1718, W. Mellar, cited as William Mellard in 1720, fined an unspecified amount for stopping a road from Walford to Eccleshall. 1875, William Mellard (ironmonger), High Street, Newcastle-under-Lyme. Finally, after the fashion of the pairing Hayward-

Millwood
Milwood

Haywood, Milward is occasionally changed to Milwood, Millwood: Star Chambe
Proceedings, 1549, William Mylward (Mylwood) of Alstonefield; 1851, Willian
Millwood (butcher) of Wesley Street, Tunstall.

Windmill
Winmill

In parts of the county where power was lacking to drive the mills, windmil
were built to grind the corn. In 1305/6 Sir Roger de Morteyn, co-owner of th
manor of Walsall with the Paganels, made a grant of two mills in the fee of Walsal
that is, the water-mill at Bescot and the windmill at Walsall, to Henry de Prestwoc
in exchange for a share in a fishery. In 1666 John Windmill was exempt from an
hearth tax at Rowley Regis.

The mainstay of any medieval family was the loaf of bread, which was take
to the communal oven or bakehouse along with anything else that needed bakin
In 1370 John Maryott farmed from the mayor and community at Newcastle-unde
Lyme the common oven at 40 shillings per annum. This was the original meanii
of the word "farm" in the Middle Ages - to let - when it was common practice to l
out a manor or estate "at farm" and the farmer paid a fixed rent for the land, and a
agent collected all the rents from it. Ironically, this surname, the most down-to-ear
of all names associated with agriculture, turns out to be of Norman origin. From tl
accounts of Standon manor court (1444-1447), Thomas Pykkyn (farmer) of Weste
owed 2 shillings in rent arrears to the lord of the manor for the first two years an
another 7 shillings to be paid for the next 7 years. In 1587 William Farmar and h
wife Margaret handed over to Robert Whilton and John Elken a substantial acreag
of land, pasture, meadow and woods in Little Fenton and Botteslow. In return the

Farmer

received 100 marks of silver. Margery Farmer and Ranulph Dakin were married
Barlaston on April 24th, 1635 and the marriage of Mr Joseph Farmer and Mrs Sara
Boulton (both of Lane Delf, Stoke) took place at Swynnerton on September 27t
1753. Trade directories: 1851, Valentine Farmer (shoemaker) of Bowers, Stando
1875, James Farmer (dealer in second-hand goods), Chancery Lane, Longton.

In 1375 William de Bradwall rented the common oven at Newcastle-unde
Lyme at 40 shillings per annum for three years, on condition, that the oven was ke
in good repair at the end of his term, and that, in any week he would bake fo
quarters of corn and would serve well and faithfully all those who came to use tl

Backhouse
Bacchus
Baccas
Bachus
Backus

bakehouse. Anyone who was employed at the bakehouse has left progeny beari
such names as Backhouse, Bacchus, Baccas, Bachus or Backus. On one market da
at Newcastle in 1320, Agnes, wife of Robert del Bakhous and others were set up
and assaulted by Henry, the clerk of the Countess of Heleigh, Henry le Peleter ai
John de Iselwalle. Thomas and John Bakhowse enlisted for Aston and Doxey in t
1539 Muster. At Ranton Thomas Bacchus (1730), is alternatively known as Thom
Backas, and at Oulton near Kibblestone it was ordered by the Officer of the Pea
in 1743, that *"widow Backhouse to be allowed 3 yards of cloth for a gown"*. Sara
illegitimate daughter of Mary Backhouse, was baptised at Church Eaton on M
8th, 1803.

The persons chiefly responsible for baking bread were the "baker" or his female equivalent the "baxter", although this term was used mainly by men. In 1383 a jury was summoned to decide whether a messuage and 60 acres of land in Checkley were free alms pertaining to the Church of St. Mary in Checkley or the lay fee of Richard Walker, held conjointly by the latter with Thomas le Baker and four other locals. Nearly three hundred years later, the manor court at Tunstall, Stoke-on-Trent, in 1663, decreed, that Henry Baker should *"...scower his ditch between the Short hey and a parcell of land called the meadowe, being Richard Sherratt's land, before December 1st, on pain of 5 shillings"*. In 1676, it was agreed by a committee at Newcastle-under-Lyme, that *"...Susanna Baker (widow), living in Mr Beardmore's cottage, whereby she is in danger from fire, is to be placed in the almshouse now in possession of John Johnson..."* 1851, Edward Baker (church clerk), Manor House, Fulford; 1875, Stephen Baker (stationer), Trentham Road, Dresden; 1887, George Baker (signalman) of Victoria Road, Basford.

Baxter is far more sporadic in its distribution. In 1413, three of the Erdeswick clan of Sandon, namely Sampson, Roger and Robert, with other malefactors, collected a large body of men, arrayed as for war, from divers parts of Chester, with a view to interfering with the King's pleas. On the outskirts of Hixon they attacked and wounded Roger Baxter, Ralph Aleyn, Richard Hille and Henry Smyth, and would have killed them had it not been for the intervention of a great "posse" from Stafford. Richard Baxter alias Marche was baptised at Stowe-by-Chartley on May 2nd, 1586 and Helen Baxter and Thomas Bailey got married at Seighford on December 30th, 1742. In 1851 Richard Baxter (boiler-maker) lived in Canal Side, Stoke and Ephraim Baxter ran a beerhouse in Bridge Street, Longton.

In the Middle Ages the loaf was changed in weight, but not in price, according to the price of corn. For instance, in the fourteenth century the average rate for a quarter of corn is calculated to have been about 5/10d, and the unit of bread was a farthing loaf. In the assize of bread only three sorts were recognised - "wastel" - "well-baked bread of the finest flour", "coket" - "the second kind of best bread", and "simnel" - "twice baked bread used only during the season of Lent". Some bakers were often named from the type of bread they made. Old French "wastel" lives on as Wastell, Wastall, Washtell, Waistell, Wassall and Wassell. William Wastall's stillborn child was buried at Cheadle on April 9th, 1633 and in 1768 Charles Waistell witnessed the marriage of John Keeling of Shifnal and Sarah Wright at Weston-under-Lizard on December 29th.

However, Wassall and Wassell spellings are jumbled up with Worzill, Wisedell and Worsdell at Codsall (1771-1838). The latter two clearly point to a derivation from Over and Nether Wyresdale in Garstang parish, Lancashire, in the valley of the river Wyre (winding river), source of the more normal Worsdale, Worsdall: 1819, June 13th, Mary Worsdale married to Thomas Arblaster at Norton-in-the-Moors; 1907, Hannah Worsdale (warehouse woman), Beaufort Road,

Longton. Yet if the Wassall, Wassell forms developed first, then they may go bac
to Walsall, recorded as "Walsall otherwise Wassall" in 1591, or to any one of sever
locatives in Worcestershire - Wassall Grove in Hagley or Warshill Top Farm an
Wassell Wood in Kidderminster, all of which exhibit early forms like "Wassa
Wassell", whilst a further source - Wast Hills in Alvechurch, occurs
"Weorsethyll" in the eleventh century. These all contain the Old Saxon compoun
"weard-setl" - "guard-house, watch tower".

     Slightly inferior in quality to "wastel" was "coket" bread, which was th
stock in trade of Geoffrey Coket, cited for Tamworth and Wigginton in

Cockett
Cockitt

Inquisition post mortem of 1266. His descendants are now called Cockett
Cockitt. In the 1539 Muster John Coket was enrolled at Coven, Thomas Cockett
Dunston and Drayton and Edmunde Cokett at Tamworth. It has been proposed, th
this kind of bread got its name from the seal or "cocket" with which it was stampe
Identical with "coket" bread is "cockin-bread", one origin of the modern Cockin(g

Cockin(g)
Cockayne
Cocaine

Cockayne and possibly Cocaine: 1532, Thomas Cokyn of Mayfield; 1532, Mess
Thomas Kokyn of Grindon. Other possibilities include Middle English "cokaygn
- the name of an imaginary country, the abode of luxury and idleness, hence
nickname for someone accustomed to such an indolent way of life: 1516 St
Chamber Proceedings, John Cokayn of Stanshope; 1851, William Cockay
(farmer) of Wetton. Also to be weighed up is the locative Cocken in Dalton-
Furness, Cumbria, recorded as "Cokayn" in the fourteenth century, and pronounc
"Cockin", and a Saxon patronymic Coccing - "son of Cocc", plus the locati
Cocking north of Chichester - "(site) of Cocca's people". In Wales Cockin is fro
"coch" - "red-haired". 1907, J.V. Cockings (ironworker) of Mayer Street, Hanle

Whitebread
Whitbread

     White bread was an expensive luxury, since it was made only of white, th
is, best bread (from wheat), hence the surname Whitebread, Whitbread: Penkrid
parish registers, Thomas Wheatbread, buried on October 10th, 1606.

     Probably most speakers of English are unaware of any connection betwe
the two words "flour" and "flower". In fact, they are variant spellings of the sa
word. "Flower" has the more recent spelling but it retains the older botanical sen

Flower(s)

whereas "flour" originally signified "the choicest among a number of persons
things", then "the finest quality of meal from wheat or other grain" and even la
"any soft powder obtained by grinding seeds or grain". The surname Flower
therefore, may refer to a maker of flour: Tatenhill manor court rolls, 1340, Willi
Flour, but in the Middle Ages "flower" was also used of persons, usually with
epithet "sweet", besides being employed as a woman's name: Tatenhill manor co
rolls. 1346, John Flowerson. A rarer source is Middle English "floer" - an arr
maker. 1664, Kingsley parish registers, Ellen daughter of John Flower of Ipsto
baptised on November 20th. 1851, Joseph Flower (farmer) of Waterfall near Cal
1907, John Flowers (house painter), Leek New Road, Cobridge; 1907, Geo
Flower (potter), Nelson Place, Hanley.

lew
day

)

The similar name Flowerdew/Flowerday is a complete mystery. Edward Flowerdewe crops up as one of the barons of the Exchequer in a Staffordshire Quarter Sessions Roll, dated 1585. The earliest known recording is a certain John Floure-dieu for Norfolk (1541), which apparently points to the French "Fleure-dieu" - "flower of God", but this makes no sense at all.

Every year, round about February, hedges had to be cut and trimmed and ditches cleared, but surnames such as Hedge(s) and Hedger probably just applied to people who dwelt by some hedge or hedges: Katherine Hedges was buried at Barton-under-Needwood on June 4th, 1609 and Edward Hedger paid tax on one hearth at Rowley Regis in 1666.

Yet with the names Ditch, Dyche, Deetch, Deykes and Dyke(s) caution is called for. A toponymic for habitation by a ditch or dyke is the norm: 1327 Inquisition post mortem, Robert atte dike (locality uncertain) and 1332 Lay Subsidies, Henry atte dych, rated at 2 shillings and 5 pence for Leigh near Uttoxeter. 1473 Assizes, Edmund Dyche of Rugeley; 1612 Feet of Fines, Francis Dyche of Crakemarsh; 1907, Richard Dyche (potter), Pleasant Street, Burslem; 1907, Albert Dyche (potter) of Nash Peake Street, Tunstall. Joseph, son of Joseph and Anne Dikes of Standon, was baptised at Lapley on September 15th, 1751, and Sarah Dyke and Charles Tyrer (husbandman) celebrated their marriage at Church Eaton on July 26th, 1784.

However, during the Middle Ages, "Dick", the pet form of Richard, often appears as "Dike, Dyke", as exemplified in the Alrewas manor court rolls, where 1269, Peter son of Dyke is recorded as Peter son of Dike in 1272. Thus surnames such as Dick(e), Dicks and Dix are derived from the pet form "Dick", but names like Dike(s), Dyke(s), plus Deeks, Deakes, Deekes and Deex have a dual origin. Thomas Deykes of Stafford(1532), enrolled as Thomas Deyx in the 1539 Muster. Betley parish registers, 1801, Ann Deekes and Jos. Hassall (widower) were married at Betley on January 1st. 1907, Thomas Deakes (potter's presser) of Leopold Street, Fenton. The Dick(s) and Dix specimens include: 1851, John Dicks (farmer), Beech, Swynnerton; 1851, Charles Dix (brick, drain and pipe maker), Salt Heath and Marston; 1887, William Dick of Cobridge Road, Burslem.

Ditcher, Dicker and Dickman are either for habitation near some ditch or dike or for a person who was employed to dig ditches. In 1308 Thomas le Dycher was paying an annual rent of three shillings and nine pence on the Audley estates at Audley for one messuage and 3 acres of land, whilst at a session of the Tunstall manor court, convened in 1326, Roger Dycchere surrendered into the hands of the lord of the manor 4 acres of land and one quarantin of land (probably a fortieth of an acre). Maria Ditcher and Jonathan James got wed at High Offley on May 9th, 1709. In the same parish registers, Thomas Ditcher (1709), husband of Anna Bayly, is alternatively entered as Thomas Dicker in 1715.

The surname Dickman could also represent "servant of Dick" - compare

John Dikeman, who in 1227, along with some others, was sued by John, son
Swain for some lands in "Langenour". This is most likely a reference to Longr
near Wheaton Aston - "the long alder copse", as opposed to Longnor in the upp
Manifold valley - "the long ridge". At any rate the surname Dickman is pre
common in the Penkridge parish registers covering the period of 1683-1708: 168

Dickman   Susanna, wife of John Dickman, buried on September 14th; 1697, Mary, daugh
of Mary Dickman, baptised on May 3rd; 1708, Anne Dickman and Henry Jacks(
married on November 10th.

HERDSMEN

From the Staffordshire Domesday survey it emerges, that meadow was m(
plentiful on the flood-plain of the Trent, flowing north west to south east across t
centre of the county, and along the main tributaries - the Dove, Tame and the So
In the north eastern region, where the limestone valleys widened out, there w
excellent meadow and pasture land, as Dr. Plot observed in 1686:"...*a short, but fi
and sweet pasture, and large oxen. Much more can they breed and feed cattle in i
rich meadows that adorn the banks of the Trent, Blithe, Teme, Churnet, Hamps a
Manifold and more especially on the famous Dove banks"*.

It is reasonable to conclude therefore, that surnames associated with t

Coward   herding of cattle and sheep should be found in good numbers in these areas, a
Cowherd   indeed they are. Take a name like Coward, for instance. The noun "cowai
implies a person of despicable character, whereas the surname Coward (rar(
Cowherd) has a more honourable calling, being but a corrupted form of "cow-her(
a tender of cattle, a role which no doubt came second nature to John le Couher(
working for the lord of the manor at Bramshall near Uttoxeter in 1327, and wh(
tax for that year amounted to 2 shillings and 6 pence. In the same returns Richa
le Couherde handed over 18 pence at Ellenhall. Elizabeth Coward and Robert No
got married at Hints on December 9th, 1559. This is a surname deeply rooted
Staffordshire's medieval pastoral economy.

Geldard   The sterile or barren cattle were looked after by the Geldard, Geld;
Geldart   Gildart, or Gelder: Barton-under-Needwood parish registers. 1797, Mary Gild;
Gildart   one of the witnesses to the marriage of James Smith and Anne Scarborou;
Gelder   solemnized on August 25th; 1872, James Gildart (farmer) of Alrewas; 1907, M
Ellen Geldard (grocer, beer retailer) of Chapel Street, Fenton.

Calvert   The calves were the responsibility of the "calf-herd" - Calvert, Calve
Calverd   Calvard: 1576, Lawrence, base son of Joane Wegley and John Calvert, buried
Calvard   Alstonefield on October 10th; 1666, Thomas Calvert charged on 2 hearths at Bradn(
1761, Rupert Calvert of Cheadle married Mary Heacock of Barlaston at Barlast(
1875, James Calvert (butter, cheese and bacon factor) of Queen Street, Burslem.

In the main, the medieval ploughman preferred to use oxen for ploughing
arable land, finding horses much more expensive to keep, despite their grea

efficiency and pulling power. 1322/23 Minister's Accounts for Tatenhill, William le Oxhirde. This is contracted to Oxer.

The element "herd" leads an independent existence of its own in the sense of "herdsman" and survives in our county in the forms Herd, Heard, Hird and Hurd, the latter being the most persistent variant. In 1532 John Hurde and wife Isabel were resident in Uttoxeter with Stanton, east of the Weaver hills, home to Thomas and Ellen Hurde and family and William Hurde, his wife Agnes and their children. In 1603 Roger Cartlage of Burslem was fined 4 pence at Tunstall manor court for making an affray on Robert Hearde. John Hurd, who died of smallpox, was buried at Ellastone on July 20th, 1636. 1875, Thomas Hurd (second hand clothes dealer) of Waterloo Road, Burslem; 1887, Daniel Hurd (coal merchant) of Sneyd Street, Tunstall; 1907, Isaac Hurd (engineer) of New Street, Longton.

Herdsman too survives, together with Herdman and Hurdman. In 1344 Hugh le Herdemon of Newton was sued by Matilda, former wife of Philip, son of William de Draycote, for certain tenements, land, meadow and woods, and six shillings rent in Draycott-in-the-Moors, which she claimed as dower. Hugh did not appear, and the Sheriff was ordered to take the dower claimed into the King's hand, and to summon Hugh for a month from Michaelmas. Hearth tax contributions in 1666 included two from John Hurdman at Kibblestone, one from Richard Hurdman at Eccleshall and another two from John Hurdman at Almington near Tyrley. Rubina Hurdman owned a grocer's shop along Sun Street, Hanley in 1887.

There is frequent interchange between Hurdman and Hardman, as illustrated by Radulphus Hardman, married to Elizabeth Austin at Burslem on October 23rd, 1678. He is buried as Randle Hurdman on June 5th, 1717. His wife is probably identical with Elizabeth Hurdman, buried on May 15th in the same year. Hardman is usually derived from the Saxon personal name Heardmann - "hard (brave) man", synonymous with Hardeman/Hardiman: 1907, Charles H. Hardeman of Brampton, Newcastle-under-Lyme.

A herdsman who drove his herd of cattle or flock of sheep to market to be sold was known as a "drover": Henry le Drovere, taxed 18 pence at Whiston near Bickford in 1327, alternatively assessed as Henry le Carter in 1332. The "driver" too may have duplicated the same tasks as the "drover", but on occasion he could have been in charge of the plough team working on the arable land. Maria Driver married David Leah at the parish church of St. James the Great, Audley on June 14th, 1709, whilst John Driver and Elizabeth Bradshaw tied the knot at Keele on June 14th, 1801. If these two Drivers are related, then the date is a very strange coincidence indeed!

In a Statute of Edward III, dated 1363, the "days" are classified alongside *"tenders of oxen, cowherds, shepherds, swineherds and all other keepers of live-stock"*. They were dairymen or dairymaids, obviously involved in all the menial jobs in the dairy, which means literally "the place where the "day" carried out his or her daily chores". Originally, however, it simply denoted a female servant wh[o] kneaded bread. In 1367 Roger le Deye of Calton near Ilam Park was sued b[y] Nicholas le Beek (chivaler) for a messuage and a bovate of land in Calton. Th[e] tenement and land were recovered two years later. The surnames Day(e) and Dey[e] are also to be traced to a pet form of the Hebrew name David - "darling, friend". I[n]

Dey(e)
Day(e)
Dye

addition Day(e), Dey and Dye go back to the Welsh "Dai, Dei", a familiar form o[f] David in Wales and the Welsh border counties. Locally, of course, the noun "day[s]" is pronounced as "dee" and this is also reflected in the surnames Dee, Dea, whic[h]

Dee
Dea

with the addition of Dye, make up the triplet Dee-Day-Dye on the analogy of Le[e-] Lay-Lye. The Irish (O) Dee - "Ó Diaghaidh" - is an attenuated form of O Dea - [Ó]

O'Dee
O'Dea

Deaghaidh". Local inhabitants in 1532 comprise Richard Day (syngulman) at Lee[k,] William Day, wife Ellen and family at Colclough near Tunstall, and Joan D[e] (singlewoman) at Prestwood near Ellastone. Thomas Day was recruited at Bishop[s] Offley in the 1539 Muster. Wydowe Dye was buried at Ellastone on November 1st 1583. Baptisms at the Church of St. Mary, Swynnerton include Ellen, daughter [of] John and Dorothy Day on March 27th, 1698, and Jenny, daughter of John and Ma[ry] Day of the Row on August 14th, 1786. Jenny was actually born on the 9th. Fro[m] the Scriven report on the employment of children in mines (1842), we learn th[at] Samson Day, aged 11, had been working at Litley Dale Colliery, Cheadle [for] eighteen months, drawing corves for the butty, his father George Day. His workin[g] day began at five or six in the morning. 1851, Joseph Day (grocer, tea dealer), Ho[pe] Street, Hanley; 1875, Jos. Day (chimney sweeper), Stafford Street, Longton; 190[0,] James Dee (labourer), Broad Street, Burslem.

Dayus
Dyas
Dias

     Dayus, Dyas and Dias may sometimes designate an employee at t[he] dairyhouse but more to the point is the Welsh "Deio", a synonym for Dafydd, fou[nd] as Deyos, Dyas etc, especially in Shropshire and Cheshire. John Dyasse enrolled [at] Horton near Rudyard in the 1640 Muster as a member of the impressed band, a[nd] William, son of William and Anna Dias was christened at Lapley on February 23[,] 1723. Dayman, too, is another medieval term for a herdsman or dairyman, althou[gh] in Devonshire the word was applied to a herder of livestock who was hired by [the] day. Richard le Deymon, rated at 12 pence for the vill of Ipstones in 1332, lived [in] the very heart of Staffordshire's pastoral community. Later on the word diverg[ed]

Daymond
Dymond
Dimond
Dimont
Diamond

into forms such as Daymond, Dymond, Dimond, Dimont and Diamond, eg 18[73] Thomas Diamond (haberdasher) of Waterloo Road, Burslem; 1873, Reverend J[?] Dimont of Milton Vicarage; 1907, William Daymond (potter) of Homer Str[eet,] Hanley; 1907, A.W. Dimond (shop assistant), Vessey Street, Newcastle-und[er-] Lyme.

Bulman
Bullman
Bullas(s)
Bullis

     The farmhand who looked after the bulls lives on in the surname Bulm[an,] Bullman: Mary Bulman, married to John Burroughs at Ellastone in 1730 (date [not] given). Some of his time would have been taken up at the bull-house, one origi[n of] Bullas(s) and Bullis, and probably Bullows: 1700, Ellin, wife of John Bullas, bur[ied]

Mellor p. 158

Mellor p. 158

Miller p. 158.

Gater p. 172

Bullas(s)
Bullis
Bullows

at Audley on November 22nd. Yet spellings such as 1577, Richard Boulas of Swynnerton, 1584, Roger Bolas of Eccleshall and George Bowlesse, incorporated in the trained band at Kibblestone and Fulford in the 1640 Muster, could be variant of Bullas, Bullis, although more acceptable bases are the two Shropshire villages of Great Bolas and Little Bolas, situated north of Waters Upton, where the rivers Ten and Meese join forces. These localities refer to a wood where bows were obtained or a wood by a river bend.

Bullard

The fieldname "Bullasland" - 1531 - in Forton near Aqualate Mere, occurs as "Bullardes landes" in the fifteenth century, where the initial element is the surname Bullard. This has been taken as a corruption of "bull-herd", but more probable is a derivative of Middle English "bole" - "fraud, deceit", plus the suffix "-(h)ard", hence a deceiver or cheat, a publisher of false bulls, synonymous with

Bullar
Buller

Bullar, Buller: Alrewas manor court rolls, 1261, Nicholaus le bolur, one of the pledges for Geoffrey by the bridge; 1590 Feet of Fines, Richard Buller of Longdon 1627, Mode Buller, daughter of Thomas Buller, christened at Cheadle on October 26th; 1666, Richard Buller (gentleman) taxed on 2 hearths at Adbaston; 187? George Buller (beerseller), Winton Terrace, Stoke.

Cattel(l)
Catell
Cattle

The surname Cattel(l), Catell, Cattle is pure bluff, for it is a diminutive of "Cat", a short form of "Catelin", from Catherine: Adam Catel, rated at 2 shillings for the vill of Hixon in 1327; 1851, Chas. Cattell (corn miller) of Stoke, with house in Trent Vale. Best is another confidence trickster, for it is often equivalent

Best
Bester

to Bester, that is, a herdsman who looked after the beasts, from Old French "beste" but, when used as a nickname, as evidenced by Henry le Beste of Newborough near Needwood Forest (1327 Subsidies), then it is either descriptive of a brutal person with a vicious streak, or its direct opposite, namely, someone prone to foolish stupid behaviour. Almond Best and Ruth Turner were married at the parish church of St. Edward the Confessor, Cheddleton on January 3rd, 1685. 1851, Henry Best (brewer), Church Street, Tunstall; 1907, James Best and Company (china and clay producers, agents for cobalt ball clay), Queen Anne Street, Hanley.

Byers
Buyers

Byres

Byrom
Byron

The rare Byers, Buyers denotes a cow-man, employed at the byre (cowhouse), although two locatives must also be considered - Byers Green near Spennymoor in Durham - "the cowhouses", and Byres in east Lothian, the old barony, which the family of Lindsay held for centuries. 1912, Thomas Buyer resident at Balterley. Byrom, Byron designate a dweller at the cowsheds or go back to Byram in the parish of Brotherton, Yorkshire - "(site) at the cowsheds", or Byrom (old manor) in Winwick parish, Lancashire, probably identical in meaning 1403, John Byrom, admitted to his liberties at Newcastle-under-Lyme; 1912, M Byron of Caroline Street, Longton, surely an unintended joke at the expense of Lord Byron and Lady Caroline Lamb! But on second thoughts....

Faulds
Fold(s)
Foldes
Fould(s)
Fouldes
Fowlds

Faulds, Fold(s), Foldes, Fould(s), Fouldes, Fowlds are either toponymics habitation at the cattle pen(s), or for a farm worker employed there, or from Fa near Hanbury or Fould south east of Rudyard Hall, both referring to a fold or farmyard. In 1345 Roger de Falde of Abbot's Bromley brought a writ against Ralph, vicar of the church at Abbot's Bromley and John Bagod (chivaler) claiming that they had unlawfully ejected him from his holdings in the neighbourhood. Catherine Foldes and Sebastian Robothome were married at Audley on September 3rd, 1542; 1912, Hendry Faulds (surgeon), Lichfield Street, Hanley.

SHEPHERDS

To the medieval farmer sheep were his greatest asset, providing him with wool for weaving his clothes, milk to make butter and cheese, mutton to eat, skin with which parchment could be made and tallow for candles. The better candles of purified beeswax he obtained from the Chandler, Chantler. No doubt, Thomas le Chaundeler, rated at 12 pence for Tutbury in 1327, catered for the lighting needs of his local community. Elizabeth, daughter of William Chantler, was baptised at Audley on January 8th, 1539; 1907, Thomas Chandler (plasterer) of Ward Street, Hanley.

The basic name for a "shepherd" exists in a number of forms - Shepherd, Shepheard, Shephard, Sheppherd, Shepard, Shepeard, Sheperd, Sheppard, Shepperd and Shippard. In 1338, Adam le Shepeherde was fined 2 pence at Standon manor court for allowing six of his sheep to stray into the lord's enclosure. The local bailiff was his pledge. In 1428 Hugh Sheperd of Oakley, drover (which Oakley is not recorded), was sued by Richard Grey (knight) and John Wilford (armiger) for taking by force from Oakley, 600 sheep belonging to them, valued at £40. 1851, George Shepherd (farmer), Flashbrook, Adbaston; 1851, Reverend Henry James Shephard, curate at Forsbrook; 1875, Walter Sheppard, licensee of the Eagle and Child Inn in Mill Street, Hanley; 1907, Isaac Shepherd (blacksmith), Shaw Street, Newcastle-under-Lyme.

In coastal regions the surname Shipman generally denotes a seaman or sailor, but in inland counties such as ours the odds favour a sheep man or shepherd, since in some English dialects "ship" was a local form of "sheep". It is still with us in the expression "spoiling a ship for a ha'porth of tar" - "marring an enterprise by skimping on little details" - a reference to when tar was smeared on sheep to protect against destructive attacks of flies. Elizabeth, wife of Thomas Shipman, was buried at Brewood on March 5th, 1642 and in 1907, E. Shipman had a newsagent's and grocer's shop along Lord Street, Etruria.

The general term for someone who looked after sheep was "looker", but this could also describe a farm bailiff. Looker, Loker and Luker come from this source, but in the north east Luker is chiefly from Lucker not far from the North Northumberland Heritage Coast - "marsh frequented by sandpipers". In 1374 Henry de Delves sued in person Peter and Hugh Loker, Hugh le Harper and 3 others, for forcibly breaking down his fences at "Le Mote" in Betley, and treading

down and consuming his grass with their cattle. Samuel Looker was one of th
witnesses to the marriage of James Moss of Cheadle and Mary Fynney, celebrate
at Cheddleton on October 23rd, 1758.

Lambert
Ewart

The lambs and ewes were the responsibility of the "lamb-herd" and th
"ewe-herd" - Lambert and Ewart, yet there are a number of problems to iron o
here. Early specimens like Hugh Lambard of Stafford (1307 Assizes) and Thom:
Lambard of Fazeley near Tamworth, sued by Thomas de Arderne (chivaler) in 137
for stealing two of his swans and five cygnets, worth £10, are probably person
names going back to the Germanic "Lambert, Lanbert" - "land bright". It was :
favourite name in Flanders, where St. Lambert of Maestricht was highly venerate
The late old Saxon counterpart "Landbeorht" may also have contributed to th
spread of the surname. However, in our county, where "lamb" is altered to "lomt
and even "lumb", there is inevitable conflict with Lombard, Lumbard, whic

Lombard
Lumbard

denotes a Lombard, an immigrant from Lombardy. In the Middle Ages such Italia
visitors to our shores were moneylenders and bankers, and thus the name may eve
refer to "a banker". In an assize of 1293 Brankeleon le Limbard is described :
canon of the Church of St. Cedde at Lichfield.   Nicholas Lumbart, who
contributing 4 shillings lay subsidy at Acton Trussell in 1332, is most likely
variant of Lambert. Judeth Lambert, who was exempt from hearth tax at Newcastle
under-Lyme in 1666, was allowed 9 pence per week from the overseers of the poc
for 1683/84. In 1767, Elener Lambert - *"a hospetel child"* - was buried at Croxde
on September 3rd. The Kidsgrove National School, where William Lambert wa
master in 1842, was supported by the children's weekly payments of 2 or 3 pend
each. The money from the boys in the school made up Mr. Lambert's salary, whic
amounted to about £50 per annum. In 1887 George T. Lambert (tinplate worke
lived in Stafford Street, Longton. In the Burslem parish registers, Thomas Lambat
signed his name as Lambart on November 11th, 1799, when he got married to Sara

Lambeth

Hall. Hence Lambeth, locally is a variant of Lambert but some families calle
Lambeth could have ancestry in Lambeth, Greater London - "harbour where lamb
were shipped".

Ewart

Now and then the surname Ewart can be a French form of the Saxon Edwar
- "prosperity guard", as in Ewardus diaconus (deacon) in a thirteenth century dee
from the Chartulary of Stone Priory. The isolated John Yward (sic), rated at 1
pence for Harlaston east of Lichfield in 1327, may just be a lazy spelling fc
"Yoward" - "ewe herd". 1907, John Ewart (lodgeman), Furnival Street, Cobridge
The herdsman who kept an eye on the wethers in a flock of sheep, that is, th
castrated rams, was the "wetherherd": 1327 Lay Subsidies, William le Wetherherd:
taxed at 14 pence for Dunston near Penkridge. This normally results in the moder

Wetherhead
Weatherhead
Weatherhed

surnames Wetherhead and Weatherhead: Brewood parish registers, 1623, Ros:
Weatherhed and Richard Hust (sic), married on November 4th, 1623, and Penkrid;
parish registers. 1707, William, son of John Weatherhead, baptised on Februar

26th.   It is in these pages, where the name undergoes some very strange transformations, for Thomas Weatherhead of Penkridge (1672), has a son called Thomas Whetherer in 1648, and John Wetherer (1679) is also known as John Weatherer in 1681, but is buried as John Weatherhogg in 1702.   1887, Sarah Jane Weatherhogg (innkeeper), Queen's Inn, Liverpool Road, Stoke and High Street, Stoke; 1907, Owen Weatherhogg (draper, milliner and outfitter), High Street, Stoke. Isabell Weatheall (sic) is baptised on December 12th 1620, and this is clearly a misprint for Weatherall, an obvious variant of Weatherer, based on the analogy of the local Tunstall-Tunster.   Hence names like Weatherall, Weatherill, Weatherhill, Wetherall etc are sometimes from this occupational source, but some of our local families bearing these surnames must be immigrants from the north west with their roots in the locality Wetheral near Carlisle - *"piece of flat alluvial land by the side of a river, where wethers were kept"*.   Roger Whetherall and Fraunces Hopton were married at Eccleshall on October 12th, 1574; 1851, Thomas Weatherhill (tailor), High Street, Longton; 1907, Enoch Weatherall (miner) of Booth Street, Tunstall; 1907, Mary Ann Weatherall of Albert Street, Chell.

SWINEHERDS AND GOATHERDS

Since pigs featured prominently in medieval life there ought to be ample evidence in the surname record, but there are no signs in our county of such names as Swinerd, Swinnard - "swineherd", Hoggard, Hoggart, Hogarth - "keeper of the hogs" or Forward, Forwood, a compound of the Saxon "for" - "pig, hog" and "weard" - "guard".   The most common term for a swineherd in medieval Staffordshire is For(e)man - the Saxon "for", as in Forward, plus "mann".   In the 1327 lay subsidy returns contributions included 6 pence from Ralph le Forman at Creighton and 12 pence from Thomas le Foremon at Cauldon.   During the sixteenth and seventeenth centuries the surname For(e)man is concentrated in the same general area, that is, around Alton, Ramshorn, Ellastone, Rocester and Uttoxeter. Rycharde, son of Thomas Forman, baptised at Ellastone on November 14th, 1541 and Richard, son of Thrustan and Alis Forman, baptised on February 25th, 1587, whilst in the 1666 hearth tax returns widdow Forman is charged on one hearth at Uttoxeter, and likewise, Robert Forman on one each at Alton and Ramshorn.   1907, Frank Foreman (plumber) of Francis Street, Longton; 1912, Harry Foreman (miner) of Oldfield Street, Fenton.   Any resemblance to "foreman" - "boss", is, of course, purely accidental.

The Saxon "gat" - "goat" gave rise to Gothard - "goat herd", as in Robert le Gateherde, rated at 18 pence for Farley near Alton in 1327 and 1851, Ann Gothard, proprietor of an academy or school in Foregate Street, Stafford, and also to the synonymous Goater, 1402 Feet of Fines, John Goter of Wolverhampton, and Gater, which exhibits the unrounded northern vowel.   Yet two other scenarios are possible here - in the Danelaw counties Gater denotes a dweller by some road, from Old

Norse "gata" - "road, path", but outside the Danelaw Gater can also refer
habitation near some gate.   In 1677 John Gater was elected headborough fo
Thursfield (forerunner of the parish constable). On October 4th, 1783 the oversee
of the poor granted 3 shillings to Hannah Gater of Betley for the purchase of
second-hand gown.   1851, John Gater (clerk), Tunnel Mouth, Ravenscliff
Tunstall; 1851, William Gater (tailor) of Gillow Heath, Biddulph. Gater, on ra
occasions, alternates with Gayter, since John Gayter (potter), who married Phoel
Smith of Leek at Burslem on July 1st, 1754 signs his name in the register as Joh
Gater.

Gater
Gayter

HORSES

The horse was such an essential part of the medieval economy, that it had
mystique all of its own.   Throughout the Middle Ages horse fairs were he
regularly all across the country. One such fair took place at Penkridge, attractir
horse breeders, dealers, buyers, sellers and spectators from miles around. The
were horses to suit all tastes and needs - lumbering cart-horses and powerful pacl
horses, impressive chargers and war-horses, nimble palfreys for the ladies ar
priests, unbroken colts with flying hooves and mares with their new foals. In tho
days, everyone who could afford to, knew how to ride a horse, but horses were ve
expensive, for, at a time when an ox could be bought for 13 shillings, an ordinar
riding horse such as a rouncy might cost over £3. Anketill le Corser of Lichfie
(1227 Assizes) - "jobber, horse dealer", may well have bought and sold horses
this prestigious fair at Penkridge, and his descendants live on in the names, Corse
Causer and Cawser: Robert, son of John and Jane Cawser, baptised at Barton-unde
Needwood on January 20th, 1801; 1851, Thomas Causer (farmer), Bromley Woo
Abbot's Bromley; 1907, William Corser (fireman), Stamer Street, Stoke.

Corser
Causer
Cawser

The surname Jobber, Jobar, Jubber actually referred to someone who let ou
horses on hire for a particular job or for a stipulated period of time, but other origir
are in the offing, including a maker of "jobbes, jubbes" - large vessels for holdin
liquor (approximately 4 gallons) or a person who made "jubes", that is, woolle
garments for men.   Elizabeth Jobber and Andrew Farecloe (probably fc
Fairclough), married at Seighford on June 21st, 1618 and Daniel Jobber and Rache
Willcox, wed at Penkridge on September 29th, 1711.

Jobber
Jobar
Jubber

In all likelihood Hors(e)man was a basic name for anyone who looked aft
the horses on the manor, and fed and groomed them, as typified by Willia
Horseman, tenant of the Audleys at Alstonefield in 1308, paying 14$^{1}/_{2}$ pence rent p
annum for one third of a messuage and 11 acres of land. 1907, George Horsma
(borough yard foreman), Albany Road, Stoke; 1539 Muster, Thomas Horskeper c
Horsley. Thomas del Stable, one of the servants of the abbot at Dieulacres Abbe
in 1414, probably performed similar tasks to William Horseman at Alstonefield
keeping the stables clean and tidy, reporting any signs of disease in the horses to th

Hors(e)man

marshall, and so on. Descendants of medieval stablemen such as Thomas survive in the names Stable(s) and Stabler: 1588 Feet of Fines, Francis Baker otherwise Stables of Bradnop; Rowley Regis parish register, 1542, Richard Stabler. Ostler, source of Hostler, Hosler, Ostler, originally signified a person who received, lodged and entertained guests, especially in a monastery, or an innkeeper. Only towards the end of the Middle Ages did it take on such meanings as a stableman. In 1423 William Osteler of Abbot's Bromley sued William Gryffyn of Walsall (pardoner) and Thomas Mitton of Wirley (yeoman) for a debt of 6 marks. Elisabeth, daughter of William and Jane Ostler, was baptised at Trentham on September 2nd, 1759. The reduced form Ostle, Hossell is from Old French "ostel, hostel" and denoted a keeper of an inn or lodging house: 1327 Lay subsidy rolls, John del Hostel, rated at two shillings at Leek.

One base for the surname Hackney is an occupational term for someone who looked after the "hackneys", a medium-sized ambling horse or mare ridden by medieval ladies who accompanied the chase. Later the name applied to a horse that was let out for hire, whence "hackney carriage", although this has also been derived from the place Hackney in north London where horses were pastured. Scott uses the word in his novel "Ivanhoe". "He rode not a mule, like his companion, but a strong hackney for the road, to save his gallant warhorse". If Hackney comes from a placename, then several candidates are at hand - Upper Hackney, north of Matlock Bank (of unknown origin), whilst also sharing the spoils are Hackney in Middlesex and Hackney in Wickhamford near Evesham, Worcestershire, both perhaps for "Haca's island". 1851, Cordelia Hackney (shopkeeper) of Hope Street, Hanley; 1851, Ralph Hackney, owner of a beerhouse in Biddulph; 1875, Georgina Hackney (dressmaker), Northwood, Hanley.

The most common word for "saddle horse, riding horse" was "palfrey", which was eminently suitable for a lady or cleric as they rode forth in a hawking party with the lord and lady of the manor. Chaucer's monk sat astride a "palfrey", which "...*was as brown as is a berrye...*" This gives the surnames Palfrey and Palfree (no examples), and the extended name Palfreyman, Palphreyman - the man in charge of the "palfreys". Originally it had been a relay horse ridden by messengers in Imperial Rome. For the privilege of holding a market and a fair at Abbot's Bromley, the Abbot of Burton Abbey (holder of the manor), gave 2 palfreys until the young King (Henry III) came of age. In 1306 Peter le Palefraymon with Peter de Fulham (chief forester of Needwood), and many others came to the house of Juliana de Myneres, broke down the fence of her park, took away all the beasts and killed two of her colts. In 1397 Alice, formerly wife of Nicholas Palfreyman of Hilderstone, was unlawfully ejected from a messuage at Stone by John Grendon of Kibblestone, William Walker of Stone and 3 others. Ffrancis, son of William and Agnes Palfreyman, was baptised on October 18th at the Church of St. Mary, Swynnerton. 1907, Charles Palphreyman (potter), Herbert Street, Burslem; 1907,

Chaucer's Wife of Bath and Prioress mounted on a Hackney and a Palfreyman (p. 173)

Isaac Palfreyman (fried fish dealer), Leonard Road, Birches Head; 1907, George Palfreyman (miner), Windmill Street, Tunstall.

Ambler is rare: 1875, Ambler and Brooks (curriers, leather cutters), Bath Street, Burslem. This is open to several interpretations; a stableman who tended the "amblers" - "ambling horses, mules", a nickname for someone with an ambling gait, or an enameller, from Old French "esmailleur" with intrusive "b".

The most valuable horses of all, of course, were the stud horses or stallions, and there are several surnames connected with the upkeep of such irreplaceable livestock. Richard Stede, assessed at 2/3d for Tunstall (Stoke-on-Trent) in 1332, was probably entrusted with their care, but William le Stede of Brewood (1315 Inquisition) could be a nickname for a person who was as high-spirited as a stallion - the modern surnames Stead, Stede, Steed, Steeds and Steede. Yet these might also be derived from the Saxon "stede" - "farm", applied to a farmer or farm worker. Christofer Stede and Hellen Blacklache got married at Ellastone on June 6th, 1548 and in 1907 Charlotte Stead sold tripe and fish at her shop in Carlisle Street, Longton. The allied name Steadman, Stedman, Steedman preserves all the senses inherent in Stead except the nickname. In 1324 Robert le Stedman of Swynnerton, and numerous others were pardoned by the King (Edward II) for the rape of Joan, formerly wife of Peter de Greseley of Drakelow, which had allegedly taken place at Swynnerton. In the sixteenth and seventeenth centuries the surname Steadman is extremely prolific around Standon, Chapel Chorlton, Slindon, Coldmeece, Eccleshall, Seighford and Chebsey. During the reign of Elizabeth I Francis Stedman had to sweep the street in Eccleshall "from the cross to Walter's Smithy" every fortnight all the year round. At Rocester, the burial took place on August 4th, 1639, of John Stedman, who *"was slaine with a sith"*, that is, a scythe. 1851, George Stedman and Company (curriers, leather cutters), The Green, Stafford; 1875, Thomas Stedman (joiner), Hope Street, Hanley.

Unfortunately, a handful of curious contradictory recordings complicate the situation at Stafford. For instance, in the parish registers of the Church of St. Mary, besides the normal Steedmans and Stedmans we find 1566, Edward Stedmore and 1640, Joan Stidmoore, which are to be examined alongside Edmond Skydmore, member of the 1539 Muster at Stafford, and Frauncis Stydman of Eccleshall (1582). Stydman and Stidmoore came about by analogy with a name like Blakeman-Blakemore, whilst a form such as Skydmore could have developed from Stydman with the common confusion between the letters "k" and "t". Nevertheless, if Skydmore is the original surname, then this is to be traced to an unidentified locality in the west or south west of England, together with its offshoot Scudamore: 1778, Elizabeth Scudamore (Newcastle-under-Lyme).

The farm worker or servant, who is most associated with looking after the stud horses is the "stod-herd", which has given us the names Stoddard, Stoddart, Stodart, Stodhart, Studart, Studdard, Studdert. In 1396 Richard Stodehard and 9

Stoddard
Stoddart
Stodart
Stodhart
Studart
Studdard
Studdert

others were sued by Thomas Beek (chivaler) for cutting down his trees a underwood at Bradnop to the value of £10. At an assembly in Newcastle-und Lyme Guildhall, April 22nd, 1653, Anthonie Stoddard and Thomas Jeninges w appointed supervisors for the highways. Bucknall cum Bagnall parish registe 1812, Mary Stoddart of Stoke (signed Stoddard); 1875, James Stodda (photographer), Gower Street, Longton; 1907, Mark Stoddart (sand merchan Louise Street, Burslem.

Stothard
Stothert
Stuttard

The very similar Stothard, Stothert, Stuttard refers to a man who kept ste or bullocks, an oxherd, since the initial element is the Saxon "stott" - originally inferior kind of horse, only later a young castrated ox or steer. John le Stothe tenant of the Audleys at Alstonefield in 1308, held one stall at an annual rent of pence and John Stott (ground collier) married Mary Gallimore at Stoke-on-Trent January 22nd, 1763. In 1907 Herbert Stott had a greengrocery business alo Lonsdale Street, Stoke. Here the name Stott probably applies to a person who w as wild and untamed as a young steer or bullock.

Sumpter
Sunter

Ancestors of anyone by the name of Sumpter or Sunter drove a packhors Old French "sometier", perhaps in one of the teams of packhorses, used for carryi salt along the ancient "saltways", that criss-crossed the Staffordshire Moorlan starting out in Congleton to the west and wending their way to Winster n Matlock. Roger le Somiter was rated at 3 shillings for Rocester in the 1332 ▮ subsidies and Anne and John Sumpter were ineligible for any hearth tax Coppenhall and Butterhill, south west of Stafford in 1666. In 1907 John Sunter listed as an agent, Arbour Street, Hanley.

Coltman

Coltard
Coltart
Colthard
Colthart
Coulthard
Coulthart

The colts were tended by the Coltman. In 1412 John Weston was claimi a debt of 16 pence from John Coltmon at Alrewas. This debt was eventua resolved when Coltmon sought a licence to concord. 1912, William Coltm (traveller), Prince's Road, Stoke-on-Trent. The "colt-herd" survives as Colta Coltart, Colthard, Colthart, Coulthard and Coulthart: 1907, E. Coulthart (engrav of Alexander Road, Oakhill.

2. FOOD AND DRINK

BUTCHERS AND COOKS

It has often been pointed out, that it was the Saxon who looked after the "ox cows, calves, sheep, swine, boar", and "poached" the "deer", all basic Germa words, but it was the Norman lord of the manor who consumed them and in so doi converted them into the Norman French "beef, veal, mutton, pork, bacon, braw and "venison". This is generally explained from the masters leaving the care of t living animals to the peasants, as we have seen, whilst they themselves feasted the cooked flesh. However, this is too naive an assumption, since it may also contended that the use of the French words is due to the superiority of the Fren cuisine, which is apparent in other imported Norman words like "sauce, boil, f roast, toast, pastry, soup" and so on. Even the humble "breakfast" is English compared with the more sumptuous Norman meals such as "dinner" and "supper".

Equally the vocabulary employed in the slaughter of the animals and the butchery of the meat in preparation for the table conveys the same wide gulf in status between master and serf. To the Saxons with their earthy turn of phrase the butcher was a "cutter" or "hewer" of flesh, in contrast to the Norman "bocher, boucher", which ultimately derives from Old French or Provençal "buc", later "bouc" - "he-goat". It was presented before the King (Henry V) at Lichfield, 1414, that John Flesshehewer of Uttoxeter, bocher, on the Wednesday, the Feast of the Nativity of the Blessed Mary, 1408, had feloniously killed one Thomas Leylond of Loxley, by striking him on the head with a staff, and that John Myners of Uttoxeter (bayly) and William Myners of the same (gentylman) and others named, had aided and abetted the said John Flesshehewer in the said felony. This is abbreviated to Flesher, which is then easily absorbed by Fletcher, as in the modern Fletcher Gate in Nottingham, formerly known as "Flesshewergate" - "the street of the butchers". 1887, Flesher and Company (wholesale druggists), Chetwynd Street, Wolstanton.

Sleigh in his History of Leek comes up with 1318, Thomas dictus (called) le Botcher of Dieulacres Abbey, who possibly slaughtered sheep and other livestock reared by the monks. The surname Butcher occurs in several forms - Butcher(s), Bucher, Boucher, Boutcher, Bowcher and Bowker. The latter is mainly a northern English variant, but it is fairly common in our county: Trentham parish register, 1627. Mathew Bowker; 1851, John Bowker (brazier, tinner), High Street, Stoke; 1875, Sarah Bowker (draper), Keeling's Lane, Hanley. Bowker could occasionally stand for Booker in the sense of a writer of books, a scribe, or even be a derivative of "bouken" - "to buck, steep in lye", hence a bleacher, e.g. 1327 Lay subsidies, Roger le Boukere, rated at 2 shillings for the vill of Ashley near Mucklestone. Richard Booker, one of the assessors for the "Pole money" at Newcastle-under-Lyme on September 19th, 1660 (a poll tax, levied at a fixed rate per head for every person in the borough), appears as Richard Bowker in 1657, appointed with 4 other burgesses to see *"that the lead that lay over the Chauncell shall be sould and a roofe of timber bought and layd over the same..."* In 1851 Thomas Booker (butcher) lived in New Street, Burslem. Butcher is somewhat scarce: 1720, Izabel Butcher and Thomas Stoakes, married at Seighford on April 20th; 1907, James Butcher (boiler maker), Cannon Street, Hanley; 1907, John Butcher (miner) of Nelson Street, Wolstanton.

The butcher who killed or slaughtered his own animals sometimes ended up with a name like Slaughter, but this is also a locative traceable to Upper and Lower Slaughter about 10 miles east of Cheltenham - "farmstead by a slough or muddy place", e.g. Register of Robert de Stretton, 1361, John de Sloughtre of Quatt near Bridgnorth. Allice Slaughter married Thomas Byby at Sedgley on May 5th, 1641.

The imported term "macegref" - "butcher" is responsible for the modern

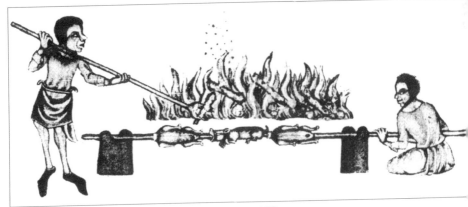

Bacon p. 179

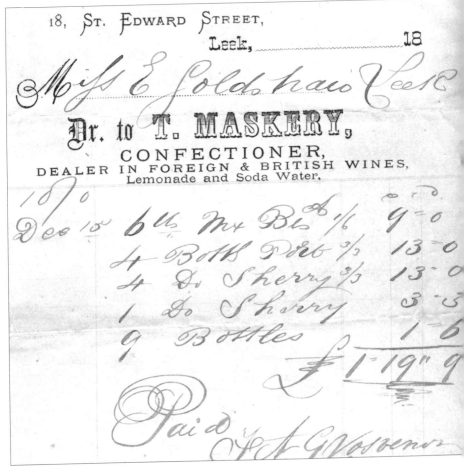

Maskery p. 179

y
ey
y

names Maskery, Maskerey and Maskrey: 1532, Richard Maskre, Agnes his wife and family, resident at Hamstall Ridware; Tatenhill manor court rolls, 1650, Robert Mascari (sic) of Callingwood; 1851, Francis Maskery (baker, flour dealer) of Spout Street, Leek; 1875, Samuel Maskrey (shopkeeper) of Mollart Street, Hanley; 1907, Harry Maskery (saggar maker) of Goldenhill Road, Fenton; 1907, William Maskery (mechanic), Bath Street, Tunstall.

The cured flesh of the pig - "bacon" - also denoted fresh pork, and so the surname Bacon usually referred to a seller or butcher of such meat. Richard Bacun, nephew of Earl Ranulph de Gernons of Chester, founded the Augustinian Abbey at Rocester circa 1142. The modern surname can also be derived from the accusative of the Germanic name "Bacco". The nominative form - "Bacus" - occurs circa 1113 in the Burton Abbey charters for Wetmore and Horninglow. In addition the name could signify a person who lived at the sign of the pig: 1327 Lay subsidies, Richard atte Bacun of Kinver. On the death of Nicholas Hyde, William Bacon became Rector at Standon in 1526. Another William Bacon (webster) who died at Alton in 1609, left *"....four weavers looms in his shoppe"*. John Bacon of Rocester and Elizabeth Cotton got married at Ellastone on October 12th, 1638; 1851, Thomas Bacon (clerk) of Compton, Leek; 1875. J.P. Bacon (master of the School of Art), King Street, Newcastle-under-Lyme.

Some obsolete names for butchers are: 1250 Assizes, Andrew Cutvel - "cut calf"; 1327 Subsidies, John Choppekoc of Yoxall - "chop cock"; 1327 Subsidies, John Cullebole of Creighton near Uttoxeter - "kill bull", a slaughterman, similar to Kellogg - "kill hog".

COOKS

Even though the Normans were supposedly more versed in the culinary arts than the Saxons, the native term "cook" was not supplanted by the Norman "queu, keu, kieu". Occasionally, however, they were employed together with reference to the same person: 1327 Subsidies, Gilbert le Keu of Lichfield, assessed as Gilbert le Cok in 1332. The former survives as Kew, Le Keux or Lequeux. In the list of names derived from trades in the 1666 Hearth tax returns, the surname Cook(e), Cookes, Coke ranks 9th after Smith, Taylor, Turner, Wright, Walker, Cooper, Clark and Hall. With the modern reliance on state-of-the-art cookers and microwaves, and so forth, it is all too easy to dismiss medieval cookery as crude and primitive. Yet, this picture would be totally false. Of course, there would be the traditional boar's head at Christmas, but in the wealthier households a wide variety of stews, soups, pies, fritters, pasties, fish and wild game of all kinds graced the lord's table. Every conceivable herb and spice was used to flavour the meals, with mustard being a special favourite. Besides the cooks in the castles of the king and his barons, there were cooks, who prepared the meals in the wayside inns and taverns, in the religious houses, in every inhabited village and hamlet throughout the land, in the woods and

forests, where outlaws took refuge from their persecutors, and of course there wa
Chaucer's cook, who accompanied the pilgrims on their journey to Canterbury an
who *"...coude rost, and seeth (boil), and broil, and frye, maken mortreux (a hash c
stew), and well bake a pie..."*. No wonder, then, that the surname proliferated in th
way it did. In 1384 Thomas Cooke was elected unto his liberties of the borough a
Newcastle-under-Lyme. He took the oath and had to pay ten shillings, half th
amount at Easter, and the remainder at Christmas. Adam Colclough was his pledge
Brother John Cooke was, very appropriately, in charge of the stores and provision
at Stone Priory in 1518 and Thomas Cook was curate at Bagnall in 1666. Mone
spent on the Kibblestone Quarter in 1745 for poor relief included one shilling an
sixpence allowed to Jane Cook for shoes for her girl (child boarded with her unl
the age of 8). 1851, Joseph Cook (blacksmith) of Cellarhead; 1875, Samuel Cook
(toll lessee), High Street, Fenton; 1887, James Cook (innkeeper and brewer), Jol
Colliers, Scotia Road, Tunstall.

Cookson
Cuckson
Cuxon
Cuxson

The patronymic Cookson, Cuckson, Cuxon, Cuxson - "son of the cook" -
not so widely dispersed. William filius coci (son of the cook) paid his 14 penc
subsidy at Caverswall in 1327. Trade directories for 1907 list: Joseph Cooksc
(carter), King's Terrace, Basford and William Cookson (platelayer) of Albert Stree
Stoke. Although definite proof has not yet been found, there could very well b
some overlap with the similar name Coxon, Cockson, Coxen - "son of Cock".

Coxon
Cockson
Coxen

1466 Richard Cokson and his wife Edith sued John Gully of Mavesyn Ridwa
(clerk) and Thomas Lyot of Lichfield (chaplain), for taking their goods and chatte
from Stafford valued at £10 and illegally detaining them. Ellen Coxon
Cheddleton married Edward Dresser of Burslem at the church of St. Edward t
Confessor, Cheddleton on May 9th. 1686. In 1841 William Coxon, aged 12, worke
6 days a week as a figure maker for John Shaw at Charles Meigh's Earthenwa
Factory, Bucknall Road, Hanley. He received a weekly wage of 2/6d. 1851, Si
Coxon (hairdresser), Chapel Street, Cheadle; 1875, Elijah Coxon,(greengroce
Marsh Street, Hanley; 1907, Edmund Coxon (kilnman), Elliott Street, Stoke.

BUTTER AND CHEESE

Two natural by-products of Staffordshire's thriving medieval pastoral econol
were butter and cheese. The surname Butter(s) has been prominent in the nol
western sector of the county since at least the 1300s - 1327 Subsidies, Richa

Butter(s)

Buttere, coughing up 18 pence to the tax collectors at Audley. This could deno
that Richard made and sold his own butter, whilst less attractive is a nickname fro
Old French "butor" - "bittern", applied to anyone with a booming voice, w
another occupational term for a keeper of the casks or bottles an also-ran. From
1500s onwards the Audley parish registers teem with the name. At the Great Co
of John Audley, Lord of Audley, held on the Friday after the Conception of
Blessed Virgin Mary, December 10th, 1512, Thomas Butter begged licence to ad

John Bolton to 5 acres of land in Bignall End, comprising pastures called "Walfeld", "Ryefeld" and "le Whetefeld", plus "le Flat". 1851, Richard Butters (gamekeeper), Blackwaters, Woodland Division, Eccleshall; 1875, Frank Butter (cashier), Lloyd's Banking Company Ltd, Cobden Street, Dresden.

The surname Cheese referred to a maker or seller of cheese, as exemplified by Alfewine Chese of Haughton south west of Stafford, quoted in a twelfth century deed from the Charters of the Priory of St. Thomas, Stafford. The registers of the Cathedral Church of St. Mary and St. Chad, Lichfield record, that Jane Cheese got married there to Francis Overton of Pattingham on April 15th, 1708. Newcastle-under-Lyme parish registers, 1797, Richard Cheese (potter) and Elizabeth Finney (both of Stoke), wed on July 30th.

HERBS AND SPICES

Today's cooks are spoilt for choice when it comes to creating tasty recipes, surrounded as they are by a seemingly endless variety of exotic herbs and spices from almost every corner of the globe. Yet medieval cooks, too, especially in the rich households, often resorted to strange-sounding spices imported from abroad to disguise the dryness and saltiness of the foods which our ancestors lived on. For example, zedoary, a ginger-like substance prepared from the rootstock of an East Indian plant, but such spices were far too expensive for the peasants eking out a living in the countryside. The cooks, here, in their rural isolation, had to make do with herbs and spices grown in their own back yard, perhaps a small piece of arable land or patch of ground close by a rickety, thatched cottage, or in some garden tended by an individual like William de Gardino, cited in an Inquisition, made at Wolverhampton on Wednesday next after the Feast of St. Peter ad Vincula (August 1st), 1294. This lives on as the surname Garden: 1539 Muster, William Garden of Stafford. Jardin(e) is from Old French "jardin" with the same meaning.

The more common name for anyone who cultivated herbs, spices and vegetables in the Middle Ages was the familiar "gardener", source of Gardiner, Gardener and Gardner. In 1306, Roger le Gardiner, indicted for stealing a colt from Joan de Myners and burning down her close at Blakenhale (probably Blakenhall near Yoxall), was acquitted. In a curious case, dated 1413, the vill of Weston-upon-Trent paid a fine of 4 shillings, the exact value of a sword with which John Gardyner had been feloniously killed by Stephen Benet of Creswalle (perhaps Creswell near Seighford rather than Cresswell not far from Saverley Green). But far more chilling than either of these is an extract from the Sessions Records of Newcastle-under-Lyme for 21st March, 1703, where Elizabeth Gardiner (widow) was accused of receiving stolen goods of and from one John Birks, a servant of Mr Thomas Burton, knowing them to be such. After she pleaded guilty to the charge, the Court decided that *"the said Elizabeth Gardiner for her said offence and misdemeanour, be, tomorrow, being the 22nd day of this instant month of March, between the hours of nine and eleven in the morning, public set and fixed in the Whipstock, and ther* *either by the Constables of this borough, or by their procurement, whipped upon he* *naked body betwixt the shoulders and the waist, until her body by such whipping b* *made bloody...."* Such brutal public floggings are a painful reminder of a inglorious chapter in the history of our island. In the 1871 Census Catherin Gardener of Stafford Street, Eccleshall, is described as a retired tanner and in 187 Jesse Gardiner (hosier) lived in Queen Street, Burslem.

Garth

In the Danelaw counties the Viking word for a garden, or any enclose ground or paddock was "garth" and so the surname Garth came to denote a perso who was in charge of such a place. In 1532 John Gargthe (sic) and his former wive Elizabeth, Phyllis and Cicely and family were amongst the inhabitants at Mavesy Ridware.

Plant

Any medieval villager who had "green fingers", so to speak, could also ver easily acquire a surname such as Plant, from the Saxon "plant" - "plant, tree". H horticultural expertise complemented the cook's culinary skills. In 1397 Peter c Legh sued eight locals including John and Richard Plont for trespassing on his lan at Quarnford with their herds of cattle and leaving them there to graze at the heart's content. He claimed damages of £10. The spelling "Plont" in the extract the Staffordshire pronunciation of "Plant", but the surname after the Middle Ages nearly always Plant, apart from Thomas and John Plont, enrolled at Swynnerton the 1539 Muster, William Plont at Maer, Thomas Plont at Stafford, and Nichola Plonte at Darlaston near Stone. In 1840 George Plant, aged 15, was drawing corve for the butty John Lowndes at Delph House Colliery, Cheadle; 1851, James Pla (corn miller), Mill Bank, Biddulph; 1851, Jonathan Plant (whitesmith), Spo Street, Leek; 1875. Thomas Plant (licensee), Saracen's Head, The Meir.

Spicer

Whether the spices were aromatic or pungent, home-grown, imported t Venetian merchants from the Far East or brought back by enterprising Crusade from the Mediterranean, it was still up to the "spicer" to build up a regular cliente and make a profit out of them. At the Great Court of Tunstall, held on Wednesda after the Feast of St Michael (4th October 1363), Nicholas Mayot, headborough Brieryhurst (between Mow Cop and Kidsgrove) proposed that John Spicer shou be fined 6 pence for insulting John, son of John de Drakeford, and 3 pence f waylaying the same. In 1375 Thomas le Spycer paid 15 shillings to the borou officials for admittance to his liberties at Newcastle-under-Lyme. A probab descendant of Thomas, Richard Spicer, was appointed sergeant to the mayor Newcastle in 1555/56, an official post that entailed serving summons, keepi prisoners safe and being at the mayor's command on all lawful occasions. 187 Gregory Spicer (tobacconist), Market Terrace, Longton; 1907, Frederick Spic (fitter), King Street, Fenton; 1907, Jos. Spicer (engine tenter), Melville St, Hanle

The medieval merchants recognised four "kinds" of spice - saffron, clov cinnamon and nutmeg, but none of these has bequeathed a surname, apparent

Cooks. Preparing and boiling meat. Pounding grain in a mortar. (Cook p. 180)

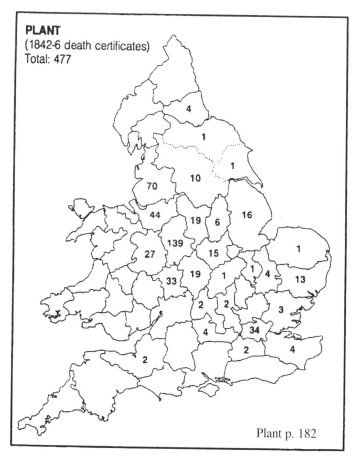

Plant p. 182

Ginger

Ginger, borne by Roger Ginger, witness to a thirteenth century deed in the Charter of the Priory of St. Thomas near Stafford, normally referred to a dealer in ginger used for flavouring fish such as herring or mixed with herbs and wine to make a rich sauce. Yet there is no reason to discount a nickname for a ginger-haired man or person, endowed with a fiery temper.

One of the favourite ingredients was mustard, which was used in enormous quantities. Thomas Ivone (mustard maker) of Wolverhampton (1457 Assizes) must have done a roaring trade. Ales Musterd married Thomas Tew at Weeford on December 2nd, 1574. The surname Mustard, besides being a maker of or dealer in **Mustard** mustard, may also have described an individual who was as sharp and as keen as mustard, that is, someone with a quick, biting wit. Pepper, too, probably preserve **Pepper** both the occupational connotation for a dealer in pepper, a pepperer or spicer, or soubriquet for a hot-tempered, easily riled man or woman. John Pepper was ineligible for hearth tax at Keele in 1666 and Aaron, illegitimate son of Jane Peppe of the Row, was baptised at Swynnerton on April 23rd, 1809. The Biblical them continues with 1851, Elisha Pepper (engraver) of Slack Lane, Hanley and Shelton and 1851, Moses Pepper (painter and gilder) of Wellington Street, Tunstall.

In his *History of Leek*, Sleigh cites Thomas Collepeper of Tittesworth for 1545 - "cull (gather) pepper", another name for a spicer, source of the modern **Culpepper** Culpepper. Sometimes pepper entered into the conditions of a feudal bargain, a characterised by Henry de Botterton, tenant of the Audleys at Audley in 130 whose tenure of a certain holding specified one pound of pepper per annum. The peppercorn rent was the absolute minimum price paid for a tenancy and Robert **Peppercorn** Peppercorn, quoted in the 1286 Pleas of the Forest for Oxley near Bushbury, could have held some land there at a peppercorn rent, but here again it might denote seller of peppercorns, a pepperer or spicer, or even a nickname for someone who was small with a dark complexion or dark hair.

Peever
Peevor

Peever and Peevor are invariably defined as occupational surnames for dealer in pepper, from Old French "peyvre" - "pepper", but more logical bases for north Staffordshire families bearing these names are Peover, Lower and Over Peover north west of Goostrey, Cheshire. All are situated on or near the river Peover, a British river name meaning "radiant" or "bright". Anna, daughter of Edward Peever, was baptised at Audley on September 9th, 1632. 1887, Charles Peever (tobacconist and general dealer) of Church Street, Silverdale; 1887, Sarah Jane Peever (smallware dealer), Princes Street, Tunstall. In Welsh Surnames Morgan and Morgan cite a pardon for murder to Oliver ap Ever alias Pever, carpenter of Middlewich, Cheshire (1522). They take this as a patronymic from the Welsh "Ifor". Oddly enough, Middlewich is only six or seven miles from Lower Peover.

Parsley, sage and fennel were all grown by peasants and gardeners throughout medieval England but the name Parsley, as we have seen, is a variant

Passelow (Age of Chivalry), whilst Sage comes from Old French "sage" - "wise", a nickname for anyone who was a fount of wisdom. In 1227 Petronilla la Sage handed over one mark for permission to withdraw her writ of novel dissein against Nicholas Duredent, that is, she had recently been ejected by Nicholas from some freeholding, although no locality is actually mentioned in the writ.

Fennel was cultivated for its fragrant seeds and fine leaves, which were used as flavourings in sauces. The surname Fennel, Fennell thus denotes a grower of fennel. Joan, daughter of Robert Fennall, was baptised at Burslem on February 7th, 1601; 1907, Hy Fennell (engraver), Mollart Street, Hanley; 1907, Frederick Fennell (potter), Brighton Street, Stoke.

Two of the most common vegetables which featured on the medieval bill of fare were onions and garlic. However, the surname Onion(s), Onians, Onyon is only rarely for a seller or grower of onions, for these names abound in all the counties bordering Wales, especially Shropshire and Cheshire, and our own county must be added to the list. Here the origin is the Old Welsh personal name "Enniaun", which also ends up as Ennion, Enion, Eynon, Inions, Anyan and Anyon: Dieulacres Charters, Thirteenth century, Eynun (Eynon, Eynoun) son of Lewellen de Berton. In 1678, William Annion, who had a wife and 2 children, submitted 4 shillings poll tax at Clayton and Seabridge towards the war effort against the French. The singular form Onion alternates with Unwin as in the Ellenhall parish registers, where Robert Onion (1682) is entered as Robert Unwin in 1686. If Unwin is the original surname, then this is traceable to Old English "unwine" - "unfriend" or "enemy", a nickname or a personal name, or to the Saxon "Hunwine" - "young bear friend", which disposes of the initial aspirate. Those called to arms in the 1539 Muster include Richard Unwyn at Swynnerton, John Onwyn at Newcastle-under-Lyme, Richard Unwyn at Betley and Balterley, and Edward Unwyn at Tunstall (Stoke-on-Trent). 1851, John Unwin (cabinet maker), Piccadilly, Hanley; 1875, Ralph Unwin (crate maker), Canning Street, Fenton. In the 1666 hearth tax returns for the county the surname Onions is spelt Onion(s), Onyon(s), Onyans and Onnyans, but out of 15 recordings, only one has any relevance to north Staffordshire - Robert Onyans, exempt from any payment at Stafford. In 1907 Ambrose Onions (tileworks fireman) lived in Cobridge Road, Hanley.

Allied names of importance here comprise the patronymics Beynon, Bennion, Binnion, Bainham/Baynham, which represent the Welsh "ab Eynon, ab Einion" - "son of Einion", and Pinion, Pinnion, Pinyon, which stand for "ap Eynon, ap Einion": Ellastone parish registers, 1628, Bartholomew, son of Gilbert Pinnion, baptised on January 12th; 1666, George Binnion, assessed on 2 hearths at Uttoxeter; 1679, Katherine Baynham and Patrick Knott, married at Penkridge on October 20th; 1810, Richard, illegitimate son of Jane Bainham (a pauper), baptised at Church Eaton on March 12th; 1851, Owen Bennion (horsebreaker) of Winnington, Mucklestone; 1851, Emma Bennion (milliner, dressmaker), New Street, Burslem.

Garlic(k)

To tempt those with stronger palates garlic was an essential seasoning fo fish, meat and game-birds of all kinds: Charters of Stone Priory, Thirteenth century Thomas Garlec clerc; 1871 Census, Henry Garlick (draper), High Street, Eccleshall 1875, George William Garlick (manager of the District Bank), Bank House Burslem. The name means a seller of garlic.

At the other extreme, people with a sweet tooth, preferred their food to b sweetened with honey or sugar. Honey was highly prized in medieval times becaus it also aided the process of fermentation of wines and ale. It was obtained, c course, from the castle or manor bees, whose hives were looked after by someon like John le Byker of King's Bromley (1347 Inquisition) - Middle English "biker" "bee-keeper", which survives as Bicker(s), Bikker: 1907, Joseph Byker (labourer) c Brownhills, Burslem. An alternative name for a bee-keeper is Beeman, Beamar Beman, Beamon: 1807, Thomas Beaman, a gardener, buried at Rocester o February 1st; 1907, James Beamon (forgeman) of Victoria Road, Fenton; 1907 Joseph Beman (carter), Boundary Street, Hanley.

Bicker(s)
Bikker

Beeman
Beaman
Beman
Beamon

Beaumont

There is an unavoidable clash with the surname Beaumont, which is spelt i a multitude of ways from the Tudor period onwards. For instance, the Beaumor family, lords of Wednesbury, occurs as Beamonde, Bemonde, Beaumont in a 150 lawsuit, dealt with by the Court of Star Chamber, whilst in the Wolverhampto parish registers, Christopher Beamonde (1605), is alternatively written down a Christopher Beamon in 1608. Beaumont in all its forms was originally brought b the Norman barons from some place in Normandy called Beaumont - "beautifu hill". The main candidate is Beaumont-le-Roger in the province of Eure, but it ha been estimated, that there are at least 46 localities called Beaumont all over Franc so the exact whereabouts of many of the English families bearing this name is ope to much speculation. Henry Beaumond, paying 4 shillings subsidy at Uttoxeter i 1327, is assessed as Henry Bemont five years later, but this time his contribution ha shot up to one mark (13/4d). He clearly belonged to one of these wealthy baroni families from across the Channel who had made it good over here. 1851, Georg Beaumont (enameller and lustrer), Albion Place, Hanley; 1851, James Beaumon licensee of the Spotted Cow, Penkhull Street, Newcastle-under-Lyme. The isolate Richard Bowmond of Old Basford (Cheddleton), who left 10 shillings to the loca benefaction board in 1866, hints at some connection with Bowman, but mor evidence is needed to prove it conclusively.

Honeyman
Hunniman

The honey, obtained from the hives, was eventually passed on to th "honeyman", who sold it to the cooks to add to the gingerbread and the jams an preserves, and to the brewers to speed up the fermentation of their ales. Thoma Hunniman of Willenhall married Frances Wheeler of Church Eaton at the Church o St. Editha, Church Eaton on May 16th, 1664, and John Hunnyman was buried a Armitage on April 29th, 1695. It may have been used to sweeten cakes and tart but usually the cooks opted for sugar, which was bought by the loaf and had to b pounded. Powdered white sugar was an expensive luxury. The surname Sugar, however, is very misleading, since in the 1500s it fluctuates consistently with Suker - Eccleshall parish registers, 1573, Joyce Sugar alias Suker, eventually becoming Shuker: 1595 Inquisition post mortem, Francis Sukar (Shuker) of Gnosall. Sugar Croft in Huntington near Cannock has been adduced as containing the Saxon word "sceacere" - "robber", pronounced something like "shackere" or "shakere", which also occurs in Sugarswell Barn and Farm in Kineton Hundred (Fexhole Hundred), Warwickshire, recorded as "Sugorswell, Shuckerswell" in the sixteenth century. Therefore, the surname Shuker, Shucker, Sugar could signify an outlaw or robber, a thief or even a highwayman, but a couple of specimens from the 1381 Poll Tax obscure the issue - Nicholaus Seuker (seuker) of Rugeley and Reginald Seukere of Gnosall, and these must be treated along with Hugh Suker of Sheriffhales (same returns). All three may be derivatives of the Saxon verb "sucan" - "to suck", hence a sucker, a blood letter, and this would make the later Sugar a voiced variant. A third possibility revolves around the Saxon "scucca" - "demon, goblin", which crops up in the locative Shugborough east of Stafford - "the fortification haunted by some demon or evil spirit". 1851, Edward Suker (bricklayer) of Knighton near Mucklestone; 1907, John Shuker (miner) of Enoch Street, Burslem; 1907, Jane Shuker (grocer) of Mark Street, Shelton, Stoke-on-Trent.

Another awkward customer is the surname Tart. It is fairly late in making its appearance, the earliest recording for Staffordshire being John Tarte of Sheriffhales, recruited for the county muster in 1539. John Tarte of Milhouse was buried at Lapley on April 27th, 1584. Trade directories for 1907 list: Joseph Tart (fried fish dealer), May Place, Fenton; James Tart (fitter), Wellington Court, Longton; Richard Tart (labourer), Castle Street, Newcastle-under-Lyme. In the fourteenth century the noun "tart" alluded to a piece of pastry with fruit or jam filling, and so the obvious deduction is that the name Tart denoted a maker and seller of such appetising items, but there might be a nickname "tart" - "sharp to the taste", possibly in the sense of "cutting, wounding, offensive, caustic", whilst on the periphery is the Old French " tart" - "late, slow", perhaps indicative of a slowcoach or stick-in-the-mud.

Pottage, thick soup or broth always provided a welcome stand-by for the cook or housewife with hungry mouths to feed on a cold, winter's day. One medieval cook who regularly served up this dish for the household was Thomas Potinger, who held one messuage and one acre of land at Audley in 1298, renting them from the Audley family for 12 pence per annum. His name now survives as Pottinger. For the fluctuation between "pottage" and "Pottinger", compare Messager-Messenger.

FRUITS

Orchard
Archard

The fruits that were made into "comfits" or "sweets", or that were added to the jam and conserves, came from the castle orchard and so a person such as Adam att Orcherd of Kinver (1327 lay subsidies) either lived near to the local orchard, or more likely was the fruit grower in charge of the orchard. In an assize of 141 Robert and Ralph Orchard of Milwich are both described as "yeomen", and in 147 William Orchard sued 5 men for breaking into his close at Salt and beating an wounding his servant John Semmell, so that he lost his services for a length of time John Orcharde of Milwich (1591 lawsuit) is recorded as John Archarde in 158. Elizabeth Orchard kept the New Bird in Hand Inn along Sun Street, Hanley in 188

Appleyard

Another familiar word for an orchard during the Middle Ages wa "appleyard" - literally "apple enclosure", again either denoting habitation in clos proximity to some orchard, or an occupational term for someone who supervised th running of the place. George Appleyard of Yoxall and Ann Harvey got married a the Cathedral Church of St. Mary and St. Chad, Lichfield on August 22nd, 172 John Appleyard (potter) resided in Selwyn Street, Stoke in 1907.

Peach(e)
Peech
Peachey
Petchey
Petch(e)

The dainty-sounding Peach(e), Peech, Peachey, Petchey, Petch(e) evoke images of soft complexions and sun-drenched orchards, and, to be sure, it ca denote a grower and seller of peaches. However, an example like Robert Pech from the twelfth century charters of Trentham Priory, who is also recorded as Robe peccatus, alludes to a nickname for anyone who had committed some sin o misdeed. Whatever its real origin, the surname Peach has its stronghold in th Staffordshire Moorlands and the Churnet valley from at least the reign of Henr VIII. Hellen, daughter of Thomas and Margerye Peache, was baptised at Ellastor on November 9th, 1547. From the 1666 Hearth tax returns for Totmonslo Hundred, it emerges, that Rowland Peach was charged on one hearth at Okeove Castern and Ilam, and John Peach, likewise at Stanton, whilst no tax was require from Richard Peach at Grindon, nor from Robert Peach at Alton. 1907 Trad directories list: Benjamin Peach (miner), Young Street, Pittshill; Alfred Peac (paviour), George Street, Cobridge; Samuel Peach (potter's placer), Clifford Stree Hanley.

Pearman

Pears were grown or sold by the pearman, a south Staffordshire name: 187 Kelly's Directory, Richard Pearman (farmer), Bannut Tree Farm, Upper Arley. H earlier namesake - Richard Perriman, member of the trained band in the 164 Muster for Clent, Broome, Amblecote and Arley, had ancestors who dwelt by a pe tree. (cf Perry in Volume 1)

Cherry

Hugh Chirie, assessed at 9 pence for the vill of Rocester in the 1327 la subsidies, grew and sold cherries - the modern surname Cherry. The marriag between Joanna Cherry and Richard Holland took place at Barton-under-Needwoo on October 4th, 1572. 1875, John Law Cherry (assistant editor of the Staffordshi Advertiser); 1907, A. Cherry (wholesale confectioner), Waterloo Road, Burslem.

Oranges, imported from Spain, were destined only for the very wealthy sections in medieval society, but the surname Orange, Orringe has nothing at all to do with the fruit, because it is taken as a woman's name, found as "Orengia, Orenga" etc during the thirteenth century. A certain William de Orange, under-tenant in the Buckinghamshire Domesday survey, has been traced back to Orange in Mayenne, south of Normandy, so this toponymic source cannot be altogether eliminated. Samuel Orange, who appears in the Newcastle-under-Lyme parish registers in 1723, is described as a "feltmaker". Unbelievably, his son, Lemon, is baptised on July 28th of that year! The surname Lemon, too, has no connection with the name of the fruit, for it is either a Saxon personal name - "Leofmann" - "beloved man", as exemplified by "Leofmon" in a ninth century Staffordshire charter for Cutsdean and Stourton, or from Middle English "leofman, leman, lemman" - "lover, sweetheart", as in Hugh called "Lemmon" of Morwhale (the lost Morghull in Streethay, near Lichfield), in a charter circa 1278, cited as Hugh Leman de Morhale circa 1268 (Great White Book of Lichfield Cathedral). In 1363 John Lemman, along with William Vernay and John atte Wode were sued by John de la Roche for the manors of Creighton and Peakstones. The modern surname Loveman/Luffman is from either of the above sources, but may also refer to "servant of Love". Other variants of the surname include: Newcastle-under-Lyme parish registers 1579, Elizabeth Lemmon and 1619, Margaret Lyman (possible forerunner of Limond, with addition of final "d"); 1652, William Leman, one of the members of the Committee for Regulating Markets at Cheadle; 1666, John Leaman, exempt from hearth tax at Madeley near Keele; 1851, John Lemon, Wesleyan New Connexion, Waterloo Road, Burslem.

ALE AND BEER

The ale of medieval times was quite different from today's ale. It was sweeter with the consistency of barley water, and well deserved its title of "the people's food in liquid form". It was consumed at all times, at home, whilst working in the fields or relaxing in the village alehouses. It took the place not only of such modern inventions as tea and coffee, but also of water. It was cheap and plentiful, and people preferred to drink ale anyway, because it was highly dangerous to drink water on account of the lack of proper sanitation. A thirteenth century writer, describing the extreme poverty of the Franciscans when they first settled in London in 1224, observes: *"I have seen the brothers drink ales so sour, that some would have preferred to drink water"*. This is an acceptable origin of the surname Drinkwater, although a better origin might be a nickname applied to a peasant who was so poor, that he or she was unable to afford to drink ale even when it was four gallons a penny, as fixed by the Assize of Ale in 1266.

With the medieval love of irony a nickname for a person who drank to excess would not be out of order, whilst another suggestion is a medieval diabetic with an insatiable thirst. The same name occurs in France as Boileau and in Italy , as Ettore Bevilacqua, former chauffeur of Federico Fellini, the film director. The surname Drinkwater in North Staffordshire is somewhat reluctant to show itself, to say the least. At a 1601 session of the Tunstall manor court, Hamlen Drynckwater (probably of Ravenscliffe) was fined 4 pence for failing to swear allegiance to his Queen (Elizabeth I). Johanna Drinkwater and Thomas Ashley were married at Audley on October 5th, 1634 and Marie Drinkewater was buried at Brewood on November 6th, 1644. 1872, Joseph Drinkwater (blacksmith) of Admaston; 1907 David Drinkwater (miner) of Newcastle Road, Stoke; 1912, George Drinkwater (labourer) of Nelson Street, Fenton.

The brewing of ale from barley, wheat or oats, or all three, was carried on in almost every medieval village, each supplying its own wants. Essential ingredients like "barley" and "wheat" were grown by peasants on a "barley croft" or "wheat croft" (see Vol. 1). In the baronial households, the lord and his retinue opted for wine, leaving the ale to be consumed by the servants. On the whole, this ale was of better quality than the ale supplied by the average village brewster, since it was brewed by an ale-wife using grain from the castle stores. Indeed, the servants and day-labourers, who were employed on the manor, and who were given food and drink as part of their wages, looked forward to drinking the ale, provided by the ale-wife after a hard day's toil in the fields, finding it much more to their taste than that supplied by independent ale-sellers.

Many ale-sellers and brewers were women: 1300, Juliana le Brewstare customary tenant of Richard de Loges at Rodbaston and renting one nook of land for 20 pence per annum. **Brewster**, **Broster** and **Bruster** is the normal feminine variant of Brewer, but it was also borne by their male counterparts, as in Peter Brewestere of Horsebrook near Brewood (1306), and John le Breustere, rated at shillings for Fenton Vivian, Longton and Hanley in the 1332 lay subsidies. 1851 George Brewster (corn miller and maltster), Water Mills, Stafford. The modern Broster is often a reduced form of "broudester" - a female embroiderer: 1851, Jesse Broster (silk twister) of Mill Street, Leek; 1851, Mrs Ann Broster (housekeeper) Park Hall, Weston Coyney.

The basic name **Brewer**, too, has alternative scenarios - a toponymic for a dweller by a heath, from Old French "bruiere": 1200 Assizes, Thomas de la Bruere of Sandon, or a topographical name from Bruyère in Calvados. Margerett Brewer and Robert Nevewe were married at the Church of St. Mary, Swynnerton on July 25th, 1570 and Thomas Brewer alias Williams was buried at Seighford on January 15th, 1700. In 1875 Joseph Brewer was the very aptly named licensee of the Duke of Wellington in Market Street, Fenton, whilst William Brewer of Newport Lane, Middleport (1907) was a butcher by trade.

Anyone who worked at a brew-house, as in Hugh del Breuhous in a list of Freeman of York for 1302, soon answered to the name **Brewis**, **Brewse** or **Browse**

Brewster
Broster
Bruster
Brewer

Brewis
Brewse
Browse

1536/37, William Brewse (sergeant to the Mayor), Newcastle-under-Lyme; 1774, Mary Brouse and John Hartelow, married at Weeford on May 29th. However, these names easily merge with Bruce later on, thereby coming into conflict with locatives such as Briouze in Orne, Normandy, from whence came Hugh de Breusia of Colton in a thirteenth century charter from the Priory of St. Thomas, Stafford, and Brix in La Manche, origin of Isabella de Bruis (1241 Assizes). Le Brus in Calvados has been adduced by some authors as a source for the name Bruce. 1851, Charles Bruce (cabinet maker), Foregate Street, Stafford; 1907, George Bruce (forgeman), Woodall Street, Cobridge.

Brew and possibly Brow(e) are interlopers, for these are Manx names, that go back to Macvriw - "son of the judge", found as "McBrow" in 1408, "McBrewe" in 1417 and "Brew" in 1616. William Brew (1755), occurs at Blymhill as William Brow in 1749. John Brew witnessed the marriage of William Standley and Elizabeth Parton at High Offley on April 12th, 1773.

One of the instruments used by the brewer in the brewhouse was a "rudder", shaped like the steering oar of a vessel. With it he stirred the mixture of malt in the vat. The Register of the Guild of the Corpus Christi of the City of York cites Robert Masherudder in 1517, which develops into the surname Masheder, Masheter. Locally, Luke, son of Thomas and Elizabeth Masheder, was baptised at Chebsey on November 1st, 1689, and Elizabeth Massiter (Masheder) got married to Edward Nicklin (carpenter) at Stoke-on-Trent on April 20th, 1792.

The obsolete John le Maltmaker of Rocester (1358 Assizes) prepared the malt before it was put into the vat for mixing.

Since the quality of ale produced varied so much from brewer to brewer, it is only natural to assume that someone such as John Goodale of Hollington near Croxden (1476 Assizes) had a reputable business in the local neighbourhood as a brewer and seller of ale - the modern names Goodale, Goodayle, Goodall and Goodhall. This, alas, was not to be, for he is also mentioned as a husbandman in the same lawsuit, accused with a whole gang of other locals from Fole, Beamhurst and Overton, of breaking by force into the close of Elena Delves at Crakemarsh, pulling down a house and taking away her goods and chattels to the value of £40. It must have been some earlier member of John's family who had originally picked up the surname Goodale bestowed on him by his regular customers. The surname persists in this part of the county throughout the 1500s: 1532, John Godhall at Stramshall, William and Richard Godhall at Cauldon, Dominus Robert Gudhall (chaplain) of Blore, Dompnus (Dan) Francis Goodhall at Dieulacres Abbey and Roger Godhall at Greatgate near Musden. In 1851 James Goodall (wheelwright) lived in Acton near Swynnerton and in the same year Jeremiah Goodall was licensee of The Lamb in High Street, Tunstall. On occasion a locative source cannot be ruled out, namely Gowdall near Snaith, south of Selby, Yorkshire, which appears as "Goldhale" in 1353 and refers to a piece of alluvial land overgrown with marigold.

WINE

Up until the Norman Conquest the English made wine in their own amateurish w
with their own grapes in local vineyards - Old English "wingeard", which surviv
Wingard
Winyard
as the surname Wingard, Winyard, Wynyard: 1539 Muster, Wylliam Whengar
Wynyard
"able man, a byllman" - of Longdon. This would denote a worker at the vineya
Wine was a common daily drink, not only in the royal and baronial households, b
also in monastic establishments, especially in those monasteries run by t
Cistercians. Their motherhouse of Citeaux, situated in the famous wine-growi
region of Burgundy, set the standard for the cultivation of vineyards during t
Middle Ages, but it was not to Burgundy that the English looked to satisfy t
enormous demands of the wine-drinking upper and middle ranks of society, but
the vineyards of Gascony. This sunny province with its sheltered villag
peculiarly suited to the vine, had been part of the king of England's realm ever sin
Henry II had married Eleanor of Aquitaine in 1152. By the beginning of t
fourteenth century the Gascon merchants virtually dominated the English wi
market, for, out of the 90,000 to 100,000 tuns of wine exported annually fro
Bordeaux, between one-fifth and one-quarter came to England.

Vinter   A clear-cut example of a French importer of wine is Robert le Franc
Vintor   (vinitor), 1182 Pipe Rolls, ie Robert the Frenchman (vinter) - the modern surnar
Vinter, Vintor: Swynnerton parish registers, 1558, Thomas Vyntor, buried
Vine(s) February 13th. Vine(s) simply refers to anyone who was employed at a vineya
or perhaps a wine-seller who dwelt at the sign of the vine: 1593, Raffe Vine, buri
at Stowe-by-Chartley on January 28th; 1907, R.W. Vine (audit inspector), Sto
Viner   Road, Hanley. Viner and Vyner indicate a vine dresser or wine grower: Aud
Vyner   parish registers, 1707, Edward Viner junior, buried on May 25th, Edward Vir
senior, buried on July 4th.

Bevin(s)   Bevin(s), Beavin and Bivins represent the French "bei vin" - "drink wine"
Beavin   phrase name on a par with Drinkwater: 1748, John Bevins and Charlotte A
Bivins   Walkerdine of King's Bromley, married on June 8th, at the Cathedral church of
Mary and St. Chad, Lichfield, but there is inevitable overlap with Bevans as in Lu
Bevans   Bevins (Bevans) of Newcastle-under-Lyme (1771). This is normally from t
Welsh "ap Evan, ab Evan" - "son of Evan", the Welsh form of John: 1851, Jo
Bevans (shoemaker) of Colton near Blithfield.

A substantial number of wine connoisseurs from Gascony settl
permanently in England during the hey-day of the wine trade (1152-1453). Inde
they were given special privileges and regularly financed the Crown out of t
profits of the wine trade. They passed on their unrivalled knowledge to th
Gascoign(e) English counterparts and some even took English brides. Their descendants are
Gascoin(e) around us now, recognisable by surnames such as Gascoign(e), Gascoin(
Gascoyne Gascoyne, Gasken, Gaskin(s): 1539 Muster, William Gascon of Hanbury, billm
Gasken
Gaskin(s) without horse harness; 1615, Edward Gascoyne (mason) of Madeley near Kee

1666, James Gaskin, exempt from paying hearth tax at Grindon. Edward Gaskin, son of William Gaskin, who was killed at the malt mill at Newcastle-under-Lyme, was buried on October 9th, 1789. In 1851 Thomas Gascoigne was licensee at the Union in Stockwell Street, Leek. In addition, Gaskin fluctuates with Gaskill, as proved by George Gascoyne of Seighford (1777), who signs his own name in the register as George Gaskill on his marriage to Mary Spencer on December 30th that year. She signs with an "X", indicating that she is unable to write. This change of "n" to "l" or vice versa is very common, as we have already seen in such surnames as Betley-Bettaney, Bradley-Bradney and Carlisle-Carnall. If the original surname happens to be Gaskill/Gaskell, then the sources include Gaitsgill south of Carlisle - "shelter for goats", Gaisgill north east of Kendal and Gaisgill near Barnoldswick in the West Riding of Yorkshire, both referring to "wild goose valley". Gaitsgill also results in the modern surname Gaitskell, Gaitskill: 1532, Dominus Richard Gatskyll curate at Pipe Ridware; 1887, Edward Gatskill (joiner), Newcastle Road, Burslem; 1907, Joseph Gaskell (decorator), Forster Street, Burslem.

Sherry has nothing at all to do with the modern fortified wine of that name but is for Irish (Mac) Sherry - "Mac Searraigh", also "O Searraigh": 1875, James Sherry (shopkeeper), Great York Street, Hanley.

INNS, TAVERNS AND ALEHOUSES

With the loss of Gascony and the subsequent collapse of the wine trade at the end of the Hundred Years War in 1453, wine shot up to 8 pence a gallon, a price that was well out of the range of the peasants' pocket. In any case, the poor contented themselves with the alehouse, which, to them, was just another meeting place, like the village church, where they caught up on all the latest happenings and drank themselves into oblivion. In the towns and along the main roads there were regular taverns, inns and hostelries, some of which provided a bed of some kind with clean straw on the floor, free from fleas. The most famous medieval tavern is Chaucer's Tabard Inn at Southwark, with its host Harry Baily, where the pilgrims assembled at the start of their journey to Canterbury. The inn-keepers and taverners went by various names, the most common being Taverner, Tavernor, Tavener, Tavenor, Tavinder. In Roman times, the original "tavern" or "taberna" was a shed constructed out of boards, a hut or workshop, later a tavern or inn. Most of the medieval Taverners are concentrated around Lichfield: 1327 Lay Subsidies, William le Taverner, rated at 12 pence, as opposed to John le Taverner, assessed at 2 shillings. In 1532 William Taverner, wife Catherine, and daughter Joan, were resident in Acton Trussell and Thomas Taverner at Baswich. Francis Tavenor witnessed the marriage between Thomas Keeling and Ann Collier at Seighford on February 1st, 1794. 1851, Joseph Tavernor (maltster) of Stowe-by-Chartley; 1907, Eliza Tavernor (dish sponger), Goodfellow Street, Tunstall; 1907, Thomas Tavernor (engineer), Milton Road, Sneyd Green.

Taberner p. 195

The roadside alehouse. Taverner p. 193

A pedlar offers his wares, p. 196

Patterned after doublets like Benison-Venison and Bickerstaffe-Vickerstaff, Taverner changes into Taberner, Tabernor, Tabenor, Tabinor, Tabbernor, Tabbiner, Tabbenor and Tabbinor, as evidenced by the Stoke-on-Trent parish registers, where Richard Taverner (1651) is written down as Richard Tabernor in 1648, reinforced by the Croxden parish registers, where Francis Taverner (1729), appears as Francis Taberner in 1731. If the original name is Taberner in all its forms, then these are a derivative of Old French "tabourner" - to drum, with reference to a drummer in the minstrelsy (see The Minstrelsy). During the Revolutionary wars against France, John Tabbernor contributed 5 shillings towards the Defence of the Nation Subscription in 1798 at Oulton near Kibblestone; 1851, Francis Tabernor (corn miller) of Okeover; 1851, Stephen Tabbernor (butcher) of Blythe Marsh, Forsbrook; 1875, Samuel Tabbinor, beer retailer, Mill Street, Hanley; 1875, Hannah Tabberner (boot and shoe dealer), East Vale, Longton.

Inman is a compound made up of the Saxon "inn" - "abode, lodging" and "mann" - "man", hence descriptive of a person who kept a lodging house, where all manner of wayfarers and travellers stayed awhile to refresh themselves before starting out again on their respective journeys. In 1666 Francis Inman paid tax on one hearth at Handsworth. Another place of shelter for these travelling salesmen, merchants and pilgrims was the Saxon "herebeorg" - literally "quarters for an army", later a lodging place. Thus, surnames such as Harber, Harbor, Harbour and Arber signify a lodging-house keeper: 1851, James Harbour (licensed victualler), Rose and Crown, Market Street, Stafford; 1875, Thomas Harber (borough rate collector), Sutherland Terrace, Longton; 1907, Arthur L. Harber (stationer), Rosslyn Road, Longton. The Old French equivalent "herberge" means exactly the same, but here the modern developments are Herbage, Harbage, Harbach and Harbidge: 1666 Hearth tax contributions comprise two at Codsall from Edward Harbage, and one each from Thomas Harbidge and John Harbridge (sic) at Brewood.

3. HAWKERS AND PEDLARS

For the peasants living in the isolated hamlets and villages in the medieval Staffordshire countryside, the only contact many of them had with the outside world was when they met the itinerant hawkers and traders who frequented the alehouses, inns and taverns along their routes. These secluded settlements, out in the wilds, miles from any shops or markets, were cosy niches for enterprising travelling salesmen to exploit. The medieval pedlar was a hardy indefatigable character, good-humoured, sharp-tongued and persuasive, employing age-old sales techniques still followed by modern door-to-door salesmen.

An idea of the goods on offer to prospective buyers can be gleaned from a bizarre incident depicted in a fourteenth century drawing, where a pedlar, asleep at the foot of a tree, has just been robbed of a box, containing caps, vests, gloves purses, girdles, hats, musical instruments, pewter pots, cutlasses and other sundr articles. The thieves turn out to be a troop of monkeys! Nevertheless, thes travelling salesmen were a godsend to the countryfolk in their rural isolation, an their regular visits were particularly welcome because they kept everyone up-tc date with all the latest news and gossip from the outside world.

Pedlar
Pedler

The basic surname Pedlar, Pedler is surprisingly very scarce Wolverhampton parish registers, 1658, William Pedler alias Fletcher; 1680, Ann Pedler and William Smith, married at the Cathedral Church of St. Mary and S Chad, Lichfield on May 6th. Note also: 1669, William Swindall, a wanderin pedler of Alstonefield. There is occasional interchange with Pedley, as in th

Pedley

Wolverhampton parish registers again, where we find 1655, John Fletcher alia Pedley of Willenhall (cf. William Pedler alias Fletcher above). North Staffordshi families called Pedley are more than likely to be traced back to any one of sever locatives in Cheshire, including Pedley House Farm on Pedley Brook, south west Alderley Edge - "the clearing of Peoda or Pedda", a meaning shared with Pedleyh Farm (Booth Green) near Adlington and Pedley House (Key Green) east Congleton: 1640 Muster, William Pedley of Horton (Rudyard); 1851, Edwa Pedley (upholsterer) of Carter Street, Uttoxeter; 1887, Thomas Pedley (smallwa dealer) of Newcastle Street, Burslem.

Pedder
Peddar

The similar name Pedder, Peddar is a derivative of Middle English "pedd - "pannier", hence, applied to a person who carried goods for sale in a pannier basket, a pedlar. In 1306 Henry, son of Thomas, son of Peter le Peddere, withdre his suit against Thomas, son of Ralph le Godrydere and others, respecting messuage and 2 acres of land in Ellastone.

Bannister
Banister
Bannester

The Pedder may have got his "panniers, baskets" from the Bannist Banister, Bannester - Old French "banastre" - "basket", with reference to a bask maker. In 1363 Thomas Banastre and 21 others were sued by Robert de Knyghte for breaking into his close at Knightley south west of Eccleshall, treading down a consuming his corn and grass with their cattle. Goods and chattels to the value 40 shillings were taken from Ralph Wolseley's property at Colwich in 1456 by thr inhabitants of Wolseley, amongst whom was William Banastre (osteler). Nychol Banester's son, John, received his baptismal rights at Ellastone on February 15 1589. Exempt from hearth tax in 1666 were Anne Bannester at Newcastle-und Lyme and William Bannester at Milwich, although Richard Bannester w responsible for two hearths at Blore near Ashley. 1851, Edward Bannister (saddl of Abbot's Bromley; 1907, David Bannister (grocer, coal dealer), Duncan Stre Fenton; 1907, John C. Bannister (signalman), Neville Street, Oakhill.

A revealing paragraph from the Newcastle-under-Lyme Corporati Minutes, dated 8th April, 1617, reads as follows: *"And further it is ordered that inhabitant of this borowghe shall suffer anie badgers or others to sell anie malte anie graine in anie of their howses either on ye markett daie or anie other daye in ye weeke untill they have paide toule of the malte or graine unto ye Belman uppon paine for everye person soe offendinge to fforfitt five shillings".* In this extract "badgers" are persons who bought corn or other commodities and carried or hawked them elsewhere to sell, hence itinerant "hawkers" who acted as middle-men between producer and consumer. The word is still in current usage in some dialects and also as a surname: Thomas Badger of the Parke Mill, buried at High Offley on February 5th, 1739; 1907, Joseph Badger (tilemaker) of Bond Street, Tunstall. Early forms waver between Badger and Bagger at Eccleshall and Pershall: 1468 Assizes, William Bagger, late of Pessale (Pershall), in contrast to 1580 Feet of Fines, Robert Badger of Pershall. If Bagger is the original variant, then this would denote a maker and seller of bags or sacks. The name Badger has no connection whatsoever with our native nocturnal mammal - badger, since this is recorded as "brocc" in placenames and fieldnames and is one origin of the surname Brock. The inference here might be to someone with nocturnal habits or maybe a cruel nickname for anyone who suffered from body odour. A locative source for Badger is provided by Badger on the river Worfe, north east of Bridgnorth, Shropshire - "Baegi's river bank". 1875, William Brock (potter's fireman), Newcastle Road, Hanley.

Bags and small sacks were also made and sold by anyone with the name Bagg(e), Baggs: 1212 Assizes, Hugh Bagge; 1875, Robert Henry Bagg (commission agent), London Road, Newcastle-under-Lyme. The phrase "to buy a pig in a poke" - "to buy or accept something without seeing it" - comes from the ancient ruse of passing off a cat for a sucking-pig, placed in a closed "poke" - bag or sack. If the unsuspecting customer opened the "poke", he "let the cat out of the bag". The surnames Poke and Poker allude to a maker of bags or small sacks. John le Poker was assessed at 16 pence for Alton in the 1332 lay subsidies. In 1532 Henry Poker resided in Mayfield north east of Calwich Abbey. Sack, Sacker and Secker all go back to a medieval craftsman who made sacks or coarse cloth, sackcloth: 1260 Manor Court Rolls at Alrewas, Richard Sac; 1907, George Sacker (miner) of Williamson Street, Tunstall.

Ironically "hawker" in its modern sense of anyone who travelled about selling goods was not used as such until the sixteenth century. Instead the surname Hawker was assigned to a falconer who tended and trained hawks for his lord: 1851, George Hawker (hardware and toy dealer) of High Street, Longton; 1875, William Hawker (dealer in fancy goods), Market Street, Fenton. The allied name Hucker and its feminine equivalent Huckster denoted a haggler, petty trader or pedlar: St. Mary's parish register, Stafford, 1586, Mary, daughter of Richard Huckster and his wife, baptised on September 29th.

The Creamer or Cramer tramped from village to village, equipped with a " cream, crame" on his back - "a pedlar's pack", but "cream, crame, craim" also

denoted a market booth or stall, occupied by a creamer or cramer. Philip, son o
Richard Cramer (shoemaker) was baptised at Castlechurch on February 26th, 162
and William Cramer (bachelor) of Stafford got married to Sarah Haywood (spinste
of Seighford at Seighford on July 3rd, 1811; 1907, Benjamin Cramer (pawnbroke
and clothier) of Congleton Road, Talke.

**Packman
Pakeman**

The most widespread surname for a pedlar who carried packs or bundles,
packman, is Packman, Pakeman, but also acceptable is "servant of Pake" from th
Old French personal name "Pasques, Paque" - "Easter". In 1412 William Neupo
(chivaler) sued in person Thomas Pakeman of Gayton near Weston-upon-Trent f
cutting down his trees at Wetmore and stealing some fish from his fishery. A
Kibblestone in 1747 the Overseers of the Poor granted Richard Pakeman's childr
an unspecified amount of money for new shirts. 1851, Sarah Pakeman (farme
Wall Heath, Woodlands, Uttoxeter. Pakeman sometimes changes places wi

Pateman

Pateman - "servant of Pate (Patrick)": Ann Pateman of Chebsey (1690), noted
Ann Pakeman in 1729, and occasionally develops an initial "S" to becom

**Spackman
Spakeman
Speakman**

Spackman, Spakeman, Speakman: Ellastone parish registers, 1598, Thom
Pakeman; 1666, Ann Spakeman; 1676, Mrs Spakman; 1851, Elizabeth Speakm
(National School), Halmerend; 1873, Thomas Speakman (beerseller), High Stre
Goldenhill, Tunstall. Usually Spackman and Speakman go back to the Midd
English term "spekeman" - "spokesman, advocate".

Tranter

Of all the medieval hawkers who roamed about the countryside the one w
was most likely to carry his wares in a horse and cart was the "tranter", since th
word goes back to Roman times and is derived from the same root as "transpor
Hardy uses it in *Tess of the D'Urbervilles* to evoke that spirit of belonging uniqu
the country-folk of Dorset in his novels: *"Once there was a old aged man over
Mellstock", recalls a dairyman to Tess, "William Dewy by name - one of the fam
that used to do a good deal of business as tranters over there...."* In our county t
surname Tranter's early evolution is virtually confined to the southern region of t
county. Moreover, in the 1666 Hearth tax returns every single instance of the na
is recorded in the Hundreds of Seisdon, Cuttlestone and Offlow. We have to w
until after the end of the Industrial Revolution before the name begins to make a
significant impact north of Stafford: 1851, William Tranter (basket and sie
maker), Stone Road, Uttoxeter; 1875, Simeon Tranter, licensee of the Sutherla
Arms, Sutherland Place, Longton; 1907, Thomas Edward Tranter (harness ma
and boot repairer), Newcastle Street, Burslem.

**Tinker
Tinkler**

In a Statute, ratified by Elizabeth I in 1572, the reputation of these wanderi
salesmen was dealt a severe blow, for in it she declared that *"...all juglers, pedla
tynkers, and petye chapmen...shal bee deemed roges, vacabounds* (vagabonds) a
sturdy beggers intended of by this present act". Tinkers were itinerants who men
pots, kettles and miscellaneous metal household utensils. In 1356 Philip Page w
indicted before John Musard, the Sheriff of county Stafford, at Tean, for feloniou

killing Philip le Tynkare at Butterton-on-the-Moors in 1352. Parrott in his account of Audley and Talke tells of Ellin Tinker who was drowned in some pool or well in 1653. In 1851 Harriet Tinker is noted as a shopkeeper of Gaolgate Street, Stafford. The variant Tinkler is also in evidence, although it is basically indigenous to northern England. Locally, Elizabeth Tinkler (spinster) of Eccleshall married Thomas Hodges (bachelor) at Seighford on October 30th, 1797.

Chapman is a very old Saxon word for a trader or merchant who bought and sold goods and wares of any kind and a good chap-man became in time a "good chap", that is, a good fellow. An allied Saxon word also survives in the phrase "to chop and change" - "to sell and exchange", and in Cheapside and placenames containing Chipping as in Chipping Ongar in Essex and Chipping Sodbury in Gloucestershire, all of which denote an original market or market town. Chapman is common enough in its own right. In the 1327 Lay subsidies, amongst those assessed for Pirehill Hundred are Hugh le Chapmon at Milwich, Symon le Chapmon at High Offley, William le Chapmon at Abbot's Bromley and another William le Chapmon at Crakemarsh. In 1360 John le Chapmon was removed from office as headborough at Stadsmorlow near Harriseahead, and John Chapman (horsekeeper) is listed as one of Sir John Harcourt's household servants at Little Bridgeford in 1536. 1851, Lancelot Chapman (baker, flour dealer), Stafford Street, Stone; 1851, George and Susan Chapman (Catholic School), Alton. Chipman is a rare variant: 1381 Poll tax returns, William Chipmon of Blymhill and Brineton near Weston Park; 1794, Joseph Chipman and Mary Gaunt (both of Drayton Basset), wed at Hints on May 19th, because the church at Drayton was under repair.

Occasionally Chapman and Mercer are used of the same person, as typified by Thomas Chapman mercer and John Chapman mercer, both assessed for Lichfield in the 1380 Poll tax. However, the surname Mercer is nowhere near as prolific as Chapman. In 1308 Richard le Mercer rented 8 acres of land at Betley from the Audleys for 4 shillings per annum. Another Richard, son of Robert and Amphillis Mercer, was baptised on October 24th, 1631 at Seighford, whilst Thomas Mercer was deemed ineligible for any hearth tax at Keele in 1666. The "mercer" was actually a dealer who specialised in lighter spun goods, textile fabrics especially silks, velvets and other costly materials. 1887, Hayden Mercer (tobacconist), Market Terrace, Longton; 1907, Edward Mercer (furnaceman) of Nash Peake Street, Tunstall.

Of all the medieval itinerants none could match the stamina and fitness of the merchants, who not only clocked up many miles in their jaunts around the English countryside, but also covered prodigious distances abroad negotiating deals with their foreign contacts in the wool, cloth and wine trades. By today's standards their travel expenses would have been astronomical! As with Clerk-Clark and Hermit-Armitt, we come across both Merchant and Marchant. John le Marchant was rated at 2 shillings for Penkridge in 1332. In 1371 Nicholas Bret of Dimsdale sued John

Chaucer's Merchant (Mercer p. 199)

Cittern.   Bagpipe.   Clarion.   Rebec.   Psaltery.   Syrinx.   Sackbut.   Regals.   Gittern.   Shalm.   Timbrel.   Cymbal

THE MINSTRELS' GALLERY AT EXETER.   [p. 20]

Minstrels p. 203

de Chesterton and John Marchant for forcibly taking and imprisoning him at Dimsdale, and detaining him a prisoner until he had paid 40 shillings for his release. C. Merchant was Curate at St. Chad's. Bagnall in 1887; 1907, Jos. Merchant (placer) of Ricardo Street, Burslem; 1907, Charles Merchant (dataller), Hot Lane, Burslem. (Dataller is most likely for "daytaler" - a man employed and paid by the day, an odd job man).

Bardsley's explanation, that Faraday, Ferriday, Ferryday, Fereday is a trader or merchant who travelled (fared) a certain distance in a day, is not convincing at all. The relevant forms for Staffordshire show quite categorically that Ferriday, Fereday are variants of Verity, which is from Old French "vérité - "truth", an abstract term, used as one of the characters in the medieval Coventry Play, alongside others such as "Mercy", "Justice" and "Peace". The Sedgley parish registers provide the necessary proof: 1599, Richard Feredy (naylor), noted as Richard Veryde in 1595. In the 1666 hearth tax returns George and Edward Ferryday are exempt at Sedgley. The change from Verity to Veridy (Veryde), where "t" becomes "d" is also exhibited in the pair Tunnicliffe-Dunnicliffe. But the switch from initial "V" to "F" is less clear. The only comparable name is Vasey-Facey. The original forms with initial "V" such as Vaisey, Vaizey, Veasey, Vesey and Voisey are derived from Anglo French "enveisé", Old French "envoisié" - "playful, wanton", or even "possessed by a demon". The "en" was jettisoned, giving us "veisé, voisié". It had been presented before the King at Lichfield at Trinity term, 1414, that John Meverel of Throwley in county Stafford, esquire, had given a livery of cloth to Robert Bayle of Calton, yeoman, and to Adam Veysey of Leek and to others at Christmas (1410) against the Statute. In the parish registers of Church Eaton we find John Vesey of Orslow (1624), who is probably identical with John Pheasy (1660), plus William Feizy (husbandman), married to Sarah Robinson on February 11th, 1798. All these variants survive as surnames. Trade directories: 1907, Thomas Vasey (miner) of Ricardo Street, Longton; 1907, Samuel Fazey (insurance agent), Wilson Street, Stoke. Facer is almost certainly another very late corruption: Mary Facer, widow, buried at Penkridge on September 14th, 1697. Other specimens of Ferryday: William Farraday (ground collier) and Martha Broadhurst, wed at Stoke-on-Trent on August 2nd, 1772; 1873, William Ferriday (beerseller) of Charles Street, Tunstall; 1907, John Fereday (ironworker), Gibson Street, Burslem.

4. MUSIC AND ENTERTAINMENT

The monotony of medieval life was relieved by festivals, pageants and tournaments of all kinds, attended by rich and poor alike. The high point of many of these fairs and festive occasions was the entertainment provided by the groups of musicians, who regaled their listeners with the latest tunes and songs. In the households of the reigning monarch and the great barons meal-times were invariably accompanied by music provided by minstrels. As Langland so succinctly puts it, in *Piers Plowman* "*...there are only two amusements at table, listening to the minstrels, and, when the are silent, talking religion and scoffing at its mysteries.*" Yet these minstrel employed by wealthy patrons, were the exception rather than the rule, for th majority were forced to make a living on the open road, wandering from village village, playing their instruments, reciting their stories and telling their jokes fellow vagabonds and travellers by the wayside, or in crowded market-places inns. The minstrels who enjoyed the patronage of the Ferrers family at the Tutbur Court of Minstrelsy during the Middle Ages were amongst the fortunate few.

In many towns the mayors appointed officials called "waits", who combine the two functions of musician and town watchman. This description would fit Hug

Wait(e)
Wait(e)s
Wates
Wayte(s)
Weight
Whait(e)s

le Waite de Eston, cited in a thirteenth century deed from the charters of Stor Priory. His descendants live on in names such as Wait(e)s, Wates, Wayte(s), Weigh and Whait(e)s. By the time of Edward IV (1461) the primary duty of the "wait" w to "pipe the watch, summer and winter, at certain fixed hours of the night". In th 1381 Poll tax returns Hugh Wayte and his wife Johanna were rated at 20 pence f Penkridge. Henry Waite's burial is recorded at Audley on August 17th, 1663. 185 John Waite (watch and clock maker), Greengate Street, Stafford; 1907, Willia Waite (borough water man), Waterloo Road, Burslem; 1907, Arthur Philip Way (accountant), Station Road, Longton.

Wait
Wheat
White
Wheat(e)
Weate
Weet
Whate

Based on the dialectal "weet" for "wait" and "wheyt" for "white", a three-wa struggle develops between the surnames Wait, Wheat and White, e.g. 1737, Hug Wheat or Waite of Seighford and 1532 John Weyte of Kinver, noted as John Whi in the 1539 Muster. Wheat(e), Weate, Weet and Whate are principally from th Saxon "hwaet" - "active, bold, brave", as in Reginald le Wete of Rickerscote in fourteenth century charter from the Priory of St. Thomas, Stafford. On the oth

White
Whyte
Whitt
Witt(e)
Witts

hand, White, Whyte, Whitt, Witt(e) and Witts denote someone with fair hair complexion: 1332 Lay Subsidies, Robert le Whyte of Bishton and Wolseley, or back to a Saxon personal name "Hwita", as borne by Hwita, Bishop of Lichfie (737 to circa 749).

The town watchman is also commemorated by names like Wake an

Wake
Wakeman

Wakeman, which mean literally "watchful" and "watchful man". The former reca the Saxon guerrilla Hereward the Wake, who had led the last resistance to th Norman invaders in the Isle of Ely. "Wakeman" was the title of the chief magistra of the borough of Ripon until 1604, when it was changed to mayor.

The town watchman at Halfcote near Kinver in 1332 was Roger le Wakem and it is in the southern region of our county that the surname Wakeman evolv From the sixteenth century onwards we find spellings such as Wakema

Walk(e)man
Wurkman
Warkman
Workeman

Walk(e)man and Wurkman around Rowley Regis, Warkeman at Kingswinford a Warkman, Workeman at Sedgley. Workman can also refer to a craftsman who w ambidextrous. Kelly's Directory 1872, Peter Workman (fruiterer and carman), Vi

Road, Handsworth. 1851, Henry Workman, Junction Station, Uttoxeter.

The extremely widespread Ward(e) can also signify a watchman, but in this case, the allusion is rather to someone placed on guard at some castle, fortress or encampment. Anketine de la Warde was Lord of the Manor at Kingsley in 1293, along with Philip de Draycote. In 1323 William le Ward of Chapel Chorlton was robbed of a horse worth one mark by Thomas, the son of Nicholas de Bromleye. Here the reference might be to a guardian or protector. At the Tunstall manor court, held on 3rd May, 1610, Richard Warde was fined 3/4d "*...for that he made an affray and drew blood from William Burne...*" and on 14th October, 1662 the Tunstall jurors presented Andrew Ward, John Sympson and William Edge for digging pits in Winghay Lane. Each was fined 12 pence. Trade directories: 1851, John Ward (police officer), Wetley Rocks; 1851, Stephen Ward (stonemason's merchant), Forebridge Wharf, Stafford.

A typical group of minstrels at any gathering comprised a hotch-potch of musicians who were adept at playing stringed, woodwind and percussion instruments of all types, ranging from harps and fiddles to pipes and drums. The term "minstrel" has not come down to us as a surname, but the status of one of these medieval music-makers is revealed in the 1271 Pleas of the Forest at Cannock, when Richard de Wemme, after being caught poaching "*......is pardoned for the soul of the King, because he is poor and a minstrel*". The impoverished Richard had obviously fallen on hard times, being an underpaid and overworked professional musician.

In the 1381 Poll tax returns John Pipere of Acton and Bednall west of Cannock Chase is also identified as "menestrallus". He was probably a skilled pipe player, either on the bagpipes or the shawm, a member of the oboe family. His progeny live on in the name Piper, Pyper. In 1306 Margaret la Piper was unlawfully killed by Nicholas de Elleford in Knutton, and Agnis Piper was buried at Mucklestone on January 7th, 1562. 1907, Henry Piper (flower painter) of Leonard Street, Burslem; 1907, Alfred Piper (miller), Ricardo Street, Longton.

In Staffordshire the surname Pipe(s) is mainly to be traced to Pipehill near Lichfield, whose springs supplied Lichfield with water for many centuries. A toponymic is also feasible for habitation by some water pipe or water course: 1348 Inquisition, John atte pipe of Horsley, or an occupational name for a player of a pipe. 1851, Edward Pipe (revenue officer) of Abbot's Bromley.

Some minstrels were proficient on horns, bugles and trumpets. At the Tunstall manor court, held on 20th May, 1326, Richard Horn was fined 2 pence because he "*...grazed his neighbour's fields by night...*" This particular Richard could have pursued any one of several occupations: he could have blown a horn in a group of minstrels, that entertained the local villagers, he could have actually made the musical horns himself, or he could have fashioned objects like spoons, bugles or combs out of horn. Other people called Horn(e) may have boasted ancestors who dwelt by a spur or tongue of land, as in 1395 Assizes, Madoc de la

Horn(e)

Horne of Salop. 1851, Thomas Horn (linen weaver), Milwich Heath; 1907, Josep Horne (engine driver), Edward Street, Stoke.

Horner

Horner most likely contains all the senses inherent in Horn except th topographical one. In 1363 Richard le Hornere and Walter de Chatewalle were sue by Roger de Ipstanes for the fifth part of two messuages, 2 carucates of land and acres of wood in Blymhill. 1887, Horner, Robinson and Company (tailors), Pa Mall, Hanley; 1907. Dr William Horner (MD), Boulton Street, Wolstanton.

Hornblower

The Hornblower summoned peasants to work with a few short blasts of h horn, a human medieval equivalent of the modern factory hooter: 1607, Catharir Horneblower and Richard Grove, married at Rowley Regis on October 4th.

Corn(e)
Cornes
Cornett
Corns

The Old French word for a horn was "corn", hence the names Corn an Corne, a player of a horn: Mary Corne, buried at Seighford on June 7th, 1729; 190 Reginald Corn (tile manufacturer), Waterloo Road, Burslem. The rare Cornett is diminutive offshoot: Matilda Cornett, rated at 7 shillings and 3 pence at Gunstor near Codsall in the 1327 lay subsidies, by far the highest contribution thereabout Around Betley, Madeley and Audley the name Corn(e) often interchanges wi Cornes: 1666 Hearth tax returns, Thomas and William Corne (Cornes) of Betley. Cornes turns out to be the original name then this describes an immigrant fro Cornwall, cf. 1517 Star Chamber Proceedings, Cornes (Cornysh) Cok of Great Bar Dorothy Cornes and Thomas Brew were married at High Offley on November 1 1662; 1887, Albert Corns (agent), Jenkins Street, Burslem.

Corner

The extended name Corner also referred to a minstrel who played the hor Robert le Cornur who killed Richard son of Wulvene in 1203 and who was declare an outlaw, may have been involved in some festivities where everything got out hand after consuming too much of the local ale. A story all too familiar down th centuries. The modern Corner also goes back to a toponymic for habitation ne some corner or angle, where two streets met: 1310 Inquisition, John de la Corne of Stafford; 1872, William Corner, New House, Acton Trussell.

Trump
Trumper

Minstrels whose preference was for the trumpet have descendants nam Trump or Trumper. In the 1327 lay subsidies Ralph Trumpe of Hints near Weefo was assessed at 12 pence, and in 1413 John Trumper (draper) of Lichfield was giv a livery of cloth by Edmund Ferrers of Chartley, squire. Ann Trumper and Samu Simister were married at Norton-in-the-Moors on December 26th, 1821.

Harper
Harpour
Harpur

Stringed instruments are also much in evidence, especially "harps". Indee during the medieval period, the "harper" was virtually another name for a minstr and this accounts for the abundance of today's families called Harper, Harpou Harpur. In 1306 Robert, son of Roger le Harpour, who had broken the arm Richard, son of Thomas at Bagot's Bromley, was known as *"a common disturber the King's peace"*. On the other hand, the more sociable Hugh le Harpor rented o cottage at Betley in 1308 from the Audleys at 3½ pence per annum. In the 1327 a 1332 lay subsidy compilations "harpers" are recorded at Rushton Spencer, Lee

GEORGE WARD,
FAMILY GROCER
AND
Provision Merchant,
27 IRONMARKET,
NEWCASTLE, STAFFORDSHIRE

FIRST-CLASS VALUE IN

TEAS @ 1/4, 1/8, 2/-, 2/6
☞ FINEST IMPORTED, 3/-.

Ward p. 203

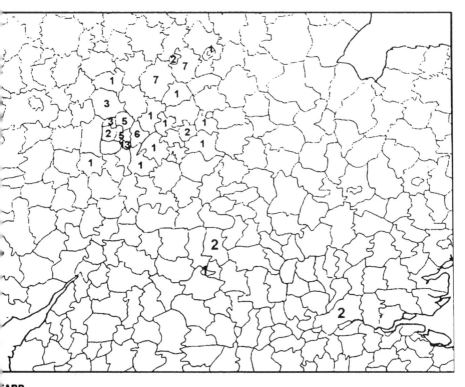

EARP
1842-6 death certificates)   Total: 75, including 2 West Derby

Earp p. 206

Harper

Bradnop, Butterton-on-the-Moors, Wolstanton, Aston and Burston, Stafford, and a Abbot's Bromley. This medieval glut continues throughout the later Middle Age and beyond, down to the present day: 1851, Sarah Harper (milliner, dressmaker Bridge Street, Longton; 1851, William Harper (upholsterer), Stafford Street, Stone 1851, Abraham Harper (tailor), Madeley, Keele.

Harp

The surname Harp on its own is not so straightforward; 1851, Maria Har (proprietor), Angel Inn, Fenton; 1875, John Harp (coalmaster), Wood Vill Longton, owner of Ubberley Hall Colliery, Old Road, Bucknall. The name normally construed either as synonymous with "harper", a minstrel who played th harp, or a toponymic for a dweller at the sign of the harp. A rare third possibility an occupational term for someone who used a harp-shaped device for sifting an cleansing salt. In our county a fourth origin presents itself. In the Rocester paris registers, for instance, Thomas Orpe (1737) occurs as Thomas Arp in 1747, ar

Orpe

these must be taken with William Horpe, one of the brethren at Rocester Abbey i 1496, and Katherin Harp (1635) in the Barton-under-Needwood parish register together with Richard Earp (1790) and Samuel Hurp (1800), both of Wychnor, the same registers. All these are variant spellings of Orpe or Earp, which go bac

Earp
Harp

to Old English "eorp, erp" - "dark, swarthy, brown". Hurp-Harp is simply reflection of Hermit-Armit, with addition of initial "H". 1851, George Ea (plumber, glazier), High Street, Tunstall; 1851, John Orpe (tailor), Charles Stree Cheadle.

Fidler
Fiddler

Fidler, Fiddler is much more scattered in its distribution than Harper. Ear specimens are concentrated in the Trent Valley, as exemplified by 1327. John Fithelere, assessed at 15 pence for Bishton and Wolseley, and Richard Fitheler a wife Agnes, rated at 2/4d for Rugeley in the 1381 Poll tax. Thomas Fydler enliste at The Rudge west of Standon in the 1539 Muster.

Crowther
Crowder
Crother
Crewther

Several obsolete terms for fiddles have left behind familiar surnames. Th "crowd" or "crouth" was an ancient Celtic musical instrument akin to the viol wi 3 strings. Later it had 6, 4 of which were played with a bow, the remaining tw plucked with the fingers. From this we get Crowther, Crowder, Crother a Crewther. In 1531 Philip Crowther (tanner) and Christopher Crowther (shoemake of Horton near Rudyard were part of a mob that "....*riotously came to ye Mil Strete in Leek, and there made assault upon Roger Smyth and Thomas Browne..* These two unfortunate victims were keepers of Macclesfield Forest. All the riote were issued with writs of "sub poena" to appear at the next Court of Star Chambe At the beginning of the seventeenth century some kind of plague ravaged Oult near Stone and in 1604 Robert Crowder lost his wife Roberta during Septembe followed by some other relative Thomas Crowder in November. 1851, Hann Crowther (straw hat maker), Oakamoor Road, Cheadle.

Rutt
Rutter

A musician whose virtuosity extended to playing the "rote", another kind medieval fiddle, was either known by the name of Rutt, as embodied by Sym

Female dancer, 15th century, p. 207

Musician and jester (Wayte p. 202)

Rutt
Rutter

Rote, rated at 8 pence for Hopwas near Tamworth in 1327, or by the far m
widespread name Rutter. In 1320 Robert le Rotour of Stafford contested a suit w
Thomas, the Parson of the Church of Weston-under-Lizard and Cecilia, former w
of Philip Nowel of Seighford, concerning 3 sacks and 4 stone of wool valued
£30. Yet the modern Rutter may occasionally go back to the medieval "rutter"
"routier" - a robber, highwayman or adventurer who hired himself out to anyc
wealthy enough to pay his wages. 1851, George Rutter (tailor) of Well Stre
Tunstall; 1907, Albert Rutter (railway guard), Edward Street, Burslem; 19
Louisa Rutter (tobacconist), Stafford Street, Longton.

Organ

The portable organs, which were sometimes chosen to add a little variety
the sound, were blown with one hand and played with the other. Symon Org
assessed at 4 shillings for Stafford in 1327, perhaps entertained the crowds w
melodic tunes played on this type of instrument. In 1872 Benjamin Organ was fa
bailiff to Mr. T. Osborne at Bramshall.

Taberer

The basic rhythm in the background was provided by the "taberers", w
beat out time on a small drum called a "tabor". One such drummer was Ralph
Taberer of Brewood (1348 Assizes). Christopher Taberer and Elizabeth Rep
were married at the Cathedral Church of St. Mary and St. Chad, Lichfield on J
5th, 1730. The Taberer's companion was the Taberner, as we have already seen
all its variations under Taverner.

Singer(s)

Very often the music was accompanied by singing and dancing. From
"caroles" or folk-songs and the ballads sung by the groups of wandering minstr
have come many of the traditional folk-song tunes heard today and of course
surnames Singer and Singers. In 1298 William le Singere held half an acre of la
in Wolstanton and rendered 3 pence yearly to his lord, Edmund of Lancaster.
1907 George Singer ran a business as a general dealer and cycle repairer in Hc

Sanger
Sangar
Songer
Sangster

Street, Hanley. Names like Sanger, Sangar, Songer and Sangster normally refer
medieval church singers or choristers. John T. Sangar was minister at Bartc
under-Needwood in 1809 and Elizabeth Sanger was married to John Edge
Norton-in-the-Moors on December 19th, 1820.

Dance
Dancer

Professional dancers live on in our Dance and Dancer: Eccleshall par
registers, Elizabeth, daughter of Richard Dance of Podmore, christened
November 21st, 1605; 1851, John Dancer (baker, flour dealer) of Broad Stre
Hanley.

Hopper

Other energetic dances or acrobatics were performed by the "hoppe
Tatenhill manor court rolls, 1344, Robert le Hopper; 1610, Margaret, daughter
John and Margerye Hopper alias Lowe, baptised at Church Eaton on January 20
1851, Christopher Hopper, licensee of the Roebuck, Greengate Street, Stafford.

Rimer
Rymer
Rimmer

In some taverns or market places stories were told and poems read out alo
usually by the "rimer", whose gifts of narration and entertaining his medie
audience live on in the surnames Rimer, Rymer and Rimmer. Yet some writ

favour an occupational term for a craftsman who made the wooden parts of wheel rims. Rimmer is especially prolific in Lancashire, where at one time the name was assumed to be derived from the occupation of cutting peat on the local bogs and mosses, but this explanation has now been discredited. In our county, Thomas Rymmer of Eccleshall (1606) is alternatively entered in the parish register as Thomas Rymer in 1610.

Whether Rimes is pertinent to our enquiry here has not been ascertained. It might just be synonymous with Rymer, Rimer in any of the senses mentioned above, but more information is needed. Rychard Rymes and Anne Dunston are included amongst the list of marriage licences for Staffordshire in 1593.

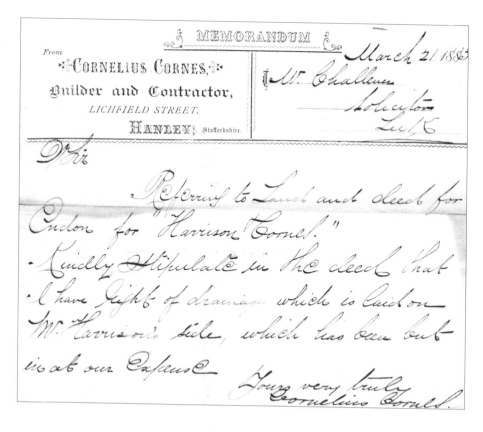

Cornes p. 204

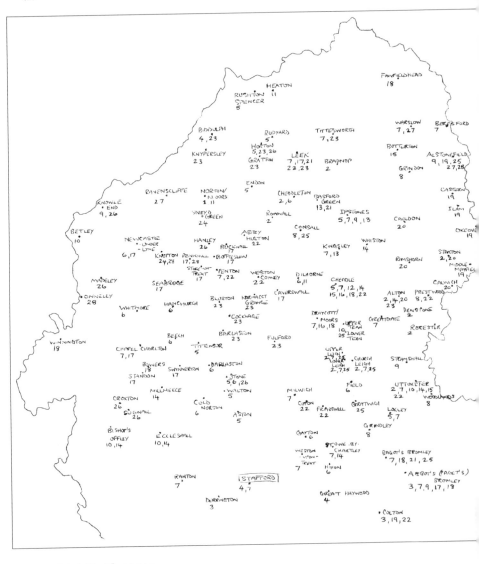

FAWFIELDHEAD
18

HEATON
RUSHTON 11
SPENCER
5

WARSLOW 7,27   BEERSFORD 7

BIDDULPH 4,23

RUDYARD 5   TITTESWORTH 7,23

BUTTERTON 15   ALSTONEFIELD 9,19,25 27,28

KNYPERSLEY 23

HORTON 5,23,26
GRATTON 23

LEEK 7,17,21 22,23   BRADNOP 2

GRINDON 8

CASTERN 19

RAVENSCLIFFE 27

NORTON/ MOORS 1,11

ENDON 5

CHEBBLETON 2,6   BASFORD GREEN 13,21

IPSTONES 5,7,9,13   CAULDON 20

ILAM 19

KNOWLE END 9,26

SNEYD GREEN 24

ABBEY HULTON 22   ROWNALL 2   CONSALL 8,25

KINGSLEY 7,13   WHISTON 14

OKEOVE 19

BETLEY 10

NEWCASTLE -UNDER -LYNE 6,17

HANLEY 26   PENKHULL BUCKNALL 17,28
KNUTTON 24,28   BOTTESLOW 17

RIMSHORN 20   STANTON 2,20
MIDDLE- MAYFIELD 19

STOKE-ON- TRENT 17   FENTON 7,22   WESTON COYNEY 22   DILHORNE 6,11   CHEADLE 5,7,12,14 15,16,18,22

CALWICH 20

MADELEY 26

SEABRIDGE 17   CAVERSWALL 17   ALTON 2,14,20   PRESTWOOD 8,22

ONNELEY 28   WHITMORE 6   HANCHURCH 6   BLURTON 23   NORMACOT GRANGE 23

DENSTONE 2

COCKAGE 23   DRAYCOTT MOORS 7,16,18   UPPER TEAN 19   GREATGATE 7   ROCESTER 2

LOWER TEAN 25

WINNINGTON 18

BEECH 6   BARLASTON 23   FULFORD 23

CHAPEL CHORLTON 7,17   TITTENSOR 5

UPPER LEIGH 2,7,18   CHURCH LEIGH 2,7,25
LONG LEIGH 2,7,25

STRAMSHALL 9

BOWERS 18   SWINNERTON 17   BARLASTON 6

STANDON 17

MILLMEECE 14   STONE 5,6,26   WALTON 5

UTTOXETER 22   WOODWARD 8

CROXTON 26   SUGNALL 26   COLD NORTON 6   ASTON 5

FIELD 6

MILWICH 7   COTON 22   FRADSWELL 22   GROATWICH 25   LOXLEY 5,7

GRINDLEY 8

BISHOP'S OFFLEY 10,14   ECCLESHALL 10,14

GAYTON 6

STOWE-BY- CHARTLEY 7,14   HIXON 6

BAGOT'S BROMLEY 7,18,21,25

WESTON -UPON- TRENT 7

ABBOT'S (PAGET'S) BROMLEY 3,7,9,17,18

RANTON 7

STAFFORD 4,7

GREAT HAYWOOD 4

DERRINGTON 3

COLTON 3,19,22

MAP 5 KEY

1. BARNISH
2. BOOT/BOTT
3. BRATT
4. CADMAN
5. CHALLINOR/CHAWNER
6. COLLIER

7. COPE
8. COPESTAKE
9. CORDEN
10. CORK
11. DRESSER
12. FLACKETT

13. HACKWOOD
14. KEY/KAY
15. LEADBEATER
16. LYMER
17. MACHIN
18. NAYLOR

19. PEGG(E)
20. POYSER
21. SHARMAN/SHERMAN
22. SPOONER
23. STONIER
24. TELLWRIGHT/TERRICK

25. THACKER
26. TYLER
27. WAIN
28. WEBSTER

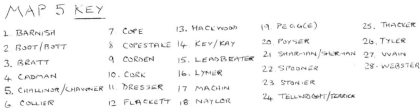

SURNAMES AT THE TIME OF THE 1666 HEARTH TAX RETURNS

CHAPTER FIVE

CRAFTS, TRADES AND OCCUPATIONS IN TOWN AND COUNTRY

1. CRAFTSMEN IN WOOD

CHARCOAL BURNERS AND WOODCUTTERS

From the time when prehistoric man discovered how to extract metals from their ores until the invention of the coke oven in the eighteenth century, the qualities of charcoal as a heating agent were essential elements to any craftsman who worked in iron, especially the smith. It is very nearly the perfect fuel, since it yields high, steady temperatures with no smoke and a small amount of ash. The ashburner's job was to make potash from the charcoal dust, which was probably used as fertiliser by medieval farmers. In 1578 William Lysatt the younger and his wife Joan remitted all rights to James Ashburner otherwise Mylles of Walsall to a messuage and a garden in Walsall, for which James handed over £40.

Barnish is unsolved but it may belong here as a phrase name - "burn ash" - equivalent to Ashburner, since "ash" - the name of the tree, often turns up as "eys, ays" in medieval scripts. In 1474, for instance, Thomas Berneys and several others were sued by Margaret, late wife of Robert Harcourt (knight) for the third part of the manors of Shareshill, Great and Little Saredon and Lache, and the third part of two parts of the manors of Coven and Brinsford which she claimed as dower. The switch from "burn, bern" to "barn" in the first syllable copies "clerk-clark" and "hermit-armit". Henry Barnish was headborough at Chell for the year 1654/55; 1907, George Barnish (saggar maker), Newport Lane, Middleport; 1907, Thomas Barnish (miner), Argyle Road, Longton. The rare Varnish perhaps arose by analogy with Bickerstaffe-Vickerstaff: 1907, James Varnish, Wedgwood Street, Smallthorne.

Brenner, too, is few and far between. In 1280 Jordan le Brenner was involved in some dispute with Alice, widow of William de Bydulf, over some tenements in the vill of Newcastle-under-Lyme, and in 1539 Thomas Brenner joined the local muster at Chebsey. The medieval "Brenner" was a burner of charcoal, lime or bricks, although the name is sometimes to be derived from the imported French term "brenier" - "keeper of the lord's hounds", that is, the running hounds which included the "braches". These hunted by scent.

The charcoal used in the firing of the forges worked by the smiths was supplied by the charcoal burner, or the "collier", as he was known then. William le Colyer (still alive in 1339), once held some strips of land in a field called "Fulfen" at Blurton at the will of the Prior of Trentham Priory. "Collier" in its modern sense of "coal-miner" did not enter the arena until the sixteenth century. The Churchwarden's accounts for Tunstall in 1648 inform us that 13 shillings were

Collier

"...paid to George Collier, a maimed souldier, upon order from the sessions...." perhaps on account of some injuries sustained during the Civil War. In 1714 two men at Hanchurch shared the name John Collier, one nicknamed "Flatback", the other called "Little". 1851, Edward Collier (dealer in old clothes), Mill Street, Stafford; 1851, James Collier (saddler) of Stowe-by-Chartley.

Minor(s)
Mynors

Surnames such as Minor(s), Mynors are from the Norman "mineur" "miner", or two locatives known as Les Minières, situated south west of Evreux in Eure, Normandy, or an unidentified "Myners", somewhere near Blakenhall west of Barton-under-Needwood; 1332 Lay subsidies, John le Myners (sic), rated at shillings there and clearly a man of high status. 1539 Muster; John Myner of Cannock cum membris; 1851, Richard Minor (farmer) of Bramshall; 1907, A Mynors (carter) of Denbigh Street, Hanley.

Coleman
Colman
Collman
Coulman

Coleman is chiefly a Kent surname, where it is a relic of the medieval charcoal-burning region centred around the Weald, hence a charcoal burner. Elsewhere the names Coleman, Colman, Collman and Coulman are liable to have sprung from other sources, such as the Old Irish personal name "Colman", earlier "Columban", which became Colman and was brought from Ireland by the Vikings but this was mainly confined to the counties of Cumberland, Westmorland and Yorkshire. In Staffordshire the possible alternatives also comprise the German "Col(e)man" or "servant of Cole". In 1298 Adam Coleman rented one messuage from the Audleys at Betley for 3/6½d per annum. In 1414 Thomas Dethek, late Sheriff of county Stafford, was attached at the suit of Thomas Colman (chaplain) for assaulting and imprisoning him at Yoxall, until he had paid a fine of 40 shillings for his release and for which he claimed £40 as damages. 1851, Margaret Coleman (milliner, dressmaker), King Street, Burslem; 1851, Samuel Coleman (pawnbroker) High Street, Newcastle-under-Lyme.

Gathercole

The exceedingly rare Gathercole might suggest a gatherer of coal or cabbage but the medieval spellings of the name include Richard Gaderecold of Suffolk (132? lay subsidies), which means literally "gather cold", perhaps a nickname for a feeble or infirm individual who was prone to catching cold. 1912, R. Gathercole (keeper) of Ashley near Mucklestone.

Hewer

Chopping down timber in the local woods for building purposes or just for firewood during the harsh winter months was undertaken by the "hewer": Tatenhill manor court rolls, 1336/37, Robert le Hewere, although some "hewers" were employed in the cutting of stone. Thomas Hewer was amongst the inhabitants Walsall in 1532. In 1338 Adam, son of Ralph le Wodehewer of Ronton was dispute with John, son of Thomas de Blorton over some holdings and land Trentham. Ralph's name means exactly what it says - "wood hewer", "cutter wood", and his descendants live on as Woodier, Woodyear, Woodyer, Woodger and possibly Woodyard by analogy with Stanier-Stanyard (see later).

Woodier
Woodyear
Woodyer
Woodger
Woodyard

Hackwood

Synonymous with Woodier is Hackwood, as exemplified by William

Hacwode, rated at 16 pence for Elford east of Lichfield in 1327 - "hack wood", a
nickname for a woodcutter. Two locatives in Derbyshire might be implicated at
some stage - Hackwood in Kirk Langley west of Derby, and "Hakewode" (1306) in
Baslow and Bubnell, north of Chatsworth House. 1851, Thomas Hackwood (china
and earthenware dealer), New Hall Works, Hanley; 1907, Samuel Hackwood
(forgeman), Sutton Street, Newcastle-under-Lyme.

Hacker refers either to a woodcutter or a maker of "hacks", that is,
agricultural implements such as mattocks and hoes: 1907, Thomas Hacker
(blacksmith), Ladysmith Road, Hanley. The Saxon "Wudumann" - "woodman"
was frequently employed as a personal name prior to the Norman Conquest and
afterwards as an occupational name. The Domesday scribes recorded that
Wodeman and Alsi were under-tenants of Robert de Stafford at Ellastone whilst
Nicholas le Wodeman of Featherstone near Shareshill appears at the Staffordshire
assizes in 1294. Edward Woodman (bank clerk) resided in Elgin Terrace, Mount
Pleasant, Newcastle-under-Lyme in 1907.

Copestake, which is characteristic of the north eastern sector of our county,
is a combination of the French "coupe" - "cut", and the Saxon "staca" - ""stake" -
"cut stake", a very apt soubriquet for a cutter of wood or timber. Unfortunately the
surname is comparatively late in its appearance. In 1521 Sampson Copstake was
servant to Walter Blount at Uttoxeter and in 1532 Dominus Roger Copstalk (sic)
was chaplain at Cauldon north of the Weaver Hills, where local inhabitants also
included Robert Copstake, his wife Agnes and their family, plus Henry Copstake,
his wife Ellen and their children. Hearth tax contributions in 1666 were made by
George Copestake at Consall (one), William Copestake at Grindon (one), Robert
Copestake at Woodlands, Uttoxeter (one), and Sampson Copestake at Prestwood
near Ellastone (two). Jane Copestick witnessed the marriage between William
Wooldridge of Stafford and Ann Foden at Seighford on September 29th, 1796. In
1851 James Copestake owned a beerhouse in New Street, Longton and in 1875
Ambrose Copestick had a business as a smallware dealer in Mill Street, Hanley

TURNERS AND POTTERS

In the past, when wooden utensils were used by all and sundry on the farm and in
the home, the craft of the "turner" was as essential in any rural community as the
skills of the blacksmith, wheelwright and carpenter. Not only did he make wooden
pails, barrels, tubs and buckets for the storage and fetching of water, milk and other
fluids, supply butter churns and milking stools to the dairyman, but he fashioned
objects of all kinds on his pole lathe out of the wood that grew in great profusion in
the forests all around. Often he worked with clay, making bowls, trenchers, cups
and jugs for rich and poor alike. Now, in the modern age of mass production the
market for domestic woodware has all but vanished and we are left with a few
tempting reminders of these ancient crafts, their surnames. Someone like Ranulph

Turner
Turnor

le Turnur, rated at 3 shillings for Bagot's Bromley in 1327, would have been adept at most of the skills outlined above. Yet the medieval "tornator" as in Geoffrey tornator (thirteenth century Okeover Deeds) signifies either "turner" or "turnspit" in a scullery, whilst Richard le Tournour of Church Eaton (1334 Assizes) was perhaps a jouster who regularly took part in a tourney or tournament. A much rarer source for the modern surname Turner, Turnor has been said to be a nickname for a hunter who was endowed with such fleetness of foot, that he could run down and turn the hare he was pursuing, or, conversely, a mocking allusion to some namby-pamby individual who was so weak that he could not even turn aside a hare, e.g. 1327 Lay subsidies, Robert Turnehare of Hilderstone. There is also a likely source with sexual connotations. In Lancashire the name Turner is occasionally to be traced to Turnagh near Rochdale in Greater Manchester. One bearer of the surname Turner whose life ended in tragedy was Sampson Turner junior of Pillaton, who "....being lunatick and drowning himself was by virtue of a licence out of the court put into the church yard, being by the rubrick deprived of the burial service in the liturgy" (Penkridge parish registers, April 4th, 1735). The manor court at Standon, convened in the 23rd year of the reign of George II (1750), on the 5th day of October, agreed that "We lay a pain of 10 shillings each upon William Turner and John Harding they don't brush the hedges and scour the ditches in the lane leading from Standon to Walford between now and Candlemas next". In 1841 Hannah Turner, aged 1 worked a twelve-hour day at George Phillips' Earthenware Factory, Longport cutting papers for John Wood, a job she had done for 2 years. She also lit the fire got the slack in and carried water in tubs to wash the ware. "Tis not very heavy" she said to the commissioners who questioned her. Trade directories: 1851, Miss Mary Turner (matron of Stafford Asylum); 1851, Samuel Turner and Son (boat builders and timber merchants), Canal Side, Barlaston; 1875, Edwin William Turner (emigration agent and writing clerk), King Street, Newcastle-under-Lyme.

In medieval London "turner" was another name for a "disher", who made wooden measures for wine and ale and whose mark had to be placed on the bottom of each measure. Samples of the marks were then submitted to the Chamberlain. Locally William Bankes, dish turner, is quoted in the Haughton parish registers for 1659, whilst John Browne dishthrowey (sic) occurs at Norton-in-the-Moors in 164. In the Audley estate surveys, William le Throwere who is paying an annual rent of 3/2½d for one and a half burgages at Betley in 1298, is contributing the identical amount ten years later for one messuage and 6 acres, but this time he is known

Thrower

William le Torner. Clearly the names Turner and Thrower are interchangeable this particular time, referring most likely to craftsmen who fashioned wooden utensils such as bowls and dishes on a lathe. However, when we alight upon William le potter (1348) at the same manor court, then the medieval trio of Turner,

Potter

Thrower and Potter are far more likely to denote local craftsmen who "turned", "threw", or simply "shaped" kitchen utensils out of clay on a potter's wheel

A potter at his wheel, and kilns (Potter and Thrower p. 214)

Elsewhere Thrower was once an occupational term from the clothing trade for a person who twisted filaments of silk, converting them into silk thread, whilst Potter also designated a maker of metal pots or a bell-founder. During the reign of King John the Pipe Rolls record under Staffordshire the purchase and dispatch of 4,000 plates and 500 cups for the king's Christmas feast held at Tewkesbury in 1204. Thomas Andrew Potter was editor-proprietor of the Staffordshire Daily Sentinel founded in 1873; 1907, Hannah Potter (confectioner) of Newport Lane, Middleport; 1907, John Potter (organ builder), Beresford Street, Shelton.

Pot
Pott
Potts

A handful of other surnames also set the tone in our county, renowned for it pottery. Pot, Pott, Potts, for instance, is certainly metonymic for Potter now and then, but it can be an abbreviated version of Philpot - "little Philip": Tatenhill manor court rolls, 1465/66, John Philipotte, or a toponymic for habitation near some pit or hole: 1539 Muster, Richard Pote, enlisted at Fradswell and John Pott at Kibblestone; 1851, James Potts (plumber, glazier, paper hanger), Queen Street, Burslem; 1907 Jabez Potts (miner), Henry Street, Tunstall.

Crocker
Croker
Crockett

Crocker, Croker and Crockett present a few problems, Crocker and Croker derive either from the Saxon "croc(c), crocca" - "an earthen pot", hence a maker of such pots, a potter, or go back to any one of three locatives called Crèvecoeur in Calvados, Oise or Nord; 1302 Assizes. Robert de Crevequer and John de Benteleye sureties for William le Sauvage and his wife Lucy in the case against Richard Costantyn; 1400 Assizes, Robert Creukere of Uttoxeter.

On the death of Edith, wife of Robert Croket at Tunstall in 1348, all her land fell into the hands of the lord of the manor and her prize bull, valued at 9 shillings, was taken as heriot. All the medieval spellings of the name occur as "Croket" at Audley, Chesterton, Penkhull, Shelton and Tunstall, and this suggests either a diminutive formed from the Scandinavian personal name "Croc (Crok)", an original byname for a crookbacked, sly, cunning individual or a diminutive of the Saxon "croc(c), crocca", mentioned above. Here a nickname is implied - a crackpot perhaps, a slightly eccentric man or woman with peculiar ways. There was a Middle English "croket" - "a lock of hair", or "a large roll of hair", much worn in the time of Edward I, which could have given rise to a name for someone who favoured a hair style of this type. Thomas Crockett was one of the "syselookers" elected a Newcastle-under-Lyme in 1565, that is, a warden of assize or "aletaster" who had to see, that the local ale was brewed according to the rules. 1875, Ann Crocke (grocer) of Normacot Road, Longton.

Bowler
Boaler

Bowler/Boaler is a surname characteristic of Derbyshire, Cheshire and Lancashire. Our own county should be added to these. It signifies either a maker or seller of bowls or a medieval tippler who "continued at the bowl" long after all the other regulars had staggered out of the alehouse. Robert le Boller of Newborough west of Needwood Forest (1332 lay subsidies) could represent either meaning. In 1666 Richard Bowler was charged on one hearth at Highfield

Workers cutting marble. (Hewer p. 212)

Turning a bowl. (Turner and Thrower p. 213/214)

(Fawfield Head) and Robert Bowler on two hearths at Ravenscliffe near Talke Pi█
1851, Thomas Bowler (farmer) of Alton; 1907, George Bowler (police sergeant█
Festing Street, Hanley.

Bowl(e)
Boule
Bowell
Bowles

     The singular Bowl(e), Boule is either synonymous with Bowler in bo█
senses or a nickname applied to anyone with a rotund physique. Robert Boule █
Butterton-on-the-Moors was ejected from his holding of half an acre of land in 13█
by William, son of Benedict de Boturdon.   1907, Ernest Bowle (corporatic█
labourer) of Liverpool Road, Burslem.   Bowell and Bowles were introduced █
Norman immigrants from Bouelles in Seine Inférieure, as in Shellow Bowells ne█
Chelmsford, held by John and Ralph de Bueles in 1249. William Boweles, one █
the members of the Bowles family, landowners in Rushall during the Middle Age█
died of the plague in 1348. In 1907, A.W. Bowles (clerk) resided in Cauldon Roa█
Shelton.

BARRELMAKERS

One of the most specialised and intricate of all woodcrafts is that of the "coope█
who makes barrels, tubs and casks for holding non-liquid substances such as flo█

Cooper
Cowper

tobacco, vegetables, fruit etc, tight casks for the storage of liquids like ale, wat█
milk and so on, and also pails, wash tubs and other utensils for dairy and househo█
use.   The craft is of great antiquity.   It is mentioned in the Bible and was known █
the ancient Egyptians. By the end of the Middle Ages, the cask was recognised █
the standard item of storage throughout most of mainland Europe. The mediev█
cooper followed no written guidelines in making his barrels or casks. He relied █
trade secrets, experience and his own impeccable judgement to calculate the exa█
number and dimensions of the staves required to make a utensil or vessel of █
particular size, ensuring at the same time that each finished article was watertig█
and strong enough to withstand any rough handling.

     Alexander le Coupere rented one messuage at Talke from the Audleys █
1308 for a sum of 20 pence per annum, and in 1432 William Hexstall and his w█
Margaret accused Thomas Couper of Ashley (husbandman) and two oth█
gentlemen of fabricating and publishing divers false charters in order to "...*distu*█
them in their possession of certain lands and tenements in Assheley". At the Gr█
Court of John Audley, held at Betley on October 28th, 1513, John Couper was fin█
12 pence "...*for that he made an affray on Ralph Roo and drew blood*". In 18█
Thomas Cooper, aged 14, earned 6 shillings a week, drawing waggons in the botto█
coal-pit at Woodhead Colliery, Cheadle, for the butty Edward Edwards. 1851, Ch█
Cooper (coach superintendent), Winton Square, Stoke; 1851, Daniel Coop█
(cratemaker), Bourne's Bank, Burslem. The variant Cowper, common up until t█
close of the seventeenth century, is now Cooper's poor relation, although m█
bearers of the surname Cowper pronounce it as Cooper: 1375 Manor court ro█
William Cowper (butcher) of Newcastle-under-Lyme; 1539 Muster, Harry Cow█

Potter 16th century (Potts p. 216)

Carver p. 220

enlisted at High Offley and Richard and Olyver Cowper at Ronton; 1653, Richar[d] Cowper, overseer of the poor at Newcastle-under-Lyme; 1697, Rugeley paris[h] registers, Richard Cowper (Cooper). In the 1666 Hearth tax returns Cooper is th[e] sixth most common surname derived from a trade in the county, behind Smit[h], Taylor, Turner, Wright and Walker.

Carver

In 1466 Richard Couper (karver) of Abbot's Bromley was one of a gang [of] eight men who broke into the property of John Gresley (knight) at Colton, poache[d] fish from his fishery, dug up and carried away earth, and stole goods and chatte[ls] valued at £20. The "karver" addition gives the game away, for Richard Couper w[as] also a wood carver, hence the modern surname Carver, but this can also mean[t] carver in stone, a sculptor. Tatenhill manor court rolls, 1523, John Bankes otherwi[se] Carver; 1907, L. Carver (grocer) of Fenton Road, Hanley. The Derbyshire locali[ty] Calver in the Derwent valley, south of Froggatt, is pronounced as "Carver", and th[is] could provide a locative source. The place means "ridge where calves grazed".

Hooper

To the "hooper" fell the task of making and fitting the hoops or staves to t[he] casks and barrels. Joane Hooper was exempt from any hearth tax at Knutt[on] Constablewick in 1666. Elizabeth Hooper of Woore was buried at Mucklestone [on] April 8th, 1694. 1851, George Hooper (coal dealer) of Rocester; 1907, Alexand[er] Hooper (ironworker) of Silvester Street, Burslem; 1907, John Hooper (shoemake[r]) Broad Street, Newcastle-under-Lyme.

Surrounded by casks, barrels and tubs all their working lives, the coopers a[nd] other craftsmen of that ilk needed little encouragement in using such words [and] similes in their conversation for colleagues of the fuller figure. Obesity a[nd] corpulence have always been natural targets for uncomplimentary nicknames, as t[he] unfortunate fat boy or girl at school knows only too well, as they are merciless[ly] tormented on all sides with taunts of "barrage balloon, barrel, barrel belly, tu[b, tubby", and so forth. Huwe Baril in a thirteenth century deed from the Rydewa[re] Chartulary may have acquired his name because of his pot belly, his resemblance [to] a barrel. But there again, it might have come about as a result of his drinking habi[ts,] that is, his ability to drink a barrel of beer in one session, or it may have sim[ply] denoted, that he was a barrel-maker by trade. Bardsley gives 1688, John Barr[ell] cited as John Barwell in 1691. Locally, Thomas Barwell of Clifton Campville s[old] a gelding for £6/13/4d to be used in the carriage of ammunition in the 1640 Mus[ter.] His ancestors probably had roots in Barwell near Hinckley in Leicestershire, ab[out]

Barrell
Barwell

15 miles away to the south east. The place refers to a stream once frequented [by] boars. For the pairing Barrell-Barwell, compare Farrell-Farewell.

Cade
Cadd

The Middle English "cade" - "cask, barrel" - was employed in exactly [the] same way. Consequently, William Cade of Dilhorne, who stole some coal fr[om] Ralph Freeman's quarry at Dilhorne in 1371, either made casks and barrels fo[r a] living or was as round as a barrel. This gives us the surnames Cade, Cadd. Oth[er] origins to be looked at include a Saxon personal name "Cada", found in Cadb[ury] near Tiverton, Devon - "Cada's fort", or an Old English byname derived from a Germanic root meaning "something lumpy or protruding", applied to someone who was stout or stumpy. In north Staffordshire dialect "cade" has the sense of "the weakest lamb". In 1532 Richard Cade, his wife Grace and five children were amongst the inhabitants at Cauldon. 1851, James Cade (tailor), Mill Street, Leek; 1875, William Cade (hatter), Tontine Square, Hanley; 1907, James Cade (labourer), Sutherland Street, Fenton.

Cadman is usually an occupational term for a maker of casks, but also feasible is "servant of Cade" in any of the senses just outlined. Some writers plump for the very rare name Caedmon, borne by the first English poet known to us by name, who was a humble servant on the estates of the abbess of Whitby (circa 680). Apparently the gift of poetry was passed on to him during a divine vision, whilst he was asleep in the abbey stables. 1539 Muster, William Cadman, enrolled at Almington, Hales and Blore; 1666, John and widdow Cadman, ineligible for hearth tax at Stafford, Joseph Cadman, charged on two hearths at Great Haywood, and Anne Cadman on one hearth at Biddulph; 1907, Ernest Cadman (ostler), Queen Anne Street, Shelton; 1907, George Cadman (marl getter), Bond Street, Tunstall; 1907, Ralph Cadman (potter's fireman), Caulton Street, Burslem.

Tubb(s) and Tubby are misleading, for they all go back to the Old Norse, Old Danish personal name "Tubbi" or the Old Swedish import "Tubbe". Richard Tubbe of Stadfold and Haselour near Elford, was rated at 2 shillings in the 1327 lay subsidies.

WRIGHTS, CARPENTERS AND JOINERS

In general the "wright" worked in wood, and was often synonymous with "carpenter" or "joiner". In the Prologue to the Canterbury Tales, Chaucer tells us that the reeve had learned a good trade in his youth, in fact "..*he was a well good wright, a carpenter*". William Wryght of Yoxall (1425 Assizes) is also styled "carpenter". The actual Wright-Joiner correspondence is not evidenced. 1601, Alice Mylwarde alias Joyner of Alstonefield; 1907, Richard Joyner of Lytton Street, Stoke. The Norman "carpenter" is thin on the ground even during the Middle Ages. His work involved the repair of the lord's ploughs and carts, building and mending houses and furniture, probably using "estovers", as in the case of John, son of Richard, son of Ralph le Carpenter of Tunstall (Dunstal), who applied for permission from his Lord John Bagot in 1310 to take reasonable "estovers" in his wood at Bagot's Bromley. This referred to wood that a tenant was privileged to take from the landlord's estate towards the reparation of houses, hedges or implements. Thomas Carpenter enlisted at Norbury in the 1539 Muster; 1851, William Carpenter (auctioneers), Foregate Street, Stafford; 1907, Alfred Carpenter (bricklayer) of Keary Street, Stoke; 1907, G. Carpentier (sic), (litho printer), Jervis Street, Hanley.

The Saxon name Wright ranks fourth on the list of the most common surnames derived from a trade in 1666, scoring 121, after Turner on 150, Taylor o 187 and Smith on 458. Another John Bagot, most likely a descendant of the Jol Bagot above, was Sheriff of the county in 1414, when he allowed 3 prisoners escape from Stafford Gaol, who were in his custody for various criminal offence Henry Wright was one of the escapees. At the Tunstall manor court, held at Bursle on May 3rd, 1610, Sissillia Wright (widow) was obliged to pay a fine of 3/4d f' assaulting and wounding Frances Smyth, wife of John Smyth. In 1841 Frederi Wright, aged 11, carried moulds for his father George at the Cliff Bank Earthenwa Factory, Stoke, owned by William Adams and Sons. He worked a 12 hour day, fro six in the morning until six at night. 1851, John Perkins Wright (hop merchan Rickerscote, Stafford; 1851, Job Wright (blacksmith), Crown Yard, Stone; 187 Francis Septimus Wright (stationer, printer), Market Place, Longton.

Wrightson

At first sight the patronymic Wrightson - "son of the wright" - looks harmle enough: 1381 Poll tax, Thomas Wrightsone (husbandman) and his wife Christian charged 16 pence at Lapley and Wheaton Aston. This develops into Wrixon: 166 Thomas, John and William Wrixon, all exempt from hearth tax at Walsall Forr Constablewick. Yet John Wrexham married Alice Jennings at Rushall on Februa 5th, 1705 and William Rixon of Walsall wed Elizabeth Booth (also of Walsall) the Cathedral Church of St Mary and St Chad, Lichfield, on April 12th, 175 Clearly, in the Walsall, Rushall area, the names Wrixon, Rixon and Wrexham a variants of the same name. Wrexham in North Wales is feasible but highly unlike

Wrixon
Rixon
Wrexham

There are numerous compounds in "-wright", many of which have no become obsolete. See accompanying table. Only two have made any significa impression on our local nomenclature - Cartwright and Wainwright, the craftsm who designed and built the medieval carts, wains (wagons) that rattled alo country lanes drawn by horses or oxen. The bigger carts, drawn by teams of up eight horses had wooden wheels with iron rims, studded with iron nails or spikes aid traction along the bumpy, muddy tracks. The lighter carts were called "wai and had 2 or 4 wheels. The surname Cartwright proliferates in virtually every no and cranny of the county at all periods. In 1356 Richard le Cartewright of Tean a 9 others were sued by Thomas de Shene for imprisoning him at Tean, where th also beat him, wounded him and generally ill-treated him. Members of the lo militia in their respective neighbourhoods in 1539 comprised Richard Cartwrigh Barlaston, Hugh Cartwryght at Whitmore and Hanchurch, Thomas Cartwright Mucklestone, Homfrey Cartwright at Stone, and William Cartwryght at Salt a Enstone. In 1693 the house of John Cartwright of Upper Hulme was licensed worship by Protestant dissenters, and in 1732 the borough officials at Newcast under-Lyme agreed that "...*Sampson Cartwright was to be paid £10 towa wainscotting the altar in the church*". 1851, Moses Cartwright (flint grind Longton Mills; 1851, Daniel Cartwright (gardener, seedsman), Leek Sheep Mark 1887, Thomas Cartwright (umbrella maker), Waterloo Road, Burslem.

Cartwright

SURNAME	WORKED WITH OR ARTEFACTS MADE	EXAMPLE	LOCATION	SOURCE(S)	YEAR
Arkwright	Ark, Wooden Chest or Cupboard	Arkwright(widow)	Wood Street, Burslem	Potteries Trade Directory	1907
Cartwright	Carts, Wagons	William Le Cartwrygthe	Trentham	Lay Subsidy Rolls	1327
Glasswright	Glass	John Glasewryth	Staffordshire (no location specified)	English Industries of the Middle Ages. L.F. Salzman	1380
Micklewright	Nickname: "The Big Wright"	Thomas Micklewright	Gaolgate Street, Stafford	Kelly's Directory	1872
Plowright	Ploughs	Robart Woode (Ploweright)	Seighford	Parish Registers	1624
Tellwright	Tiles	Frederick Tellwright (miner)	Darnley Street, Hanley	Keates's Gazetteer and Directory	1873
Wainwright	Wains – Carts, Wagons	Mary J. Wainwright (dressmaker)	Albert Street, Tunstall	Keates's Gazetteer and Directory	1873
Wheelwright	Wheels and Wheeled Vehicles	John Whelewryght	Lapley and Wheaton Aston	Poll Tax Returns	1381

Compounds of Wright. (E. Tooth, F. Daniels)

A COMMON CART.

Cartman p. 226

Iron mill with water hammer for making blooms. (Bloomer p. 234)

A 14th century English carriage. (Cartwright p. 222)

A 14th century reaping cart or wain. (Wain p. 227)

Cart(e)

The people who drove the carts and wagons went by any one of a number of names, e.g. the basic Cart(e): 1532, Thomas Carte of Meaford or Cartman: 190? Charles Edward Cartman (shopman), Hamilton Road, Birches Head.   Yet ? Yorkshire Cartman, together with Carman and Cartmal are corruptions of Cartme? which is a locative derived from Cartmel with its ancient priory and square belfr? west of Grange-over-Sands, Cumbria. This represents the Scandinavian compour "kart-melr" - "sandbank on rocky ground", where the initial element recalls the fir? part of our own Cartlidge, discussed in Volume 1.

Cartman
Cartmel
Cartmale
Cartmail
Cartmill
Carpmail
Carpmael

The locative Cartmel results in the modern surnames Cartmel, Cartma? Cartmail and Cartmill, whilst a coarse kind of cloth once manufactured in the are? known as "Carpmeals" or "Carptmeals" survives as Carpmail, Carpmael: 18? Samuel Cartmail (shopkeeper) of Kingstone, Uttoxeter; 1866, John Carpma? paying an annual sum of £1/4/9d for freehold land near Wetley Rocks; 1912, Jose? Cartmill of Waterloo Street, Hanley.   If the original name is Carman, then this stan? either for "carman, cartman, carter" or the Old Norse "karmann", variant "karlmann" - an adult male, used as a personal name.   John Carmon held one gard? in Abbot's Bromley at the will of the lord in 1402 and paid 9 pence rent per annu?

Carmon
Charman
Cherman
Churman
Charme
Churm(e)

Charman too signified a carter or carrier, as typified by Geoffrey le Charmo? assessed at 2/6d for Haughton south west of Stafford in 1327.   Around Tipton a? Wednesbury the spelling Charman interchanges with Cherman and Churma? eventually becoming Charme and Churme: Tipton parish registers, 1654, Elin? Cherman (1655, Charman; 1604, Churme); 1666 Hearth tax returns, Henry Charn? exempt at Wednesbury.   Note also 1872 Kelly's directory, Joseph Chirm, Fair Vie? Beech Lane, Harborne.   However, an early instance such as 1539 Muster, Geffr? Cherme of Sheriffhales may be derived from Saxon "cearm" - "cry, shout",? nickname for a boisterous person.

Carter

The basic Carter - "carter, cartman" - is almost as widely dispersed ? Cartwright.   In an assize, dated 1319, the Abbot of Burton Abbey appeared agai? more than a dozen defendants, who had come by night in a hostile manner to ? manor of Ilam, where they broke open his doors, took away certain cattle, st? goods and chattels to the value of £40 and assaulted one of his servants Nicholas? Cartere.   At the Standon manor court in 1338 Thomas Ball sought a debt of ? shillings from Thomas le Carter and Nicholas de Boures.   Carters recruited in ? 1539 Muster include Edward at Blithfield, Thomas at Norbury, William at Ron? and Thomas at Stafford.   Elyzabeth Carter, *"a poore laboring wench"*, was bur? at Ellastone on July 30th, 1600.   The first incumbent of Christ Church, Tunst? consecrated by Bishop Ryder in 1832, was the Reverend William Carter.   18? John Carter (enameller, lustrer), Mill Street, Hanley; 1851, George Carter (join? of Trentham.

Charter

The rare Charter is a survival of the Old French "charetier" - "car? wagoner": 1323 Assizes, William le Charetter of Uttoxeter; 1640 Muster, Edw?

Charter, member of the trained band at King's Bromley.

The archaic Saxon "wain" - "cart, wagon", as portrayed in the famous painting *The Hay Wain* by Constable, was constructed by the wainwright, also spelt Wainewright and Wainright. It was a large, open wagon, with either two or four wheels, drawn by horses or oxen, and used for carrying heavy loads, usually of agricultural produce. Apparently the surname Wainwright established itself in the Danelaw shires wherever the ash tree flourished, since its wood, when steamed, was pliable and well adapted to the making of "wains". Henry Waynewright was elected sergeant of the borough at Newcastle-under-Lyme in 1497, his pledges being Thomas Crockitt and Edmund Mathowe, and in 1500 this same Henry was appointed constable. The Audley parish registers give the following: Elizabeth Waynewrighte, buried on January 19th, 1567, Agnes Weanwright married to James Howarthe on October 26th in the same year and Delicia, wife of John Wainwright (parish of Lawton), buried on February 17th, 1709. Trade directories: 1851, Samuel Wainwright (farmer), Winnington, Mucklestone; 1907, Alfred Wainwright (fireman), North Staffordshire Railway, of Maclagan Street, Stoke and the very apt Richard Wainwright, carting contractor of High Street, Tunstall.

"Wain", when employed on its own, signifies a builder or driver of a cart or wagon, and exists today as the name Wain(e), Waines and Wayne. In 1327 subsidies paid at Castern and Wetton in the Manifold valley comprised 2 shillings from Richard Wayn and 2/6d from William Wayn. Thomas Wayne was one of the brethren at the Priory of St. Thomas, Stafford in 1524. Naturally accidents occurred from time to time involving these heavy contraptions, and one such took place at Hints in 1614, when "*Jhon (sic) Addams, son of Rodger Addams, beeing kilde with a wayne, was buryed*". The date was September 28th. From a post office run by Isaac Wain at Longnor in the Staffordshire Moorlands in 1834, letters were sent to Leek 3 days a week by horse post. 1851, George Waine (coal dealer), Clarence Street, Hanley; 1851, Richard Wain (chair maker, turner), Derby Street, Leek; 1875, Mary Wain (beerseller) of Canal Street, Longport.

Wainman, Wenman, Whenman denote a wagoner, driver of a cart: Betley parish registers, 1563, Nicholas Weinman, buried on July 4th. George Wenman was rector of Kingsley from 1716 to 1725.

The construction of the wooden wheels for the carts and wagons involved not only great dexterity in the use of a wide range of hand tools, but also accuracy of measurement and considerable knowledge of all the different stresses and strains on joints. This is where the "wheelwright" could show off his consummate craftsmanship. John Whelewryght and his wife Sibilla were assessed at 2 shillings for Lapley and Wheaton Aston in the 1381 Poll tax; Weston-under-Lizard parish registers, 1742, William Wheelwright of Castle Bromwich. But here the principal name associated with the craft is Wheeler, as evidenced by William le Weler, rated at 16 pence for Bishop's Offley in 1332, and noted down by the Norman scribes as

Wheeler

"rotarius" in 1327 - "wheelwright". Interestingly, in the 1381 Poll tax, Rober Cartwryght of Brewood is also known as "rotarius", and so these two surnames ma be interchangeable during medieval times. One remarkable fine imposed by th Staffordshire assizes of 1414 amounted to 2/6d, the exact value of a cartwhee which had caused the death by accident of Adam de Mutton at Ingestre. Th surname Wheeler is essentially a south Staffordshire surname, but examples for th northern sector are in good supply: 1608, Thomas Wheeler, paying 3 pence pe annum rent for his house in the Iron Market, Newcastle; 1666, Francis Wheele charged on one hearth at Haughton near Stafford; 1851, James Wheeler (tailor Brownhills, Burslem; 1907, Edward Wheeler (barman), Erskine Street, Longto 1907, Alfred Wheeler (terra cotta maker), Clarence Street, Stoke.

Wildsmith

Tirer
Tyrer

Spokes

Tyers
Tyas
Tyes
Tiece
Teice

The Wildsmith was responsible for making the iron parts of the wheels, th rims: 1907, H. Wildsmith (engine driver), Cambridge Street, Fenton; 1912, Dani Wildsmith (potter), Dunrobin Street, Longton. The original form is something lik "wheolsmith". The Tirer, Tyrer too may have fitted iron rims or tyres to the whee Eccleshall parish registers, 1602, John Tyrer of the Ridge; Castlechurch paris registers, 1638, Richard Tyrer of Forbridge. Yet a spelling such as John Tireha (1332 lay subsidies) for Lancashire, could represent "tire hare", hence a hunter hares (Compare Turner). Spokes would then denote a craftsman who made th wooden spokes of the wheel: 1539 Muster, Robert Spokes, enlisted at Burton ar Rickerscote. Incidentally the names Tyers, Tyas and Tyes all go back to Old Frenc "tieis", the Norman description for a German, and pronounced "tea-ace" or "ti ace": 1324 Assizes, Henry Tyes (Tyers); Pelsall parish registers, 1775, Thom Tiece, 1810, Charles Teice. Note also the fieldname "Tiersplace" (1462/63) Blymhill.

Dowler
Dowley
Dooley

Dowell
Dowall

The headless pins, pegs or bolts, used to fasten together the separate piec of wood, were called "dowels", and made out of wood or iron by the Dowler: 185 Thomas Dowler (baker, flour dealer) of Bridge Street, Newcastle-under-Lym 1907, G. Dowler (police sergeant), Uttoxeter Road, Longton. However, Pet Dowler of Stowe-by-Chartley (1618), is also recorded as Peter Dowley in 161 which inevitably clashes later on with the Irish Dowley and Dooley. These a derived from "O Dubhlaoich" - "descendant of Dubhlaoch" (black hero). Dow and Dowall are Scottish or Irish forms of Dougal - "black stranger": 1872, Jo Dowell (farmer) of Acton Trussell.

Pegg(e)
Peggs

Peg-making also attracted the attention of anyone called Pegg(e), Peggs, t these names are often from a pet name for Margaret. One of the indictments ma before the Justices on the Monday, the Feast of St. Michael, 1306, concern William and Adam Pegge, who had unlawfully killed John, son of Walter Turgis Stafford. Thomas Pegg was one of the churchwardens at Ellastone in 1639, a Catherine Pegg married Robert Ford of Swynnerton at Seighford on June 15 1756. 1851, George Pegg (auctioneer), High Street, Uttoxeter; 1873, Edward Peg (station master), North Staffordshire Railway, Milton; 1873, William Pegg (house painter), Buxton Street, Sneyd Green.

There is some overlap with Page, since Ann, daughter of John and Mary Page alias Peg, was baptised at Weeford on May 26th, 1771. The John and Mary here are almost certainly the same John Pegge, bachelor, aged 21, and Mary Cope, spinster, married at Weeford on September 30th, 1769.

Much of the timber used by all the aforementioned woodworkers and craftsmen may have been supplied by the "sawyer", who sawed the wood and timber at the local saw-pit. In 1312 Gladusa, formerly wife of William de la Pole, sued Henry le Saghere for an acre of land in Hatherton near Cannock as her right. Sawer is the original form, but Sawyer with intrusive "y" as in Bowyer wins the day. Henry le Sawyer and his wife Alice were assessed at 2 shillings for Lichfield in the 1380 Poll tax. In the 1539 Muster Roger and Thomas Sawyer enrolled at Knighton near Adbaston, whilst in the 1640 Muster one gelding, priced at £4/10/- was purchased from Christopher Sawyer of Colton for Mr Wilson's division. At the township of Bignall End and Eardley End the Overseers of the poor in 1729 granted 1/3d a week to Ann Sawyer, who was 45 years of age, lame and had "one child to tend her". 1851, Henry Sawyer (grocer, provision dealer), Lower Hadderidge, Burslem; 1851, William Sawyer (beerhouse owner), Smallthorne; 1875, Mary Sawyer (coal dealer), Broom Street, Hanley. Sawyer often develops into Sayer: Haughton parish registers, 1731, Edward Sawyer, cited as Edward Sayer in 1743. Nevertheless, if the original name started out as Sayer, then a number of other solutions must be sought. For example, 1302 Feet of Fines, Saer de Harecurt of Quixhill is a Norman personal name of Germanic origin, possibly from "Sigiheri", but Sayer, along with Sayers, Sare, Sear(s), Seers and Seear can also be derived from Middle English "saier" - a professional reciter of poems or songs, a shortened form of "assayer" - a person who assayed or tested metals, or a foretaster of food, or even a derivative of Old French "saie" - "silk, serge", a maker or seller of such materials: 1539 Muster, William and Richard Sare of Eccleshall; 1875, Thomas Sear, White Swan Inn, Church Street, Longton; 1887, Abraham Sayer (grocer) of King Street, Tunstall.

The rare Cleaver/Cleever is either for a worker who split boards with wedges instead of sawing, or for a dweller by a cliff: 1907, William Cleaver (hairdresser), Carlisle Street, Longton.

2. CRAFTSMEN IN METALS

IRONWORKING

Almost every medieval community had its own iron smithy, domain of the local "blacksmith", or "smith" as he was better known. If it were not for his skill in forging metal in his workshop, all other craftsmen would have had no tools with

which to carry on their own trade. Not only was he concerned with shoeing hors
and oxen, but he also made and repaired ploughshares and harrow tines for t
ploughman, the scythes that cut the corn, the shears that clipped the wool, t
chisels that shaped the stone and axes that chopped the wood. He made fittings
all kinds for wagons and tackle and spurs for horses, armour for the knights a
soldiers, iron arrowheads for the arrow-makers, not forgetting a whole host
weapons for hunting and war. Anything made of metal was put to use and the wa
of his forge must have been crammed with old bits of metal from discarded too
and all sorts of odds and ends. More than any other inhabitant in a medieval villa
he was the mysterious devil-like figure with mastery over fire. Just how wide

Smith(e)
Smyth(e)

dispersed the surname Smith was during the Middle Ages in north Staffordshire c
be seen immediately from the map, charting the 1327/1332 lay subsidy rolls for t
two northern hundreds of Pirehill and Totmonslow. In 1341 Adam le Smyth a
two others, armed with swords and bows and arrows, took away some marl, cl
and sand from the soil of Thomas de Wasteneys at Colton in the Trent valley. At t
Tunstall manor court on September 14th, 1372, Alice le Smyth was fined thr
pence for brewing once against the assize of beer, that is, brewing and selling be
of inferior quality. The claim, that the spelling Smyth(e) is proof of aristocra
ancestry, simply does not ring true, since Smyth(e) is merely an older form of Smi
dating back to the period when "i" and "y" were used for the same vowel soun
usually next to the letters "m" and "n", e.g. Standon manor court rolls, 1355, Hen
le Smith, quoted as Henry le Smyth in 1356 and as Henry le Smithe in 1361.
selection of noteworthy incidents and episodes involving people called Smith etc
as follows: At Newcastle-under-Lyme in 1584 Homfry Smyth was denied h
liberties "...*for breakinge the peace against Robert Halpeny and John Woddall a*
strikinge them with a cay and a clogge tyed to the same in the tyme of election
officers..." George Smyth, otherwise Nayler, late of Audley, nayler, was indicted
the Quarter Sessions for discharging a fowling piece, charged with powder and na
shot at the conies (rabbits) in a warren belonging to Edward Egerton at Wrinehi
on January 6th, 1599. Two years later, having evaded capture, he was declared
outlaw. One tragic tale concerns Ann, wife of John Smith of Stanton, who w
buried at Ellastone on July 9th, 1638. The parish clerk tells us that she "...*fi*
unnaturally killed hir owne child and having nott ye feare of God before her eay
hanged herself in a chamber with a slipping of yarne". Trade directories: 185
Noah Smith (basket-maker), Derby Street, Leek; 1851, William Smith (cheese a
bacon dealer), Navigation Road, Burslem; 1875 Bickerton Smith (sugar boile
Dale Street, Hanley; 1887, Richard Smith (tinplate worker), High Street, Longto

Smithson
Smisson

Male heirs of medieval "smiths" did not always inherit the surname Smit
but were often designated quite mundanely "son of the smith", resulting in Smithso
and Smisson. In 1350 John le Smythesone of Amerton near Weston-on-Trent, o
of the executors of the will of Adam atte Pyrye (chaplain), sued Robert son and h

Blacksmiths (Smith p. 229)

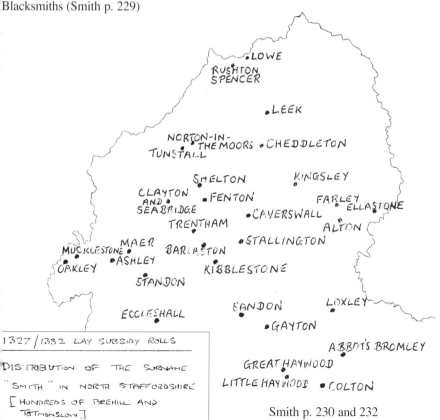

Smith p. 230 and 232

SURNAME	METAL WORKED WITH OR ARTICLE(S) MADE	EXAMPLE	LOCALITY	SOURCE(S)	YEAR
Arrowsmith Harrowsmith	Arrows, Iron Arrowheads	John Le Arwesmyth	Betley	Audley Estates Survey	1298
Goldsmith Gouldsmith	Gold	Henry Le Goldsmyth	Stafford	Lay Subsidy Rolls	1327
Greensmith	Copper and Brass	Thomas Greenesmythe	Alstonefield	Parish Registers	1549
Locksmith	Locks	William Le Locksmyth	Newcastle-under-Lyme	Manor Court Rolls	1369
Naismith Naysmith	Knives	William Le Knyfsmyth	Newcastle-under-Lyme	Assize Rolls	1348
Shoesmith	Horseshoes	Henry Shewsmyth	Tamworth	Parish Registers	1613
Sixsmith	Scythes	John Sixsmith(collier)	Fegg Hayes	Potteries Trade Directory	1887
Whitesmith	Tin	Richard Le Whytesmith	Walsall	Assize Rolls	1309
Wildsmith	Wheels, especially the Iron Parts	Daniel Wildsmith(potter)	Dunrobin Street, Longton	Potteries Trade Directory	1912

of Robert de Say for a debt of £6. Christobell Smithstun (sic) was buried at Standon on the 22nd March, 1578.

Less common surnames for a worker at the smithy include Athersmith, that is, "atter smithe", but an alternative origin might be a toponymic for habitation at some smooth place: 1763 Tithe Map, R. Athersmith of Walsall.

The medieval "smithy" supplies us with the names Smithies, Smithyes and Smythyes, plus the self-explanatory Smythyman, Smytheman, Smitherman. William Smythies (clerk) was admitted to his liberties at Newcastle-under-Lyme in 1371; 1435, John Bothum (smythyman) of Froghall; 1579, Elenour, daughter of Raphe Ratchdale and Margery Smythyman, baptised at Ellastone on March 20th; 1666, Humfrey Smythiman, exempt from hearth tax at Cannock.

Competing with the indigenous Saxon "smith" was the Norman "fevere, fevre", from Latin "faber", or "ferour, ferreor" - "worker in iron". Yet neither comes anywhere near the total domination of the home-grown Smith. The former survives as Feaver(s), Fever(s), or Le Fevre, Le Fever. In 1295 Edmund, brother of Edward I, appeared at the Staffordshire assizes against a number of defendants, including Hugh le Fevre of Mucklestone, claiming, that they had entered his free chase at Needwood and had killed and carried away game and done other damage amounting to £200. 1907. Dr Le Fevre (physician, surgeon), Trentham Road, Longton.

In 1320 William le Ferour sued Swane de Snoxton regarding nine acres of land in Meaford. Modern variants of the name comprise Ferrer, Farrar, Farrow, Faro and Pharaoh: 1532, Thomas Ferrer, householder in Sandford Street, Lichfield; 1577 Feet of Fines, Francis Farrowe of Lichfield; 1667, Sussana Pharoe, servant of Thomas Nabb of Alton (yeoman), left 2 shillings in his will; 1851, Ralph Farrar (clog and patten maker), Piccadilly, Tunstall. Robert Farrow (1822-1906), who settled in Leek in 1847, first worked as a tallow chandler, then was appointed sanitary inspector in 1867 by the improvement commissioners, also serving as supervisor of markets, school attendance officer and secretary to the fire brigade.

French interest here is also focussed on names such as Ferrers/Ferris and Fourniss/Furnace. Ferrers and Ferris are to be traced back to any one of umpteen localities on French soil called Ferrières, meaning "the smithies" whilst Fourniss and Furnace are sometimes from places called Fourneaux in Calvados or La Manche - "the furnaces". During the Middle Ages, the Ferrers family, who hailed from Ferrières-Saint-Hilaire in the province of Eure, Normandy, held a considerable amount of land in eastern Staffordshire, centred around their castle at Tutbury, but George Ferris (potter), resident in Wellington Street, Burslem in 1907, probably had ancestry in one of the many other locations called Ferrières in France.

Besides the French connection, the surname Furnace, together with Furness and Furniss, is also to be derived from Furness in Cumbria - "Fuththernessa" - circa 1150 - "headland near the island of Futh (Old Norse Futhar-ey)": Chebsey parish registers, 1664, Bennet Furnace (male) of Walton near Eccleshall; 1851, Thomas

Ryder Furniss (Catholic schoolmaster) of Swynnerton; 1887, James Collins Furnes (surgeon) of Heathcote Street, Kidsgrove.

Ovens

Remarkably the surname Ovens lives on, testimony to some mediev worker who lived near or worked at an oven or furnace. Church Eaton paris registers, 1578, Robart Ovens and Katerina Edwardes, married on January 20th 1872, Peter Ovens (shopkeeper) of Gnosall. Even more extraordinary is the survival of the name Doubtfire: 1332 Subsidies (Lincolnshire), Thomas Doutefi

Doubtfire

This stands for "do out the fire", hence someone who was in charge of a furnace, c who enforced the curfew, originally "couvre-feu" - "cover fire", a custom institute by William the Conqueror in 1068, at the hour of 8pm. A bell was rung ever evening at this particular hour as a signal to put out fires and go to bed. Bardsle gives 1771, William Flude and Mary Doubtfire, married (Records of St. George' Hanover Square, London).

Bloomer

Since ancient times iron had been extracted from iron ore by "smiths" i "bloom-smithies", where there were open charcoal-burning hearths, on which th ore was heated, and, by constant blowing of the bellows, small amounts c malleable wrought iron or "blooms" were formed by the "bloomer", who sold ther to other smiths for fashioning into whatever finished product was required. In 129 Richard le Blomare rented half a rood of land for $^3/_4$d per annum on the Audle estates at Betley. The "blooms" he made could well have gone to William Naylare, also resident at Betley in the same year, who obviously made nails ar may have been a joiner or carpenter himself (see Naylor). Anne Blumer's buri took place at Mucklestone on February 20th, 1648, whilst Allice Bloomer ar

Bloom

William Pool got married at Penkridge on June 24th, 1703. The rare Bloo contains the same meaning as Bloomer: 1907, Mark Bloom (tailor) of Lichfie Street, Hanley, but nowadays a Jewish name going back to the German for "flowe takes precedence in some instances.

Blower(s)

The worker who operated the bellows in the bloomery earned himself th name Blower(s), but as we have seen, this is often a local pronunciation of Blo near Swinscoe or Blore south of Mucklestone, or even descriptive of an entertain in the minstrelsy who blew a horn of some sort. A bloomsmithy at Horton ne Rudyard, held on a lease by the Abbot of Hulton Abbey, was broken into by riv claimants in 1528, and the "blow hearth", the "smith wheels" and most of the wal were damaged. Anna Blower married William Bentley at the parish church of S James the Great, Audley on November 28th, 1680; 1875, Thomas Blower (assista to Dr Dawes), Chadwick Street, Longton.

Bowdler

Some writers associate the surname Bowdler with the process of ir manufacture, taking it as an occupational term for a man who cleansed ore in buddle (shallow vat or tumbrel). The latter was certainly used by Derbyshire le miners during the seventeenth century, but this origin has never been validated. C the contrary, greater emphasis must be laid here on two Shropshire localities - Ho

Bowdler near Church Stretton and Ashford Bowdler south of Ludlow. Both places preserve a modified form of the Norman family name "de Bulers" or "Boulers", landowners here during the Middle Ages. Locally we find Robert Boudeler, late of Wolseley, and his wife Margaret, accused by Thomas Wolseley in 1461 of causing waste and destruction to some houses demised by him to them for a term of years. Mary, daughter of John and Mary Boudler, was baptised at Seighford on August 22nd, 1725; 1907, Stephen Bowdler (miner) of Leek New Road, Cobridge. The English verb "bowdlerize" - to expurgate a book, is attritutable to Thomas Bowdler, who, in 1818, published a 10-volume edition of Shakespeare's works *"in which nothing is added to the original text, but those words are omitted which cannot with propriety be read aloud in a family"*.

The dealer or trader in ironware was of course the "ironmonger". In 1294 John, son of Henry de Casterne sued John de Knotton for a messuage in Newcastle-under-Lyme, in which John de Knotton had no entry except by a demise which Henry de Casterne (his father) had made to one Elyas le Ironmongere for a term which had expired. Humphrey Iremonger was buried at Standon on March 6th, 1560, and Anne Iremonger, daughter of Richard Iremonger, was baptised at the same place on 11th May, 1572.

One of the most difficult surnames to unravel in this category is Blundred with variants such as Brundred, Brundrett, Burndred and Burndrett. A convenient starting point is a fieldname called "The Brundrit" in Baguley near Wythenshawe Hall, Greater Manchester. William Brond(d)ret held land here in 1282, and the place is recorded as "Brundrett(e)" in 1838. It is derived from "branderith" - a gridiron, grating, grate, that is, an iron tripod fixed over a fire on which a pot or kettle was placed. The surname would thus indicate a maker of such an iron framework. Additional localities in Cheshire of a similar nature include "Brondurthfyld juxta Altryncham" - 1423, which probably survives in Brundrett's Flatts in Altrincham, Blundretts Moor in Rostherne, Brundreth in Great Budworth, The Brundrett in Hatton near Runcorn and Burnt Yard Field in nether Knutsford, which occurs as "le Branderth" in 1440, "the Brente erthe" in 1571 and "The Brundearthes" in 1634. All these, however, go back to the Saxon "brend, eorthe" - "burnt earth" - scorched earth or land cleared by burning, and eventually converted to arable. Besides these, Brundred Farm in Prestbury - "Brundritt House" (1692), owes its name to the Brundrett family, amongst whom were Robert Brundrett (1602) and John Brundreth of Bollington (1686).

The obvious conclusions to draw from this mass of information is that the surname Brundred, Brundrett, Burndred and Burndrett, and finally Blundred is either an occupational term from "branderith" for a craftsman (smith) whose forte was hammering out gridirons or gratings, or a toponymic for habitation by a plot of land which had been cleared by burning: 1539 Muster, Richard Brondret, enlisted at Biddulph; 1658, James Brundreth of Trentham; 1712, Anna Brundred of Keele;

Burndred
Blundred

1882, Miss Annie Burndred, appointed mistress at Foxt village school; 1887, Josep Burndred (photographer), Market Street, Hanley; 1907, Sampson Blundred (co. dealer, carter, furniture remover), Upper Normacot Road, Longton; 1907, Arthu Blundred (labourer), Helena Street, Fenton.

Brandreth
Brandrick

Brandreth and Brandrick specimens are a little thinner on the ground: 166 John Brandreth, charged on one hearth at Bagot's Bromley, whilst Richar Brandrike was exempt at Gayton. In the 1532 list of families in the Archdeacon of Stafford, Bronrede is coupled with Bronrege at Lichfield, and Alyzawnd Brownryge is numbered amongst the Lichfield contingent in the 1539 Muster. S this suggests that the modern Brownridge is just another corrupted form o

Brownridge
Brownrigg(e)

Brundred, rather than for a dweller at a brown ridge, cf. 1588, Symon Brownridg of Ellenhall, noted as Brownrigge in 1611. If Brownrigg is the original name the we must consider a derivation from Brownrigg north east of Whitehaven ar Brownrigg near Moricambe Bay (both in Cumbria).

Trevitt
Trevett
Trivitt
Treffett

The surname Trevitt, Trevett, Trivett and Treffett is also liable to catch o the unwary researcher. The first reaction is to connect it with the old word "trive - a three-legged stand or support for a pot or kettle made out of iron and placed ov a fire, just like the "brandreth", but this is too premature. All the evidence points a modified variant of Trafford, which is first altered to Trefford: St. Mary's pari

Trafford

registers Stafford, 1639, Geoffrey Traford (1637, Trefford), then sharpened Traffort: 1539 Muster, Lewys Traffort of Brereton near Rugeley, and simplified Traffott etc: Cheadle parish registers, 1662, Ann Traffett, Jeffery Traffott; 157 Thomas Treffett of Lapley. The letter "f" is finally hardened to "v": 1685, Sar Trevit of Keele; 1907, Charlotte Trevett (tilemaker) of William Street, Bursler 1907, W. Trevitt (pointsman) of Alma Street, Fenton; 1907, Walter Trivett (min of Jervis Street, Fenton. Trafford is usually a shortened version of Stratford

Stratford
Stretford

Stretford - "ford crossed by a Roman road", but it is also traceable to Mick Trafford and Bridge Trafford near Chester - "ford in a valley", or Trafford Chipping Warden, Northamptonshire - "ford by a trap": 1851, Charles Traffo proprietor of a temperance eating house in Derby Street, Leek; 1875, Alfr Trafford (agent for the Shropshire Union Railways Company), Station Stre Burslem.

Besides horseshoes, the smith made other equipment for horses, includi buckles, spurs and stirrups. Reaney cites John Bokelsmyth of London (138 although the buckles were generally made by someone called Buckle or Buckl

Buckle
Buckler

1736, Thomas Buckler and Elizabeth Longslough married at the Cathedral Chur of St. Mary and St. Chad, Lichfield on July 26th; 1907, Frederick Buckler (mo man), London Road, Trent Vale.

Spurrier

In an assize of 1461 William Sporyour of Wolverhampton - "spur maker is also designated as "smyth". His name lives on as Spurrier. In 1381 Willia Wasteneys sued Ralph Sporyere for breaking into his close and houses at Staffo and taking his goods and chattels valued at 40 shillings; 1532, Henry Sporear, resident at Bromley Hurst near Blithfield Reservoir; 1731, Elizabeth Spurrier and Thomas Bladen, married at Barton-under-Needwood on April 20th. The equivalent Norman term for a maker of spurs, a spurrier - "loremier", supplies the modern Lorimer, Lorrimer, Loriner: 1435, Roger Sporyour (lorymer) of Walsall; 1539, Robert Lorymer, member of the local militia at Abbey Hulton; 1582, Agnes Lorymeire of Hanchurch; 1628, Richard Phillips alias Lorimer of Milwich.

The stirrup maker has bequeathed names such as Stirrup, Stirrop and Sturrup, although some of these must be derived from Styrrup north of Worksop in Nottinghamshire - "(site) at the stirrup-shaped hill". Stirrups crop up at Newcastle-under-Lyme regularly covering the period 1490-1688: 1490, Richard Sturrope, warden of the assize of bread and beer, appointed sergeant to the mayor in 1495 as Richard Stirrop; 1688, Thomas Stirropp, firelooker. In 1851 Thomas Stirrup (coal master) resided in Cinder Hill, Longton.

NAILS, LOCKS, KEYS AND KNIVES

The main centre of the nail-making industry in Staffordshire has always been the south of the county, yet nail-making was also undertaken at Newcastle-under-Lyme, Audley and Betley during the thirteenth and fourteenth centuries, since at that time nails and other iron ware were being transported from Newcastle to North Wales for the construction of castles to keep the Welsh insurgents in check. The individual craftsmen worked on their own, making the nails by hand, taking advantage of the abundant charcoal, iron ore and limestone, essential requirements in the process, and their nails were passed on to the local farriers, joiners, carpenters and shoemakers. On the Audley estates at Audley in 1308 William le Naylere rented one messuage at 3/7d per annum, whilst William, son of Walter le Nayler held 5 acres of land at Betley at an annual rent of 2/5d. In 1380 Henry Nayler stood as one of the pledges for John Boothland, admitted unto his liberties at Newcastle-under-Lyme that year. The surname Naylor, Nayler, Naylar, Nailer persists in this north western region for over three centuries, even before the advent of the Industrial Revolution: 1539 Muster, John Nayller enrolled at Trentham, and Ralph Nayler at High Offley; 1555, John Neyler and Margery Loloe (sic), married at Audley on June 18th; 1669, Thomas Nayler, juror at Standon manor court; 1702, Maria, daughter of Jos. And Maria Naylor, baptised at Audley on April 6th; 1873, George Naylor (potter) of Macclesfield Street, Burslem; 1907, Thomas Naylor (postman) of Ford Street, Shelton.

The enormous numbers of nails produced included "tingle-nails", a very small kind of nail or tack, which gives the modern surname Tingle, a maker of such nails: 1576, John Tingle of Newcastle-under-Lyme; 1618, Thomas Tingle and Ann Depper, wed at Seighford on September 1st; 1875, William Tingle (beerseller) of Hope Street, Hanley. Rivett(s) and Revitt designate either a maker of rivets or

Rivett(s)
Revitt

possibly a nickname for someone as hard and as stumpy as a rivet: 1385, William Rivett, pledge for John le Fletcher junior, received unto his liberties at Newcastle-under-Lyme; Betley parish registers, 1596, Thomas Ryvet; 1851, Reuben Reve (grocer, tea dealer), Watergate Street, Tunstall. A locative source might be Rea west of Burnley - "Revet" (1202) - "roe headland".

Nail
Neal(e)

Although evidence is lacking the surname Nail could well be a local varia of Neal(e) - Gaelic "Niall" - "champion" - compare especially 1532. John Ney householder at Wall near Lichfield and of course the dialectal "neel" for "nail".

Lokesmith

The manufacture of locks and keys has been an important industry Wolverhampton since at least the early 1600s, but "locksmiths" do occ sporadically in north Staffordshire from time to time. Richard Lokesmith wa appointed one of the wardens of the assize of bread and beer at Newcastle-unde Lyme in 1395 and John Sillitoe (locksmithe) was buried at Audley on Decemb 7th, 1643.

Lock(e)
Locks

Lock(e), Locks on its own is somewhat misleading, for the sens inherent in the names comprise a nickname applied to someone renowned for his her fine, curly locks and an occupational term for the keeper of the lock (barrier) a river or the bridge-keeper who took the tolls. In 1430 Rose, late wife of Willia Lok, sued William Snape for a third of a croft, 30 acres of land, 8 acres of meado and 10 acres of pasture in Uttoxeter and Abbot's Bromley, which she claimed dower. 1907, Frederick William Lock (tramways inspector), Wade Street, Bursle 1907, Albert R. Lock (motor man), Victoria Road, Stoke.

Locker
Lockyer
Lokier

Locker, too often contains the occupational meaning, but, in addition, it ca also be synonymous with Locksmith or Looker (a shepherd). In 1476 Hugh Lock and two other yeomen from Newcastle-under-Lyme were accused by James L (knight) of stealing his horse, valued at 40 shillings. John Lokker was chaplain Ipstones in 1539 and Richard Locker was charged on one hearth at Kingsley 1666. 1851, Samuel Locker (coal dealer), John Street, Longton; 1887, Jam Locker (hairdresser), Market Street, Fenton. Many of the Lancashire Locke derive their name from Locka Farm near Arkholme in Lonsdale Hundred, found "Lokker" in the Middle Ages. Lockyer, Lokier - "locksmith, lock maker" is ve scarce: 1412 Manor court rolls, John Lokyer and his wife acknowledged a debt

Makeblyth

22 shillings to Richard Makeblyth, vicar of Alrewas; 1471 Assizes, Nichol Dyngeley late of Walsall (sporyour) alias called Nicholas Lokeer of Walsall; 190 William Lockyer (joiner) of Lower Hartshill, Brick Kiln Lane, Stoke.

Shacklock

The compound Shacklock is probably for a shaker of locks, either in t sense of a gaoler, or, less likely, for someone who had a habit of shaking back his her long hair. In 1227 Robert Shakeloc and William Turgis appeared at the loc assizes, charged with ejecting Philip and his brother Geoffrey, from their fr tenement in Stafford. William Shakeloc paid his subsidy of 16 pence at Alton 1332 and in 1532 Robert Shakelok, his wife Dorothy and family were householde at Mayfield several miles to the north east, descendants in all probability of Willia

The noun "locket" - a small ornamental case of gold or silver, containing a miniature portrait etc, worn around the neck, was originally a diminutive of "lock", a small lock, a catch or spring, used to fasten a necklace or other ornament. However, the surname Lockett, Lockitt and Luckett is a diminutive of "Luke" from the Greek name Lucas, "the man from Lucania", a west coast region of southern Italy. Its popularity is down to the apostle St. Luke: 1532, Edmund Lokett, wife Margaret and children, resident at Horton near Rudyard; 1666, William Lockett charged on one hearth at Botteslow, Hanley, John Lockett likewise at Meir Lane End, Christopher Lockett exempt at Stone, William Locket assessed on one hearth at Longsdon, whilst those at Horton Constablewick include John Locket, rated at one hearth, Timothy Lockett at 2 hearths, with Walter, Francis and widdow Lockett all ineligible for any tax. John Lockett was one of the overseers of the poor at Betley in 1726. 1851, Samuel Lockett (farmer) of Dilhorne; 1875, Ann Lockitt (stay maker), Lichfield Street, Hanley.

The concept of left-handedness has always been surrounded by an air of mystery and suspicion. Latin "sinister", for example, originally meant simply "left (hand side)", but later "foreboding of ill, ill-omened", because, according to the augurs, birds etc that appeared on the left-hand side were a sign of bad luck, but on the right-hand side they presaged good luck. Similarly the imported French "gauche" - "left-handed", came to mean "awkward", and both senses are contained in the surname Gauche. The equivalent notion in the Danish language is "kei", a dialect word, which referred to anyone who was left-handed or left-footed. This occurs in the medieval romance *Sir Gawain and the Green Knight* - line 422 : "*...the kay fote on the folde he before sette*". Survivals of this Danish word are probably represented by Henry Kay, contributing 3/4d lay subsidy at Whitmore and Hanchurch in 1332, and Robert Kay, who sued Ralph de Makley and his brothers Richard and John in 1349 for taking him by force and imprisoning him at Uttoxeter and ill-treating him until he had paid to them a fine of 40 shillings for his release and for detaining 80 florins belonging to him, worth 20 marks (£13/6/8d). This is one origin of the surname Kay(e), Kayes, Keay(s), Keeys, Key(e), Keyes, Keys and Keyse.

Another common source of Kay in northern counties such as Yorkshire and Lancashire and also Lowland Scotland is Old Norse "ka" - "jackdaw", but in the Midlands and in Staffordshire the usual development is "co(o), ko", the modern Coe: 1887, William Coe (mining engineer), Brownhills, Tunstall. Key and Kay often alternate with one another, as in Eccleshall parish registers: 1578, Katheren Key (Kaye), so we are also dealing with a maker of keys. Other Keys had ancestors who used to reside by some quay or wharf, or who were employed there in some capacity or other, whilst not to be ignored is the Old Welsh personal name "Cai", Middle Welsh "Kei", which is ultimately from the Latin "Caius". Of the numerous Keys recruited in the 1539 Muster, mention must be made of John Key at

Key(s)
Keay

Millmeece, George Key at Shugborough and Crystofer and William Key at Newto near Blithfield. Robert Key was a member of a local Quaker family, who practise as a physician in Leek during the 1730s and 1740s. 1851, James Keys and So (brass and coppering etc, sheet roller manufacturers), Brookhouses, Cheadle; 187. William Keay (cabinet maker), Sneyd Street, Tunstall; 1875, Josiah Key (grocer Marsh Street, Hanley.

Kear
Keer
Care

Kear, Keer, Care - "keysmith, maker of keys" - is not noted for nort Staffordshire, but see Codsall parish registers, 1682, Jane Care and Thomas Co married there on November 30th.

Naismith

Knives of all description were made by the Naismith - "the knife smith". 1347 William le Knyfsmyth held one messuage for life at Rugeley. Indeed, Rugele seems to have been the focus of a thriving cutlery industry during the 1300s, judgin

Cut(t)ler
Grinder

by the presence there of the surnames Cutler and Grinder. In 1327 William Cotyler contributed 18 pence lay subsidy at the vill, Henry le Grynder was i possession of one tenement there in 1347, and inhabitants at Rugeley in the 138 Poll tax returns include Adam Gryndere cotiller, William Grindere cutler, I Grynder cutiller, Adam Eliot cotiller and several more besides. The "grinde actually sharpened iron tools of all kinds on a grindstone or grindlestone. In th north west of the county John le Cotiller was unlawfully killed in 1306 by John c Meudon by night in his bed at Newcastle-under-Lyme. Richard and Thomas Cotel were enrolled at Maer in the 1539 Muster and Ellen Timmins alias Cutler marric Thomas Berkes at the parish church of St. James the Great, Audley on July 14 1612. In 1907 Joseph Cutler (miner) lived in New Street, Wolstanton.

LEAD, TIN, COPPER AND BRASS

Leadbeater
Leadbeeter
Leadbitter

The more malleable metals have handed down few surnames of note in nor Staffordshire, apart from Leadbeater, Leadbeeter, Leadbitter. In 1692 lead an copper mining were revived by the Earl of Shrewsbury in partnership with local an London investors, and lead and copper ore began to be mined at Ilam, Onecote ne Bradnop, Ribden, south of Cauldon Lowe and Swinscoe near Blore. Yet lead o and the remains of a smelting furnace have been found at Wetton in the Manifo valley on the site of an extensive Romano-British settlement in this particular are Wetton itself is situated on the edge of the old lead-mining district of the Derbyshi Peaks, which was concentrated mainly around the Derbyshire villages of Bakewe Matlock, Crich, Ashford and Wirksworth. No fewer than seven smelters are list under entries for these localities in the Derbyshire Domesday survey. With countrywide upsurge in building in the twelfth and thirteenth centuries the Pe: district was intensively exploited for its pigs of lead. Medieval laws enabled t leadminer to search out and to mine ore almost anywhere he wished, save churchyards, gardens, orchards and the highway. These lead miners and worke were known as "leadbeaters", hence the modern surname. In an assize, dated 133

John de Beaufey sued Robert Tochet in a plea, that he should warrant to him 7 acres of land and an acre of meadow which Hawise, formerly wife of Walter le Ledebeter of Derby claimed against him. Unfortunately the surname does not appear in north Staffordshire until 1532, when heads of households comprise John Ledbeter at Okeover and Henry Ledbeter at Rushton Spencer. In fact the name Leadbeater is virtually confined to the north eastern sector of the county bordering on the Derbyshire Peak district prior to the Industrial Revolution: Ellastone parish registers, 1599, Thomas, son of William and Elyzabeth Leadbeater, baptised on May 6th. In the 1666 hearth tax returns for Totmonslow Hundred, Richard and widdow Leadbitter were exempt at Cheadle, although John Leadbitter was charged on one hearth here, another John Leadbitter paid tax on one hearth at Butterton-on-the-Moors, whilst at Uttoxeter, the Constable Richard Turner excused Thomas Leadbitter by reason of his poverty. After the Industrial Revolution the surname invades other areas in the northern half of the county: 1851, Thomas Leadbetter (baker, flour dealer, confectioner), Market Street, Longton; 1851, Edward Leadbetter (butcher), Eastgate Street, Stafford; 1875, Benjamin Leadbeater (greengrocer, coal dealer), High Street, Hanley. (See also Plummer).

One of the most famous sites in the Manifold valley is the Ecton copper mine, which re-opened in 1723 and which was worked more or less continuously until the 1890s. But the medieval coppersmiths used imported copper to make their utensils and their legacy lives on in the name Copper/Cupper: 1539 Muster, Ralfe Copper of Bromley Hurst; 1554 Feet of Fines, Richard Cupper of Paget's Bromley; 1907, John Copper (potter) of Ashford Street, Shelton. The most widespread surname for a worker in copper is Greensmith: 1550, John, son of Roger Greenesmythe, buried at Alstonefield on April 4th; 1872, William Greensmith (hop and seed factor), Tipping Street, Stafford; 1907, Lawrence Greensmith (miner), Garden View South, Longton.

Workers in brass or brass founders are commemorated by the names Brasier, Brazier, Braizier, Brasher. In 1428 Richard Brasyer (potter) of Lichfield broke into the house of Thomas Stanley (armiger) at Lichfield and stole goods and chattels valued at 100 shillings. The addition "potter" here could well refer to a "bell-founder" (see Potter). 1887, Nancy Brazier (milliner and dressmaker) of Knutton; 1907, John Brazier (grocer) of Hall Street, Newcastle-under-Lyme. There may be some overlap with Bracer, Brasher, from Old French "braceor, brasseur" - "brewer" as in Hugh le Brasur, rated at 12 pence for Castern and Wetton in the 1327 lay subsidies. The unattested Brass is perhaps from Welsh "bras" - "stout, fat".

Cann and Canner both refer to makers or sellers of cans, although the Dorset Canns get their name from the locative Cann near Shaftesbury - "(site) in a deep valley", whilst Canner also crops up occasionally as Ganner, with the common medieval confusion between initial "C" and "G", found also in Cannock-Gannock: 1327, William le Cannere of Church Eaton, compared with 1381 Poll tax, John

Gannere husbandman of High Onn. These two places are no more than one mil[...] apart. Other examples of the two names include: Tatenhill manor court rolls, 142[...] Margaret Canne; 1532, Agnes Canner syngulwoman of Longnor in the Upp[...] Manifold valley; 1907, Jesse Cann of Sun Street, Tunstall.

GOLD AND SILVER

The English craftsmen in gold, the goldsmiths, were renowned for their outstandin[...] workmanship long before the Norman Conquest. For example, at the time [...] Edward the Confessor Theodoric the Goldsmith was an extremely wealth[...] landowner. With the arrival of the Normans the goldsmith's trade soon flourished [...] all the great towns, and indeed the Goldsmiths' Company of London was given th[...] exceptional privilege of inspecting all the gold and silver work made in Englan[...]

Goldsmith Thomas le Goldsmyth was appointed one of the wardens of the assize of bread an[...] beer at Newcastle-under-Lyme in 1373. When John Goldesmith of Tamworth wa[...] indicted in 1422 for fabricating 40 nobles of base money (gold coins first minted [...] 1351), one Roger Wilnehale of Lichfield (gentleman), the clerk of the Justices of th[...] Peace at Stafford, abstracted and embezzled the indictment with a view of favourir[...] the said John Goldesmyth. Dorrothy Gooldsmith and Edward Abell got married [...] Stowe-by-Chartley on February 15th, 1655. In 1851 George Goldsmith was static[...] master at Rushton Spencer; 1907, John Goldsmith (groom) of Festing Street, Hanle[...]

Offer
Orfeur The Norman counterpart of the Saxon "goldsmith" was "orfevre", as in 13[...] Assizes, Geoffrey le Goldsmith, quoted as Geoffrey le Orfeure in 1295, hence th[...] rare modern surname Offer, Orfeur - eg Antony Orffever, enrolled at Audley in th[...] 1539 Muster, who was head of the frankpledge at Wedgwood in 1549 (Tunsta[...] manor court rolls), written as Anthony Orfer.

Gold
Gould
Goold Gold, Gould, Goold as an independent surname is open to sever[...] interpretations: a nickname for someone of wealth, as typified by 1220 Patent roll[...] Thomas withe Gold of Staffordshire; another nickname for a person who had gold[...]

Goldylockes hair, Ellen Selbye, alias Goldylockes, a poore woman, buried at Ellastone Septemb[...] 19th, 1599; or a personal name such as the Saxon "Golde" (female) or "Gold[...] (male). Up until the seventeenth century the Gold(e), Goold spellings predomina[...] but henceforward Gould strides away into an unassailable lead: 1448 Assize[...] William Goold of Grindon (yeoman); 1532, Dane Gold of Adbaston; 1532, Joh[...] Golde, William Gold and John Goold, all from Elkstone near Warslow; 1539 Must[...] James Golde of Kibblestone; 1666, Hearth tax contributors include Edward Goul[...] charged on one hearth at Wootton-under-Weaver, Bartholomew Gould likewise [...] Waterfall, William Gould exempt at Bradnop. 1851, Ann Gould (cow keeper), Spo[...] Street, Leek; 1875, Joseph Gould (cratemaker), Leek New Road, Hanley.

The extended name Golden, Goolden, Goulden refers either to a golde[...] haired individual or is a late variant of the Saxon personal name "Golding", [...] evidenced by Thomas Golden of Audley (1662), also written down in the pari[...]

register as Golding in 1667 and as Goulding in 1672. This switch recalls a couplet such as Holden-Holding. 1851, Josiah Golden (coal dealer) of Middleport; 1851, Joseph Goulden (boot and shoe maker), Hassells Street, Newcastle-under-Lyme; 1875, Israel Golding (dealer in paper hangings), Stafford Street, Hanley; 1875, Jesse Goulding (grocer), George Street, Newcastle-under-Lyme.

The compound Shergold, Sheargold is probably synonymous with Golden, i.e. descriptive of someone with shining, golden hair: 1872, Henry Sheargold, Cleveland Arms, Cleveland Street, Wolverhampton, whilst Threadgold, Treadgold - "thread gold" - is a name for an embroiderer: Francis Threadgold (chimney sweeper) of Stoke-on-Trent married Jane Taylor on February 3rd, 1803; 1912, A. Threadgould (police constable) of Windsor Street, Hanley.

Some goldsmiths may have excelled at making garlands, chaplets or circlets for the head, adorned with gold or silver and worn on special occasions by the ruling monarch and the nobility - the modern surname Garland, but also pertinent is a maker of garlands composed of greenleaves awarded to the King or Queen of the May-day ceremony. In 1359 Katrine, wife of Thomas Garlaund was unjustly ejected from six acres of land in Colton near Blithbury by John Wymour. 1907, George Garland (watchmaker) of Caroline Street, Longton. Some authors have derived the name from the Saxon "garland" - a triangular piece of land, with reference to a dweller there.

This dual origin is also exhibited by Silver, which is either an occupational name for a silversmith or a toponymic for habitation by a silvery (clear) stream: 1612, Mrs Anne Sylver and Mr Laurence Woodde, married at Codsall on June 11th, 1612; 1907, Philip Silver (plumber), Alfred Street, Burslem.

3. THE BUILDING TRADE

DAUBERS, PARGETERS

Nothing brings home more dramatically the threefold division of medieval society than the dwellings of our ancestors - the palaces and castles of the ruling elite, the houses of the middle classes with their magnificent halls and outbuildings and the squalid cottages of the peasantry. These hardly protected the occupants from the cold and driving rain, for they were nearly always made of "wattle and daub", that is rows of upright stakes with the spaces in between filled with interwoven twigs and branches, hazel rods, osiers, reeds and so on, forming a lattice-work. On top of them were daubed layers of earth and clay, or mud mixed with straw, all of which was thrust well into the gaps and left to dry. The whole process was then completed by the "dauber", who smoothed down the surfaces, usually treating them with plaster or whitewash. In 1327 this was the occupation, followed by William le Daubor, rated at 6 pence for Tutbury in the lay subsidy rolls for Offlow Hundred, the lowest tax band in the neighbourhood. His progeny live on as Dauber, Dawber

Dawber
Dauber
Dowbar
Doorbar
Durber

or possibly Dowbar. William Hill, churchwarden for Stoke-on-Trent in 1633 records that William Wotten, the dawber, was paid 3/- for some unspecified work i that year. The surname Doorbar/Durber has been proposed as a variant of Daube but no proof is forthcoming. Nor is there any foundation in the theory, that it wa introduced by some Anglo-Indian immigrants at the height of the Raj, who arrange the "durbar" (reception) for Indian princes. One other alternative beckons - a lat local variant of Derby, which is pronounced by many north Staffordshire natives a "Durby". The change to Durber would then be child's play, since Grubber's Ash nea Alsager's Bank (Bowen's map, 1777), occurs as Groby Ash in 1691 (Audley paris registers). As we have seen, the endings "-er, -ey" often interchange in loc surnames - Pashler-Pashley, Dowler-Dowley, Powner-Powney, so Durber-Durbey i perfectly feasible. The only trouble is no actual written evidence has yet come t light to confirm my suspicions. Despite that, the two variants Durber and Doorba are now well established in north Staffordshire: 1851, James Durber (omnibu proprietor), Amicable Street, Tunstall; 1887, John Doorbar (fishmonger), Broa Street, Hanley; 1907, Emmanuel Durber (teacher of music), Maddock Stree Burslem; 1907, James Henry Doorbar (miner), Upper Mount Street, Tunstall.

     In many ways the craft of "pargetting" was similar to that of "daubing", b the "pargeter" used plaster instead of clay or loam, modelling it into patterns ar completing the work with a coat of whitewash or roughening the surface with sar

Pargeter
Pargiter

or small stones. Pargeter/Pargiter is definitely a south Staffordshire surname, but 1596 the churchwardens at Stoke-on-Trent - Richard Lovat and Bartholomew Boy paid someone called Rawlins 4 shillings for pargetting, and his labourer receive half that amount for 4 days work. In the 1666 hearth tax returns, John Pargiter listed as collector at Rowley Regis, Mr William Pargiter is charged on 6 hearths Mavesyn Ridware, whilst Robert Pargiter is not chargeable at Arley. In 1872 Josep Pargeter, grocer and provision dealer, resided at Quarry Bank, Brierley Hill.

THATCHERS, TILERS, SLATERS

The roofs of the peasants' dwellings were usually thatched with straw or other ra materials which grew in the vicinity such as reeds or sedge. For instance, in Ea Anglia and Essex the most commonly used roofing material was reeds, especially

Reader
Reeder

Norfolk, hence the prevalence of the surname Reader, Reeder in that county. The two names are also of regular occurrence in north Staffordshire: Wolstanton pari registers, 1691, William Reader and Elizabeth Handley married on January 4 1907, William C. Reader (clerk) of Hartshill Road, Stoke.

Redman
Reedman
Readman

     Richard le Redemon, taxed at 12 pence for Water Eaton, south west Penkridge in 1332, could have been a "reedman" - a cutter of reeds, a thatcher or may have had red hair - the modern surname Redman, Reedman, Readma Redmayne, although the latter is usually traceable to Redmain near Cockermouth Cumbria (of disputed meaning). Trentham parish registers, 1620, Raphe, son

an
an
an
yne

Robert Redman, baptised on October 10th; 1875, William E. Redman (joiner, builder, contractor), Edensor Road, Longton; 1907, Philip Redman (plasterer), Hill Street, Fenton.

Reed, together with Read(e), Reid, Rhead and Red(d) have nothing at all to do with "reeds", for they are nicknames for a person with red hair or complexion. In the annals of children's folklore, red-headed people have always been singled out for more adverse comment than anyone else, unaware of course, that the tradition was actually based on the fact, that Judas had red hair. Their repertoire ranges from the basic "Rusty" and "beetroot" to the more picturesque "coppernob, ginger nut" and "carrot top". The following rhyme has been recited (with minor variations) for generations by youngsters all over the British Isles: *"Rusty nut fell in the cut and frightened all the fishes, a fish jumped up and bit his nut and made him wash the dishes"*. The medieval counterpart of "ginger" was the straightforward "le rede" - "the red-headed one", as in David le Rede, paying $4^1/2$d rent per annum for one messuage on the Audley estates at Betley in 1298.

Reed and allied spellings are also derived from several locatives, comprising Read west of Burnley in Lancashire - "roe headland" (see also Rivett), Rede south of Bury St. Edmunds in Suffolk - "the reed bed" and Reed near Royston, Hertfordshire - "rough common", with a toponymic for habitation by a clearing to be considered besides. Reid is the Scottish variant. At Newcastle-under-Lyme in 1688 John Read, the miller, was ordered by the borough officials "*....to amend his unhandsome, careless grinding and neglect in his place and if he do not, then another miller to be appointed*". In 1690 Thomas Cliffe, churchwarden at Stoke-on-Trent, paid a fee of 2/6d to William Reade of Thornfield near Stafford "*...who had a letter of request for grate losse by fire*". The parish clerk at Chebsey records that John Read, a West Indian Black, was baptised there on June 30th, 1778. Was he a servant at Eccleshall Castle, by any chance? 1851, Alfred Read (police officer) of Caverswall; 1875, Sampson Rhead (auctioneer and valuer), Old Road, Bucknall.

r

Strange as it may seem, the surname Thatcher in north Staffordshire shuns the limelight. At Standon in 1361 John le Thatcher was fined 2 pence for letting his colt stray into the lord's corn, but thereafter instances are very hard to come by in the northern half of the county. 1641, Luke Thatcher, resident at Barton-under-Needwood; 1907, Anne Thatcher, licensee of The Globe Inn, Bryan Street, Hanley.

Centre stage is taken by Thacker, a derivative of the Saxon "thacian" - "to thatch", with a hard "k" sound, or Old Norse "thack" - "thatch". In 1472 the sheriff of county Stafford was ordered to arrest Roger Thakker (yeoman), late of Alton and 2 other former inhabitants of the same place, to answer for a number of miscellaneous felonies, trespasses, insurrections and riots, of which they had been indicted in county Warwick. After the Middle Ages the surname Thacker goes from strength to strength, whilst Thatcher fades into the mist. Robert Thacker died of "the sickness" (probably plague) at Kibblestone in 1604. Eventually the north eastern region of the county becomes the real home of the name, for in the 1666 hearth tax returns payments on one hearth apiece are made by Zachary Thacker at Gratwich, Anthony Thacker at Tean, John Thacker at Consall, widdow Thacker at Leigh and Richard Thacker at Beresford (Alstonefield). During Lent 1764 George Thacker was sentenced to transportation to the American colonies for seven years for stealing game birds at Checkley and Stone. 1907, William Thacker (gardener) Temple Street, Fenton; 1907, John Thacker (potter), Uttoxeter Road, Longton.

Theaker

The exceedingly rare Theaker, from Old Norse "thekja" - "to cover", hence a craftsman who roofed buildings with thatch of straw, still survives for a thatcher or roofer in the dialects of northern England and Scotland. 1199 Assizes, Walter son of Thecker; 1875, George Theaker (master of the School of Art, Wedgwood Institute), Burslem; 1907, Mrs Mary Ann Theaker of Marsh Road, Wolstanton.

Tiler
Tyler

The devastating fires, that frequently destroyed houses with thatched roofs in many medieval towns, gradually led to the use of tiles and slates for roofing purposes. It has been surmised, that some 74,000 roofing tiles were supplied by a tilery at Hulton Abbey in 1332-1334 towards the renovation of Croxden Abbey. Roofing tiles were certainly produced in kilns at Sneyd in 1300. Richard le Tyler held one tenement at Great Saredon near Cannock in 1372 and Walter, son of William Tyler received his baptismal rights at Audley on August 26th, 1641. Trade directories: 1875, Rowland Tyler (contractor), Elm Grove, Cobridge; 1907, Thomas Tyler (potter), Bradwell Lane, Wolstanton.

Tellwright

Tellwright - "a maker of tiles or bricks" - is as characteristic of north Staffordshire as potbanks and oatcakes. In the Tunstall manor court rolls (1512-1693) it occurs in a wide variety of forms: 1512, Thomas Telrik; 1549, James Telryk(e); 1572, Thomas Telreight of Sneyde; 1603, Alice Telright; 1641, William Telwright. In 1851 James Tellwright of Market Square, Hanley, specialised in groceries and tea-dealing and in 1873 John Tellwright (miner) lived in Alexandra Road, Oakhill.

Slater
Slatter

The craft of slating roofs demanded not only considerable skill in the correct positioning and accurate nailing of the slates, but also an intimate knowledge of the different shapes, angles and sizes of the roofs. The carboniferous slates that occur in north Staffordshire (Alton rock) may well have been utilised by local slaters during the Middle Ages. Richard Sklatter, admitted unto his liberties at Newcastle-under-Lyme in 1388, had John Smyth and Adam Granehonger as sureties. Members of the 1539 Muster included Humfrey Sclater at Whitmore and Hanchurch, Peter Slater at Stafford, Ralph Sclater at Aston and Doxey and William Sclater at Betley and Balterley. John Sclater of Stanton, buried at Ellastone on July 17th, 1625, lost his life "....*being killed with the thunder*". On August 10th, 1628, the churchwarden at Stoke-on-Trent paid someone called Prince the slater 10 shillings "....*for part of the worke about the porche and slate to slate it*". The spelling Slater does not impose itself with any authority until the seventeenth century: 1666 Hearth tax

WILLIAM SLATER,
FAMILY GROCER,

BAKER, CONFECTIONER
AND
Provision Merchant,

NEW STREET, WOLSTANTON.

Slater p. 246

G. W. RHEAD,
CERTIFICATED

At the Government Art Classes, Longton, Fenton & Chesterton.

ATTENDS PRIVATE SCHOOLS.

TERMS ON APPLICATION.

Special Terms for Private Pupils at their own Residences; or at—

Foulhay Cottage, Hartshill,
STOKE-ON TRENT.

Rhead, Reed p. 245

Slater
Slatter

returns. William Slater taxed on one hearth at Rownall, Richard Slater likewise at Denstone near Rocester, with Raph and Joane Slater ineligible at Cheadle. 1851 George Slater (watch and clock maker) of St. John's Square, Burslem; 1875, Fran Slater (butcher), Nile Street, Burslem. The rare Slatter occurs at Codsall in 1700 where Margret Slatter married John Humfrison on April 10th.

The "pointer" worked in the building trade putting down overlapping tiles c slates and "pointing" them, that is, rendering them with mortar. However, the ter "pointer" was used in the clothing trade for someone who made "points" - tagge laces or cords for fastening hose and doublet together, so either meaning i

Pointer
Poynter
Painter
Paynter

applicable for families called Pointer or Poynter: 1872, George Pointer (joine wheelwright), Biddulph Park; 1875, Henry Poynter (beerseller) of Waterloo Roa Burslem. At Hanbury Pointer is a variant of Painter: 1532, John Peynter, wi Margaret and family, householders there, whilst Robert Poynter is charged on hearths at Hanbury in 1666. Indeed, in the Rowley Regis parish registers, Richar Painter (1610), appears as Richard Poynter in 1618. If the original surname Painter then this refers to the worker who brightened up the interiors of the bigg medieval buildings, churches and castles. The couplet Painter-Pointer (Poynter) an echo of Painting-Pointon in Volume 1. In 1306 William le Leche (doctor) wa indicted at the local assizes for the unlawful killing of Thomas le Peyntour Stafford. John Peyntour, gaoler at Stafford prison in 1414, is probably a descenda of the unfortunate Thomas. The marriage between Jane Painter and John Lomma was celebrated on New Year's Day, 1701 at the parish church of St. Edward tl Confessor, Cheddleton. 1851, John Painter (race-horse breeder and farmer) Deans Hill, Castlechurch; 1851, Thomas Painter (coal dealer), Canal Street, Leek

The dialectal "spon new" - "brand new", comes from the Old Norse "spa nyr" - "chip new" or "as fresh and as clean as a chip or splinter newly chopped off This word, or the allied Saxon "spon" - "chip, splinter", is the basis of tl

Spooner

occupational term Spooner - a maker of roofing shingles (wooden tiles). A le common origin is a person who made spoons (kitchen utensils). This particul surname has been immortalised by the Oxford don, W.A. Spooner, famous for h slips of the tongue such as "*I have in my bosom a half-warmed fish*" - instead of *half-formed wish*" and "*You were fighting a liar in the quadrangle*" instead "*lighting a fire*". These have now entered our dictionaries as Spoonerisms. Tl name Spooner is fairly well dispersed across north Staffordshire from the lat Middle Ages onwards. In 1479 Nicholas Mountgomery, late sheriff of coun Stafford, sued several yeomen, including James Sponer of Milwich, for a debt of marks. 1851, Eli Spooner (butcher), Market Street, Hanley, plus a stall in Hanl market; 1851, Thomas Spooner (boot and shoe maker), Tean Street, Cheadle.

Shingler

Thin boards of wood with parallel sides and one end thicker than the oth are called "shingles" in the trade and these too were often used as tiles for roofir hence the name Shingler, the workman who cut them and roofed buildings w them. Richard Bordehewer of Madeley (Salop) in an assize of 1468, is also classified as a "shyngeler" - a hewer of boards of wood and a tiler, whilst in the 1381 Poll tax William Shyngelere, assessed at 2 shillings for Brocton by Baswich, is entered on the rolls as "carpentarius" - "carpenter". In the Middle Ages, Avery Sulny, chief forester of Needwood, was ordered to deliver from the park at Agardsley as much timber as would suffice to make 10,000 shingles for roofing the houses within the castle of Newcastle-under-Lyme, and Robert atte more, receiver of Tutbury, was to pay for making the shingles and also for the carriage of them to Newcastle. On the 1844 Tithe Map for Kibblestone Joseph Shingler occupied a garden and a stable, owned by Edward Barlow. 1907, Reuben J. Shingler (potter) of Slater Street, Middleport; 1907, Annie Shingler, British Volunteer Inn, Lockett's Lane, Longton.

WORKERS IN STONE

During the Middle Ages domestic buildings made out of stone were relatively rare, and stone, as a building material, was mainly reserved for the construction of castles, churches, cathedrals, abbeys and city walls. Furthermore, in view of the cost, time and effort involved in such formidable building projects, it was only natural, that the stone should be obtained from the nearest available source. Indeed, the medieval church at Biddulph was built of stone excavated from the quarry at Mow Cop, whilst in the thirteenth and fourteenth centuries local stone from the nearby quarry at Hollington served in the construction of buildings at Croxden Abbey about a mile away. Stone quarries were in operation at Tunstall (Stoke-on-Trent) in 1272, at Talke in 1278 and at Balterley in 1280. The stone first had to be quarried, by someone like Henry Quarrior of Newcastle-under-Lyme (1383 Manor court rolls), who is probably identical with Henry de le Delves (1371) - see Delves Volume 1. The name Quarry/Quarrie denotes either a quarryman or a nickname for a squarely built individual: 1306 Inquisition post mortem, Thomas le Quarre of Longdon near Rugeley.

The labourer who actually cut or hewed the rough blocks of stone out of the quarry face was the "stonehewer". In 1513 Richard Stonehewer of Rushton Grange near Cobridge was fined 2 pence for default of appearance at Tunstall manor court. Joshua Stonehewer was vicar at Audley from 1784 until 1790. 1851, William Stonehewer (plasterer), Mill Street, Leek; 1907, Samuel Stonehewer (drayman), Sneyd Street, Cobridge. Other variants evolve later on. First of all Stonehewer is trimmed down to Stonier/Stonyer: 1539 Muster, Roger Stonyer, recruited for the vills Almington, Hales and Blore; 1603, William Stonyer of Wedgwood surrendered some pasture, unenclosed crofts and one tenement for the use of Richard Drakeford; 1719, John Stonier of Horton parish and Katherine Myott of Woolstanton (sic) married at Cheddleton on 13th April; 1851, William Stonier (beerhouse), Slack Lane, Hanley; 1907, John Stonier (tram conductor), Argyle Road, Longton.

Stanier
Stanyer
Stanyard

Stonier/Stonyer are then unrounded to become Stanier/Stanyer and eventually Stanyard with the almost obligatory addition of final "d" :Seighford parish registers. 1791, Richard Stonier, noted as Stanyard in 1793 and as Stanier in 1799; 1796, Joseph Stanyard of Armitage near Rugeley; 1851, Thomas Stanyer (nailmaker), Sharpley Green, Hilderstone; 1873, Noah Stanier (farmer, grocer) of Packmoor; 1887, Samuel Stanyer (marine stores), Church Street, Newcastle-under-Lyme; 1907, Thomas Stanier (carter) of Talbot Street, Fenton.

Dresser

In the past the surname Dresser has been assigned several divergent roles comprising a "dresser" of textile fabrics, that is, a finisher who gave such fabrics a smooth, nap surface, whilst Bardsley suggests a "dresser" of plants, a gardener, with Salzman favouring a "dresser" of leather, whose work involved treating raw hide with lime to remove the hair, and then washing them again before they were placed in the tan vat. Yet in north Staffordshire the name Dresser coincides almost exactly with Stonehewer in the early recordings and is clearly associated with the "shaping" or "dressing" of the stone blocks or even cutting an intricate pattern of grooves in limestone blocks in preparation for their use as millstones.   In 1690 the churchwarden at Stoke-on-Trent paid John Wilkinson 1/4d per day for 24 days for getting, dressing and setting stone for some reparations to the church. Mr. Thomas Dresser (vicar) paid tax on 2 hearths at Dilhorne in 1666.

Mason

After the Norman conquest the Saxon "stonehewers" found themselves competing against the skilled stone workers from all over France, who had brought their own building terms with them. The "mason" - Old Central French "macon" soon became one of the most essential craftsmen in medieval times, and the foreman mason or "master" mason was very nearly equivalent to the modern architect with total control over the design and erection of buildings. He was in charge of the freemasons who worked with freestone, the rough masons who were involved with the less skilled operations such as dressing stones outlined above, and the gangs of labourers on the site.

In 1295 Richard le Mason of Stafford and several other inhabitants swore upon oath that "..*it will not be to the damage of the King's town of Stafford, nor of any other person, if the King grant to Master John de Cadamo, Dean of the King's Free Chapel of Stafford, that he may stop and enclose with a wall a certain lane in Stafford contiguous to the chamber of the said Dean, which extends itself from the highway towards the church of St. Mary in the town aforesaid..*" Masons enrolled in the 1539 Muster include William at Keele, Roger at Stone, Ralph and Harry at Eccleshall, John at Great Sugnall and Ralph at Podmore; 1574, Edward Mason appointed syselooker (aletaster) at Newcastle-under-Lyme; 1688, Elizabeth Mason and George Davenport married at Seighford on June 7th; 1851, John Mason (scythe stone maker), Sheen; 1875, Elijah Mason (basket maker), Pool Dam, Newcastle-under-Lyme.

Mason can also be a variant of Mayson, which normally stands for "son of May", where May is a shortened form of Mayhew, the Norman version of Matthew.

Mason p. 250

Masons, dressers and
stonehewers. p 249-250

Glassmaking (Glazier p. 256)

Ellastone parish registers, 1564, Thomas Mayson and Alice Burton, parents of Margerye, baptised on March 2nd.

Even more prolific than Mason is its Norman counterpart Machin. In 1307 John Machen and Richard de Dokeseye (Doxey) and his wife Margaret were embroiled in a lawsuit centred around the raising of a mill-pool, which unduly narrowed the right of way of John, the vicar of the church of Seighford. The latter complained, that, whereas he had been accustomed to having a wide road from his house in Seighford as far as Doxey, and also as far as Stafford for his horses, carts and wagons in the conveyance of his tithes from Doxey as far as Seighford, the present situation had been made intolerable because of the narrowing of his right of way. Unfortunately, the vicar lost his claim since his own account was not in accordance with the facts of the case. In 1379 Benedict le Machon, William Geffesone and John de Clayton took over a coal-mine at Shelton, Hanley for a period of 20 years, paying the lord of the manor 13/4d rent per annum. Members of the local militias in 1539 comprised Hugh Machyn at Fenton and Longton, Henry Machyn at Abbey Hulton, Roger Machyn at Fulford and Great Fenton, William Machyn senior and junior at Chapel Chorlton, and Humfrey and Thomas Machyn at High Offley. During the reign of James I, two Machins incurred the displeasure of the manor court at Standon, for in 1616 Thomas Machin was fined 2 pence "...*for gettinge claye in Bowers, without lycense...*" whilst in the following year William Machin coughed up a fine of 4 pence for angling in the enclosed fishery and taking fish without the owner's consent. Not far away at Mucklestone in 1629, during the bishop's visitation, Thomas Machin got censured "...*for playinge upon a treble violl upon the Saboth Day upon the greene*". 1851, Aaron Machin (blacksmith, manufacturer of agricultural machines and implements), Castle Street, Eccleshall; 1875, Theophilus Machin (cratemaker) of Nelson Place, Hanley; 1887, Joseph Machin (teacher of music), America Street, Tunstall. Other variants like Macham, Meacham and Meachem are well evidenced but Meachen and Meachin are not: Ellenhall parish registers, 1772, Edward Machin, cited as Edward Macham in 1774; 1887, Henry Meachem (fishmonger), Sneyd Street, Tunstall; 1907, Frederick Meacham (wholesale and retail fishmonger) of King Street, Tunstall.

Lodge is either an occupational term for the warden of a mason's lodge or a toponymic for a dweller at some cottage :Wolstanton parish registers, 1804, Joseph Lodge (cordwainer) and Ann Taylor, married on December 17th; 1907, Mrs A. Lodge (fried fish dealer), Harley Street, Hanley. The famous physicist and spiritualist, Sir Oliver Lodge, was born at Penkhull on June 12th, 1851. His experiments in wireless communication, which preceded those of Marconi's, brought him world-wide acclaim, whilst some of his other research proved invaluable to Einstein in his formulation of the Theory of Relativity.

The medieval "paver" or "paviour" paved the floors of chapels, cathedrals and palaces with marble or ornamental tiles. For example, in 1308 Hugh le

Paver
Pavier
Pavior
Paviour
Pavyer

Peyntour and Peter the Pavier were engaged in "making and painting the pavement at St. Stephen's Chapel, Westminster. In 1443 Thomas Paver (walker) c Newcastle-under-Lyme and a gang of ne'er-do-wells lay in ambush at Newcastle fo John Kyngesley with the intention of killing him, but they only succeeded i thrashing him within an inch of his life. In 1666 William Pavier paid tax on on hearth at Great Wyrley near Cannock.

Limeburner

Whenever building operations of any importance were decided upon, th normal procedure was to build a limekiln on the spot for the burning of lime fc mortar. In the north of the county limestone has been used for centuries for farmin and building purposes, as testified by the limekilns scattered around the Moorland such as those at Consall Forge and Froghall in the Churnet valley, for the Cauldo Lowe limestone quarries. Until the late eighteenth century most of the limeston produced was almost certainly burnt and the lime used either as a fertilizer or fc the making of mortar. The basic name Limeburner is nowhere to be seen, but no 1912, William Limeburn (sic), labourer of Chapel Court, Longton.

Kilner
Killer

Kilner and Killer denote a person in charge of a kiln, where lime was burne 1532, Richard Kylner, wife Margery and children, householders at Barton-unde Needwood; 1666, Edward Killer, charged on one hearth at Rolleston. The Kilne Killer interchange is mirrored in Milner-Miller. To local potters "kiln" has alway been "the kill".

Lymer
Limer

Lymer/Limer is widely accepted as a trade name for someone who used lim in whitewashing houses, but in the light of all the historical evidence outline already, a better option is a worker who burnt lime in the kiln, and consequently o a par with Limeburner and Kilner. Admittedly, the surname is very late in comin to prominence, but this does not detract from the alternative notion. In the reign c Elizabeth I, Richard Lymer otherwise Willcoxson handed over £40 to Richar Mylles and his wife Jane for rights to 2 messuages, 2 gardens, 2 orchards and substantial acreage of land, meadow and pasture in Cheadle. In another disput three years later, in 1587 he goes by the name of Richard Wilcockson otherwis Lymer. Three horseloads of lime and one strike (bushel) of washing lime were use to point the church and steeple at Stoke-on-Trent in 1657. Local Lymers/Lime who tied the knot centuries ago include: James Lymer, married to Elizabeth Botte Ellastone on July 16th, 1595, and William Limer, wed to Betty Davenel at Seighfor on August 11th, 1777. Ann Lymer was mistress at the Catholic day-schoo Cobridge in 1841. 1851, Thomas Limer (nailmaker) of High Street, Longton; 190 Ralph Limer (potter's slipmaker), Shelton New Road, Stoke.

Chalk(e)
Chaulk

Although chalk was often used for masonry, more often than not it w converted into lime. However, the surname Chalk(e), Chaulk, probably refers habitation near some hills where chalk was quarried or goes back to Broad Chalk or Bowerchalke south west of Salisbury, Wiltshire or Chalk near Gravesend, Ken All localities allude to the nearby chalk or limestone downs. In 1907 Cecilia Cha (widow) resided in Wellington Street, Burslem.

During the medieval period most industries were dominated by the master craftsman, who supervised the training of a number of apprentices in his own trade, often requiring to give them some form of education, besides providing bed, board and clothing, until their apprenticeship was completed and they were accepted by the craft guild. At the head of the guild was the "alderman", one origin of the surname Alderman, but there might also be a trace of the Saxon "ealdorman" - a noble or person of rank: Charters of Dieulacres Abbey, Thirteenth century, Aldermanus de la Ward. Note also "Aldermans Hill" (1570) in Rugeley.

The surname Master could signify the master mason or any master in charge of a group of apprentices, the master of a ship, the master of a farm or great household, or even a schoolmaster. Hence, Henry le Mayster, assessed at 2/- for Grindon near Wetton in 1327, might have held any one of these positions. The plural form Masters, Marsters refers to a servant or an apprentice who lived at the master's house: 1347 Inquisition post mortem, William atte maistres of Penkridge. In 1615 Edward Masters (gentleman) and his wife Katherine held one acre of copyhold land called Broadwithies Close at Penkhull for an annual rent of 10 pence. 1907, Tom Masters (clerk) of Princes Road, Stoke; 1907, George Masters (plumber) of Woodland Street, Tunstall.

The patronymic Masterson, Marsterson represents "son of the master" in any of the senses aforementioned: 1605, William, supposed son of Richard Masterson and Isabella Knight, baptised at Betley on February 28th; 1612, Bennetta Masterson, buried on August 8th at Milwich; 1666, Margrett Masterson, exempt from hearth tax at Leek; 1875, William Masterson (draper) of High Street, Newcastle-under-Lyme. Masterman - "servant of the master" - seems to be absent from local documents.

The Norman import "aprentis" - "apprentice", shortened to "prentis", gives us the modern names Prentice and Prentis(s): 1340, William le Prentys, chaplain at the church of Leek. In 1360 Richard Prentys paid a fine of 2d. for failing to appear at Tunstall manor court. 1617, John Butler, a prentice, buried at Seighford February 4th; 1704, Ann, daughter of Thomas Prentice, baptised at Penkridge on March 30th.

The curious Twentyman is a tough nut to crack. Bardsley proposes "twynterman" - a herdsman, who tended "twinters" - cattle, sheep or colts that were two winters old. Another solution focusses on a foreman, probably on some medieval building site, head of a gang of twenty labourers: 1872, Alfred Charles Twentyman of Castle Croft House, Lower Penn.

WORKERS IN GLASS

The cottages of the peasants, made of flimsy timber frames and covered with wattle and daub, had small apertures to let the light through but no proper windows of glass. During the harsh winter months the cold and damp were kept at bay by

Windows
Windus
Winders

wooden shutters or pieces of cloth stretched across the gaps. The surname Window may look like a throw-back to these hard times, but is in fact a variant of Windus Winders - a worker at the winding-house, where threads and yarn were wound. The Register of the Freeman of the City of York cites 1458, William Wyndowes, weaver. In 1872 Joseph Windows (farmer) lived at Mitton Lodge, Penkridge.

Glasswright
Glasewright
Glassman

Most of the glass, made during the Middle Ages, went to enhance the appearance of the great Gothic churches and cathedrals with their majestic towers and spires. Surnames such as Glasswright - "glass maker": 1396 Muniments and manuscripts of Lichfield, John Glasewright, and Glassman - "dealer in glass ware" Richard le Glasmon, rated at 3/4d for Abbot's Bromley in 1327, are apparently obsolete. However, Glasier, Glazier, Glazyer, Glaisher and Glaysher - "glass

Glasier
Glazier
Glazyer
Glaisher
Glaysher

maker" - is alive and well: Tatenhill manor court rolls, 1415, William Glasyer; 1539 Muster, Thomas Glasier, recruited at Mitton and Longnor near Wheaton Aston 1580, Emma, wife of Thomas Glasier of Milton near Norton-in-the-Moors, buried on September 15th.

Verrer
Verriour

The Norman equivalent of the Saxon "glasier" is "verrer, verrier", origin of Verrer and Verriour: 1356 Inquisition, Hugh le verer of Lichfield.

Glass(e)
Glaze

Glass(e) and probably Glaze are derived from the Welsh "glas" - ""blue green or silver grey". John, son of Edward Glasse, buried at Burslem on January 27th, 1614; 1701, Deborah Glass and Charles Whithead, married at Wolstanton on February 10th; 1875, Mr Robert Glass (Inspector of markets and nuisances), office in Market Terrace, Market Place, Burslem.

Glassmaking in Staffordshire was monopolised in the last quarter of the sixteenth century by "gentlemen glaziers" from Lorraine in north east France, driven out of their native country on account of their Huguenot backgrounds. They settled in Bishop's Wood near Eccleshall and their distinctive Huguenot surnames like Hennezel (Henzey), Thisac (Tyzak), Thietry and Houx stand out like sore thumbs the Eccleshall parish registers during the 1500s and 1600s. By the end of the first decade of the seventeenth century these Lorraine glassworkers had all migrated other midland counties or put down roots around Newcastle-on-Tyne.

4. THE CLOTHING INDUSTRY

THE WOOL TRADE

Throughout the Middle Ages England was basically an agricultural nation, whose economy was dependent to a large extent on the export of raw materials and the import of manufactured goods. The main source of the country's wealth at this time was the wool trade. Indeed, English wool was held in such high repute by European buyers, especially clothworkers in the Low Countries that it became known as *"the flower and strength and revenue and blood of England"*. A modern reminder, that wool was England's chief staple for so long is the Woolsack in the House of Lords

16th century glass and below, glassblowing. (Glasier, Glazier p. 256)

Tiler p. 246

Dyer p. 263

Furthermore, how much poorer our literature and everyday speech would be were it not for the many phrases and metaphors borrowed from the manufacture of cloth - "web of life", "homespun philosophy", "thread of discourse", "unravel a mystery" and so on. So universal was the craft of "spinning" that "spinster" became the general description for any woman who had no particular rank or trade and who was independent, that is to say, unmarried, for in the eyes of the law a married woman had practically no existence apart from her husband. The phrase "spinning a yarn" harks back to the time when the "spinsters" gathered at one another's houses during the long evenings of a medieval winter, spinning and making up stories as they worked.

Sometimes wool was spun straight from the fleece, but, as a rule, the fleece was washed to get rid of all the dirt and grease, then greased artificially, using goose fat, butter or vegetable oil. When it had been washed the tangled wool was pulled apart by hand and "carded" - placed between two "cards" held in the hand - wooden blocks, whose inner surfaces were covered with fine, wire hooks. This was the job of anyone called Card(e) or Carder: 1907, H. Card (owner of a sweet stall), Hanley Borough Market. Note also John Cardemaker and wife Matilda, rated at 12 pence in the 1380 Poll tax returns for Lichfield. In North Staffordshire the name Carder could also be a reduced variant of Cardall from Cauldwell (see Volume 1). This process may have even been undertaken by the Comber, Coomber, but these names are generally derived from The Compa in Kinver, recorded as "Coumbere" in 1332 or are toponymics for habitation in a small valley.

Kember and its feminine counterpart Kempster denote a comber of wool or flax: Tatenhill manor court rolls 1345, Sibilla le Kemster; 1414/15, John Kempster. 1907, Bertram Kempster (car conductor) of Hartshill Road, Stoke; 1907, F. Kempster (car inspector) of Windmill Street, Tunstall. The source of Kimber is unknown, unless it is another form of Kember: 1851, William H. Kimber (tailor), Union Street, Hanley.

Before the spinning wheel was introduced the "spinner" availed herself of the distaff and the spindle. This was the method employed by someone like Lucia Spynner, assessed for an unrecorded amount at Barton near Alstone in the 1381 Poll tax. On the other hand, Alice le Whelspynner (1345 Tatenhill manor court rolls) would have found things much easier.

For all intents and purposes, the "roper" too was involved in the process of "spinning", but his craft called for the twisting or plaiting of fibre or strips of hide or animal hair. When Britain's maritime power was at its height during the expansion of the Empire, ropeyards were a feature of almost every coastal town and village. Closer to home rope-spinning can still be seen at Peak Cavern in Derbyshire. In 1326, at the Tunstall manor court, Thomas le Ropere surrendered into the hands of the lord a messuage and all the land with its appurtenances, which he held in Chatterley, to the use of his daughter Ellen and the heirs of her body

lawfully begotten. Another of Thomas's fellow craftsmen, John le Roper, w
elected bailiff at Newcastle-under-Lyme in 1377. Later recordings include: 18
William Roper (cattle dealer) of Croxton, Eccleshall; 1907, Lawrence Ro
(boilermaker) of Fletcher Road, Stoke. The form Raper is chiefly a northern varie
but it does occur sporadically in north Staffordshire: 1637, William, bastard son
Raper   Jane Raper, baptised at Brewood on March 8th; 1907, Jas. Raper (carter) of Cobc
Street, Longton.

Dependent on fine quality wool, the woollen trade and commercial she
farming were integral elements in the economy of medieval Staffordshire. F
example, the best grades of wool produced by the flocks of sheep on the esta
owned by Dieulacres Abbey were selling at £10/13/4d per sack abroad, compan
with £14 per sack from the herds reared by the monks at Croxden - each sa
contained 26 stones of wool.

Weaving was the most important of all the processes in clothmaking a
almost every medieval rural locality had its own weavers, who were responsible :
meeting the local demand for all types of cloth, blankets, materials and so for
The general term "weaver", a derivative of the Saxon "wefan" - "to weave" - is n
very common at all in north Staffordshire in the Middle Ages. When it does cr
up, it is usually an addition to someone's name, as typified by 1442 Assizes, Thon
Stacy wevere of Newcastle-under-Lyme, 1468 Assizes. Thomas Whitgreve, late
Stafford, wever, and 1472 Assizes, Thomas Overton wever of Biddulph. Used
Weaver   its own, it occurs at Walsall in 1377, when Richard Wever is listed on the Burge
Wheaver   Roll. The baptism of Richard Weaver took place at Standon on November 15
1568. In 1840, Thomas Weaver, aged 14, had already served 5 years at Litley Da
Colliery, Cheadle, as a drawer of corves (small coal tubs). At the same pit Sime
Wheaver, aged 17, hauled wagons for the butty, Thomas Flowett. Neith
complained to the Commissioners about the heavy work. 1851, John Weaver (mc
catcher), Waste, Barlaston; 1887, Lydia Weaver (dressmaker), Edward Stre
Burslem. A locative origin for the surnames Weaver and Wheaver is provided
Weaver Hall near Winsford, Cheshire, situated on the river Weaver - "windi
river". This is identical in meaning with a lost stream which gave its name to t
Weaver Hills south of Cauldon, and, of course, to Wootton-under-Weaver.

By far the most persistent occupational term for a weaver during t
Webb   "surname period" is Webb, from an archaic Germanic word, allied to the Sax
"wefan" - "to weave". In 1329 Richard le Webbe was indicted for breaking into t
church of Colton near Blithfield Reservoir, and stealing some chalices a
vestments, valued at 100 shillings. He pleaded not guilty to the charges and w
acquitted by a local jury. By contrast, Maud le Webbe, was fined 3 pence by t
manor court at Tunstall in 1366 for brewing poor quality beer in contravention
the assize of bread and ale. Webbs who swelled the ranks of the local militias
1539 comprise Thomas Webbe at Aston-by-Stone, Thomas Webbe at Swynnerto

John Webbe at Barlaston, Randall Webbe at Madeley (Keele), Robert Webbe at Stone, William and John Webe at Stafford, Richard Webe at Amerton, William Webe at Chartley and Stowe, and John Webe at Hixon. 1851, Richard Webb (corn miller) of Great Haywood; 1851, Peter Webb (farmer) of Crowborough, south of Biddulph Moor; 1875, Josiah Webb (machinist, engineer, tool maker), Gower Street, Longton. Obsolete compounds of Webb are: Great White Book of Lichfield Cathedral, 1318, Henry le Poghwebbe - "weaver of bags", and 1380 Poll tax, Matilda Keuchyfwebbe of King's Bromley - weaver, maker of kerchiefs.

The feminine form was "Webster": 1380 Poll Tax, Adam Webbester and wife Johanna, rated at 16 pence for Penkridge; 1453 Assizes, William Webster of Ilam; 1539 Muster, John Webster, enrolled at Stafford; 1640 Muster, John Webstere, member of the impressed band for Bradnop and Caverswall. In 1666 John Murrall, churchwarden at Stoke-on-Trent, allowed Thomas Webster 2 shillings for "...*beinge in povertie with his wife and ffive children*". On January 27th, 1742, the marriage took place at the Church of St. Mary, Swynnerton between Ann Webster and William Vernon (both of Stone). 1851, Hannah Webster (straw hat maker) of John Street, Tunstall; 1875, William Webster (coal dealer) of Sandford Hill, Longton.

Webber - "weaver" - is a surname characteristic of south western counties such as Devon and Somerset, and is absent from the early material for Staffordshire. In all likelihood the north Staffordshire Webbers were originally migrants from down south.

"Slay" - the reed or shuttle which the weaver used to beat up the weft - was made by the Slaymaker (not evidenced), but it may also survive in the surname Slay, Sleigh. However, the principal source for these is the Scandinavian import "slaegr", a nickname for a wily, cunning individual, as exemplified by 1307 Assizes, Richard Slegh of Gnosall; 1532, William Sleghe of Stowe-by-Chartley; 1532, Agnes Sleghe syngulwoman of Prestwood near Ellastone; 1666, Charles Sleigh (gentleman) charged on one hearth at Kibblestone Constablewick and widdow Sley on two hearths at Burton-on-Trent; 1851, Robert Sleigh (shopkeeper) of Great Haywood; 1851, Hugh Sleigh (silk manufacturer) of Spout Street, Leek. In the northern counties of the Danelaw the chief spelling is Slee, so this, together with Slay/Sleigh and Sligh/Sly would then recall the triplet Lee/Leigh-Lay-Lye: Lichfield Cathedral Registers, 1744, Thomas Slee and Sarah Weast of Drayton Basset, married on August 5th; 1512, Tunstall manor court rolls, Roger Slye, fined 2 pence for default of appearance; 1568, Joane Slighe of Rocester. The trio Sleet/Sleath/Sleith-Sleight-Slight also comes into the equation: Lichfield Cathedral Registers, 1731, Henry Sleet and Martha Rogers, married on January 24th; Church Eaton parish registers, 1593, Frannces Sleight of Norbury; Armitage parish registers, 1733, Jonathan Sleith; Church Eaton parish registers, 1769, Mary Sleeth; 1539 Muster Roll, William Slyght of Hixon. The modern surnames Sleath, Sleith should be compared with the pronunciation of Keighley in the West Riding of Yorkshire - "Keathley".

On leaving the loom, the cloth was in the condition known as "raw" - n[e] ready for use but marketable, and many of the lesser clothmakers preferred [t]o dispose of their products at this stage rather than incur the expense of any furth[er] processes. This raw cloth was transferred to the fulling mills, where it was trample[d] in a trough to soften and cleanse it. Only then was it fit for subsequent handlin[g] along the production line. This trampling process was known as "walking", and th[e] workers engaged in such an activity were called "walkers", "tuckers" and "fullers[,]" depending on which part of the country they came from. Generally speaking, th[e]

Walker

surname Walker is characteristic of the Midlands and the north of England, wi[th]

Tucker
Fuller

Tucker prevailing in the south west and Fuller having the upper hand in the sou[th] east. In our county Walker is streets ahead of both competitors. In 1323, on th[e] Feast of St. Ceadde, several inhabitants of Eccleshall, Pershall and Sugnall bro[ke] into the house of Thomas le Walker at Offley, and carried away linen, 12 silv[er] spoons, five mazers, 40 shillings in money and other goods to the value of £20 [(a] mazer is a hard wood bowl, richly carved and ornamented). At the Tunstall man[or] court in 1353, John Wolryche was fined 12 pence because he "...*fell upon Richa[rd] le Walker and drew blood...*" Richard paid a similar fine for defending himself a[nd] drawing blood on his attacker. Richard Walker of Calwich near Ellastone, yeom[an] and servant of Sir John Cokayn, indicted as an accessory to the death of Jo[hn] Normon, killed at Abbot's Bromley in 1409 by Walter Gilberd of Marchingto[n] surrendered and produced a general pardon in 1415. Two burials worthy of n[ote] from the Ellastone parish registers are as follows: 1619, December 11th, Jo[hn] Walker "...*of the age of five score and five...*" and 1636, August 10th, Pruden[ce] Walker, who died of small pox. 1851, Mary Walker, owner of an eating house in [St.] John's Square, Burslem; 1857, Hugh Walker, killed by an explosion of a cylinder [at] Alton Paper Mill; 1875, Aaron Walker (saddler), Anchor Terrace, Longton.

In Northumberland the name has also originated in Walker on Tyne a[nd] Wear, recorded as "Walkyr" in the thirteenth century: "marsh by the Roman wal[l]" 1347 Assizes, Adam Barat (Baret) of Walker, Northumberland.

By the later Middle Ages there were fulling mills at Burton-on-Tre[nt,] Tutbury, Rolleston, Barton-under-Needwood, Uttoxeter, Rocester, Betley a[nd] Himley. In 1307 John le Folur rented one messuage on the Audley estates at Betl[ey]

Fuller

for 5 pence per annum, and in the same year the Sheriff was ordered to arrest Jo[hn] de Somerville of Wychnor, Lord of Stockton, Warwickshire, and Philip Somerville of Wychnor, county Stafford "...*if they are laymen, and to keep them [in] safe custody until they had rendered to William le Fullere and Robert de Kynto[n] sacks of wool or the value of them, at 10 marks a sack...*" Peter Walkere, assess[ed] at Brewood and environs in the 1380 Poll tax, is also classified as "fuller". 190[5,] Arthur Fuller (shoemaker), Sant Street, Burslem; 1907, William Fuller, Cr[oss] Princess Street, Tunstall. Yet several recordings around the Tipton area need to [be] addressed, e.g. Tipton parish registers, 1661, Richard and Avery Fulwood; 16[

Alice Fullerd (sic). These must be taken along with Reaney's examples: Salt Archaeological Society, 1703, 1719, Avory Fullward, Fuller, alias Fullwood. Richard Fullord is quoted in the 1666 hearth tax returns for Tipton, as well as Richard Fullward. If Fulwood, Fullwood is the original surname, then the locatives to be looked at comprise Fulwood Coppice in Cannock, Fulwood in Preston, Lancashire, Fulwood near Mansfield, Fulwood in Sheffield (West Riding of Yorkshire) and possibly Clay Hall in Tanworth, Warwickshire, recorded as "Folewode" in the thirteenth century. All locations refer to a dirty or muddy wood. Ellastone parish registers, 1635, Elizabeth Fulwood and Hugh Lummas, married on June 27th; 1907, William Fullwood of High Street, Brindley Ford. In order to cleanse the cloth properly the "fullers" resorted to the peculiar absorbent earth known in the trade as "Fuller's Earth", alternatively noted as "Walkerherth" in the Victoria County History for Nottinghamshire. This is a plausible origin of the familiar expression, *"I don't know whether I'm on this earth or Fuller's earth"*.

The surname Tucker - "tucker or fuller" - is hardly in the picture: 1907, John Tucker (market gardener), Wholesale Market, Market Square, Hanley.

When wool or cloth was ready for dyeing, it was handed over to the "dyers". In 1293 Geoffrey Gryffyn was involved with Robert le Deyere and John le Deyere in a dispute concerning an acre of land in the town of Clayton Gryffyn (later known as Clayton Griffiths). 1875, Michael Dyer (coal dealer), Bourne's Bank, Burslem; 1907, W.E.Dyer, licensee of the Unicorn Inn, Higherland, Newcastle-under-Lyme.

The female counterpart was "dyster": Ralph le Deystere of Stafford appeared in a plea, dated 1298, against Alan, son of Simon de Acton, that the latter should warrant to the said Ralph the third part of 4 acres in Acton Trussell. Householders at Shugborough in 1532 included Roger Dester (sic), his wife Agnes, and three children - Edward, Alice and Elizabeth. The modern spelling of the surname is Dexter: 1907, Ted Dexter (potter) of Bold Street, Northwood.

Another occupational term for a "dyer" is Lister, Lyster, Litster, Lidster, Ledster, Lester, a derivative of Middle English "lit(t)e" - "to dye". In 1338, on the Morrow of St. John the Baptist (25th June), Henry Flygh and his wife Alice acknowledged that a certain messuage in Burton-on-Trent was the rightful property of Robert, son of Ralph le Listere, for which Robert gave them 20 marks. 1907, Thomas Lister (blacksmith), Bath Street, Longton; 1907, Robert Lister (boot and shoe maker), High Street, May Bank, Wolstanton. There is some confusion with Leicester (see Volume 1).

Being a specialist trade in the Middle Ages, confined mainly to towns and cities, the dyeing of cloth relied on a whole range of dyestuffs from home and abroad. The purple or red dye known as "cork" supplies us with the names Cork(e) and Corker, both denoting a worker who dyed cloth with "cork" or a person who sold purple dye, acting as a middle man between the "fulling" and "dyeing" processes. 1521, Ralphe Corke, novice at Ranton Abbey; 1539 Muster, John Corke,

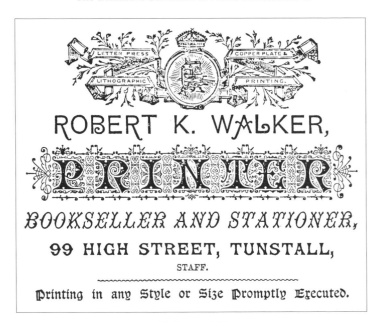

Walker p. 262

Pargeter p. 244

1634, May	14.	Cathar. f. Wm. Whitall & Janæ.
,, May	14.	Anna f. Wm. Hildiche & Doroth.
,, May	14.	Maria f. Henrici Woodland & Mariæ.
,, May	16.	Thomas f. Rogerii Skellet & Doroth.
,, June	1.	Jana f. Thomas Walklate & Emmæ.
,, June	29.	Margareta f. Nicholai Woodcocke & Anna.
,, July	16.	Gratia f. Wm. Mobberley & Ellenæ.
,, Aug.	17.	Thomas f. Wm. Bagnall & Winefridd ⎱ gemelli. Jana f. ejus dem Wm. & Winefridæ ⎰
,, Sept.	7.	Wm. f. Randulphi Boone & Ellenæ.
,, Sept.	29.	Maria f. Rogeri Ellys & Joanna.
,, Oct.	6.	Michael f. Wm. Hulme & Elizab.
,, Oct.	13.	Jana f. Rogeri Dale & Margeria.
,, Oct.	13.	Wm. f. Wm. ffisher & Annæ.
,, Oct.	14.	Isaac f. Thomas Greatbatch & Annæ.
,, Oct.	20.	Margareta f. Wm. Cradock & Annæ.
,, Oct.	20.	John f. John Lovatt & Margaretæ.
,, Oct.	27.	Elizab. f. Wm. Baddeley & Aliciæ.
,, Nov.	3.	Isaac & Samuel, gemelli John Poulson & Margaretæ.
,, Nov.	17.	John f. Wm. Allen & Aliciæ.
,, Nov.	17.	Robert f. Sampsonis Anson & Joannæ.
,, Nov.	17.	Robert f. Roberti Mills & Joannæ.
,, Nov.	17.	Margareta, illegitima f. Margaretæ Passe.
,, Nov.	24.	Thomas f. Thomæ Rowley & Joannæ.
,, Dec.	1.	Jana f. John Beech & Annæ.
,, Dec.	19.	John f. Rich. Nicols & Joannæ.
,, Jan.	10.	Ellena f. Rich. Walklate & Margaretæ.
,, Jan.	24.	Jana f. Jacobi Whitehurst & Janæ.
,, Feb.		Thomas f. [too faded] & Margaretæ.
,, Feb.	8.	Wm. f. Wm. Poulson & Mariæ.
,, Feb.	8.	Robert f. Thomæ Parker & Margaretæ.
,, Feb.	15.	John f. John Asburie & Joannæ.
,, Feb.	15.	Anna f. Henrici Heaton & Margaretæ.
,, Mar.	8.	Rich. f. Thomæ Hommersley & Doroth.

CONIUGIA.

1634, May	5.	Georgius Loe & Emma Baddeley.
,, June	2.	Humphridus Cooper & Margareta Lee.

Copied from Stoke on Trent Parish Register

Cork(e)
Corker

enrolled at Maer, Raulf and Humfrey Corke at Horsley near Eccleshall; 158⁹ Thomas Corke, buried at Stowe-by-Chartley on January 10th; 1685, Mary Cork an Jonathan Loe, married at the parish church of St. James the Great, Audley on Ne⋁ Year's Day: 1851, Samuel Cork (farmer), Hamil, Burslem; 1851, John Corke (watch and clock maker), Greengate Street, Stafford. (See also Madders und⋿ Mather, Chapter 4 - Rural Society).

Blatcher
Blacker
Blaxter

The bleaching of the cloth was the domain of the Blatcher, Blacker or th⋁ Blaxter: 1199 Assizes, William de Blakestere (sic). On the Monday before the Fea⋊ of the Invention of the Holy Cross, 1370, Roger Blechere and a whole host of loca⎹ from the villages of Waterfall and Cauldon, cut down some trees at Cauldoⁿ belonging to the Abbot of Burton Abbey, valued at £10.

One of the most outstanding of the ancient fairs of Staffordshire wa⋁ Wolverhampton Wool Fair, which was accompanied by much pomp and ceremon⋎ After a religious service attended by the mayor, bailiffs, constables, burghers an⋁ merchants, the entire congregation set off in a procession, at whose head was th⋁ Crier and a band of musicians, followed by all the dignitaries. The rear was brougl⋁ up by the groups of sheep shearers, fell mongers, wool-combers, dyers, fuller⋅ weighers and packers. The "packers" made up packages of wool for transport ⋅

Packer

sale. In 1609/1610 Lewis Packer contested two suits, first with John Goodwyn an⋁ his wife Anne, and secondly with George Cotton (gentleman) concerning a variou⋅ assortment of tenements, gardens, orchards, pasturage for cattle and meadowlan⋅ centred around the vills of Gayton, Weston-on-Trent, Forsbrook, Dilhorne an⋁ Caverswall. 1887, Frederick George Packer (photographer), Trinity Street, Hanle⋎ 1907, Eliza Packer of Heron Street, Fenton.

Woolhouse

The "packers" worked in some kind of warehouse or wool-house, and so th⋁ name is perhaps identical with Woolhouse: 1614 Feet of Fines, John Woolhowse ⋅ Hardwick and Sandon. The wool storer or warehouseman also went by the name ⋅

Storer
Storah
Storrer
Storror
Storrow

"storer", but the modern Storer, Storah, Storrer, Storror, Storrow may also be trace⋁ to an antecedent who supervised the stores or provisions of a household: Tatenhi⋅ manor court rolls, 1365, Adam le Storour; 1631, Bennet, wife of Raphe Store⋁ buried at Seighford on March 26th; 1808, Elinor Storah, witness to the marriage ⋅ Robert Ward and Sarah Aston at Barton-under-Needwood on April 18th; 187⋊ George Storer (grocer), Hawkesmore Street, Hanley; 1907, John Storer (coac⋁ painter), Aynsley Road, Hanley.

Sterr(e)y

In the 1700s Storer and Storey occur side by side at Barton-under-Needwoo⋁ and Dunstall, whilst in the West Bromwich parish registers, Richard Storey (1648⋅ appears as Richard Stery a year later. The latter survives as Sterry, Sterrey. If th⋁

Stor(e)y
Storie
Storry

original surname is Story, Storie, Storry, then this was brought over during th⋁ Scandinavian invasions of the 9th century. It stands for Old Norse "Stori" - "strong Luke Story became curate at Longnor in 1769; he was already assistant curate ⋅ Alstonefield. 1851, Henry Storey (camel hair pencil maker), Old Hall Street, Hanle⋁

The "weighers" in the procession are probably represented by the modern surname Poyser, from Anglo French "peiser, poiser" - "weigher, an official in charge of the public weighing machine". One of the regulations in force at the Wolverhampton Wool Fair stated that "*when ye merchandise is to be exported, it shall be brought to ye staple to be weyed by ye standard, and everie sack and sarplet of woole so weyed shall be sealed under ye seale of ye Maior of ye staple*". (A "sarplet" is a large sack of coarse canvas). Before the Industrial Revolution the surname Poyser becomes well established in the Staffordshire Moorlands: 1532, Richard Poyser, wife Ellen and family, resident at Wetton and Thomas Poyser, wife Agnes and children, householders at Blore near Ilam. Hugh Poyser of Stanton, who was killed by Captain Watson's soldiers during the Civil War, was buried at Ellastone on January 15th 1644. Payments on one hearth were made in 1666 by Richard Poyser at Calwich and Norwood, widdow and John Poyser at Stanton, Nicholas Poyser at Cauldon, and John Poyser at Ramshorn, with no tax at all levied on Thomas Poyser at Alton, and Dorothy Poyser at Cauldon. 1851, Jonathan Poyser (farmer), Weston Coyney; 1851, Daniel Poyser (agent), Woodhead Colliery, Farley.

Ballance could be synonymous with Poyser, signifying a person who used a "balance" whilst weighing merchandise, including wool or cloth: Great White Book of Lichfield Cathedral, 1285, Thomas Balaunce. Elizabeth, daughter of John and Ann Ballance was baptised at Kingsley on December 3rd, 1719; 1851, Joseph Ballance, owner of a beerhouse at Drointon; 1907, George Ballance of Weston Road, Meir. But, at Armitage near Rugeley, Joseph Ballance is also written down as Vallance in the parish register in 1811, bringing into play once again the familiar interchange B-V, seen in Bickerstaffe-Vickerstaff etc. If the original surname happens to be Vallance, Valance, then it was brought to our shores by the Normans, from Valence in Drôme, or any French place so called: 1286 Pleas of the Forest, William de Valence; Seighford parish registers, 1775, George Vallance and Elizabeth Mills, married on September 23rd. In those counties bordering on Wales, Ballance can also be a variant of Ballins, Bollins, from Welsh "ab Iolyn", where "Iolyn" is a pet form of "Iorwerth".

MATERIALS AND ARTICLES

The cheapest woollen cloth available during the Middle Ages was called "borel" or "burel" cloth. It was reddish brown in colour and was worn by virtually all the poorer classes of society. Indeed, garments made out of this particular material became so popular amongst the peasantry, that they came to be known as "borel-folk", or "borel-men" - "plain men, laymen". Chaucer's "Franklin" beseeches his listeners to excuse his rude speech because he is "*a borel man*" - "unlearned". Hence, surnames such as Burrel(l), Burrill and Borrell refer either to a maker of "borel" cloth or they may be a nickname for someone with a reddish brown complexion or an unlearned, rude individual. Muniments and manuscripts of

Burrel(l)
Burrill
Borrell

Lichfield, 1457, Peter Burrell; 1907, Frederick Burrell (chemist), Gilman Street Hanley.

On the other hand, "burnets" were cloths of superior quality, wool-dyed and originally dark-brown in colour, and so, just like Burrell, the surname Burnet(t) Burnitt alludes either to a maker or seller of such material, or a nickname is involved

Burnet(t)
Burnitt

for anyone of a brownish complexion. William Burnet witnessed the signing of a deed in 1369, by which Edmund Giffard of Chillington granted his manor of Walton near Chebsey with the homages, rents etc of all his free tenants and natives(bonded tenants) to Philip de Lutteleye. The account of John Cartwright, churchwarden at Stoke-on-Trent in 1648, states, that 13 shillings was allowed to "...*William Burnett a maimed souldier by order of ye sessions*". Widdow Burnett was deemed ineligible for any hearth tax at Colton near Blithfield in 1666. 1851, Sarah and Martha Burnet (shopkeepers) at Grindon; 1851, John Burnett (farmer) at Rownall.

Another cloth, named from its colour is "scarlet", associated with the medieval clothmakers of Lincoln and Stamford. Again, the surname Scarlet(t) is metonymic for a dealer in scarlet cloth. Amongst the goods and chattels claimed as

Scarlet(t)

her rightful inheritance in 1277 by Avice, widow of Robert de Mapelton, from Robert de Wodehuses, were 4 mantles, one of scarlet furred with miniver. 1875 William Scarlett (lamp and oil dealer), Lichfield Street, Hanley; 1894, Joseph Scarlett of Sandy Lane, Brown Edge, trustee of the Wesleyan Chapel.

Fine garments made of silk were the preserve of anyone named Silk, a maker or dealer in silk. In a robbery which took place in 1282 at the manor house of William de Mere in the vill of Mere, the stolen items included 4 girdles of silk, 2

Silk

being of black silk barred with silver and the other 2 of red silk barred with silver (total value 100 shillings). In this context "vill of Mere" is very vague, although the most likely location is Maer near Ashley. At a general meeting held at the Swan Inn Hanley on the 27th April, 1798, William Silk and 42 other gentlemen were enrolled as members of the local troop of volunteer cavalry in the Potteries, who pledged themselves to bear true allegiance to the King, and to act on all occasions in aid of the Civil Power. This association was formed rather hastily in response to some very alarming reports of an imminent invasion by Napoleon Bonaparte. 1907 Charles Silk (boot maker), Anchor Terrace, Longton.

One of the most prosperous towns on the Continent during the Middle Ages was Chalons-sur-Marne, east of Paris in the province of Champagne, renowned for the manufacture of woollen and worsted stuffs, particularly blankets or coverlets known as "chalons". These were imported or made here by the "chaloner". Symon le Chaloner, assessed at 5 shillings for the vill of Cheadle in the 1327 lay subsidie was undoubtedly one of the wealthier residents hereabouts, probably running a thriving woollen and clothing trade in that part of our county. John Chaloner, also called "webbe", of Rugeley, rated at 2 shillings in the 1381 Poll tax, pursued a similar line of business in the Trent Valley. By way of contrast, in 1414, the vill of

Leek was fined 12 pence, the value of a sword, by which William Chaloner had been feloniously killed by Edmund de Sutton and in 1423 Elizabeth Grey sued Richard Chaloner of Cheadle (husbandman) "*...to render to her a reasonable account for the time he was her bailiff in Cheadle*". The modern surname has ramified to a considerable extent in north Staffordshire since the close of the Middle Ages, producing variants such as Challener, Challenor, Challinor, Challender, Chawner and Channer. Thomas Chawner, the last abbot at Croxden Abbey, also appears as Chauner, Chalner and Challinor in the 1530s, whilst his brother William, abbot at Hulton Abbey in 1532, is spelt Chalner in that year. Francis Chawner and Alice Boughey got married at Audley on November 16th, 1624. Another Chawner by the name of Edward, wed Susannah Bowyer at Cheddleton on July 26th, 1773. The Reverend William Chawner (BA) was incumbent at Quarnford and Hollinsclough in 1851, whilst George Chawner (pawnbroker) traded from a shop in Waterloo Road, Burslem in 1907. Challinor is easily the most widely dispersed form of the name: 1851, Francis Challinor (basket and sieve maker), Friar's Lane, Newcastle-under-Lyme; 1871 Census, William Challinor (plumber, glazier), Chebsey Lane, Eccleshall; 1887, Arthur Challinor (Clerk of the Peace), Court of Quarter Sessions, Hanley.

Flackett too covers more or less the same territory as Challinor in north eastern Staffordshire from the later Middle Ages onwards, but the meaning of the name is far from settled. A Middle English "flakette" is one possibility - a linen or flax cloth covering for a bed, hence a maker or seller of such material. "Flacket" also denoted a bottle, flask or vessel, now usually found in dialects with reference to a barrel-shaped container for holding liquor, but what the actual significance here is anybody's guess. The most interesting idea is the verb "flacket" - "to flap about" - employed in some dialects for a woman whose clothes hang loosely about her, hence a nickname for a female of easy virtue. The matter is unresolved. In 1438 Robert Holynton, prior of St. Margaret of Calwich and Thomas Flaket of Calwich (husbandman), were attached at the suit of James Olde for forcibly taking 10 oxen and 8 cows belonging to him at Calwich, for which he claimed £20 as damages. In 1666 John and Thomas Flackett were both exempt from any hearth tax at Cheadle. 1907, Albert Flackett (potter), West Parade, Fenton; 1907, Thomas Flackett (bricklayer), Woodland Street, Stoke.

The "cope", a long cloak or cape worn as an outer garment, was donned chiefly for outdoor use. These two words "cope" and "cape" are variants of one another. Cape is the northern form, with Cope typical of the midland counties, including Staffordshire. Both surnames designate a maker or seller of capes or copes. In addition the "cope" could be the special attire of a monk or friar, whilst in ecclesiastical circles it referred to a vestment of silk or other material somewhat like a long cloak, made out of a semicircular piece of cloth, worn on special occasions or at Vespers. In a dispute over an acre of land in the vill of Clayton

Cope
Cape(s)

Gryffyn in 1293, between Geoffrey Gryffyn and Richard Cope, the latter called to warranty Edmund, brother of the Lord King (Edward I). Jonathan Cope of Ranton Abbey was Sheriff of Staffordshire in 1657. 1760, Isaac Cope (surgeon), Sheepmarket, Leek; 1887, Samuel Cope (fustian cutter, plaster manufacturer), Butt Lane Mill, Talke; 1907, Charles Cape (grocer, confectioner), Bucknall New Road, Hanley; 1907, Adrian Capes (professional footballer), Corporation Street, Stoke. For an alternative locative origin of the surname Cope, see Cowpe in Volume 1.

Bratt

The Anglo Saxon "bratt" - "pallium, cloak, pinafore" - was probably a loan word from Celtic - compare the Irish "bratt" - "cloth, especially as a covering for the body, a mantle". This term may have been used in the same way as Cope/Cape as an occupational name for someone who made or sold cloaks, mantles or pinafores. In northern dialects it is still in common usage for a child's bib or apron, but the most vivid use of the word occurs in Charles Shaw's autobiography "When I was a Child", in which he says: *"When I went to the workhouse all my clothes were taken away, after having a cold bath on a cold day. I was then supplied with stockings, clogs, moleskin breeches, roughly put together, and over these I wore a grey "brat' or pinafore, which served as waistcoat and jacket".* In 1455 John Gresley (knight) and William Bukkenale sued Nicholas Bratte of Dimsdale (yeoman) and 15 others for breaking into their houses at Stoke and helping themselves to goods and chattels valued at £20. 1851, James Bratt (wheelwright) of Roebuck Lane, Newcastle-under-Lyme; 1875, Edward Bratt (beerseller), Albion Street, Burslem.

Brett

However, there is occasional interplay with Brett, since Margaret Brett (spinster) of the parish of Seighford, who married Samuel Wiggin of Cheadle (bachelor) on July 8th, 1782, signed her own name in the register as Margaret Bratt. This was clearly how she herself pronounced her own name. If the actual surname in this instance is Brett, then this signifies an immigrant from Brittany, as exemplified by Geoffrey le Bret, chief tax-payer at Knutton and Hanford in 1327 rated at 4/6d. Moreover, the Nicholas Bratte of Dimsdale, quoted above, is probably identical with the Nicholas Brette of Dimsdale, mentioned in an assize of 1470. By the seventeenth century the surname Brett is well established in north Staffordshire: 1666, Hearth tax payments include Thomas Brett - 2 at Great Bridgeford near Stafford; Margaret Brett - 1 at Eccleshall; William Brett - 1 at Aston and Doxey; Randle Brett - 1 at Stoke-on-Trent; Edward Brett Esquire - 9 at Dimsdale; widdow Brett - 5 at Abbey Hulton; Edward Brett exempt at Cheddleton.

Mantle
Mante(l)l

Bearers of the surname Mantle, Mantel(l) possess ancestors, who worked in the cloth trade making mantles or cloaks for the local populace or even some great medieval landowners: Lichfield Cathedral Registers, 1676, Sarah Mantell and Thomas Cope, married on September 6th. By some curious quirk of fate, both bride and groom most likely descended from a long line of medieval cloak makers! 1875 Mary Mantle (greengrocer), Mill Street, Hanley; 1907, Walter Mantle (potter) Alexandra Road, Oakhill; 1907, George Mantle (platelayer), Granville Place, Cobridge

With the immense assortment of cloths and materials at his disposal, the medieval "tailor" was spoilt for choice. But this was an occupational term introduced by the Normans, meaning literally "the cutter", equivalent in fact to the Saxon "Shearer" and "Shearman" - someone who sheared woollen cloth or who removed the nap on the cloth and brought it to a smooth finish ready for use. Before the arrival of the Normans the high-ranking chieftains wore knee-length tunics and fur cloaks and thick stockings cross-gartered with leather thongs, whilst the wealthiest women in society were dressed in long gowns or mantles. During this period clothes were basically simple and loose-fitting, hardly requiring any shaping or designing or any real skills from the Shearer or Shearman. Shearer and Shearman are undocumented, but other variants such as Sherman and Sharman are well in evidence. On the Sunday (the Vigil of St. Matthew the Apostle), 1304, a mob came by night to the house of Henry le Schermon at Stafford and wounded and ill-treated Hugh Gregory of Salop, so that his life was despaired of. In 1387 Roger Shermon was one of the wardens of the assize of bread and ale at Newcastle-under-Lyme. Ann Sharman of Wolstanton, who married Thomas Owen (butcher) at Burslem on January 9th, 1770, signed her name in the register as Sherman. 1887, Thomas Sharman (general draper), Congleton Road, Talke; 1907, David Sharman (potter's dipper), Russell Street, Hanley.

The Norman import "tailor" quickly put both of these native Saxon terms in the shade, and by the compilation of the hearth tax returns in 1666 it had attained second position behind Smith in the list of the most common surnames derived from occupations, chalking up 187 behind the 458 of Smith. On the Audley estates at Audley in 1298 Robert le Taillour paid 2/6d rent per annum for one messuage and one toft. In 1350 John le Taillour of Knightley and five others were sued by Richard, Prior of Ronton, "*...for forcibly rescuing cattle which he had impounded according to the law and custom of the kingdom*". A more serious case involved Joan Taillour, servant of James Lee (armiger), who was abducted from the latter's property at Aston near Stone in 1469. Timothy Taylor was a member of the trained band at Ilam in the 1640 Muster. The overseers of the poor, decided in 1730, that Samuel Taylor of Talke hamlet, who was blind "*shall have his house thatched and repaired and shall have a pail bought to carry water*". One of the most celebrated local Taylors is John Taylor, bellman and town crier of Hanley, born in 1769. Nicknamed "Tambourine John" on account of his predilection for this particular musical instrument, he is remembered by the following rhyme: "*Oh, John Taylor, your like was seldom seen, riding on a pony, through the streets of Hanley Green*". 1851, Daniel Taylor (hairdresser), King Street, Longton; 1851, William Taylor (coachman), Bishton, Colwich; 1875, Frederick Taylor (bill poster), Railway Street, Newcastle-under-Lyme.

The patronymic Tailorson - "son of the tailor" - is extremely rare. In 1328 John de Ruycroft appeared by attorney against William le Tailloresone and five

Tailorson

other gentlemen, in a plea, that they had forcibly broken open a chest belonging to him at Hilton (probably Hilton near Essington), and taken from it goods and chattel to the value of £10 and certain charters and deeds.

Hattrell
Haddrell

"Haterel", used circa 1440 in the York Plays of "dress, attire", perhaps come from the Saxon "haeteru" - "clothes" with reference to a tailor. It survives as th surname Hattrell, Haddrell: Newcastle-under-Lyme parish registers, 1689, M Harry Hattrell and Mrs Amey Shaw, married on October 14th; 1907, Georg Haddrell (tram inspector), Coronation Road, Stoke.

Souster

The bulk of the sewing of the garments was done by the "souster": 1298 Emma la Souster, charged $2^1/2$ pence rent per annum by the Audleys on their estate at Betley. At the Standon manor court in 1361 the Lord of the manor gav permission to Alice le Soustere to take 3 waste lands adjoining her cottag "*...rendering for the said waste lands 12 pence at the terms of the Annunciation an St. Michael, beginning to pay rent at the Feast of the Annunciation of St. Mary la: past, at the will of the lord*". These examples end up as the modern surnam Souster.

Simester
Simister

"Seamster", the feminine form of "seamer" - "sewer, tailor" results in name such as Simester and Simister: 1380 Poll tax, Julia Semster, rated at 12 pence fo Lichfield; 1851, John Simister (smallware dealer), Custard Street, Leek; 1907 Daniel Simister (placer), Gibson Street, Burslem; 1907, William Simeste (waterman), Raymond Street, Hanley.

Butner

The numerous buttons to be sewn on all the different types of apparel wer made by the Butner: 1380 Poll tax, John Botoner and his wife Alice, assessed at shillings for Lichfield. Anyone called Button manufactured the same articles: 153: Giles Button, head of the household at Alstonefield; Ellenhall parish registers, 171-Ellen Button.

Button

Draper

At the very heart of all this medieval trade in wool and cloth was th "draper", who not only made woollen cloth himself, but also sold cloth an materials of all sorts to his own clientele in the local towns and villages. Richard Draper, for instance, contributing 12 pence lay subsidy for Maer and Aston in 133: would have known all the best contacts and customers on his own patch of territor William Draper was recruited for Shugborough in the 1539 Muster and John Drape was churchwarden at Stowe-by-Chartley in 1623. 1851, John Draper (baker, flou dealer), Forebridge, Stafford; 1907, Thomas Draper (carter), Sandon Street, Etrurie

Capp(s)
Capper

Surnames derived from headgear do not feature as prominently as some c the other names we have looked at thus far. Coverings for the head like hats, cap hoods and bonnets were probably made of woollen cloth or felt. Cappers, hatte and feltmakers crop up frequently in the sixteenth century corporation minutes fo Newcastle-under-Lyme, when there must have been a flourishing hat-makin industry already in existence: 1533, John Smyth capper; 1569, Richard Morto hatter; 1588, John Woddall feltmaker, etc. Cap-making has given us the name

Shearer cutting cloth.
(p. 271)

Knifegrinder p. 240

Skinners p. 275

Capp(s)
Capper

Capp(s) and Capper: 1332 Lay subsidies, Robert Cappe, contributing 3 shillings a Tillington near Stafford. According to the Bishop's visitation in 1629, Franc Capps, vicar of Wolstanton, was censured "...*for not wearinge the surplice, as also the said vicar for at divers and severall times wittingly and willingly administring the Holy Communion to one that doth refuse to kneele.....*"

At Stafford the manufacture of caps was an important industry by th sixteenth century, although in decline by 1575: 1541 Star Chamber Proceeding Richard Gibbons capper of Stafford. At the height of the Chartist movement i 1842, regular meetings were convened locally at Joseph Capper's smithy nea Tunstall Market Place, where Joseph aired his radical views on politics and th rights of the workers. 1851, Sarah Capper (milliner, dressmaker) of King Stree Burslem; 1907, Albert Capper (lamplighter), Seymour Street, Hanley.

Bonnet(t)

Anyone named Bonnet(t) had an ancestor who made bonnets: John Bone viscount of Stafford - circa 1224. Caller, Callear and Callier denote a maker c close-fitting caps for women - Middle English "calle" from French "cale": 132

Caller
Callear
Callier

Assizes, Elias le Callere of London; 1875, John Callear (grocer) of Newcastl Street, Burslem; 1907, Albert Callear (carter) of Elm Street, Hanley; 1907, Danie Callear (insurance agent), Biddulph Road, Pittshill, Tunstall. However, thes recordings are very late, and I suspect another derivation is in the offing, such as a unrounded version of Collier, on the analogy of Mall-Moll, Fallwell-Follwell. Bu alas, no evidence is at hand.

Horhod

Throughout the Middle Ages the obligatory headwear of rich and poor wa the "hood", an immediate reminder of the most famous medieval outlaw of all Robin Hood, who may have got his surname from some distinctive head protectio he wore. Similar nicknames were borne by 1293 Assizes, Richard Horhod (possibl of Whitgreave), who wore, made or sold grey hoods, and 1394 Manor court rolls

Redehodes

Richard Redehodes of Newcastle-under-Lyme, whose passion extended to the mor fashionable red hoods. In 1303 Hugh Hod and a whole host of local inhabitant were summoned to the assize court to answer the charge, that they had unlawfull dispossessed Henry son of Thomas de Shirford of a messuage, mill and some lan in Ellastone. Hugh's descendants live on in the modern surnames Hodd(s), Hoddes

Hodd(s)
Hoddes
Hodes
Hood(s)

Hodes and Hood(s): Ellastone parish registers, 1539, Raphe Hoode and Margeri Ratchdale, married on November 9th; 1540, Johane, daughter of Lawrance Hoode baptised on August 28th, etc. In 1704 the Lords of Leek Frith manor licensed Ralp Hood of Leek and some others to dig for lead and copper ore on the waste near th Roches. 1851, John Hood (boot and shoe maker) of Wetley Rocks; 1875, Edmun Hood (agent for the Midland Railway Company), Bradwell Street, Burslem.

Hudd

But there is inevitable overlap with Hudd, a very common medieval pet forr of the Germanic "Hugh": 1327 Lay subsidies, Thomas filius Hudde of Handsacre noted as Thomas filius Hugonis (son of Hugh) in 1332. 1539 Muster, Richar Hudde of Shugborough; Rocester parish registers, 1598, Mawde Hudd, alias Hoode

1666, William Hudd, exempt from hearth tax at Penkhull cum membris Constablewick.

Hodder - "maker of hoods" - is very scarce: 1887, William Hodder of Market Place, Burslem, rather conveniently sold hats for a living!

THE LEATHER TRADE

Ranking second in importance to the clothing industry during the Middle Ages was the dressing of animal skins and the making of leather, an item of manufacture for which there was a seemingly insatiable demand all those centuries ago, not only from military circles and the rural sphere, where every horse required a new saddle every now and again, but also from the wealthier classes, who could not do without their new gloves, boots, shoes, purses and pouches.

Two different processes were involved in the preparation of skins and hides, depending on which animal they were taken from. Ox, cow and calf hides were tanned by immersing them in a liquor containing oak bark, whilst the skins of deer, sheep and horses were treated with alum and oil. The task of stripping the skin or hide from the carcase and passing it on to the "tanner" was carried out by the "skinner". In a medieval pastoral county like Staffordshire sheep skins and cattle hides would be plentiful in many areas, offering good opportunities for the evolution of a surname such as Skinner, Skynner, Skyner. For instance, two of these "skinners" occur at Sandon and Little Sandon in the 1327 lay subsidies, in the heart of the Trent Valley - Thomas le Skynnere charged 12 pence tax compared with the 15 pence of William le Skynnere. In 1414 the vill of Betley was fined 6 pence, the value of the skin of a horse, which had caused the death of Robert de Ruggeleye, killed by accident. 1532, Richard Skyner, householder at Ellastone, with his wife Joan, and daughters Agnes and Isabel; 1685, Richard Skinner ran Tib Green finery forge on Checkley Brook between Wrinehill and Checkley Wood for Sir Philip Egerton of Oulton; 1851, James Skinner (butcher) of Stoke Road, Stoke; 1875, Herbert Skinner (grocer, beer retailer), Mill Street, Hanley.

The archaic "fellmonger" dealt in animal hides or skins, especially sheep-skins. The initial element "fell" still exists in the surname Fell(s) with the same meaning, although in the Danelaw counties a much more amenable origin is a toponymic for a dweller by a hill or fell, from the Old Norse "fell, fjall": Stoke-on-Trent parish registers, 1764, John Fell (peruke maker) and Mary Baddiley, married on May 28th; 1907, Benjamin Fell (fitter), Garner Street, Stoke; 1907, Arthur Fell, licensee of the Three Horse Shoes, York Street, Hanley.

The Norman equivalent for a fellmonger, dresser of fells, hides or skins - "peletier", survives as Pelter or Pilter. A Staffordshire assize reports, that "....*Henry, the clerk of the Countess of Helegh, Henry le Peleter and John de Iselwalle at Newcastle, on a market day in 13 Edward II (1319), came like common malefactors and beat and wounded Agnes the wife of Robert del Bakhous and Adam, son of*

Adam de Lanton...." 1714, Edward Peleter of Cheadle.

Pilcher

The native "pilch" - "an outer garment made of skin dressed with hair" - w made and sold by the "pilcher". In 1306 the chattels of Henry le Pylchere (unknown address), outlawed for felony, were valued at 47/2d. In 1666 Elizabe Pilcher was not chargeable for any hearth tax at Rugeley.

Tanner

The tougher hides of the cow, ox and calf, which were steeped in a liqu containing oak bark, were the responsibility of the "tanner" himself. In 1294 Ra de Kerswall and his wife Margaret recovered the third part of a messuage and bova of land in Fenton Culvert, as Margaret's dower, against Adam, son of William Tannur of Newcastle-under-Lyme and his wife Eva, by default of the defendan Ralph le Tannor was rated at 2 shillings for the vill of Abbot's Bromley in the 13 lay subsidies. After the Middle Ages the surname Tanner struggles to make presence felt. Sleigh's *History of Leek*, Temp. Henry VIII, William Tann Dieulacres; 1666 Mr John Tanner, paying tax on 6 hearths at Stafford; 1907, M Tanner (dressmaker), Lawson Terrace, London Road, Stoke; 1907, Henry Tann (engine driver), Oxford Road, Wolstanton.

Whittier
Whittear

The "white-tawer", the leather dresser, who tawed the skins into whi leather, gives us modern names like Whittier and Whittear. In 1458 John Mille, la of Trysull near Wolverhampton, is described as a "whittawer", in a case, where is sued for a debt of £10 by John Hampton (armiger).

Barker

Medieval villagers who lived in close proximity to the hunting forests Kinver, Cannock or Needwood, were not permitted to tan the skins of slaughtere beasts. Instead, they had to take them to the tanning pits in Stafford, Walsall a Lichfield. This was to prevent the local inhabitants from destroying the oak bar which was such an essential part of the tanning process on account of its high tann content that the alternative name for a tanner was "barker". For instance, John Barkere of Abbot's Bromley (1327 lay subsidies) most likely got his bark fro Needwood Forest, whereas William le Barker, taxed at Cannock in the same list, ha the woodlands of Cannock Chase at his disposal. In 1686, Plot observed that in th villages of Norton-in-the-Moors, Milton and Baddeley Green, the oak bark wa stripped between April 1st and June 30th, and then allowed to stand naked a summer, drying in the sun. Naturally some "barkers" succumbed to temptation an poached the deer running free in the local forests, using the hides for their ow benefit. William Stikbuk barker, resident at Lichfield in 1433, is a classic exampl of a medieval poacher, who seized his chance when he could, for his name mear literally "stick (kill) buck". Further, Richard Couper barker of Uttoxeter (1415) n only stripped the oak bark for tanning, but also used the timber for making barrel

The high incidence of the surname Barker in most regions of the county accounted for by another factor. The Normans imported their own word "berche - "shepherd": 1307 Audley Inquests, Henry le Bercher, renting one plot of land Betley for 2 pence per annum. In medieval records it is often written down a "berker" or "bercar", as evidenced by 1267 Assizes, Richard le Berker of Little Aston near Stone, and 1338 Manor court rolls, Adam Bercar of Standon, alternatively known as Adam le Shepeherde. When "er" coalesced with "ar" as in "clerk-clark", "berker" - "shepherd" became "barker" and thus was indistinguishable from "barker" - "tanner": 1306 Assizes, Roger Barker (bercarius - shepherd) of Wootton (probably Wootton-under-Weaver), indicted for stealing 3 sheep from the Abbot of Croxden, found guilty and hanged. In 1840 Thomas Barker, aged 16, was employed at Woodhead Colliery, Cheadle, drawing wagons in the bottom coal pit for Edward Edwards, the butty; 1851, Edward Barker (nail maker), Cheadle Mill; 1887, James Barker (tinsmith), Waterloo Road, Burslem. Some Lancashire Barkers are said to trace their ancestry back to Higher or Lower Barker, north of Goosnargh, although there are no references to either locality before the sixteenth century.

dle   Leather belts or girdles for breeches or trousers were made by anyone with the name Bracegirdle: Stoke-on-Trent parish registers. 1640, Dorothea Brasegirdle, buried on January 2nd; Church Eaton parish registers, 1741, Mary Bracegirdle of Church Eaton and William Bren (or Brew) of the parish of Bradely (sic), married on February 4th; 1907, George Bracegirdle (labourer) of Wellington Street, Fenton. Anne Bracegirdle, one of the first English actresses (circa 1663-1748) and called the Diana of the Stage, was suspected of having been secretly married to William Congreve, the playwright.

's)   The surname Leather(s) simply denotes a dealer in leather or a craftsman who used leather in his work: Newcastle-under-Lyme parish registers, 1802, Ellen, daughter of John Leather, baptised on March 14th. However, in the Wolstanton parish registers Richard Leather (1738) is noted as Ledder in 1746, and Bainton Leader of Norton appears in the registers for 1756. Ledder is applied to a worker in lead, a plumber, which also survives in Leader, Leeder and Lader, but these can also be derived from an old Saxon term for a driver of a cart, a carter. The Leather-Ledder interchange is based on Mather-Madder: 1876, Matthew Leader (china and earthenware decorator), Hanover Street, Burslem; 1907, Mrs Mary Leader (grocer), Keeling Street, Wolstanton.

The tanner could not complete his work without the assistance of the "currier", for tanned leather is stiff and badly coloured. The job of the "currier" was to dress the hides with tallow, thereby rendering them smooth and supple, so that they could be passed on to the real craftsmen in leather, namely, the saddlers, glovers, and shoemakers. 1380 Poll tax, Nicholas Coriour, rated at 12 pence for Lichfield.

With the reliance on the horse in medieval times, not only as a draught animal on the farm, but also for hunting and warfare, the craft of the saddler was as essential in any community as the skills of the blacksmith and wheelwright. During his apprenticeship the saddler was taught how to cut out the different leathers for collars and harness as well as saddles, and he was not a fully fledged member of the

fraternity until he had mastered the various techniques. In 1354 the prior of ,
Thomas the Martyr, Stafford, and brother Richard de Aldelyme (Audlem), monk
the said priory, brought a suit against a number of local residents including Elias
Sadeler of Stafford, for beating, wounding and ill-treating brother Richard at Cotc
near Hopton. They put in a claim for £100 damages. Richard Sadeler and sc

Sadler

enrolled at Stafford in the 1539 Muster, are most likely descendants of the accus
mentioned in the above extract. An infant whose name is not recorded, son
daughter of George and Elizabeth Sadler, was buried at Standon in 1632. Tra
directories: 1851, Edward Sadler (cabinet maker), Piccadilly, Hanley; 1873, Har
Sadler (drayman), Malkin Street, Burslem; 1875, Benjamin Sadler (agent for Nor
Staffordshire Canal Company), Etruria Vale Wharf.

Glover

The tawed soft leathers made from the skins of deer, sheep and horses, we
ideal for luxury articles such as gloves, worn by the falconers in the popular spc
of hawking, and by the wealthier classes whenever they went out riding and huntin
The high numbers of Glovers in our modern telephone directories are sufficie
testimony to the importance of this particular craft during the Middle Ages. Indee
in the 1327 lay subsidy rolls the taxpayers comprise Thomas le Glovere
Eccleshall, Richard le Glover at Abbot's Bromley, Richard le Glovere at Staffor
and a third Richard le Glover at Newcastle-under-Lyme. In 1412, three members
the Erdeswick family of Sandon, several yeomen from Milwich and Ston
including Richard Glover, "....*with other disturbers of the peace, who we
unknown, had been purposely collected from divers parts of England, Ireland ar
Wales, rebels of the King, to the number of 1,000 men, with a view to killing Edmu
de Ferrers, the lord of Chartley.....*" On a lighter note, in 1625, the manor court
Tunstall urged John Walton and Richard Glover of Burslem to "...*secure the wat
and scour the ditch between the new meadowe and the Bothom Lane by Penteco.
on pain of 6/8d*". Directories: 1851, Joseph Glover (chair maker, turner) of His
Street, Stone; 1851, George Glover (farmer, maltster), Peartree Lake, Balterle
1851, William Glover (corn miller), Stanley, Endon.

Ganter
Gaunter

The Normans attempted to challenge the monopoly of the Saxon "glover
with their own "gantier" - "maker or seller of gloves" - Ganter, Gaunter, but fail
miserably. Medieval specimens of this name are as hard to find as a needle in
haystack. In 1295 John le Gaunter of Tillington near Stafford was ordered by t
local sheriff to explain exactly by what service he held a tenement in the said vi
The root of ̌"gantier" - "gant" - occasionally survives in the modern surnai

Gant
Gaunt

Gant/Gaunt, synonymous with Ganter/Gaunter -"manufacturer or seller of glove
but these can also represent a nickname for someone who was tall and slim wi
haggard features, or even a locative from Ghent, one of the great industrial cities
Belgium during the Middle Ages, famous for its cloth. This place is recorded
"Gant" in the Domesday survey and as "Gaunt" in the thirteenth century:1227 Assiz
Maurice de Gant of Himley near Wombourne, cited as Maurice de Gaunt (same ye

in the Great White Book of Lichfield Cathedral. The most celebrated bearer of the name, John of Gaunt, was born at Ghent in 1340, the fourth son of Edward III. As inheritor of the Duchy of Lancaster, he was resident at Tutbury Castle from 1374. The marriage between Margery Gaunt and William Ratchdall (freemason) took place at Ellastone on January 15th, 1611. Sleigh cites John and James Gaunt of Summerhill (buttonmen) for the year 1767. 1851, John Gaunt (silk manufacturer), Globe Factory, Spout Street, Leek; 1851, William Gaunt (farmer) of Alton.

Apart from the richer classes of society who habitually travelled on horseback, the vast majority of the population during the Middle Ages walked from place to place, and of course, all this walking called for a decent pair of shoes or boots, that fitted correctly. The medieval shoemakers were divided into a number of branches, the most important being the "cordwainers", who got their name from the town of Cordova in Spain, where the shoemakers fashioned leather footwear of unrivalled quality for the elite. In 1456 Richard Cordwaner sued Humfrey Swynarton, late of Swynarton (armiger) and John Hethe, late of Swynarton (yoman), for taking by force from Clent 3 horses, 4 oxen and 2 cows belonging to him and worth £6. The normal modern spelling of this name is Cordner or Codner (no local examples). Several specimens taken from seventeenth century documents are ample proof of the shoemaking industries at Newcastle-under-Lyme and Stafford: 1608, John Harrison (cordwainer), appointed sergeant to the Mayor; 1654, Randall Vernon (cordwainder), "*a borne burgesse, tooke his oath*"; 1666, Edward Rathbone (cordwayner), exempt from hearth tax at Stafford.

The Middle English "cordewan" - Spanish leather made at Cordova - results in names like Corden, Cordon, Cordwent and Corwin. Richard Cordewan (1199 Assizes) obviously used this type of best leather for his clients' boots and shoes. Yet these names can also be derived from Old French "cordon" - "cord, ribbon", hence a maker of such items, synonymous with Corder: 1280 Assizes, Adam le Cordur of Packington. Householders in 1532 comprise John Cordon, wife Margery and family at Leek, with William, Robert and John Cordon and their respective families settled over at Betley. 1851, Uriah Corden (corn miller) of Whitfield (Fegg Hayes); 1851, Zachariah Corden, licensee of the Arblasters Arms, Wetley Rocks; 1907, Albert Corden (forgeman), Cobridge Road, Hanley.

In the Barton-under-Needwood parish registers, covering the period 1682-1790, the spellings Corden, Cordin, Caudin mingle with forms such as Corodine, Corrodine, Coradine and Carodine. Clearly, these are corrupted variants of each other, but which version takes precedence - the shorter or the longer one? If the latter turns out to be the answer, then we are dealing with the modern Cawarden Springs between Hill Ridware and Rugeley. Stebbing Shaw claims that the place took its name from an ancient coppice owned by the Cawardens. But Horovitz favours an enclosure or homestead frequented by jackdaws. Yet, if the Cawarden family is responsible for the name, then they could trace their ancestry back to

Corodine
Corrodine
Coradine
Carodine
Carwardine

Higher and Lower Carden in Tilston parish, Cheshire, not far from the Welsh border. This locality is found as "Cawardyn" in the fourteenth century and denotes an enclosure by a rock - cf 1408 Assizes, Owyn de Cawardyn and Master Robert Cawerden of Mavesyn Ridware (1532). The modern surnames Carden, Cardon and Carding are generally derived from the Cheshire locative as well, but also involved is a nickname from Old French "cardon" - "thistle", with allusion to someone of a stubborn nature: 1332 Lay subsidies, Richard Cardon of Lichfield; 1851, Joseph Carding (shopkeeper), Workhouse Street, Leek.

Carden
Cardon
Carding

Corviser

Another typical medieval term for a shoemaker - "corveiser, corviser" seems to have died out and left no progeny at all, although it does occur locally a late as 1851, when William Corvesor is recorded as "wharfinger" - keeper of the wharf, resident at Stowe-by-Chartley. In 1342 Adam, son of Geoffrey le Corviser acknowledged some tenements at Betley to be the rightful possessions of Beatrice de Wovere (Woore) and her heirs, for which she handed over 20 marks. It is interesting to note, that some of these medieval "corvisers" are appended to other names, such as 1364, John le Sadler corviser of Lichfield, and 1478, Thomas Taillour corveser of Wolverhampton, and it is reasonable to conclude, that the "corvesor" was absorbed by "taylor" and "sadler" in these two instances. In the 1381 Poll tax returns, Richard Corviser of Great Wyrley, rated at 2/4d, is also cited as "sutor" - Latin "sutor" - "shoemaker", used to translate the Saxon "sutere". In the lay subsidies Adam le Souter, of Betley (1332) is noted down as Adam le Cornise (sic) by the tax collectors in 1327. This is clearly for "Corviser" with the common medieval confusion between "n" and "v". Nowadays the most regular spellings of

Souter
Soutar
Sowter
Suter

the surname are Souter, Soutar, Sowter and Suter: 1559 Lawsuit, Agnes Sowter widow of Hanbury; Madeley parish registers, 1567, Lawrence Suter (webster); 1665, John Sowter and Mary Blackam, married at Penkridge on June 26th; 1873, Benjamin Souter (agent), The Grove, Wolstanton.

Shoemaker
Shumaker
Shoemark
Shoesmith

Shoemaker/Shumaker is very scarce: 1539 Muster, Nycolas Shomaker, recruited for the Stafford militia. The contracted form Shoemark was still prevalent at Stafford in the 1987 telephone directory for Stoke-on-Trent, Stafford and Crewe: 1872, Edward James Shoemack (sic) of Mellish Road, Walsall.

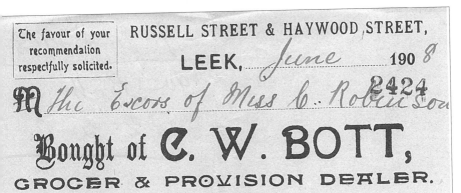

The favour of your recommendation respectfully solicited.

RUSSELL STREET & HAYWOOD STREET,

LEEK, *June* 190 8

2424

M *the Excors of Miss C. Robinson*

Bought of C. W. BOTT,

GROCER & PROVISION DEALER.

⚬⚬ HOME-CURED HAMS AND BACON. ⚬⚬

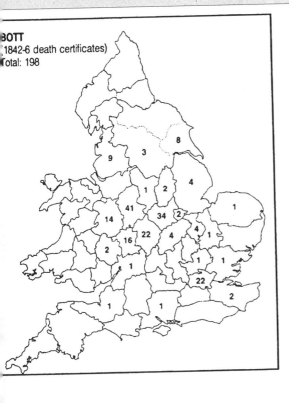

BOTT
(1842-6 death certificates)
Total: 198

Poyser and Ballance p. 267

Bott p. 284

Scales and Weights.

Shoesmith

Redschoz
Horssho

Boot(e)
Bott

Boot(e)

Bott

Bodfish

Shoemaker is quite distinct from Shoesmith, since the latter designate farrier who made horseshoes: 1666, Henry Shewsmyth, taxed on one hearth Hopwas near Tamworth. Obsolete names here are: 1332 Lay Subsidies, Willi Redschoz of Newcastle-under-Lyme and 1379 Assize rolls, William Horssho a called William de Burton of Rugeley.

Superficially the surname Boot(e) is just a plain and simple survival of so medieval craftsman in leather who made and sold boots of all shapes and sizes. 1350 Nicholas Bote was sued by John Stykebuk of Colton and Juliana, daughter Margaret, daughter of Robert, son of Hugh de Colton, for the rightful ownership one acre of land in Colton in the Trent valley; 1640 Muster, Lyonell Boote, mem of the trained band at Cheddleton; 1851, Abraham Boote, owner of a beerhouse Bagnall Street, Longton; 1907, Charles Boote (waggoner), Hitchen Street, Bursle 1907, David Boote (groom), Union Street, Pittshill.

Yet, in the 1532 list of families in the Archdeaconry of Stafford, the na Boot(e) is indexed alongside Bott, but, most significantly of all, the Boot(e), Bott spellings are concentrated around Alton, Denstone near Rocester and Uttoxet John Botte contributed 3 shillings lay subsidy at Denstone in 1327. This fluctuati between Bott and Boot persists well into the 18th century: Kingsley parish registe William Bott (1694), entered as William Boot in 1696 and in the High Offi registers for 1787, where George Bott of the parish of Lilleshall, Shropshi married to Frances James on February 12th, signs his own name as George Bo From the close of the Middle Ages, the surname Bott ramifies in north ea Staffordshire, especially in the Churnet valley. Authorities are divided as to the tr source of the name - some favour a Saxon name "Botta", or another Saxon nam "Butt(a)", or a nickname from "butt" signifying a short, stumpy person, or even a Old French "bot"-"toad" with some obscure meaning. However, the most reveali clue for our own local families called Bott lies in two recordings from an assize r of 1461, in which Thomas Botfysshe of Froghall (labourer) and William Botfyss of Kingsley, also a labourer, together with some other malefactors from Cheadle a Whitehurst near Dilhorne, broke into the property of Robert Cuny (armiger) Weston Coyney, and terrorised Robert's servants so much, that they went into hidi for a length of time. The spelling "Botfysshe" lives on in the name Bodfish. T initial component is Middle English "butte", which comes from the same root a Swedish "butta" - "turbot", and Dutch "bot" - "flounder, flatfish". Thus it wou denote a trader who sold such fish at the local market. Halibut contains the sam word - originally "holy butt", presumably because it was eaten on holy days. Bo too, could preserve the word, and hence refer to a fishmonger who sold flounde or flatfish at his market stall. In 1636, Katherin Bott, servant at Mr. Hugh Sheldon' was buried at Ellastone on June 8th, having succumbed to small pox. In 184 Lydia Bott, mistress at the National day-school at Longton, gave instruction to th girls in writing, reading the scriptures, needle-work, marking and knitting. 185

William Bott (parish clerk), Swinscoe; 1851, Arthur Bott (plumber, painter) of Wetton.

Wooden-soled shoes or clogs were crafted by anyone called Clogg: Rowley Regis parish registers, 1645, William Meanely called Clogg - cf. 1875, John Moston (clog and shoemaker), Newcastle Street, Burslem. The ancient Staffordshire "clog almanacs" were constructed of a "log", or square piece of wood, made out of box, fir or oak, which had four edges, on each of which were marked out three months of the year. Very similar to the "clog", the "patten" had a wooden sole, rimmed with iron. They were often worn by members of the clergy to protect their feet from the cold bare stones in the medieval churches.

The shoemaker who made these "pattens" has left progeny bearing such names as Patten, Pattin or Pattern: 1845, Thomas Patten and Company, allotted pew number 10, sitting 9 (south gallery), Cheadle church; 1912, F.P. Patten (pianoforte tuner and organ repairer), King Street, Leek. cf. 1851, Ralph Farrar (clog and patten maker), Piccadilly, Tunstall.

Yet there might be some confusion with Patton, traceable to Patton near Easthope on Wenlock Edge, Shropshire - "village of Peatta's people", or Patton in Westmorland - "village of Patta" or "homestead by a path". A diminutive of "Pat" from Patrick, the patron saint of Ireland, also ends up as Patton or Paton: 1292, Nicholas Patun of Enville; 1912, Bridget Paton (widow) of Malkin Street, Burslem.

Hoser and Hosier may sometimes refer to a dealer in or maker of "hose" - "stockings, socks", but more to the point is a shoemaker, especially someone who made boots, and hence synonymous with the famous name Chaucer, our most renowned medieval poet. His name is a derivative of Middle English "chawce", which was a general term applied to anything worn on the feet - boots, shoes and so on. In all probability the medieval "Chaucer" worked in leather, making breeches and boots, cf the obsolete 1272 Feet of Fines, William Letherhose of Lichfield and 1306 Assizes, Peter Streythose of Thursfield, killed by Nicholas Wyrhof of Biddulph at Tunstall. The latter probably refers to close-fitting tights or boots. In 1407 John Saxsy of Betley, chaplain, was indicted for assaulting John Hosyer with a baselard and cutting off a finger of his right hand. (A "baselard" was a long dagger, worn from the girdle). Of course, the modern "hosier" deals exclusively with socks and stockings or knitted and woven underwear, as indicated by 1428 Assizes. William Sherman hosyer of Lichfield, who cut his own woollen cloth, out of which he made socks, etc for his customers. 1605, William Davenport (hosier) was buried at Seighford on March 5th; 1666, Richard Hosier, charged on one hearth at Brewood; 1742, John, son of John and Elizabeth Hosier, baptised at Oaken near Codsall on March 28th.

Latin "hosatus" - "booted", a nickname for someone who wore unusual boots, was taken up by the Normans as "hosed, hoset" and shortened to "hose, husse", etc: Staffordshire Cartulary, circa 1149, Hugo Hosatus; 1203 Assizes,

Husey
Hussy
Hussey
Hosey

Radulfus Huse (Hose) of Colton. This is one origin of the surname Husey, Hussy, Hussey, Hosey, preserved in Albright Hussey near Shrewsbury, where Walter Hussey held land circa 1165. The latter is most likely to be identified with Walter Hosatus, cited in the *Black Book of the Exchequer*, 1166. Also to be considered is a reduced form of "housewife" - "hussy", a complimentary name when applied to a woman during the Middle Ages, but when aimed at a male it hinted at his ineffectuality as "man of the house": Henry Hoswyf, who rented one plot of land from the Audleys at Betley in 1308 for an annual sum of one penny. "Hussy" in its sense of a bold, shameless woman did not emerge until the 17th century. Richard Hussey, probably one of the Husseys of Longdon near Rugeley, was one of the MPs for Newcastle-under-Lyme in 1558, and Joseph, son of John Hussie of Foxt, was baptised at Kingsley on October 24th, 1663. 1851, Thomas Hussey (joiner) of Charnes near Gerrard's Bromley; 1907, John Hussey (collier), Commercial Road, Hanley; 1907, Stephen Hosey (miner), Audley Street, Tunstall.

Shorthose
Shorthouse
Shorters

Shorthose, Shorthouse, Shorters is either a nickname for anyone who habitually wore a short boot, as opposed to a long boot, as in 1277. Robert Langhose of Suffolk, or a corruption of the Saxon "sceort, hals" - "short neck". 1666, Anne Shorthose (widow) charged on two hearths at Stretton near Burton-on-Trent; 1887, Frederick Shorthouse (turner) of Campbell Road, Stoke; 1907, George Shorthouse (police constable), Leek New Road, Cobridge.

Master mason and apprentices, 13th century, p. 255

INDEX